Revolution and Class Struggle
A Reader in Marxist Politics

GW00362462

Revolution and Class Struggle:
A Reader in Marxist Politics

Edited by
ROBIN BLACKBURN

Fontana/Collins

This selection first published in Fontana 1977

Copyright © in the Preface, arrangement of the selection
and all original material Robin Blackburn 1977

Made and printed in Great Britain
by William Collins Sons & Co. Ltd, Glasgow

Contents

Acknowledgements

For permission to reprint the texts contained in this Reader the Editor wishes to thank the following publishers and copyright-holders:

The *International Socialist Review*, New York, for permission to publish 'The Leninist Theory of Organization' by Ernest Mandel.

Pathfinder Press, New York, for permission to publish 'Peaceful Coexistence and World Revolution' by Ernest Mandel.

The *Socialist Register*, edited Ralph Miliband and John Saville, published by Merlin Press, London, for permission to publish 'The Coup in Chile' by Ralph Miliband.

The Isaac Deutscher estate and Oxford University Press, London and New York, for permission to publish 'Maoism – Its Origins and Outlook' by Isaac Deutscher.

New Left Books, London, for permission to publish 'Lenin's *State and Revolution*' by Lucio Colletti and an extract from *The Legacy of Rosa Luxemburg* by Norman Geras.

New Left Review, London, for permission to publish 'The Origins of Marxist Politics' by Robin Blackburn; 'Marxism and the National Question' by Michael Löwy; 'The Turin Workers' Councils' by Antonio Gramsci; 'The Question of Stalin' by Lucio Colletti; 'Communism in Czechoslovakia: 1938–68' by Jiři Pelikan and 'The Anatomy of the Labour Party' by Tom Nairn.

'Proletarian revolutions . . . constantly engage in self-criticism, and in repeated interruptions of their course. They return to what has apparently already been accomplished in order to begin the task again; with merciless thoroughness they mock the inadequate, weak and wretched aspects of their first attempts; they seem to throw their opponent to the ground only to see him draw new strength from the earth and rise again before them, more colossal than ever; they shrink back again and again before the indeterminate immensity of their own goals, until the situation is created in which any retreat is impossible and the circumstances themselves cry out: *Hic Rhodus, hic salta!* Here is the rose, dance here!'

Karl Marx *The Eighteenth Brumaire of Louis Bonaparte*

'The class struggle, which is always present to a historian influenced by Marx, is a fight for the crude and material things without which no refined and spiritual things could exist. Nevertheless it is not in the form of the spoils that fall to the victor that the latter make their presence felt in the class struggle. They manifest themselves in this struggle as courage, humour, cunning, and fortitude. They have retroactive force and will constantly call in question every victory, past and present, of the rulers. As flowers turn towards the sun, by dint of a secret heliotopism the past strives to turn towards that sun which is rising in the sky of history. A historical materialist must be aware of this most inconspicuous of all transformations.'

Walter Benjamin *Theses on the Philosophy of History*

Preface

To assemble a reader in Marxist politics is an ambitious, problematic, even presumptuous undertaking. Marxism has transformed the politics of the twentieth century and engaged the talents of many profound revolutionary thinkers. Something like a third of the world's population now lives in countries where there has been a socialist revolution and whose leaders claim that they are inspired by the teachings of Marx and Lenin. In most parts of the world Marxism has been a seminal force within the workers' movement. The ideas of Marx and Lenin have also been drawn upon by revolutionary movements that have won the support of the mass of peasants and of the downtrodden rural poor. Many of those who have fought for the equality and liberation of women, or against national and racial oppression, have been attracted by the Marxist critique of capitalism. Marxism draws on a wide range of sources, from the achievements of classical bourgeois thought to the popular traditions of rebellion in many lands. It has fascinated intellectuals across five continents, yet it has proved capable of transmitting its essential message to millions of toilers, often without any formal education, in every part of the world.

In changing the history of the world Marxism itself has been transformed, often in ways that have yet to be adequately accounted for. For the prodigious impact of Marxism on world politics has not been matched by a corresponding development of Marxist political theory. It is this circumstance that makes especially difficult and necessary a critical Marxist reflection upon the experience of the workers' movement – its victories and defeats, and those various combinations of victory and defeat embodied in the institutions it has created, the compromises it has made and the frustrations it has encountered. This collection seeks to account for the originality and potency of Marxist political thought and to furnish some notable Marxist analysis of the history it has made and suffered. It can be no more than a somewhat arbitrary selection, some of whose unifying themes will now be discussed.

The Theory of Revolution

Marx himself only produced the basic elements for a political theory; these are discussed in the first essay in the collection. He saw the bourgeois democratic revolution as necessarily incomplete, since the regime of capitalist private property would continually reproduce inequality and exploitation, misery and servitude. The hierarchy of the state machine, rather than any democratically constituted legislature, would rule society in the interests of the possessing classes. Marx vigorously supported every genuine democratic reform, since a workers' movement which had fought for such measures would be able to use them to place some check on the power of capital. But reforms within the framework of the bourgeois regime could not stop the juggernaut of capital since its implacable progress was determined, not by votes or parliamentary legislation, but by the imperatives of capital accumulation. Expropriating the capitalists required a new revolution and a qualitatively more democratic state that would be directly answerable to the mass of producers. Lucio Colletti argues that Lenin's 'State and revolution', inspired by the Russian soviets, was a reaffirmation and renewal of this radical democratic impulse in Marxist politics. Soviet delegates had no lengthy fixed terms but were recallable at the wish of the workers, peasants and soldiers who had elected them; state officials were to be paid no more than average workman's wages; the soviet itself was an executive as well as legislative body; sustaining the soviet was a network of committees elected in the various places of work and residential districts. It was this novel political form that made possible the improvised creation of a Red Army that could defeat the White Guards, despite the lavish help the latter received from Britain, France and other imperialist states.

Antonio Gramsci's writings on the Turin workers' councils, set up in the aftermath of the First World War, provide another vivid image of proletarian political creativity. Yet in this instance there was no revolutionary party within the councils which could offer them a coherent political purpose and social programme. At the height of the factory occupation movement in 1920 it seemed possible that the workers' movement could lead Italian society out of the depths of the post-war economic and social crisis, with its mass unemployment, slashed living standards and the growing menace of fascism. In September of 1920 an at-

tempted lock-out by employers in Milan led to the occupation
of most of the heavy industrial plants throughout the country
and many smaller plants as well. The Factory Councils which
Gramsci had advocated controlled production and began to
elaborate a new system of distribution, while a workers' self-
defence force protected the occupations from the security forces
and from the fascist bands. The leaders of the Socialist Party
who had so often declaimed against the evils of capitalism – the
untold misery and suffering caused by the war and the economic
crisis – refused to form a Socialist government based on this
movement and offering solutions to the afflictions of the peasants
and middle classes. Instead it abdicated responsibility to the
trade union federation which in turn organized a referendum
among its members, asking them whether they wanted to open
negotiations or to move to revolution. By a narrow majority the
workers endorsed the recommendation of the trade union
leadership to open negotiations. The Italian Government headed
by Giolitti, having witnessed the ardour and power of the workers'
movement, was prepared to support any economic concession to
restore bourgeois law and order – Giolitti even introduced into
Parliament a bill ratifying the 'principle' of workers' control of
the factories. The occupation movement was successfully
demobilized; the Socialist Party, which had always been regarded as an ultra-radical force, had made a purely negative
contribution, helping to resolve the crisis in favour of the
employers. Before long it became clear that the true victor in
this conflict was neither the leadership of the workers' movement,
nor Giolitti, but the fascist leader Mussolini. Gramsci argued
that a socialist programme, and a workers' democracy opposed
to bourgeois rule, must be given a firm foundation in the organization the workers' movement had actually achieved in
struggle. But for this, as he soon recognized, a specially organized
revolutionary party was needed that could dispute the leadership
offered by the reformists.[1]

In 'The Leninist theory of organization' Ernest Mandel seeks
to synthesize the theory of revolutionary organization to be
found in the writings and practice of Lenin, and to integrate the
insights to be found in the writings of some of those who criticized Lenin, notably Rosa Luxemburg and Leon Trotsky.[2]
Mandel focuses on the crucial significance of political organization
for the working class, based on the grass-roots leadership and
informed by a clear programme for society as a whole. The

development of capitalism spontaneously generates mass resistance and popular anger, but this resistance is not necessarily co-ordinated with a programme for a new society and popular anger does not inevitably find the right target. Racism, chauvinism, sexism and narrow craft pride can fatally undermine unity within the ranks of the oppressed and exploited. As Mandel points out, the capitalist class has its own means of achieving unity and agreeing on a programme for society as a whole – it controls the major means of communication, it finances political parties, above all its will is centralized by the tops of the state apparatus itself. The workers' movement needs to develop a counter-organization to these instruments of the capitalist class. It needs to achieve common action at the right moment and to develop a workers' democracy in which alternatives can be discussed, elaborated and decided upon. A plurality of currents within itself and an ability to compete with the bourgeois parties for mass support is indispensable for the vitality and effectiveness of the workers' movement. In any developed bourgeois society the path of workers' democracy is the only path to socialist revolution, since it is the only way of fully tapping the collective energies of the working class and its allies. The extra-parliamentary power of the ruling class – its control or influence in every sphere of society – is the fundamental basis of its power within parliamentary assemblies. Similarly for the workers' movement, its representation in national assemblies of any type is only effective to the extent that it is based on a wide-ranging extra-parliamentary organization and mobilization.

Mandel argues that the rank-and-file activist is the crucial lynch-pin of working-class organization. The activist furnishes the point of concentration for popular resistance to the encroachments of capital in everyday life. The capitalist manager, editorialist and police officer are lavishly endowed with resources by the class whose interests they defend. The working-class activist has no resources that do not derive from those he represents and organizes: he or she depends, not on their passive consent, but upon their active support. As Mandel points out, the whole pressure of bourgeois society tends to encourage the passivity of the underlying mass of the population; it is in this soil that the roots of bureaucracy are nourished. A bureaucratization of the workers' movement arbitrarily arrests its capacity to check the power of capital; it defensively freezes popular gains, inhibiting further advance and eventually jeopardizing even that which has been achieved.

The Fate of Socialism in the East

These general principles of proletarian organization are exemplified and tested in the historical case studies, surveys and documents which comprise the second and third part of the volume. Neither the defeats nor the victories of revolutionary socialism can be explained simply in terms of the original propositions of Marxism and Leninism. The path of socialist revolution has not passed through the most advanced capitalist countries where bourgeois development and power has been at its greatest; neither has it erupted in the most oppressed and subjugated zones of the third world. Rather socialist revolution has triumphed in those countries where the failure of capitalist civilization provoked popular opposition from a society which had some degree of historical development and some margin of independence. The combination of local history and imperialist depredation brought these conditions together in Russia, Yugoslavia, China, Vietnam and Cuba in the period of their socialist revolutions. In each of these cases the revolution was a decisive democratic advance upon prevailing conditions, releasing and canalizing popular energies for a remaking of the social order. In each of these cases age-old scourges of mass illiteracy, endemic famine and curable disease, capitalist exploitation, landlordism and military or feudal despotism, have been overcome. Yet as Lucio Colletti points out in his essay on Stalin these societies have not enjoyed the historical prerequisites for a genuine socialist society: a modern economy with high social productivity of labour. This material scarcity has usually been accompanied by international isolation and imperialist blockade. These unavoidable limitations have often been compounded by avoidable political deformations which have qualified or even destroyed revolutionary democracy. In the struggle for survival there has been a bureaucratization or militarization of the revolutionary movement itself. In the Soviet Union most of the worker activists upon whom the revolution depended were either killed at the front, or promoted into the administrative apparatus. Russian industry itself was brought to a virtual standstill by the end of the civil war. The emergency measures taken by the Bolshevik leadership itself in 1920–1 gained a temporary respite, but at the terrible cost of destroying the lively democracy of the soviets and the Party itself. Stalin was able to exploit these conditions and to erect upon them a bureaucratic despotism exercised by the top leadership of the Party as representative of the newly privileged layers in society. The ideology which he developed to justify this bureaucratic usurpation has at least partially corresponded to those other countries where the socialist revolution was itself produced by a military process. Moreover in these other countries the old order was so weak and fractured that it could be overthrown without the prior development of soviets or properly democratic organs of popular power.

The consolidation of the Stalinist regime, its survival in essentials down to the present day in the Soviet Union, and the incorporation of certain Stalinist components within other post-revolutionary regimes, pose a new problem. The phenomenon of political bureaucracy in this instance acquires an autonomous organization and ideology of its own. The Leninist activist is replaced at best by the Communist partisan or guerrilla, at worst by the Stalinist cadre. He, or she, is now placed in authority over the mass of producers and no longer has to gain their support or submit to their approval. Whereas the rank-and-file Bolshevik in the early days of the Russian revolution participated in, and arbitrated upon, all the disputes and debates that animated the Party, the Stalinist cadre is invigilated from above by an obsessively secretive party leadership which exercises a monopoly of all substantive discussions and decisions. However, so long as the cadres retain a highly charged ideological commitment, and faith in the wisdom and competence of the Party leadership, they will continue to be capable of feats of military valour and economic mobilization.

To a certain extent the bureaucratization of the first socialist revolutions can be explained within the terms of the original schemes of Marx and Lenin. That capitalism would break at its weakest link was clear at least to Lenin on the basis of his study of imperialism. Trotsky actually predicted that a socialist revolution was possible in Russia, despite its backwardness compared with overall social development in western Europe and North America. Both Lenin and Trotsky conceded that a certain degree of bureaucratization was inevitable so long as the revolution remained confined to this relatively backward and absolutely war-devastated country. They both argued, as Mandel points out in 'Peaceful Coexistence and World Revolution', that the

Soviet government in its isolation should draw as much support as possible from the anti-capitalist workers' movement of the advanced countries and the anti-imperialist movement of the colonial and semi-colonial world. The success of these movements would furnish the Soviet Union with its only reliable allies and would alone make possible the construction of a truly socialist society. Until such a time the socialist regime in Russia would be as far from socialism as the bourgeois regime of Cromwell or Robespierre was from fully developed capitalism.

The comprehensive economic and social powers of the workers' state gave enormous scope to its bureaucratic leading stratum. By far the most important source of Marxist analysis of this phenomenon is Trotsky's critique of Stalinism. Trotsky argued that despite Stalin's horrendous crimes he had not been able to cancel out entirely the gains of the Bolshevik revolution. The bureaucratic regime itself rested not on private property but on a planned economy and a regimented workers' movement. Within the Soviet Union this political system would still be compatible with social and economic advances – indeed it would be capable of outpacing capitalist development. In the international arena the role of the Soviet Union would also be contradictory; it would always timidly seek to collude with the major imperialist states, but such major events as wars or revolutions would bring out the objective antagonism between imperialism and the bureaucratized workers' state. Trotsky argued that the Stalinist regime could only pervert the conquests of the October revolution for a limited time. Since the regime was not itself a class embedded in production relations but only derived its power at second hand by manipulating and terrorizing the underlying mass of producers, its rule was highly precarious. To defend this rule it would rely on the most extreme measures but once these failed it would have few resources to fall back upon. Even in the economic sphere it could only feed off the original momentum for a certain time, since the planning system would be increasingly undermined by bureaucratic irrationality and growing mass apathy. Trotsky concluded that the rule of the Stalinist bureaucracy must be overthrown. A political revolution was needed to spring the bureaucratic apparatus in the air and restore an integral soviet democracy. The hallmark of such a revolution would be that freedom of discussion and association would again regulate the life of the soviets.[3]

In the decades since Trotsky first advanced his critique of Stalinism much has happened and his ideas have given rise to much controversy even within the movement he founded – the Fourth International. In the Second World War and its aftermath Stalinism seemed to gain a new lease of life. Faced with the terrible alternative of fascist occupation the majority of the Soviet people rallied to the regime and sustained the Red Army and partisans in their ultimately victorious struggle. In the immediate post-war period the Stalinist system extended into eastern Europe while socialist revolutions in Yugoslavia and China seemed to offer further evidence of the potency of Stalinist organization and ideology. Yet these apparent triumphs for Stalinism contained within them the seeds of a generalized crisis for its ideology and institutions. For the most part they were achieved only as a consequence of some relaxation of the monolithic system of Stalinist tutelage. Stalin himself soon openly clashed with Tito and privately distrusted the Chinese Communists. Within four years of his death Khruschev, who had been political commissar at Stalingrad, delivered a lengthy and detailed denunciation of Stalin's tyranny in his celebrated 'secret speech' to the Twentieth Congress of the CPSU.[4] Subsequent explosions of mass unrest in Hungary, Czechoslovakia, Poland and China have indicated that the post-Stalin bureaucracy is perennially haunted by the true spirit of the proletarian socialism it proclaims and falsifies.

The challenge to capitalism in the West

If the fate of socialism in the East is still open, it will be partly determined by the progress of revolution in the West. The advanced capitalist states represent a different and, in some respects, more formidable obstacle to socialist revolution than was faced by revolutionaries in Russia, China or Vietnam. This does not mean that the lessons of previous socialist revolutions are irrelevant, but it will demand a further development of Marxist political strategy and tactics based upon an understanding of the more developed capitalist social formations.

Lenin's last major political text, *Left-wing Communism*, was specifically addressed to the problems of Communist strategy in the advanced countries. He stressed the importance of carrying socialist agitation into every institution through which the bourgeoisie exerted its influence over society. He strongly

supported Communist participation in parliamentary assemblies
on the grounds that this platform must be used to popularize the
socialist programme and institutions of the Soviet type – the
qualitative extention of democracy that would be required to
effect a socialist transformation. However Lenin did not live to
see the formation of a workers' government within a bourgeois
democratic regime proclaiming the need for a break with
capitalism. In the thirties the growth and radicalization of the
workers' movement in certain European countries for a time
seemed to offer the possibility of socialist governments being
elected within a bourgeois democratic framework. However the
rise of fascism eliminated this possibility in all those countries
where it existed, along with the destruction of all independent
workers' organizations. As Norman Geras argues, the rise of
fascism posed in a new and more extreme form the question of
different types of bourgeois political regime. Trotsky held that
bourgeois democratic governments rested on the consent of the
masses and that bourgeois democracy incorporated 'elements
of proletarian democracy' (i.e. trade unions, workers' parties),
albeit in embryonic form. Trotsky concluded that it was imperative for the entire workers' movement to unite to oppose the
mortal danger of fascism whose programme was the elimination
of all these embryos of proletarian democracy within bourgeois
society.[5] Geras explores the further implications of Trotsky's
theses on the nature of bourgeois democracy.

The defeat of the major fascist states in the Second World War
led to a reintroduction of bourgeois democratic regimes. The
war functioned as a belated last act of the bourgeois democratic
revolution in the advanced capitalist countries. The potential
radicalization that the struggle against fascism carried within it
was to be frustrated by a combination of Stalin's cynical power
politics and the massive Cold War mobilization of the West.
The post-war boom of the capitalist economies enabled important
economic concessions to be made to the workers' movement. In
Britain the first majority Labour Government was formed. But,
as Tom Nairn argues, Labourist politics had always narrowly
concentrated on the parliamentary terrain at the expense of the
mass movement and the socialist activist. Socialism was confused with a nationalization and welfare programme, installed
from above and congruent with the interests of capital accumulation. Some major reforms were achieved but mass
enthusiasm for a new society was dissipated: capitalism re-

mained to cancel out all that had been achieved.[6]

However the apparent success of the capitalist social order in containing the threat of socialism in the post-war world also contained within it seeds of disintegration and failure. During and after the war there was an insistent appeal to democratic ideology and to the need to build a new society in which there could be no return to the Depression or to fascism. Before long capitalism was to find itself haunted by the democratic and social ideals that it proclaimed but proved incapable of sustaining in practice. In the immediate aftermath of the war, fascism and doctrines of racial superiority were utterly discredited. Yet before long the rulers of the major western states decided to do nothing about the remaining fascist regimes in the Iberian peninsula and to maintain the European colonial regimes where no acceptable successor was available. A series of bloody colonial wars ensued. Throughout southern Africa colonialist and racialist regimes thrived within the capitalist world community and were supported by military alliance. Even where decolonization was conceded the capitalist order in these lands became increasingly dependent on military or neo-fascist regimes.[7]

Within the advanced capitalist countries the prolonged boom itself threw up old and new forms of inequality and irrationality. The continuing struggle for existence even in a supposedly affluent society bred anew poisonous doctrines of racial and communal oppression. Full citizenship was effectively denied to women, blacks, immigrants, national minorities in nearly every advanced bourgeois democracy. Invariably an important layer of capitalist enterprise battened upon the super-exploitation of these groups. Access to education, health and the good things in life continued to be determined by class membership. The chief workplace institutions of the 'Free World' continued to be run on hierarchic and authoritarian principles. In the sixties and seventies the major capitalist states witnessed the birth or rebirth of a whole series of movements for substantive equality and democracy. In most of these states there was also a great movement of support for the struggles of national liberation in the third world. Blanket bombing of peasants, systematic torture and assassination of political opponents caused widespread revulsion from the arrogant politics of imperialism. With the onset of renewed capitalist crisis and its train of mass unemployment, rampant inflation, falling living standards and decaying public services, the democratic ferment in the West began to mingle with a proletarian revolt. Just at this point most bourgeois governments stepped in to redefine, qualify or retract hard-won trade union rights and to seek to impose state-sponsored incomes policies.

At different times the reawakening democratic and proletarian movement has threatened to break the prevailing governmental formula: May 1968 in France, the Divorce Referendum in Italy of 1974, the trade union mobilizations that brought down the Heath Government in Britain, the vast popular acclaim for the overthrow of fascism in Portugal in 1974, the turbulent opposition to Francoism, with or without Franco. None of these movements pressed for a socialist transformation, yet each of them was incipiently anti-capitalist. In each case those who were expert in parliamentary combinations, and operating in the corridors of power, were rudely surprised by the vigorous assertion of the popular will. In consequence western Europe now faces the prospect of an unprecedented test for the bourgeois political system in a string of important states. That test will be the formation of governments based on the major workers' parties – the Socialists and Communists – and pledged to fundamental social programmes. It may, of course, be that such governments can be absorbed by the political system; but in a context of capitalist instability and awakened popular aspirations it is also highly possible that they will lead to a widespread extra-parliamentary mobilization of both the bourgeoisie and the working class.

There can be little doubt that the impasse of the post-Stalin regimes in the East and the disarray of the post-boom regimes in the West underline the continuing relevance of the fundamental themes of the classical Marxist tradition of political thought: from the days of the *Communist Manifesto* to the debates of Rosa Luxemburg with Karl Kautsky, from Lenin's underground pamphlets to Trotsky's searing indictment of the Stalinist regime. In the East there have been many and varied attempts to alleviate or 'improve' the Stalinist model: but in default of a full inauguration of workers' democracy these have all foundered. In the West every conceivable reform and panacea has been proposed and applied to eliminate the recurrent evils of capitalism and yet they have stubbornly reasserted themselves. In the capitalist third world old-style colonialism has been thrown back and there is a developing working class in both town and countryside. Opposition to prevailing forms of imperialist hegemony is bound to be based on democratic and anti-capitalist themes and its horizon will be a socialist revolution. Thus in all the major world zones the bold contours of classical Marxist political theory have an evident actuality. The thought of Marx, Engels, Lenin, Luxemburg, Trotsky and Gramsci remains an essential starting point for those who wish to grasp the underlying dynamic of world politics.

A critical recovery of classical Marxist political thought has been made no easier either by the intervening epoch of Stalinist obfuscation or by the circumstance that the recent reawakening of interest in Marxism remained for a time limited to a predominantly non-proletarian social milieu. It is not difficult to identify a residual influence of Stalinism and of petty bourgeois radicalism and revolutionism in both the new and the old left. One of the aims of this reader is to make available a contemporary restatement and appraisal of the classical Marxist political tradition. It is also to present Marxist analysis of certain major developments in world politics that were not, or could not, be anticipated by the generation that grew up before the outbreak of the First World War and the triumph of the Russian revolution: among them the Chinese revolution, the fate of socialism in Czechoslovakia, the new pattern of international relations, the experience of the first Socialist government elected within a bourgeois democratic framework. In the selection of texts and topics there is an emphasis upon the problems of socialism in the advanced countries, since this question tended to be neglected while the colonial revolution provided the major theme of world politics. Another limitation should be acknowledged. Marxist politics are, of course, based on an economic and historical analysis of capitalism and imperialism and a cultural critique of bourgeois civilization. The texts in this reader rest on such an underlying social theory, but are themselves concerned with the strictly political domain. A special strength of the articles assembled here is that they theorize a particular problem or experience, distilling the general significance it has for the contemporary socialist movement. Finally it should be emphasized that the various authors represented are each contributing to a wider framework of Marxist debate and discussion in which they are responsible only for what they have themselves written.

Robin Blackburn   London, January 1977

Notes

1. A comprehensive edition of Gramsci's writings is being published by Lawrence and Wishart (London) under the editorship of Quintin Hoare; admirably presented and translated, it furnishes a valuable guide to the historical and political context of Gramsci's work. The evolution of Gramsci's thought, and its relationship to the classical Marxist debates on strategy, is much illuminated by Perry Anderson's study, 'The Antinomies of Antonio Gramsci', *New Left Review*, 100, November 1976–February 1977.

2. A succinct conspectus of Lenin's thought is provided by Georg Lukacs, *Lenin: A Study on the Unity of his Thought*, New Left Books (London 1977). A scrupulous account of Lenin's practice, and its relationship to his theories, will be found in Marcel Liebman's major historical synthesis, *Leninism under Lenin*, Jonathan Cape (London 1975).

3. Trotsky memorably declared his conclusions and analysis in the fundamental text, *The Revolution Betrayed*, Pathfinder Press (New York 1973). Trotsky's life and work are magisterially surveyed in Isaac Deutscher's three-volume biography: *The Prophet Unarmed, The Prophet Armed, The Prophet Outcast*, Oxford University Press (paper edition, London 1970). A stimulating interpretation of Trotsky, bringing out the profound significance of his theory of permanent revolution, is provided by Denise Avenas 'Trotsky's Marxism', *International* (London), vol. 3, No. 2, winter 1976 and *International*, vol. 4, No. 1, spring 1977.

4. A searching historical investigation of the Stalin era is provided by the Soviet oppositionist Roy Medvedev in *Let History Judge*, Macmillan (London 1972). Soviet foreign policy, and the policy of the Communist Parties, is reviewed by Fernando Claudin in *The Communist Movement: from Comintern to Cominform*, Penguin Books (London 1976). These two studies, published after the composition of the essays in this volume by Colletti and Mandel on Stalin and Soviet foreign policy, contain new data which confirm their argument.

5. Trotsky's texts on the German conjuncture are now collected in *The Struggle Against Fascism in Germany*, Penguin Books (Harmondsworth 1975). The vital contemporary significance of Trotsky's conception of the united front and of a workers' government is discussed by Ernest Mandel in 'A Political Interview', *New Left Review*, 100 November 1976–February 1977.

6. The grotesque survival of every type of capitalist inequality, despite many years of Labour government, is amply documented by John Westergaard and Henrietta Resler, *Class in a Capitalist Society*, Heinemann (London 1976); Tom Nairn has himself eloquently extended his indictment of the misery of Labourism, and of the decaying bourgeois society to which it clings, in *The Break-up of Britain*, NLB (London 1977).

7. The explosive implications of an authentic realization of democracy for the major zones of world politics are explored in the pioneering work by George Novack, *Democracy and Revolution*, Pathfinder Press (New York 1971).

PART ONE
Origins

The essays in this section examine the formation of Marxist politics in the writings and activities of Marx, Engels, Luxemburg, Lenin and Trotsky and seek to assess their contemporary relevance.

Robin Blackburn argues that the novelty of Marxist political theory has been underestimated: the theory of proletarian revolution first outlined in the *Communist Manifesto* was quite distinct both from the ideas that previously dominated the workers' movement and from even the most radical political and social thinkers of the Renaissance and Enlightenment. Marx and Engels identified the modern industrial proletariat as a class capable of emancipating itself through political institutions of a fundamentally new type. The elements of a theory of proletarian representation were elaborated in their writings as they grappled with the problems of the first working-class parties and trade unions.

The crucial distinguishing feature of revolutionary Marxism has been the strategy it advocates for confronting the capitalist state. Marx himself insisted that the working class could not simply lay hold of the ready-made state machinery and employ it to install socialism. Reformists have by contrast identified socialism with nationalization and welfare measures carried through by the capitalist state. Marx insisted that the successful overthrow of capitalist property relations would require a 'dictatorship of the proletariat', a new political power directly based upon, and answerable to, the working class and its allies. Lenin's pamphlet 'State and Revolution' was a vigorous re-statement of these Marxist theses on the capitalist state and the need for a revolutionary proletarian democracy. Lucio Colletti's essay insists on the profound democratic inspiration of Lenin's ideas and their subversive implications in the lands that have had a socialist revolution, as well as in the capitalist West.

Ernest Mandel's study of the Leninist theory of organization seeks to draw out the universal element in Lenin's theory of class consciousness and class organization. He argues that the necessity for a revolutionary party stems from the heterogeneity of the oppressed and exploited in capitalist society, the uneven domination of bourgeois ideology and the political centralization imposed by the existing state. Mandel shows that the Leninist conception of a revolutionary party, far from contradicting the spontaneous class combativity of the proletariat, was designed to give it coherence and durability. Mandel's original discussion of class consciousness and revolutionary organization integrates the theoretical contribution of Luxemburg, Trotsky, Lukacs and Gramsci in addition to the basic theses advanced by Lenin.

Marx and Engels initially assumed that the advance of the bourgeois democratic revolution would eventually lead to the establishment of independent nation states throughout the world. The failure of the revolutions of 1848, the subsequent uneven development of capitalism and the emergence of the first national liberation movements of the modern type induced them to begin revising their views. However, as Michael Löwy shows, they never developed an adequate theory on the national question. Lowy surveys the contribution made to the study of the national question by Luxemburg, Bauer, Trotsky and Stalin but concludes that only Lenin understood the need for an unequivocal commitment by Marxists to national self-determination. Although national independence was undoubtedly a goal of the bourgeois democratic revolution, the working-class movement must be prepared to fight for bourgeois democratic goals where the bourgeoisie has failed to achieve them itself.

Marxism: Theory of Proletarian Revolution

ROBIN BLACKBURN

(Reprinted from *New Left Review*, 97, 1976)

The real focus of the work of Marx and Engels was political, not economic or philosophical. They were the first to discover the historical potential of the new class that capitalism had brought into existence – the modern proletariat, a class that could encompass a universal liberation from all prevailing forms of oppression and exploitation. The modern workers' movement, capable of self-determination and self-emancipation, able to draw on the best of bourgeois culture and science, would have no need of utopias or religious exaltation. The political capacity of the proletariat sprang from its objective position within bourgeois society. Thus the analysis of capitalism, and of its historical antecedents and consequences, to be found in the writings of Marx and Engels – however necessarily partial its initial formulations – was a necessary underpinning for their political theory. But the decisive contribution made by the founders of historical materialism was the theory of proletarian revolution. There has been an increasing tendency in twentieth-century Marxism to identify the philosophical method or epistemology employed by Marx or Engels as their crucial contribution, and to represent these as the touchstone of Marxist orthodoxy. In different ways this is done by the Lukacs of *History and Class Consciousness*, the exponents of Soviet Diamat and Louis Althusser and his collaborators in *Reading Capital*. There is little equivalent insistence on the originality of the political conceptions of Marx and Engels. Indeed, often attempts are made to suggest that their political ideas are essentially a continuation or development of those of Machiavelli or Montesquieu or Rousseau. This is especially curious since in no domain has Marxism been more original than in that of political theory. Historical materialism either discovered or thoroughly reworked every important political concept: class, party, state, nation, revolution, bureaucracy, programme and so on. Such concepts have developed in conjunction with Marxist political practice and in the course of vigorous political polemics. Moreover, it is evident that all the major divisions of Marxism have arisen over directly political questions, which have thereby furnished the critical determinants of Marxist 'orthodoxy'. This does not mean that philosophical or epistemological disputes have had no significance for Marxism. It does mean that they have emerged as secondary by-products of conflicts over substantive political questions. Since Marxism adopts a completely consequent and complete materialism, this should not be so surprising. No standpoint in philosophy can *produce* proletarian revolutionary politics – but in the long run only materialism is fully consistent with them.[1]

The theory of proletarian revolution developed by Marx and Engels sets them quite apart from those who have been claimed as their precursors in matters of political science. The fact that their political theory was deeply grounded in an analysis of social and economic forces is in the greatest contrast to Machiavelli's arbitrary and self-sufficient notion of politics. Their insistence that the working class could emancipate itself and all other oppressed groups is sharply at variance with the Machiavellian conception of the state as a simple instrument of princely manipulation, with its peremptory maxim to the effect that, as Machiavelli writes in the *Discourses*, 'in all states, whatever their type of government, the real rulers are never more than forty or fifty citizens'. There is no valid analogy between the Marxist conception of the party of proletarian revolution and Machiavelli's Prince. Rousseau's political ideas, based on a profound critique of social inequality, are discrepant with Marxism in a quite different way. With Rousseau, the critique of all political institutions is so radical and sweeping that the very notion of valid political representation or delegation is denied. Thus the sovereignty of the people is only possible if there are no parties or factions within the state and no communication between its citizens. Rousseau declares in the *Social Contract*: 'It is therefore essential, if the general will is to express itself, that there should be no partial society within the state, and that each citizen should think only his own thoughts.' Again, as we shall see, there is no valid analogy between Rousseau's vision of the General Will, inaugurated by the Wise Legislator, and proletarian democracy forged in class struggle.[2]

Marxist politics could not possibly spring fully armed from the heads of Marx and Engels, but required decades of participation in the workers' movement. The development of capitalism and of the class struggle was constantly presenting them with new problems and new solutions. In those texts written by

Marx or Engels as interventions in the workers' movement, it is possible to trace their increasing awareness of the great variety of tactics and instruments of struggle that the working class would need if it was to carry through a successful socialist revolution against such a powerful antagonist as the world capitalist system. These works by Marx and Engels lack the brilliant paradoxes of their philosophy, the literary polish of their journalism or the intricate abstraction of their economics, but they are unsurpassed in clarity and vigour: they have proved to be the iron rations of revolutionary socialism. It is hoped that this account of the origins of Marxist politics, although unavoidably cursory and selective in its reference to the historical context of the writings of Marx and Engels, will nevertheless underline their crucial significance within the Marxist corpus.

The discovery of the proletarian revolution

If the definitive tenet of Marxism is the proletarian revolution, then it is possible to give a precise date to Marx's first announcement that he had become a Marxist. In the early part of 1844 Marx published his last text as a critical philosopher and radical nationalist: 'The Introduction to the Critique of Hegel's Philosophy of Right'. In this he declared war on the stifling conditions that prevail in Germany in the name of philosophy and the proletariat. The material base, the 'passive element' in this revolution, will be supplied by the proletariat, the radically oppressed class, while philosophy will determine the revolution's goals. 'Just as philosophy finds its *material* weapons in the proletariat, so the proletariat finds its *intellectual* weapons in philosophy . . . The *emancipation of the German* is the *emancipation of man.* The *head* of this emancipation is *philosophy*, its *heart* the *proletariat.*'[3]

Marx spent the first part of 1844 studying political economy and filling his notebooks with the 'Economic and Philosophical Manuscripts'. In June 1844 there was an armed revolt by the weavers in Silesia. It was to be dismissed as an event of little consequence by Marx's closest collaborator, Arnold Ruge, writing under the name 'A Prussian' in the Paris émigré newspaper *Vorwarts*. Marx was provoked into an instant response: 'Our so-called Prussian denies that the King "panicked" for a number of reasons, among them being the fact that few troops were needed to deal with the feeble weavers . . . In a country

where banquets with liberal toasts and liberal champagne froth
provoke Royal Orders in Council . . . where the burning desire
of the entire liberal bourgeoisie for freedom of the press and a
constitution could be suppressed without *a single soldier*, in a
country where passive obedience is the order of the day, can it
be anything but an *event*, indeed a *terrifying* event, when armed
troops have to be called out against feeble weavers? And in the
first encounter the feeble weavers even gained a victory. They
were only suppressed when reinforcements were brought up. Is
the uprising of a mass of workers less dangerous because it can
be defeated without the aid of a whole army? Our sharp-witted
Prussian should compare the revolt of the Silesian weavers with
the uprisings of the English workers. The Silesians will then stand
revealed as *strong* weavers.' Much of this article is still written
in the old philosophical jargon and involves an argument about
the nature of the German revolution. But Marx concludes from
the weavers' revolt that the proletariat is the 'active agent' of the
revolution and the political consciousness they revealed is
greatly superior to 'the meek, sober mediocrity' of the political
literature of the German bourgeoisie, 'for all their philosophers
and scholars'. Marx points out that 'however limited an industrial revolt may be it contains within itself a universal soul'.
Ruge had maintained that Germany needed 'a social revolution
with a political soul'. Marx in conclusion replies: 'whether the
idea of a *social revolution* with a *political soul* is paraphrase or
nonsense, there is no doubt about the rationality of a *political
revolution* with a *social soul*. All revolution – the *overthrow* of
the existing ruling power and the *dissolution* of the old order – is
a *political act*. But without revolution *socialism* cannot be made
possible.'[4]

Marx's reply to the article by 'A Prussian' is dated Paris, 31
July 1844. Naturally, it ended Marx's collaboration with Ruge
and the other critical philosophers. Some days after publication
of the article, on 26 August 1844, Marx met Engels in Paris and
talked at length with him for the first time. They discovered a
profound community of views and interests. Engels, who had
been living in Manchester, was deeply impressed by the Chartist
movement and the working-class politics it represented. They
both rejected the vacillation and vapourings of the critical
philosophers and looked upon the working class as a potent
revolutionary force. The fully-fledged idea of proletarian revolution was to develop subsequently during the course of extensive

practical experience in the workers' movement in Brussels, Paris, London and Manchester.

Although the encounter with the workers' movement was to be decisive for Marx and Engels, they certainly did not simply adopt its politics. Within the workers' movement at this time, it was held that the emancipation of the labouring classes would be accomplished essentially by some external agency. For the disciples of Proudhon or Robert Owen, co-operative schemes devised by enlightened reformers were to be the salvation of the workers: this was the resolution of the 'social' question. For the followers of Blanqui or Weitling, it was the revolutionary conspiracy that would deliver the proletarian masses from their bondage: this was the path of 'political' revolution. None of these thinkers advanced the idea of the working class as the conscious, leading force in a revolution that would unite the 'social' and the 'political'. Indeed, they lacked a precise conception of the proletariat as a class: for Blanqui the term covered all those who worked, including the mass of the peasantry, while for Weitling the most revolutionary social category was the lumpen proletarians or 'dangerous classes'. For Marx and Engels the emergence of the propertyless industrial working class opened up the possibility of a new type of politics no longer subordinated to conspiracy or utopia. The workers were organized into giant industrial armies by capitalism itself. They participated in a global system of production and exchange. A conscious movement of this class could alone destroy capitalism and establish a new society, free from exploitation and oppression, because based on mastery of the new social forces of production. Marx and Engels first presented an integrated account of these ideas in the *Communist Manifesto*.

The *Communist Manifesto* was drafted and redrafted by Marx and Engels during the course of nearly a year of lectures and discussions with the members of the German Workers' Educational Association. These German immigrant workers – nineteenth-century *Gastarbeiter* – were in the main skilled propertyless artisans drawn by the rapid economic advance taking place in England and Belgium. Originally they organized themselves as a classic revolutionary conspiracy – the League of the Just – on the model of the French revolutionary secret societies; but they learnt from the English Chartists the advantages of open mass organization and agitation. The Educational Associations were established for this latter purpose by a decision of the League. However, Marx and Engels opposed the authoritarian structure and cabalistic paraphernalia of a secret society – with codes, passwords and hierarchies – which still governed the operations of the League of the Just. The supporters of Marx and Engels successfully proposed a new organization, to be called the Communist League, with a new programme, which was to be the *Manifesto*. The new League was to have a democratic constitution with elected officials and annual congresses. On grounds of security the League was to be secret, but it was to make full use of all available means of public propaganda and organization.

The politics of the 'Communist Manifesto'

The first section of the *Manifesto* is an eloquent tribute to the historic achievements of capitalism and the bourgeoisie. In the economic field, Marx and Engels insisted that capitalism 'has accomplished wonders far surpassing Egyptian pyramids, Roman aqueducts and Gothic cathedrals'. They summarize these wonders as follows: 'The Bourgeoisie, during its rule of scarce one hundred years, has created more massive and colossal productive forces than have all preceding generations together. Subjection of nature's forces to man, machinery, application of chemistry to industry and agriculture, steam navigation, railways, electric telegraphs, clearing of whole continents for cultivation, canalization of rivers, whole populations conjured out of the ground – what earlier century had even a presentiment that such productive forces slumbered in the lap of social labour?' Referring to the most advanced capitalist countries, Marx and Engels declare that these accomplishments are here crowned by the appropriate political structure in the course of the bourgeois revolution: the modern representative nation state. 'Independent or but loosely connected provinces, with separate interests, laws, governments and systems of taxation, become lumped together in one nation, with one government, one code of laws, one national class interest, one frontier and one customs tariff.' The new nation state is increasingly responsive to the bourgeoisie, 'which has at last, since the establishment of modern industry and the world market, conquered for itself, in the modern representative state, exclusive political sway'.[5]

The sweeping away of feudal particularism and fragmentation produces a simplification of the social order: 'society as a whole is more and more splitting up into two great hostile camps, into two great classes directly facing one another: bourgeoisie and proletariat'. With the development of the modern forces of production, the modern working class 'becomes concentrated in greater masses, its strength grows and it feels that strength more'.[6] The workers find their conditions of existence continually threatened by the anarchic fluctuations of the capitalist economy. The *private* ownership of the means of production, super-imposed on increasingly *socialized* forces of production, generates harsh inequality and recurrent crisis.

To begin with, the working class does not act for itself but is mobilized by the bourgeoisie. The bourgeoisie, 'in order to attain its own political ends, is compelled to set the whole proletariat in motion, and is moreover yet, for a time, able to do so'. At this time, 'the whole historical movement is con-centrated in the hands of the bourgeoisie; every victory so obtained is a victory for the bourgeoisie'. But with the develop-ment of capitalist industry and the resulting economic fluctuations, 'the workers begin to form combinations (trade unions) against the bourgeoisie; they club together in order to keep up the rate of wages; they found permanent associations in order to make provision beforehand for these occasional revolts . . . Now and then the workers are victorious, but only for a time. The real fruit of their battle lies, not in the immediate result, but in the ever expanding union of the workers. This union is helped on by the improved means of communication that are created by modern industry, and that place the workers of different localities in contact with one another. It was just this contact that was needed to centralize the numerous local struggles, all of the same character, into one national struggle between classes. But every class struggle is a political struggle . . . This organization of the proletarians into a class, and consequently into a political party, is continually being upset again by competition between the workers themselves. But it ever rises up stronger, firmer, mightier. It compels legislative recognition of particular interests of the workers, by taking advantage of the divisions among the bour-geoisie itself.'[7]

The class struggle could only be resolved by a victory for the working class and the suppression of capitalism. The working class alone had the collective, co-operative character required to master the new forces of production and to ensure that they did not dominate those who had created them. With the accentuation of the crisis of bourgeois order, the workers as a class would be joined by 'a portion of bourgeois ideologists who have raised themselves to the level of comprehending theoretically the historical movement as a whole'. The working class would become the basis for a new type of political movement. 'All previous historical movements were movements of minorities or in the interests of minorities. The proletarian movement is the self-conscious, independent movement of the immense majority.' Without any stake in capitalist private property, the proletariat's historical mission is to destroy it. But to do this a revolutionary seizure of political power is necessary: 'the first step in the revolution by the working class is to raise the working class to the position of ruling class, to win the battle of democracy'. Once the workers had conquered political power, they would be forced to embark on a programme of 'despotic inroads on the rights of private property and the conditions of bourgeois production'. Because the bourgeois political framework was that of the nation state, 'the proletariat of each country must, of course, first settle matters with its own bourgeoisie'. But this was the 'form' not the 'substance' of the proletarian revolution. With the generalization of the proletarian revolution, the global productive forces developed by capitalism would be brought under social ownership and regulation: 'In place of the old bourgeois society, with its classes and class antagonisms, we shall have an association, in which the free development of each is the condition for the free development of all.'[8]

It would seem to be implied by the *Communist Manifesto* that the workers' movement would develop most rapidly, and the socialist revolution first erupt, in the most advanced countries, where capitalist contradictions were present in the most acute and purest form. Certainly this was a view expressed by Engels in a speech made at about the time the *Manifesto* was written: 'The English Chartists will rise up first because it is precisely here that the struggle between bourgeoisie and proletariat is at its fiercest . . . thus the struggle has been simplified, thus the struggle will be resolved at one decisive blow'.[9] Certainly this is one outline of proletarian revolution which can be drawn from the *Manifesto*. However, there is also an indication of a different perspective. When the *Manifesto* was written, capitalist social relations were spreading throughout the world. The economic advance of capitalism, combined with the political impact of the French revolutionary and Napoleonic wars, had undermined feudal domination throughout most of Europe. But a full-scale bourgeois revolution, of the sort invoked in the *Manifesto*, had only triumphed in a handful of countries (Britain, France, Belgium, the Netherlands). The *Manifesto* implicitly acknowledges this by insisting that Communists will fight for the victory of the bourgeois-democratic revolution in all the countries where it had not yet been achieved. Moreover, the *Manifesto* states that a social revolutionary dynamic must underlie the movements for national liberation. Thus in Poland the Communists support 'the party that insists on an agrarian revolution as the prime condition for national emancipation'. More surprising than this is the assertion that Communist hopes are pinned on Germany, where no bourgeois revolution had yet taken place. 'The Communists turn their attention chiefly to Germany because that country is on the eve of a bourgeois revolution that is bound to be carried out under more advanced conditions of European civilization, and with a more developed proletariat, than that of England in the seventeenth or of France in the eighteenth century, and because the bourgeois revolution in Germany will be but the prelude to the immediately following proletarian revolution.'[10] In this conception, the political turmoil and social instability attendant upon a belated bourgeois revolution, superimposed upon the fundamental contradictions of capitalist advance, combined to open the way for a proletarian revolution. However, this idea was not further developed in the *Manifesto*.

The directly political concepts contained in the *Manifesto* are spare and rudimentary. The advancing sweep of the bourgeois revolution was clearing away all the debris of pre-capitalist social relations and political forms. The bourgeoisie was creating a world in its own image. The state was 'but a committee for managing the common affairs of the whole bourgeoisie'. The essential function of the state could be defined in a similarly peremptory fashion: 'Political power, properly so called, is merely the organized power of one class for oppressing another.' The simplification of all social relations in the wake of the bourgeois revolution meant that the proletarian movement could develop in a straight line from economic combination to the socialist revolution. The programme of the Communists could be summed up in one slogan: 'The abolition of private property'. Within the workers' movement, the Communists distinguish themselves only by the fact that they see the future development of the class struggle and bring to the fore the interests of the working class as a whole, 'independently of all nationality'. The Communists are practically 'the most advanced and resolute section of the working-class parties of every country' and theoretically 'they have over the great mass of the proletariat the advantage of clearly understanding the line of march, the conditions and the ultimate general results of the proletarian revolution'. But since the forward development of the movement is prepared by the development of capitalism itself, the Communists will be cutting with the grain of bourgeois society in carrying through their tasks; hence, 'The Communists do not form a separate party opposed to other working-class parties.'[11] There is little need to labour the point that the *Manifesto*'s abrupt formulations on the bourgeois state or the proletarian movement were over-simplified. Less evident, perhaps, is that each of these formulations retains a definite value on the basis of a more complex analysis of historical development and bourgeois society.

Permanent revolution

The Communist League itself, for which the *Manifesto* had been written, did not function as a party during 1848 itself. The members of the League mostly returned to Germany, where they were caught up in the fragmented revolutionary process in the different German states. The League was too newly formed to withstand such pressures as a coherent force. Marx and Engels subsequently declared that 'A large number of members who were directly involved in the movement thought that the time for secret societies was over and that public activity alone was sufficient.' This undoubtedly reflected their own attitude. The first set-backs persuaded Marx and Engels of the necessity of regrouping the League's forces. They thought there was still a possibility of a new revolutionary upsurge, led by the democratic middle class, who would be forced by monarchical reaction to adopt more radical measures than hitherto. In an Address dispatched in March 1850 Marx and Engels defined the tactics that they thought should be developed by the League, and in doing so gave more precision to their concept of a proletarian revolution. In the coming revolution, 'As far as the workers are concerned one thing, above all, is definite: they are to remain wage labourers as before. However, the democratic petty bourgeois want better wages and security for the workers, and hope to achieve this by an extension of state employment and welfare measures; in short they hope to bribe the workers with a more or less disguised form of alms and to break their revolutionary strength by temporarily rendering their situation tolerable . . . While the democratic petty bourgeois want to bring the revolution to an end as quickly as possible, achieving at most the aims already mentioned, it is our interest and our task to make the revolution permanent until all the more or less propertied classes have been driven from their positions, until the proletariat has conquered state power and until the association of proletarians has progressed sufficiently far – not only in one country but in all the leading countries of the world – that competition between the proletarians of these countries ceases and at least the decisive forces of production are concentrated in the hands of the workers.' In order to achieve this radicalization of the revolution, the League must 'drive the proposals of the democrats to their logical extreme (the democrats will in any case act in a reformist and not revolutionary manner) and transform these proposals into direct attacks on private property. If, for instance, the petty bourgeoisie propose the purchase of railways and factories, the workers must demand that these railways and factories simply be confiscated by the state without compensation as the property of reactionaries.' Pursuing these tactics would make it necessary for the proletarians to develop complete political independence. Through the initiative of the League the workers must be 'independently organized and centralized in clubs'. These clubs should put up working-class candidates for any elections that are held: 'Even where there is no prospect of achieving their election the workers must put up their own candidates to preserve their independence, to gauge their own strength and to bring their revolutionary position and party standpoint to the public attention.' The workers' clubs should have a clear programme for developing a new type of armed power: 'the workers must try to organize themselves independently as a proletarian guard, with elected leaders and with their own elected general staff; they must try to place themselves not under the orders of the state authority but of the revolutionary local councils set up by the workers'.[12]

This astonishing scenario of proletarian revolution was, of course, hopelessly unrealistic, as Engels was subsequently to admit. Not only had the revolutions of 1848 been definitively defeated, but 'the state of economic development on the Continent at that time was not, by a long way, ripe for the elimination of capitalist production'.[13] Nevertheless, the Address of 1850 did provide a remarkable anticipation of certain elements of a proletarian revolution, either one arising from the turmoil of an unfinished bourgeois-democratic revolution, or one deriving from the contradictions of a reformism based on the extension of state employment and welfare.

Marx and Engels were soon persuaded, by their sense of political reality and their insight into the historical process, to adopt a more sober perspective. However, a strong group within the Communist League remained wedded, against all evidence, to the idea that new revolutionary outbreaks were imminent – and that the determined action of revolutionaries could hasten their arrival. Marx was to refer to this conception as follows: 'For them revolutions are not the product of the realities of the situation but the result of a mere *effort of will*. What we say to the workers is: "You will have fifteen, twenty, fifty years of civil war and national struggle and this is not merely to bring about a change in society but also *to change yourselves* and prepare yourselves for the exercise of political power." Whereas you say on the contrary: "Either we seize power at once, or else we might as well take to our beds." Just as the word "people" has been given an aura of sanctity by the democrats, so you have made an idol of the word "proletariat". Like the democrats you ignore the idea of revolutionary development and substitute for it the slogan of revolutions.'[14] Marx's concern to establish the real workings of the economic and political order was directly associated with his understanding that the working class would only realize its potential as a revolutionary force in the course of an extended series of class struggles in which it would develop its political capacity. The manifold contradictions of the established order would have to be measured and mastered by the workers' movement, if it was really to make a conscious revolution and to ensure itself the leadership of all the oppressed and exploited.

The uneven development of capitalism

The fact that the bourgeois-democratic revolutions of 1848 were all to fail upset the picture of bourgeois advance contained in the *Manifesto*. Already in that text there are certain hints of the uneven character of historical development, such as the concluding remarks on Poland and Germany, and it is these which indicate what were to become the crucial problems for Marxist politics. Of course, the failure of the 1848 revolutions certainly did not mean that the epoch of bourgeois advance was over. Whether we consider only the subsequent decades or the whole subsequent century, capitalism was able to achieve – albeit at a rising cost to mankind as a whole – striking economic and political advances. Henceforward, most bourgeois transformations of state and society were not to have a revolutionary democratic character: they were to be imposed from above by an alliance of the bourgeoisie and the old ruling classes, or from 'outside' by war, rather than from inside and below by popular revolution. One important reason for this was that the bourgeoisie could itself see that any revolutionary democratic upheaval could easily spill over into a generalized revolt against all forms of property and privilege. Moreover, at the economic level the capitalist could not, and did not, immediately seek to displace pre-capitalist forms of exploitation and oppression, but instead incorporated them in a wider system of exchange dominated by capitalist production. Indeed, at the time the *Manifesto* was written capitalism coexisted with – and battened upon – plantation slavery in the Americas, serfdom in Russia and most of eastern Europe, and a web of pre-capitalist forms of dependence in India. While the eventual consequence of the ascendancy of capitalism would be to undermine these anterior modes of production, the first effect was to give them a more concentrated, systematic and extensive character. In the general context of capitalist ascendancy a feudal aristocracy could, by stages, convert itself into a special fraction of the capitalist class, in the manner of the Prussian Junkers. Moreover, as the case of the Tsarist autocracy was to prove, a feudal absolutism could continue to hold political power while capitalism became dominant in the Russian economy as a whole.

In the *Manifesto*, the relations of the advanced capitalist states to the rest of the world were summed up by the formula that capitalism 'compels all nations, on pain of extinction, to adopt the bourgeois mode of production; it compels them to introduce what it calls civilization into their midst, i.e. to become bourgeois themselves'. But the *Manifesto* adds that capitalism was making 'barbarian and semi-barbarian countries dependent on civilized ones, nations of peasants on nations of bourgeois, the East on the West'.[15] The experience of capitalist expansion was greatly to accentuate the implied inequality of these relations. Marx's account of the dynamic of capitalism stressed that it accumulated wealth at one pole and poverty at another, but it did not involve a detailed and direct analysis of how these processes worked themselves out within the world economy capitalism was creating. Instead, Britain was taken as a paradigm and some of the seeds of the later Marxist theories of capitalist imperialism are to be found in the sections of *Capital* dealing with Britain's domination of Ireland. While capitalism developed forces of production on a global scale, the political framework concentrating and guaranteeing the relations of production was that of the nation state. And as imperialism strengthened the process of capital accumulation in the metropolitan countries, so it undermined the development of an indigenous bourgeoisie in the dependent areas. Imperialism, as a superstructure upon capitalist and pre-capitalist social relations, not only produced and intensified uneven development but also combined the most various social forces, locking together the most backward and the most modern forms of economic activity, exploitation and political institutions, in different combinations in every different area. Within this pattern and patchwork of uneven development a fundamental divide, however, can be defined in terms taken from the *Manifesto*. That is the divide between those areas that had a bourgeois revolution, early or late, and those which did not. However, there remains an important distinction between those countries which had a bourgeois *democratic* revolution and those which had a bourgeois revolution imposed from above or from outside.

The complexity of the social formation

The development of the social structure within each capitalist state further complicated and confounded the theses set forth in the *Manifesto*. The notion that capitalism had already, or would soon, simplify the class structure was not borne out. Thus a peasantry with its own internal differentiations continued to exist, even in most of the more advanced countries, and to pose a crucial problem for revolutionary strategy. Both Marx and Engels were to recognize this and combat the anarchist slogan of abolition of all property inheritance mainly on the ground that it would prevent the workers' movement reaching an alliance with the peasantry. In the *Critique of the Gotha Programme* (1875), Marx vigorously rejects the formula that relative to the working class 'all other classes are only one reactionary mass', demanding with particular emphasis whether *peasants* should be lumped together in this way with bourgeois and landowners.[16]

Even if we turn to the urban population, the simplification thesis was not to hold. In the *Manifesto* itself, the thesis was qualified by the statement that there was 'a new class of petty bourgeois ever renewing itself as a supplementary part of bourgeois society'. However, this category of persons was to be progressively supplanted by the advance of modern industry and replaced by 'overseers, bailiffs and shop assistants'.[17] The precise class interests and positions of these overseers, bailiffs and shop assistants was not specified. In *Capital*, Marx did not explicitly abandon the polarization thesis, but the impetus of his research was away from it. So far as the working class was concerned, he acknowledges the tendency of capitalism to produce a whole series of internal divisions 'the better paid strata', the 'nomad' workers, the 'reserve army of unemployed', etc. (see *Capital*, volume I, chapter 25). Marx's analysis of the mode of production hinged on the latter's ability to integrate science with the productive process, and on the increasing discrepancy between socialized forces of production and private relations of production. This has necessarily thrown up a series of thorny topics for Marxist class analysis, concerning the exact class attributes of such diverse categories as scientists, technicians, supervisors, teachers, civil servants, salesmen and so forth. Marx was greatly preoccupied in *Capital* and *Theories of Surplus Value* with the distinction between productive and unproductive workers, but he did not come to any systematic conclusions in the matter. Within the working class, competition on the labour market puts one group of workers against another and encourages differentiation on the basis of a whole series of secondary characteristics: age, sex, religion, language, ethnic origin and so forth. Meanwhile, between the bourgeoisie and proletariat the involution of the relations of production throws up a series of intermediate strata.

The uneven progress of the bourgeois revolution meant that there was considerable heterogeneity among the possessing classes as well as among the masses. Marx identifies a whole series of factions within the French ruling class in his accounts of 1848 and its aftermath. These factions reflected both the historical experience of the French bourgeoisie and the different types of property (land, industry, commerce, finance). In *Capital*,

Marx was to explore the underlying processes by which capitalism took over and absorbed pre-capitalist forms of land rent. However, diversity within the possessing classes did not prevent the different factions rallying round the state power whenever the interests of property were threatened. A vivid demonstration of this had been supplied by the bloody suppression of the popular insurrection in Paris in June 1848, identified by Marx as a turning-point in the revolutionary process throughout Europe. 'The defeat of the June insurgents prepared and flattened the ground on which the bourgeois republic could be founded and erected.'

Marx had characterized the constitutional republic as the dictatorship of the 'united exploiters', exploiters united by fear around the state and the constitution. Concerning the liberties enshrined in the constitution of the French Republic, Marx points out that they were hedged around with provisos that ensured that they could only be effectively enjoyed by the possessing classes: 'each paragraph of the Constitution contains its own antithesis, its own upper and lower house, namely freedom in the general phrase, abolition of freedom in the marginal note. In this way, as long as the *name* of freedom was respected and only its actual implementation prevented (in a legal way, it goes without saying), its constitutional existence remained intact and untouched however fatal the blows dealt to it in its actual physical existence.' Although formal sovereignty resides in the Constitution itself, its physical guarantor is the executive and repressive power of the state. This power is concentrated in the person of the President, with 'the whole of the armed forces behind him', and the extensive bureaucracy of the state administration, to which the President had power of appointment.[18]

The historical analysis of 'The Class Struggles in France' and 'The Eighteenth Brumaire of Louis Bonaparte' explain the particular circumstances that led to a strengthening of the relative autonomy of the state – from, and in the interest of, the possessing classes. But although this phenomenon took the peculiar French form of Bonapartism, Marx's general analysis of the capitalist mode of production suggested that it would be, in some degree, a feature of any social formation dominated by capitalism. This analysis implied a necessary separation of the economic and political level in bourgeois society. A consideration of this thesis will establish more exactly the nature and the specificity of the political order.

Politics and economics in capitalist society

Some essential features of the capitalist mode of production were spelt out in the *Manifesto* itself, but a more thorough account of Marx's views at this time was given in *Wage Labour and Capital*. It is in this latter text that Marx defines the modern proletariat as a class of 'free labourers', in contradistinction to the slave or the serf. 'The slave, together with his labour power, is sold once and for all to his owner. He is a commodity that can pass from the hand of one owner to that of another ... The serf belongs to the land and turns over to the owner of the land the fruits thereof. The *free labourer*, on the other hand, sells himself and, indeed, sells himself piecemeal ... The worker belongs neither to an owner nor to the land, but eight, ten, twelve, fifteen hours of his daily life belong to him who buys them. The worker leaves the capitalist to whom he hires himself whenever he likes, and the capitalist discharges him whenever he thinks fit, as soon as he no longer gets any profit out of him, or not the anticipated profit. But the worker, whose sole source of livelihood is the sale of his labour power, cannot leave *the whole class of purchasers, that is the capitalist class, without renouncing his existence*.'[19]

Given that the capitalist class owns the decisive means of production, they will always be able to exploit the mass of proletarians on the basis of a free and equal exchange of wages for labour power. Marx was, of course, only to develop the concept of labour power, in all its implications, in his later writings. But already in *Wage Labour and Capital* Marx was stressing the vital distinctions quoted above between the position of the direct producer in capitalism and in previous modes of production. Marx's later insistence on the fact that the worker sold the capitalist, not a definite quantity and type of labour, but rather his general capacity to work during a given period, served to reinforce the analysis of the worker under capitalism as a free labourer. A crucial feature of the labour process under developed capitalism was that surplus value was pumped out of the direct producer without the use of physical coercion by the immediate exploiter. This permits an increasing separation of the *organization of production* from the *organization of violence* – or, to put it in other terms, of *economics* from *politics*. The slave owner required

teams of armed overseers, the feudal lord an armed retinue, if
they were to extract surplus labour from the direct producer. All
the capitalist needed, once the conditions of capitalist production
had been established with private ownership of the decisive
means of production, was a free and equal contract to exchange
wages for labour power. Under these conditions the worker would
accumulate capital for the capitalist and reproduce the conditions of his own exploitation. Of course, capitalist private
property would itself have to be defended from individual or
collective attacks against it and a specialized body of armed men
would be required for this purpose – but this specialized repressive
force would not be at the command of the individual capitalist.
The essential function of the state was to guarantee the conditions of capitalist production. In this context, the original
formulations of the *Manifesto* take on a precise significance. The
state executive was indeed a mechanism for managing the common affairs of the whole ruling class – and first and foremost the
organized power of this class for oppressing another.

The nature of the capitalist state

Following from Marx's analysis of the capitalist mode of production, we can therefore define the capitalist state as a specialized
organization of force to guarantee the conditions of capitalist
production. If it is to manage the common affairs of the whole
bourgeoisie, it needs an unchallenged monopoly of force within
its own territory. Such a conception is, of course, close to that
maintained by classical bourgeois sociology, notably Max
Weber. This is not so surprising, since Weber acknowledged that
his own definition of the state as the institution successfully
claiming a monopoly of legitimate force in a given territory was
taken from the speech of a Russian Marxist, namely Trotsky.[20]
Weber's conception was an abstract and ahistorical version of
the Marxist original. Marx and Engels rooted the emergence of
the state in the historical development of a surplus product. The
specific features of the capitalist state could only arise on the
basis of capitalist relations of production. Some of these features
are already present in the late feudal Absolutist state, on the
basis of a developing market economy and under pressure from
the early bourgeois revolutions in the Netherlands and England.
But a unitary, stable and distinct state apparatus only appeared
after the bourgeois revolution. Modern police and armed forces

required an efficient system of taxation as well as a minimum industrial and communications infrastructure. By the middle of the twentieth century, every capitalist state is engaged in a wide range of social and economic activities and it might be thought that this dilutes or qualifies its essential function of monopolizing the organization of force. Certainly these social and economic functions are very important in late capitalist society. But they in no way weaken or qualify its monopoly of violence. It is this monopoly that allows the state to be the arbiter and guarantor of the social formation as a whole. Even though this function of the state is only fully revealed in a period of war or counter-revolution, it is the constant underpinning of social relations, defining the context in which all transactions take place.

The capitalist economy extends on a global basis – only with capitalism did a world economy come into existence. It mediates production and exchange relations in a highly abstract manner. The law of value, the market, the rate of profit – all these economic mechanisms operate in an opaque and mysterious fashion. They bring vast populations into contact with one another, but only through complex and indirect mechanisms. This fundamental characteristic of economic relations in capitalist society is partly concealed by an ideology which insists on a few simple, direct relationships: that between the worker and the boss, the buyer and the seller, one group of workers and another in competition with them. But in each case the truth about such relationships can only be unravelled by reference to the economic context as a whole. By contrast, the state apparatus is said to be governed by abstract principles – the rule of law, constitutional formulae, the mechanisms of popular representation. In reality the state constitutes a sphere of compressed and direct authority within a given territory, constituted by chains of command, orders, police patrols, prison bars, frontier guards. It is because the state is an instrument of this sort that it brings all social classes into direct relations with one another. Thus in the *Poverty of Philosophy* Marx already characterized the state as 'the official resumé of society'.[21] Each capitalist state thus constitutes and defines a particular relationship of class forces. Any fundamental discrepancy will lead to displacement of the prevailing political regime.

It will be recalled that in the *Manifesto* Marx and Engels speak of the 'modern representative state' as the culmination of bourgeois political power.[22] They also refer to the historical

movement in which the bourgeoisie of the more advanced
countries in their battles with the feudal aristocracy – and with
one another – seek to enlist the support of the mass of proletarians. Marx's later writings analyse the economic foundation
of the bourgeois democracy that first appeared in the bourgeois
revolutions. The absence of physical coercion in the productive
process requires its concentrated presence patrolling the perimeter
of the social formation and guaranteeing its basic institutions.
But this does not mean that the separated-out apparatus of
repression must necessarily govern society. Indeed, there are
good reasons why the apparatus of repression should be a
generally subordinate instrument of government in a developed
capitalist society that is not faced with an immediate threat to its
existence. Marx's analysis of the rise of Louis Bonaparte had
stressed that the reason for the super-added independence of the
state power was the comparative weakness and division of the
French bourgeoisie, as well as the strength of the popular
challenge to them from below. Bonapartist bureaucracy was
'only the low and brutal form of a centralization still burdened
by its opposite, feudalism'.[23] In those countries where the bourgeoisie was accumulating tremendous economic and social power,
such as England and the United States, the state machine could
not acquire the same preponderance. In a developed capitalist
country, the repressive power of the state would always be there
to underwrite the integrity of the social order, but it would not
direct public or private affairs.

As Marx insists many times, capitalist exploitation is perfectly
compatible with juridical equality and freedom. The sphere in
which labour power is bought and sold as a commodity is,
Marx declares in a famous passage of *Capital*, 'a very Eden of the
innate rights of man . . . the exclusive realm of Freedom, Equality,
Property and Bentham'.[24] If the innate rights of man are not
violated by the sale of labour power, then they do not need to be
suppressed by the capitalist political regime. Moreover, as both
the *Manifesto* and later economic writings make clear, the
capitalist mode of production is also defined by the constant
application of science to industry and a consequent rise in the
productivity of labour. In these circumstances, capitalists –
whether spurred by competition among themselves or by combination among their workers – can afford to grant economic
concessions to their employees. There are, of course, strict limits
to the concessions they can make; but Marx was to emphasize

that trade unions can raise wages and the working class could extract legislation in its interest even from a purely bourgeois government.

The separation of the economic and political levels in bourgeois society produces a segmentation of the social formation. The economic organization of the working class more or less directly produced by capitalism itself will be pitted against the employer in wage-bargaining – but it will not necessarily challenge the property system or the capitalist state. As Marx was to put it in *Wages, Price and Profit*, trade unions defended the immediate interest of the workers but they did not generally pose a fundamental challenge to capitalism: 'Trades Unions work well as centres of resistance against the encroachments of capital. They fail partially from an injudicious use of their power. They fail generally from limiting themselves to a guerrilla war against the effects of the existing system, instead of simultaneously trying to change it, instead of using their organized forces as a lever for the final emancipation of the working class, that is to say, the ultimate abolition of the wages system.'[25] In these words, addressed to English trade unionists, it is not clear whether the general failure and limitation of the trade unions can be overcome by a purely internal development of the workers' movement. But Marx's very presence before the General Council implied that this could not be the case. Even in the *Manifesto*, the developing organization of workers was strengthened by the adhesion of bourgeois intellectuals who had 'raised themselves to the level of comprehending theoretically the historical movement as a whole'. The development of capitalism did lead to the increasing integration of science into production, but it also led to a complex division of labour. Culture and science developed outside the sphere of direct production – especially in an increasingly ramified educational system. And the schools and universities did not only produce science and technology, but also reproduced workers and managers, scientists and teachers, rulers and ruled. Naturally the ruling class would secure for itself, and for its immediate subalterns, a privileged access to education, science and culture. If the working-class movement was itself to become the ruling class, it would need to break this monopoly, initially by drawing on the specialized knowledge of renegade 'bourgeois ideologists'. Moreover, Marx was well aware of the paradox that if the workers' movement did not take advantage of these more or less individual defections from the bourgeoisie, then it would remain subordinate to the bourgeoisie as a *class*. Again the *Manifesto* had stressed that the initial political formation of the working class was dominated by the bourgeoisie.

The International

Marx's activities within the International Working Men's Association (1864–72) were designed to induce the trade unions to overcome their economic limitation and corporate narrowness. The Inaugural Address drafted by Marx praised such political campaigns as that to limit the length of the working day by legislation and the movement of solidarity with the Polish insurrection of 1863. The Address referred enthusiastically to the simultaneous efforts being made in a number of countries 'at the political reorganization of the working men's party'. It declared 'the lords of land and the lords of capital will always use their political privileges for the defence and perpetuation of their economical monopolies . . . To conquer political power has therefore become the great duty of the working classes'.[26] The Instructions drafted by Marx for the Geneva Congress of the International in 1867 criticized the trade unions for having 'kept too much aloof from general social and political movements'. They should 'consider themselves as the champions and representatives of the whole working class' and 'convince the world at large that their efforts, far from being narrow and selfish, aim at the emancipation of the whole working class'. However, Marx did not imply that the local struggles of trade unions against employers were unimportant: they were 'guerrilla fights between labour and capital' in which a broader organization and understanding could develop.[27] Marx continually urged the English trade-unionists to set up an independent political party of their own and to cease serving as the tail of the Liberal party. Though Marx underestimated the potential strength of reformism, he cannot have doubted that a party set up by the English trade unions would initially be reformist in character. Marx was confident that the important question was whether a real workers' political party was brought into existence or not, rather than its initial political philosophy. An independent proletarian movement would be able to learn from its own experience in a way that was precluded either for small socialist sects or for a workers' organization still under the tutelage of a bourgeois political party. Marx's conception of the proletarian party combined two essential elements. It must be based on the experience and organization forged in the struggles at the point of production. But it must learn how to take up all the questions, national and international, that affect any exploited or oppressed group. To this end it must use every available channel of political action, including the bourgeois electoral process.[28] In his Report to the Basle Congress of the International in 1869, Marx stressed the significance of the wave of strikes that had broken out in Europe, notably in France. Even where, as in Normandy, the strike failed, this was 'compensated for by its moral results. It enlisted the Norman cotton-workers into the revolutionary army of labour, it gave rise to the birth of trade unions'. Marx pointed out in this report that the successful participation of workers' candidates in the General Elections subsequently helped to stimulate the strike movement: 'The only strange feature about those strikes was their sudden explosion after a seeming lull, and the rapid succession in which they followed each other. Still the reason of all this was simple and palpable. Having, during the elections, successfully tried their hands against their public despot, the workmen were naturally led to try them after the elections against their private despots. In one word, the elections had stirred their animal spirits.'[29]

Marx clearly envisaged the ideal form of organization of the workers' movement as one which overcame the capitalist division of the economic and political spheres. This necessitated the co-ordinated activities of diverse forms of organization: trade unions, co-operatives, educational associations, socialist societies, working-class political parties. Marx devoted his energies to the International because it combined these different elements in such a way as to permit a process of political development. The political heterogeneity of the International was a consequence of the fact that it was an expression of the real workers' movement. Because of the objectively antagonistic character of capitalist social relations, a real workers' movement would continually be subject to experiences from which it could learn. Engels was later to explain this in a new introduction to the *Manifesto* written in 1888: 'Marx, who drew up this programme [that of the International] to the satisfaction of all parties, entirely trusted to the intellectual development of the working class, which was sure to result from combined action and mutual discussion. The very events and vicissitudes of the struggle against capital, the defeats even more than the victories, could not help bringing home to men's minds the insufficiency of their various favourite nostrums, and preparing the way for a more complete insight into the true conditions of working-class emancipation.' Although Marx made tactical concessions in drawing up the International's statement of aims, he was able to ensure that it opened with a ringing declaration of the necessity for an independent workers' movement; in this same introduction, Engels explains 'our notion, from the very beginning, was that "the emancipation of the working class must be the act of the working class itself".'[30] When the International was founded, Marx had a low opinion of the existing working-class parties and socialist societies. He evidently hoped that the trade unions which belonged to the International, stimulated by their contact with it, would become the prime instruments of the self-emancipation of the working class. As we have seen, such an expectation was somewhat at variance with his economic analysis, which stressed that the defensive activities of trade unions were both necessary and effective. Although economic dislocations might impel them to more general political aims, they were essentially organizations for securing economic concessions and this was the source of both their strength and weakness. The Paris Commune of 1871 was to impress on Marx the necessity for the proletarian movement to develop its own forms of political organization for seizing and securing power.

The lessons of the Commune

The uprising of the Parisian masses in 1871 in the aftermath of the Franco–Prussian war was a decisive event in the development of Marx's political ideas. In a foreword to the *Communist Manifesto* written in 1872 Marx wrote that, while the political principles contained by the *Manifesto* were generally correct, the experience of the Paris Commune – 'where the proletariat for the first time held political power' – had rendered it 'antiquated' in at least one important respect. The *Manifesto* had given no detailed account of the political form of the proletarian revolution and its consequences for the existing state machinery. The Commune gave a vivid demonstration of what was meant by the 'dictatorship of the proletariat'. Above all, it had shown that 'the working class cannot take hold of the ready-made state apparatus and wield it for its own purposes'.[31]

From the days of his earliest political activity, Marx had a strong antipathy to the state bureaucracy and was critical of the political abstraction of the representative state. He had described the function of the bureaucracy as that of protecting the '*imaginary universality of particular interests*'. It was in the nature of the state bureaucracy to raise itself above society: 'the bureaucracy holds the state, the spiritual essence of society in thrall as its private property. The universal spirit of bureaucracy is *secrecy*, it is mystery preserved within itself by means of the hierarchical structure . . . The principle of its knowledge is therefore *authority*, and its patriotism is the adulation of authority. Within itself, however, spiritualism degenerates into *crass materialism*, the materialism of passive obedience, the worship of authority, the *mechanism* of fixed, formal action, of rigid principles, views and tradition. As for the individual bureaucrat, the purpose of the state becomes his private purpose, a hunt for promotion, careerism!' But Marx insists that 'the bureaucracy is only a "formal system" for a content lying outside it'. That content was the particular interests of property. Marx's conclusion was that 'bureaucracy can be superseded only if the universal interest becomes a particular interest in reality'.[32] The political institutions of the representative state do not produce such a result, rather they produce an abstraction from civil society in favour of the dominant particular interests: 'The separation of the political state from civil society takes the form of a separation of the deputies from their electors . . . The deputies of civil society are a society which is not connected to its electors by any instruction or commission . . . They have authority as the representatives of *public* affairs, whereas in reality they represent private interests.'[33] This critique of bureaucracy and the representative state was made by Marx prior to his identification of the working class as the fundamental revolutionary class. This latter discovery was made by Marx at the same time as he identified the state as an apparatus of *force* that would have to be overthrown. The text in which Marx first outlined these two positions was his article on the revolt of the Silesian weavers. Prior to this he had criticized the political abstraction represented by the state: from this time onwards he attacked the state as an instrument of repression, which thereby *concentrated* social relations.

In 'The Civil War in France', the Address of the General Council drafted by Marx in response to the Commune and its suppression, he for the first time indicates the fundamental

features of a workers' state. Each of these features arises out of
the necessity of overthrowing the old state power: 'The centralized state power, with its ubiquitous organs of standing army,
police bureaucracy, clergy and judicature – organs wrought after
the plan of a systematic and hierarchic division of labour.' In
the wake of the development of capitalist industry and its
attendant class struggle, 'the state power assumes more and
more the character of the national power of capital over labour,
of a public force organized for social enslavement, of an engine
of class despotism. After every revolution marking a progressive
phase in the class struggle, the purely repressive character of the
state power stands out in bolder and bolder relief.' Marx insisted
that the parliamentary republic had played a decisive part in
this strengthening of the state power, 'in order to convince the
working class that the "social" republic meant the republic
ensuring their social subjection'. Since the state apparatus of
repression was the lynch-pin of the bourgeois order – whether in
the form of the parliamentary republic or the Bonapartist
Empire – the first task of a real workers' revolution must be that
of settling accounts with it: 'The first decree of the Commune,
therefore, was the suppression of the standing army, and the
substitution for it of the armed people.'[34]

The political institutions of the Commune represented a
qualitative advance over even the most democratic bourgeois
republic. 'The Commune was formed of the municipal councillors,
chosen by universal suffrage in the various wards of the town,
responsible and revocable at short terms. The majority of its
members were naturally working men, or acknowledged representatives of the working class. The Commune was to be a
working not a parliamentary body, executive and legislative at
the same time . . . From the members of the Commune down-
wards, the public service had to be done at *workmen's wages* . . .
While the merely repressive organs of the old governmental
power were to be amputated and its legitimate functions were to
be wrested from an authority usurping pre-eminence over
society itself, and restored to the responsible agents of society.
Instead of deciding once every three or six years which member
of the ruling class was to misrepresent the people in parliament,
universal suffrage was to serve the people, constituted in Communes, as individual suffrage serves every other employer in
search for the workmen and managers of his business.'[35]

Through the political form of the Commune, the working

class could lead all those classes menaced by capital in an assault on the old order. 'The Commune was perfectly right in telling the peasants that "its victory was their only hope" . . . The Commune would have . . . transformed his (the peasant's) present bloodsuckers, the notary, advocate, executor, and other judicial vampires, into salaried communal agents, elected by, and responsible to, himself. It would have freed him of the tyranny of the *garde champêtre*, the gendarme and the prefect; would have put enlightenment by the schoolmaster in place of stultification by the priest.' These were the 'immediate boons' that the Commune offered the peasant; but Marx also points out that the Commune alone would be able to cancel peasant debts and offer long-run economic salvation in the face of 'the competition of capitalist farming'. The Commune had also proved that the middle strata could be won to the side of the working class: 'this was the first revolution in which the working class was openly acknowledged as the only class capable of social initiative even by the great bulk of the Paris middle class'.[36]

Marx declares that the modest social measures which the Commune was able to implement during its two months of embattled existence could only 'betoken the tendency of a government of the people by the people'. Among the most significant of its plans were those concerning education and culture: 'The whole of the educational institutions were opened to the people gratuitously, and at the same time cleared of all interference of church and state. Thus not only was education made accessible to all, but science itself freed from the fetters which class prejudice and governmental force had imposed on it.' Marx privately thought that the Commune should have undertaken bolder economic and military measures – in particular it should have launched an attack on Versailles while the relationship of forces was in its favour. But whatever the limitations of the Commune's policy, its greatest achievement 'was its own working existence'. Even its errors were open to scrutiny and correction: 'the Commune did not pretend to infallibility, the invariable attribute of all governments of the old stamp. It published its doings and sayings, it initiated the public into all its shortcomings.' The Commune had a number of incompetent and inadequate leaders, including 'survivors of and devotees to past revolutions'. 'They are an unavoidable evil: with time they are shaken off; but time was not allowed to the Commune.' Marx summarizes the significance of the Commune in the following terms: 'The multiplicity of interpretations to which the Commune has been subjected, and the multiplicity of interests which construed it in their favour, show that it was a thoroughly expansive political form, while all previous forms of government had been emphatically repressive. Its true secret was this. It was essentially a working-class government, the product of the struggle of the producing class against the appropriating class, the political form at last discovered under which to work out the economical emancipation of labour. Except on this last condition the Communal constitution would have been an impossibility and a delusion. The political rule of the producer cannot coexist with the perpetuation of his social slavery.'[37]

In 'The Civil War in France' Marx was making propaganda for the Commune, highlighting what he saw as its most significant features. But at the same time he was irrevocably and publicly defining the Marxist conception of the dictatorship of the proletariat. Marx emphasized the immense potentialities of the Commune in order to indicate the future path of social revolution. Breaking the power of the capitalist state and destroying its repressive apparatus was an essential pre-condition for any generalized expropriation of the bourgeoisie. In Marx's account of the Commune it has seemed to some that there is an echo of Rousseau and of his own earliest writings on the state. Thus the delegates to the Commune are not like parliamentary representatives since they are 'at any time revocable and bound by the *mandat impératif* (formal instructions) of his constituents'.[38] Moreover the 'particular interest' reflected in the Commune was at the same time capable of leading a universal emancipation. However, it would be misleading to imagine that the old philosophical critiques had now merely discovered an active historical protagonist. The new social forces reflected in the proletariat gave it the possibility of producing valid and effective forms of political representation and of controlling 'the responsible agents of society'. They did not need to fear representation. For Rousseau and the young Marx, all forms of representation were a falsification and an abstraction. For the mature Marx, the truly collective character of the working class had to find collective political expression if the productive forces of modern society were to be mastered. Because the working class was the motor force of socialized forces of production, it had the possibility of controlling the necessary forms of political abstraction, of which the Commune itself was only the elementary and primitive form. In the first draft of 'The Civil War in France' Marx points out: 'As the state machinery and parliamentarism are not the real life of the ruling classes, but only the organized general organs of their dominion, the political guarantees and forms and expressions of the old order of things, so the Commune is not the social movement of the working class and therefore of a general regeneration of mankind, but the organized means of action. The Commune does not do away with class struggle . . . but it affords the rational medium in which that class struggle can run through its different phases in the most rational and humane way.'[39]

In the aftermath of the Commune, Marx was certainly aware that the workers' movement would have to develop politically if the battle of the Communards was to be taken up again and pressed to a victorious conclusion. The Commune had positively indicated the outline of a workers' state. But there can be no doubt from Marx's accounts of the Commune that it needed to develop a more clear-sighted social and economic programme. In the aftermath of the Commune the English trade unions withdrew from the International, which had been the target of ruling-class hysteria throughout Europe. What remained of the International was riven by the disputes with the anarchists over the necessity for 'political action'. Marx was more convinced than ever of the need for the workers' movement to develop adequate political forms. The Commune would have survived longer and accomplished more if there had been a stronger political leadership within it. The anarchists were opposed to the workers' movement developing open political parties and instead regressed to the stage of revolutionary conspiracies. Although Bakunin opposed Marx's hegemony within the International in the name of democracy, his own conceptions of revolutionary organization envisaged no internal democratic structure at all. In some areas Bakunin's representatives did establish real workers' organizations which Marx and Engels ignored to their cost. But for the most part his conspiratorial activities led to fiasco and fantasy – or worse. The anarchist refusal of 'political action' also had the consequence of removing the revolutionary organization from developing authentic forms of proletarian representation. This was certainly a drastic antidote against reformism, but, as it turned out, not an effective one.

Programme and party

When the two wings of the German workers' movement – Lassallean and semi-Marxist – united, adopting a common programme, at Gotha in 1875, Marx and Engels were forced again to define the essence of their conception of revolutionary proletarian politics. They had consistently opposed the influence of Lassalle, who had built up a considerable following among German workers by adulterating the theories of the *Manifesto* with an accommodation to the Prussian state and Bismarck's policy of uniting Germany under Prussian hegemony. The key points in Lassalle's agitation had been the demand for universal suffrage and advocacy of workers' co-operatives to be financed by the state; in return for satisfaction of these demands Lassalle was prepared to support Bismarck's policy. As soon as Marx saw the orientation of Lassalle's policy he broke relations with him. After Lassalle's death, Marx successfully encouraged the leaders of the Lassallean party to develop a trade-union organization that would enable the German workers to discover their own strength. Marx and Engels repeatedly urged the need for a co-ordination of the divided forces of the German movement, so that it is all the more significant that they were to react so strongly to the programme of unification.

The main grounds on which Marx and Engels objected to the Gotha programme were that it failed to take up a revolutionary position on the state, that it failed to place the German workers' struggle in an internationalist perspective and that it failed to base the party's strategy on proletarian class struggle. Each of these failures was rooted in Lassallean confusions which spurred Marx to produce one of the most succinct and peremptory statements of his politics. The Gotha Programme declared that: 'The German workers' party, in order to pave the way for the solution of the social question, demands the creation of producers' co-operatives with state aid.' Marx's riposte was as follows: 'The existing class struggle is discarded in favour of the hack phrase of a newspaper scribbler – "the social question", for the solution of which one "paves the way". Instead of being the result of the revolutionary process of social transformation in society, the "socialist organization of the whole of labour" "arises" from "state aid" to producers' co-operatives which the *state*, not the workers, is to "call into being". The notion that state loans can be used for the construction of a new society as easily as they can for the construction of a new railway is worthy of Lassalle's imagination.' The Programme also substituted a list of democratic demands addressed to the existing German state for any reference to the necessity for a revolutionary dictatorship of the proletariat. Moreover, even these democratic demands were half-hearted: 'Even vulgar democrats, who see the millennium in the democratic republic and who have no inkling that it is precisely in this final state form of bourgeois society that the class struggle must be fought to a conclusion, even they tower mountains above this kind of democratism which keeps within the bounds of what is allowed by the police and disallowed by logic . . . Despite its democratic clang, the whole programme is thoroughly infested with the Lassallean sect's servile belief in the state, or, what is no better, by a democratic faith in miracles, or rather, it is a compromise between these two sorts of faith in miracles, both equally far removed from socialism.'[40]

In the *Manifesto*, Marx and Engels had declared that 'united action, of the leading civilized countries at least, is one of the first conditions for the emancipation of the proletariat'.[41] The celebrated call 'Proletarians of all countries, unite!' had always been the motto of their political activity. In the Inaugural address to the International, Marx had pointed out: 'Past experience has shown how disregard of that bond of brotherhood which ought to exist between the workmen of different countries, and incite them to stand firmly by each other in all their struggles for emancipation, will be chastised by the common discomfiture of their incoherent efforts.'[42] The internationalist practice elaborated by Marx in the International in principle called for opposition to the militarism of capitalist states and support for the struggles of oppressed peoples. In his Address on the Paris Commune, Marx remarked the significance of the fact that it had given responsible commands to foreign revolutionaries and that 'to broadly mark the new era of history it was conscious of initiating . . . the Commune pulled down that colossal symbol of martial glory, the Vendôme column'.[43] Marx's German co-thinkers had distinguished themselves at the time of the Franco-Prussian war by opposing the war, despite Bismarck's adroit stage-managing and the outburst of popular war fever.

Marx found the Gotha programme to lack completely the internationalist proletarian spirit: 'And to what is the internationalism of the German workers' party reduced? To the consciousness that the result of their efforts "will be the international brotherhood of peoples" – a phrase borrowed from the bourgeois League of Peace and Freedom and which is intended to pass as an equivalent for the international brotherhood of the working classes in the joint struggle against the ruling classes and their governments. Not a word, therefore, about the *international role* of the German working class . . . In fact, the programme's commitment to internationalism is *infinitely smaller* even than that of the free trade party. The latter also claims that the result of its efforts will be the "international brotherhood of peoples". It is also *doing* something, however, to internationalize trade and is certainly not content with the mere consciousness that all peoples are carrying on trade at home.'[44]

Marx and Engels had themselves usually regarded the formation of a united workers' movement as good and desirable in itself. However, in the battle with the anarchists over 'political action' and as a consequence of the Commune, they had become more attentive to the problem of the authentic political expression and representation of proletarian politics. A clear and coherent programme was of vital significance in defining a party. Marx argued in his prefatory note to the 'Critique of the Gotha Programme' that if his supporters could not persuade the ADAV to abandon its Lassallean nostrums, then 'they should simply have concluded an agreement for common action'.[45] Engels had commented shortly before German unification on the fact that political differentiation in the workers' movement was unavoidable and healthy: 'Hegel said long ago: a party proves itself victorious by *splitting* and being able to stand the split. The movement of the proletariat necessarily passes through different stages of development; at every stage part of the people get stuck and do not join in the further advance.' Recalling later the struggle against the influence of Lassalle, Engels commented: 'It seems that every workers' party of a big country can develop only through internal struggle, which accords with the laws of dialectical development in general.'[46]

Although the German Social Democrats came to see themselves more and more as Marxists with the passage of time, their relations with Marx and Engels were often strained. A characteristic episode illustrating the problem of proletarian representation as well as the necessity of internal struggle was the dispute over the conduct of the party's parliamentary representatives and the principles governing the editing of its theoretical journal. Max Kayser, a Reichstag deputy for the Social Democratic Party, voted in 1879 for one of Bismarck's taxation proposals; the other deputies had given him permission to do this, despite the fact that it was in violation of the party's programme. The man nominated to edit the party's theoretical journal openly attacked Kayser's action, to the consternation of the party leadership. The party leadership, therefore, nominated a supervisory commission to vet the contents of the journal. These proceedings scandalized Marx and Engels. It seemed to them that the real violation of discipline was that committed by Kayser and that the reaction of Hirsch, the proposed editor of the party journal, was entirely justified and necessary. They asked: 'has German Social Democracy indeed been infected by the parliamentary disease and does it really believe that with the popular vote the Holy Ghost is poured out over the elect, that meetings of the parliamentary party are transformed into infallible councils and party decisions into inviolable dogmas?'. So far as Marx and Engels were concerned, the party's parliamentary representatives were elected not in their personal capacity but as champions of the party's programme. Unlike other representatives in a parliament, they possessed a *mandat impératif*, formal instructions embodied in the party's programme. The workers' party should embody a proletarian democracy opposed to the authority of an alien class embodied by the bourgeois parliament's mechanisms of political abstraction. The Social Democratic deputies enjoyed full political rights – but as members of the party, like any other, not because they were deputies. Marx and Engels found the critical position of Hirsch to be exemplary and attacked the editorial commission set up by the party leadership for attempting to suppress an entirely healthy and necessary discussion inside the party on the scandalous behaviour of its parliamentary representatives: 'they are already revelling so much in the feeling of bureaucratic omnipotence that in reply to . . . Hirsch they are already claiming the new power to *decide* on the acceptance of articles. The editorial commission has already become a commission of *censorship*'.[47]

The attitude of the proposed 'editorial commission' met with vigorous opposition from Marx and Engels on the grounds of the political content of its proposals, as well as its bureaucratic methods. The editorial commission had declared that it was opposed to 'a one-sided struggle for the interests of the industrial workers' and wished the party to become an organization of 'all honourable democrats . . . at whose head the independent representatives of science and all men filled with a true love of humanity were to march'. They praised the activity of the party for rejecting 'the path of violent bloody revolution' and instead pursuing 'the path of legality, i.e. reform'. Marx and Engels were outraged at the blatant rejection of the class struggle advocated by the editorial commission: in attacking it, they again underlined their fundamental axiom that the true source of all proletarian politics was the elemental force of the class struggle. They summarized the argument of the editorial commission as follows: 'Thus, if 500,000–600,000 Social Democratic voters, one tenth to one eighth of the whole electorate, dispersed furthermore, far and wide across the whole country, are sensible enough not to run their heads against a wall and to attempt a 'bloody revolution', one against ten, this proves that they forever exclude the possibility of making use of a tremendous external event, of a sudden revolutionary upsurge which might result from it, indeed of a *victory* gained by the people in a conflict arising from it! If Berlin should again be so uneducated as to have another 18 March [1848], the Social Democrats, instead of taking part in the struggle as "rabble with a mania for barricades", must rather "pursue the path of legality", curb the movement, clear away the barricades and, if necessary, march with the splendid army against the rough, one-sided, uneducated masses. If the gentlemen maintain that this is not what they meant, then what did they mean?'[48]

In the view of Marx and Engels, the party should prepare itself and its followers for such an explosion of popular revolt precipitated by some 'external event' (war, crisis of the ruling order, etc.). It should be continually bringing forward in all its public agitation, including in the Reichstag, demands and proposals calculated to stimulate the organization and combativity of the extra-parliamentary movement and to expose the rotten workings of the capitalist system. The editorial commission by contrast wished to limit the party's agitation to certain 'immediate goals' acceptable to the ruling power. As Marx and Engels put it: 'The programme is not to be *abandoned* but only *postponed* – for an indefinite period. It is accepted, but not actually for oneself and for one's own lifetime, but posthumously, as an heirloom for one's children and one's children's children. In the meantime one applies "all one's strength and energy" to all sorts of petty trifles and to patching up the capitalist order, so that at least it looks as if something is happening and at the same time the bourgeoisie is not alarmed. Compared with that I would much prefer the Communist Miquel, who proves his unshakable belief in the overthrow of capitalist society in a few hundred years by indulging in swindles for all he is worth, making an honest contribution to the crash of 1873 and thus *really* doing something to bring about the collapse of the existing order.'[49]

Marx and Engels emphatically conclude: 'We cannot ally ourselves, therefore, with people who openly declare that the workers are too uneducated to free themselves and must first be liberated from above by philanthropic big bourgeois and petty bourgeois.' They point out: 'If these gentlemen constitute themselves as a social-democratic petty-bourgeois party, they have a perfect right to do so; it would be possible, then, to negotiate with them under certain circumstances and to form a common front with them under certain circumstances.'[50] Marx and Engels always stressed that the workers' movement should seek collectively to appropriate the best in bourgeois science and culture. Individual bourgeois intellectuals should be welcome in the workers' movement and could 'supply it with educative elements'. But such renegades from the ruling class could only make a genuine contribution if they accepted the self-emancipation of the working class. Marx and Engels certainly did not underestimate their own theoretical contribution to the workers' movement, and indubitably their privileged cultural background made this contribution possible. But from the 1840s onwards, they did strive to study and learn from the real, historical proletarian movement and its experience of class struggle: the revolt of the Silesian weavers, the Chartists, the revolutions of 1848 and their aftermath, the Fenian movement in Ireland, the development of the English trade unions, the Commune, the experiences of the first workers' parties. To begin with, their politics were highly schematic and often at variance with their own subsequent political standpoints (e.g. on colonialism). But they did in the main base themselves on the real development of the workers' movement and not seek to impose upon it some favoured nostrum or utopia of their own. As their analysis of the bourgeois order became more elaborated, so did their political conceptions. They favoured a combination of tactics for developing the workers' movement as the leader of the conscious independent movement of the immense majority. They had confidence that the workers' movement had the capacity to control the political structures that were needed to destroy the bourgeois order. They insisted that ultimate sovereignty belonged to the workers' movement itself in its struggle against the prevailing order.

However, the political theory that Marx and Engels developed was in many respects incomplete. From the mid-forties onwards, they were generally hostile to most manifestations of nationalism. Their failure to analyse the international dimension of capitalist expansion, the imperialism of the first capitalist powers, meant that they did not anticipate the importance of movements for national liberation. It also meant that they did not anticipate the intense economic and military rivalry that would increasingly develop between the major imperialist states. In his writings on France, Marx had identified militarism and a powerful apparatus of repression with the backward features of French society, when compared with England or the United States. He saw Bonapartism as the antithesis of bourgeois democracy. Yet before long Britain and the United States were to develop a bureaucratic military complex at least as large as that of France. Meanwhile, France was to adopt a bourgeois parliamentary system similar to that prevailing in the Anglo-Saxon states. Even Germany and Italy were to adopt parliamentary forms, though less securely. In his early writings on France, Marx had insisted on the practical impossibility of a parliamentary republic 'with social institutions' on the model of February 1848. Given the economic development of France at this time he was right. But by the time of Marx's death the first capitalist states were beginning to discover not only that they could afford social and economic reforms, but that these reforms were a convenient way of obtaining a more educated and contented labour force. The original accumulation of capital had been greatly boosted in these countries by various forms of colonial plunder. The application of science to industry and the growth of a more elaborate and differentiated economy had greatly raised the social productivity of labour. On this basis a parliamentary republic with 'social institutions' was not at all impossible. These were the conditions that were to shape the workers' movement in the years preceding the First World War. They were, however, also to be accompanied by more advanced forms of proletarian class struggle than had ever been witnessed by Marx and Engels – the first-class actions of an industrial proletariat.

In one of his last major political texts, the 'Introduction to Marx's *Class Struggles in France*', Engels reviewed the political trajectory that he and Marx had followed. He conceded that the majority revolution that they had worked for had not been a historical possibility in 1848, but maintained that the later development of capitalism, with its 'revolutions from above' and its great expansion of capitalist industry, had now put it on the agenda. 'The time of surprise attacks, of revolutions carried through by small conscious minorities at the head of unconscious majorities, is past. Where it is a question of complete transformation of the social organization, the masses themselves must also be in it, must themselves have already grasped what is at stake, what they are going in for, body and soul.' Engels insists in this text that the prevalence of bourgeois democratic forms offers a tremendous opportunity to the workers' parties: 'The *Communist Manifesto* had already proclaimed the winning of universal suffrage, of democracy, as one of the first and most important tasks of the militant proletariat.' Engels pointed out that electoral agitation provided a gauge of the strength of the workers' party and 'a means second to none for getting in touch with the mass of people where they still stand aloof from us; of forcing all parties to defend their views and actions against our attacks before all the people; and, further, it provided our representatives in the Reichstag with a platform from which they could speak to their opponents in parliament, and to the masses without, with quite other authority and freedom than in the press or at meetings.' This text by Engels has sometimes been regarded as a sign of incipient reformism. It was written for legal publication in Germany and is therefore cautious in its formulations – though it was not cautious enough for the Social Democratic leaders, who cut out its numerous hints about the necessity for the workers' party to be well prepared for a future test of force between itself and the state. However, the whole argument of the 'Introduction' makes it clear that all possible legal means are to be employed to enhance the capacity of the working masses to take their destiny into their own hands and to ensure a victorious outcome to the eventual confrontation between the workers and the ruling power. Engels certainly did not forget that the state was essentially an organization of force defending the interests of the possessing classes. He warned that the bourgeoisie would break its own democratic constitutional

forms if these threatened its property. He also predicted that the
next war which capitalism was preparing could only be 'a world
war of unheard-of cruelty and absolutely incalculable outcome'.
The last section of this text uses an analogy with the role of the
early Christian Church in the Roman Empire to advocate social
democratic agitation within the armed forces. He points out that
the early Christians were at this time 'a dangerous party of
overthrow' who carried out both 'seditious activities in secret'
and open agitation, including in the imperial armed forces. He
declares that eventually this party of overthrow were forced to
respond to persecution by 'burning the Emperor's palace at
Nicomedia over his head'. Whatever the limitations of this ruse
for evading the censorship, Engels's Aesopian language speaks
clearly enough and the message is not a reformist one.[51]

The reason that some of the later utterances of Marx and
Engels were capable of being given a reformist interpretation is
that they did not live to see the first nationwide actions of a
modern working class. As we have seen, they responded warmly
to the Commune – but this was still essentially a revolt sustained
by artisans, journeymen and petty bourgeois. During the lifetime of Marx and Engels, there was no national general strike
anywhere in Europe, nor was there any generalized movement of
factory occupation. The soviets and workers' councils of the
twentieth century were to represent an advance upon the Commune because they had this firmer class basis. Without any
experience of such proletarian explosions, Marx and Engels
could not complete their theory of the proletarian revolution,
even if they could clearly distinguish it from Blanquism and
'democratic faith in miracles'. The task of developing their
theory fell to the revolutionary Marxists who learnt the lessons
of 1905 and 1917.[52] However, as we have sought to show, those
who came after Marx and Engels did not start from scratch
when it came to formulating proletarian strategy and tactics.
They were equipped not simply with a philosophical standpoint, a
method of social analysis or an economic doctrine, but also with
the elements of a revolutionary political theory premissed upon
the capacities of the modern workers' movement.

Notes

1. cf. Sebastiano Timpanaro, *On Materialism*, London 1976.
2. Lucio Colletti has claimed: 'It is Rousseau to whom the critique of
Parliamentarism, the theory of popular delegacy and even the idea of the

state's disappearance can all be traced back. This implies in turn that the true *originality* of Marxism must be sought rather in the field of social and economic analysis than in political theory.' Introduction by Lucio Colletti to Karl Marx, *Early Writings*, London 1975, p. 46. The claims of Machiavelli as pre-eminent precursor of Marxist politics have been advanced most notably by Antonio Gramsci, and it is the Machiavelli of *The Prince* rather than *The Discourses* to whom he most often refers (see 'The Modern Prince' in Antonio Gramsci, *Selections from the Prison Notebooks*, edited by Quintin Hoare and Geoffrey Nowell Smith, London 1971, pp. 123–205). A certain tendency to reduce Marxist politics to Jacobinism is often apparent in these identifications. On the other hand, the notion of 'totalitarian democracy' confected by the anti-Marxist historian J. L. Talmon insists on the identification of Rousseau and Marx, doing a serious injustice to both thinkers in the process: J. L. Talmon, *The Origins of Totalitarian Democracy*, New York 1960, and *Political Messianism: the Romantic Phase*, New York 1960.

3. Karl Marx, 'Critique of Hegel's Philosophy of Right. Introduction' in *Early Writings*, London 1975, pp. 252, 257 This text is sometimes quoted as defining Marx's conception of the proletariat's role in revolution (cf. the remarks of Alvin Gouldner in 'The Metaphoricality of Marxism', Amsterdam 1974, a chapter of Gouldner's forthcoming study *On Marxism*). This is most misleading and involves ignoring practically everything that Marx and Engels subsequently wrote about the working class. Marx had not at this time encountered the workers' movement or adopted the standpoint of socialist revolution, hence the largely passive and subordinate role ascribed to the proletariat in the revolution.

4. Karl Marx, 'Critical Notes on the King of Prussia and Social Reform' in *Early Writings*, pp. 403, 415, 416, 420.

5. Karl Marx and Frederick Engels, 'Manifesto of the Communist Party' in *The Revolutions of 1848*, edited and introduced by David Fernbach, London 1973, pp. 70, 72, 69, 72.

6. ibid. pp. 68, 75.

7. ibid. pp. 75, 76.

8. ibid. pp. 77, 78, 86, 78, 87.

9. Frederick Engels, 'Speech on Poland', *The Revolutions of 1848*, p. 101. Marx was later to imply a similar perspective in his letter to the Chartist Labour Parliament in 1855. This text also contains a succinct formulation of the reasons why the working class was the fundamental revolutionary force: 'It is the working millions of Great Britain who have first laid down the real basis of a new society – modern industry, which transformed the destructive agencies of nature into the productive power of man. The English working classes with invincible energies, by the sweat of their brows and brains, have called into life the material means for ennobling labour itself, and of multiplying its fruits to such a degree as to make general abundance possible. By creating the inexhaustible productive powers of modern industry they have fulfilled the first condition of the emancipation of labour. They have now to realize its other condition. They have to free those wealth producing powers from the infamous shackles of monopoly, and subject them to the joint control of the producers . . .' *Surveys from Exile*, p. 278.

10. 'Manifesto', *The Revolutions of 1848*, pp. 97, 98.

11. ibid. pp. 69, 87, 80, 79–80. The schematism of the *Manifesto* represents in part a residue of the paradoxical mode of philosophical reflection which

is mocked in the section on 'Socialist and Communist Literature'. It also led to sweeping declarations about the significance of the nation and the family (ibid. pp. 77–8). The economic theory of Marx and Engels at this time contained the following assumption: 'Wage labour rests exclusively on competition between the labourers' (ibid. p. 79). For this reason simply by combining into trade unions the proletariat 'cuts from under its feet the very foundation on which the bourgeoisie produces and appropriates products' (ibid. p. 79).

12. Karl Marx and Frederick Engels, 'Address of the Central Committee to the Communist League (March 1850)', *The Revolutions of 1848*, pp. 323–4, 326, 327, 329.

13. Frederick Engels, 'Introduction to *The Class Struggles in France*' in Marx/Engels, *Selected Works*, London 1968, p. 656. For an evaluation of the political activity of Marx and Engels during the early period, see in particular two important recent studies: Michael Löwy, *La Théorie de la Révolution chez le Jeune Marx*, Paris 1970, and Fernando Claudin, *Marx, Engels y la Revolucion de 1848*, Madrid 1975. These works supply a necessary corrective to the forced interpretation of this period to be found in Richard N. Hunt, *The Political Ideas of Marx and Engels*, London 1975. Thus Hunt argues that many positions adopted by Marx and Engels in the *Manifesto* and the Address of March 1850 were mere tactical concessions inconsistent with their overall political strategy. Hunt fails to explain why Marx and Engels should choose to adopt tactics at variance with their strategy and he does not explain how it was that both texts were subsequently republished without disclaimer. Throughout their life Marx and Engels referred to the *Manifesto* in the warmest terms, regarding it as the first comprehensive statement of their position. The March 1850 Address certainly does not have the same status as the *Manifesto*, but it is absurd to deny that Marx and Engels were responsible for this text. Both in style and content the Address is very similar to Marx's 'Class Struggles in France'; see also the remarkable letter by Engels to Wedemeyer, 12 April 1853, with its presentiment of the necessity and perils of a premature proletarian revolution: Marx/Engels, *Selected Correspondence*, Moscow 1965, pp. 77–8.

14. Karl Marx, *The Cologne Communist Trial*, London 1971, pp. 62–3.

15. Karl Marx and Frederick Engels, 'Manifesto', *The Revolutions of 1848*, pp. 71, 72.

16. Karl Marx, 'Critique of the Gotha Programme', *The First International and After*, edited and introduced by David Fernbach, London 1974, p. 349.

17. 'Manifesto', *The Revolutions of 1848*, p. 89. In his *The Leninist Theory of Organization*, London 1974, Ernest Mandel discusses the class position of technicians and intellectual workers. See also Nicos Poulantzas, 'The Petty Bourgeoisie: Traditional and New' in *Classes in Contemporary Capitalism*, London 1975, pp. 191–327; and Erik Ohlin Wright 'Contradictory Class Locations' *New Left Review* 98, July–August 1976.

18. Karl Marx, 'The Eighteenth Brumaire of Louis Bonaparte', *Surveys from Exile*, edited and introduced by David Fernbach, London 1973, pp. 155, 160, 161.

19. Karl Marx, 'Wage Labour and Capital', Marx/Engels, *Selected Works*, pp. 75–6. The labourer is 'free' also in the sense of being without property. Once inside the capitalist factory the labourer is subject to the authority of the capitalist or his manager. However, this fact does not cancel out the significance of the free contract by which the labourer sells

his labour power to the capitalist, especially since the transformation of the labour process produced by technical advance continually encourages both sides to redefine the terms of the original sale. Although the organization of workers at the point of production will seek to set limits to the arbitrary power of management, in the end, so long as the capitalist ownership of industry remains effective, this authority has to be accepted in some form. A tendency to reduce capitalist social relations simply to authority relations within the factory or workplace is to be found in the Frankfurt school of critical social theory: see Herbert Marcuse, 'A Study On Authority', in *Studies in Critical Philosophy*, London 1972, pp. 128–43. However, it must be conceded that Marxists have not sufficiently studied the everyday struggle over authority in the workplace that takes place within the general framework of capitalist social relations. But see Harry Braverman, *Labor and Monopoly Capital*, New York 1976, for a discussion of this problem; unfortunately this important study does not adequately analyse union power in the workplace.

20. Max Weber, 'Politics as a Vocation' in *From Max Weber*, edited by H. H. Gerth and C. Wright Mills, New York 1946, pp. 77–128. Trotsky first singled out the organization of violence as the essential monopoly of the state in his defence speech before the Tsarist court in September 1906 (printed as an appendix to Leon Trotsky, *1905*, London 1974). The celebrated Marxist formula that the state will wither away in the future socialist society refers essentially to the disappearance of physical coercion in social relations.

21. Karl Marx, *The Poverty of Philosophy*, London 1957, p. 156.

22. 'Manifesto', *The Revolutions of 1848*, p. 69.

23. Karl Marx, 'The Eighteenth Brumaire of Louis Bonaparte', *Surveys from Exile*, p. 245. However, Marx's analysis of the significance of Louis Bonaparte's coup for France was not accurate; see the interesting discussion of the Second Empire in E. J. Hobsbawm, *The Age of Capital*, London 1975, chapter six.

24. Karl Marx, *Capital*, vol. 1, new translation by Ben Fowkes, with an introduction by Ernest Mandel and the first English translation of the 'Results of the Immediate Process of Production' ('Chapter Six'), London 1976, p. 280. See also ibid. pp. 1031–2 and Marx's discussion of freedom and equality in bourgeois society in 'The Chapter on Capital' in *Grundrisse*, London 1973, pp. 241–9.

25. Karl Marx, 'Wages, Price and Profit', Marx/Engels, *Selected Works*, p. 229.

26. Karl Marx, 'Inaugural Address', *The First International and After*, p. 80.

27. Karl Marx, 'Instructions for Delegates to the Geneva Congress', *The First International and After*, pp. 91–2.

28. For the development of Marx's political ideas at this time see Angiolina Arru, *Clase y Partido en la International*, Madrid 1974.

29. Karl Marx, 'Report to the Basle Congress', *The First International and After*, p. 105.

30. Frederick Engels, 'Preface to the English Edition of the Communist Manifesto', *The Revolutions of 1848*, pp. 63, 65.

31. Quoted ibid. p. 66. Hunt, op. cit. p. 190, by taking the single word 'antiquated' out of context, manages to imply that Marx was abandoning 'many points' in the *Manifesto*.

32. Karl Marx, 'Critique of Hegel's Doctrine of the State (1843)', *Early*

Writings, pp. 108, 109.

33. ibid. p. 195. For an interesting commentary on this passage, see the introduction to the volume by Lucio Colletti, especially pp. 28–46. However, Colletti here makes the mistake of equating the real abstraction of social relations brought about in the economic sphere by the law of value with the concentration of social relations produced by a given form of the state. The latter is an effect of the state as an organization of violence, a crucial phenomenon not discussed by Colletti (see pp. 38–9).

34. Karl Marx, 'Address of the General Council: The Civil War in France', *The First International and After*, pp. 206, 207.

35. ibid. pp. 209, 210, 211.

36. ibid. 215, 216, 214.

37. ibid. pp. 217, 209–10, 217, 219, 212. For Marx's private reflections on the Commune, see Marx/Engels, *Selected Correspondence*, Moscow 1955, pp. 261–5.

38. Karl Marx, 'The Civil War in France', *The First International and After*, p. 210.

39. Karl Marx, 'First Draft of the Civil War in France', *The First International and After*, pp. 252–3. Colletti has developed his theses on the relationship between Rousseau and Marx in *From Rousseau to Lenin*, London 1972, especially in Part Three of this work, as well as in the previously quoted Introduction to Marx's *Early Writings*. Despite the criticisms made here, it should be said that there is much of value in Colletti's discussion, including a valuable critique of Galvano Della Volpe's use of Rousseau. Colletti has elsewhere conceded that his attempt to reduce Marxist politics to Rousseau was deliberately provocative: see Lucio Colletti, 'A Political and Philosophical Interview', NLR 86, July–August 1974.

Moreover, it must be conceded that Marxist politics do contain a suitably transformed version of the Rousseauian concept of popular sovereignty; namely the concept of the dictatorship of the proletariat. As we have seen, Marx's explanation of this concept unambiguously insists on the sovereignty of the proletariat and its allies within the revolutionary process. Proletarian representatives or delegates are subordinate to the mass of electors, who retain sovereignty via the *mandat impératif* and the right to recall their delegates when they please. In his otherwise valuable study of the Social Contract, Althusser fails to register at all this vital Rousseauian contribution. It is true that Rousseau's intransigent defence of the inalienable nature of popular sovereignty is apparently discrepant with his preparedness to envisage special, and even dictatorial, measures to sustain this sovereignty, such as the ban on factions and parties. Althusser's study is, however, chiefly concerned to establish the 'discrepancies' of this sort which characterize the thought of the Genevan democrat (see Louis Althusser, *Politics and History*, London 1972, pp. 113–60.) Non-Marxist scholars have, of course, clearly grasped the revolutionary significance of Rousseau's concept of sovereignty, despite its contradictory features: 'the destruction of the contract of rulership cleared the way for the destruction of every right of the ruler; and from the permanent and absolute omnipotence of the assemblage of the people, suspending the executive power and the whole jurisdiction of government as soon as it is assembled, he developed his programme of permanent revolution.' Otto von Gierke, *The Development of Political Theory: on the life and work of Johannes Althusius*, London 1939, p. 98. The most comprehensive Marxist evaluation of Rousseau is the essay by Valentino Gerratana in *Ricerche di Storia del Marxismo*, Rome 1972, pp. 3–69.

40. Karl Marx, 'Critique of the Gotha Programme', *The First International and After*, pp. 353, 355.

41. Karl Marx and Frederick Engels, 'Manifesto', *The Revolutions of 1848*, p. 85.

42. Karl Marx, 'Inaugural Address', *The First International and After*, p. 81.

43. Karl Marx, 'The Civil War in France', *The First International and After*, p. 217. A Hungarian supporter of Marx, Leo Frankel, was appointed 'Minister of Labour' by the Commune. In 'The Eighteenth Brumaire' Marx concluded by declaring that the elevation of Louis Bonaparte would be fatal to the Napoleonic cult: 'when the emperor's mantle finally falls on the shoulders of Louis Bonaparte, the bronze statue of Napoleon will come crashing down from the top of the Vendôme column'. *Surveys from Exile*, p. 249. The demolition of the Vendôme column decreed by the Commune was carried out with the assistance of Gustave Courbet, who had been elected a member of the Commune. (See Jack Lindsay, *Gustave Courbet: his life and work*, London 1973, chapter 14.)

44. 'Critique of the Gotha Programme', *The First International and After*, p. 350. For a vivid account of Lassalle's political ideas and activity, see Theodore S. Hamerow, *The Social Foundations of German Unification*, Princeton 1969, chapter 6.

45. 'Critique of the Gotha Programme', *The First International and After*, p. 340. Engels also wrote an important letter on the Gotha Programme: Engels to Bebel, 18–25 March 1875, Marx/Engels, *Selected Correspondence*, pp. 290–5.

46. Engels to Bebel, 30 June 1873, and Engels to Bernstein, 20 October 1882, Marx/Engels, *Selected Works*, pp. 285, 353.

47. Marx and Engels, 'Circular Letter to Bebel, Liebknecht, Bracke et. al.', *The First International and After*, pp. 366, 363–4.

48. ibid. p. 368–70.

49. ibid. p. 371. Engels writes to Bebel on 16 December 1879: 'world history is taking its course regardless of these wise and moderate philistines. In Russia matters must come to a head in a few months from now. Either absolutism is overthrown and then, after the downfall of the great reserve of reaction, a different atmosphere will at once pervade Europe. Or a European war will break which will bury the *present* German party beneath the inevitable struggle of each people for its national existence. Such a war would be the greatest misfortune for us; it might set the movement back twenty years. But the new party that would ultimately have to emerge anyhow would in all European countries be free of a mass of dubiety and paltriness that now everywhere hampers the movement.' Marx/Engels, *Selected Works*, p. 331.

50. Marx and Engels. 'Circular Letter', *The First International and After*, p. 373–4.

51. Engels, 'Introduction to Karl Marx's *The Class Struggle in France*', in Marx/Engels, *Selected Works*, pp. 664, 660, 658, 667.

52. The turning-point represented by the 1905 revolution in Russia is discussed in Norman Geras, *The Legacy of Rosa Luxemburg*, NLB London 1976, especially chapters two and three, and in Marcel Liebman, *Leninism under Lenin*, London 1975. As both authors point out, the full implications of the experience of 1917 were not adequately reflected in Bolshevik theory.

State and Revolution powerfully restated and elaborated the argument of Marx's writings on the Commune, but did not examine the precise functioning of the soviets. Thus Lenin had nothing to say about the relationship between soviets and the parties that operate within them. Precisely for this reason, it is possible to represent Lenin as a disciple of Rousseau if only this work is considered. The first text to address itself to the problem of the relations between the soviet and the party was Trotsky's *The Revolution Betrayed*, New York 1945, see pp. 265 ff. In this passage Trotsky spells out the need for pluralism and free political competition within the Soviets.

Lenin's State and Revolution

LUCIO COLLETTI

(Reprinted from *From Rousseau to Lenin,* London 1972)

The basic theme of *State and Revolution* – the one that indelibly
inscribes itself on the memory, and immediately comes to mind
when one thinks of the work – is the theme of the revolution as a
destructive and *violent* act. The revolution cannot be restricted
to the seizure of power, it must also be the destruction of the old
state. 'The point is whether the old state machine shall remain,
or be *destroyed*,' says Lenin.[1] *Sprengen, zerbrechen,* destroy,
smash: these words capture the tone of the text. Lenin's polemic
is not directed against those who do not wish for the seizure of
power. The object of his attack is not *reformism.* On the contrary,
it is directed against those who wish for the seizure of power but
not for the destruction of the old state as well. The author he aims
at is Kautsky. But not, let it be clear, the Kautsky who was to
emerge after 1917 (in *Terrorism and Communism,* for example),
but rather the Kautsky of the writings devoted to the struggle
against opportunism: the Kautsky who *wants* revolution, and yet
does not want the destruction of the old state machine.

At first impression the text seems an implacable but sectarian
essay, primitive, steeped in 'Asiatic fury' – a kind of hymn to
'violence for violence's sake'. What seems to emerge from it is a
reduction of revolution to its most elementary and external
features: the capture of the Winter Palace, the Ministry of the
Interior in flames, the arrest and execution of the political
personnel of the old government. It was precisely this interpretation that ensured the success of *State and Revolution*
throughout the Stalin era, for more than a quarter of a century
from 1928 to 1953, not only in Russia but in all the Communist
Parties of the world. The revolution is violence. Kautsky is a
social-democrat because he does not want violence. It is impossible to be a Communist if your aim is not the violent seizure
of power. Until 1953, any militant in a Communist Party (the
Italian Party included) who had dared to cast doubts on this
necessity of violence would have found himself in the same
position as anyone today who expresses doubts about the
'peaceful, parliamentary road'.

I shall not be so stupid as to suggest that Lenin was *against* violence. He was in favour of a violent insurrection, just as in June 1917 he had supported the peaceful development of the revolution. He was for one or the other, according to the circumstances. But on one point his thought was immutable: in each and *every* case, the state machine must be *destroyed*.

The ways in which the revolution can be achieved are to some extent contingent: they depend on a constellation of events which it is useless to discuss beforehand. Nor does the amount of bloodshed in itself indicate the thoroughness of the revolutionary process. The essential point of the revolution, the *destruction* it cannot forego (and of which violence is not in itself a sufficient guarantee) is rather the destruction of the bourgeois state as a power *separate* from and *counterposed* to the masses, and its replacement by a power of a new type. This is the essential point.

According to Lenin, the old state machine must be destroyed because the bourgeois state depends on the *separation* and *alienation* of power from the masses. In capitalist society, democracy is, at best, 'always hemmed in by the narrow limits set by capitalist exploitation'. 'The majority of the population is debarred from participation in public and political life.' All the mechanisms of the bourgeois state are restrictions that 'exclude and squeeze out the poor from politics, from active participation in democracy'.[2] A socialist revolution that maintained this type of state would keep alive the *separation* between the masses and power, their *dependence* and subordination.

If the socialization of the means of production means that, emancipating itself from the rule of capital, the society becomes its own master and brings the productive forces under its own conscious, planned control, the political form in which this economic emancipation can be achieved can only be one based upon the initiative and self-government of the producers.

Here we have the really basic theme of *State and Revolution.* The destruction of the bourgeois state machine is not the Ministry of the Interior in flames, it is not the barricades. All this may take place, but it is not the essential point. What is essential to the revolution is the destruction of the diaphragm that separates the working classes from power, the emancipation and self-determination of the former, the transmission of power directly into the hands of the people. Marx said that the Commune had proved that 'the working class cannot simply lay hold of the ready-made state machinery, and wield it for its own purposes'. It cannot:

for the aim of the socialist revolution is not 'to transfer the bureaucratic-military machine from one hand to another'[3] but to transfer power directly into the hands of the people – and that is impossible if this machine is not first smashed.

These few lines require the most serious reflection: the socialist revolution does not consist in transferring 'from one hand to another' the military-bureaucratic machine; the destruction of the military-bureaucratic state machine is, according to Marx, 'the preliminary condition for every real people's revolution', and, comments Lenin, a 'people's revolution' is one in which 'the mass of the people, its majority, the very lowest social groups, crushed by oppression and exploitation, rise independently and place on the entire course of the revolution the impress of *their* own demands, of *their* attempts to build in their own way a new society in place of the old society that is being destroyed'.[4]

The sense of the passage is clear. The destruction of the old machine is the destruction of the *limits* imposed on democracy by the bourgeois state. It is the passage from a 'narrow, restricted' democracy to full democracy. And, adds Lenin, 'full democracy is *not*, qualitatively, the same thing as incomplete democracy'. Behind what might seem formally a difference in quantity, what is actually at stake is 'a gigantic replacement of certain institutions by other institutions of a fundamentally different type.'[5]

The significance of the polemic against Kautsky emerges here too. The clash with Kautsky is important because it reveals a dilemma which has since become the crux of the whole experience of the workers' movement after Lenin. Kautsky wished for the seizure of power but not the destruction of the state. What is essential, he said, is purely and simply to take possession of the state machine which is already there, and to use it for one's own ends. Anyone who reflects on the diversity of the two formulae will find, behind the innocent verbal difference, a far more substantial and profound divergence. For Lenin, the revolution is not only the transfer of power *from one class to another*, it is also the passage from *one type of power to another*: for him, the two things go together because the working class that seizes power is the working class that governs itself. For Kautsky, on the other hand, the seizure of power does not mean the construction of a *new power*, but simply the promotion to the use of the *old* power of the political personnel who *represent* the working class, but are not themselves the working class. For the former, socialism is the self-government of the masses: in socialism, says Lenin, 'the *mass* of the population will rise to taking an *independent* part, not only in voting and elections, *but also in the everyday administration of the state.* Under socialism *all* will govern in turn and will soon become accustomed to no one governing.'[6]

For the latter, socialism is the management of power *in the name* of the masses. For Lenin, the socialist revolution has to destroy the old state because it must destroy *the difference between governors and governed itself.* For Kautsky, the state and its bureaucratic apparatus is not to be destroyed, because bureaucracy, i.e. the difference between governors and governed, cannot be suppressed and will always survive. For Lenin, the revolution is the end of all masters; for Kautsky, it is merely the arrival of a new master.

I repeat, the Kautsky against whom Lenin directed this polemic was still a Marxist, holding firmly to the class conception of the state. His political vision, indeed, had a rigidly *ouvrièrist* cast. As with all the Marxists of the Second International, his class position was, in fact, so strict that it often turned into a closed corporatism. What Lenin wrote in opposition to Plekhanov *et al.*, on Marx's concept of the 'people's revolution', could easily have been extended to Kautsky as well.

And yet, despite its rigid class standpoint, Kautsky's idea of *power* already contained the germ of all his subsequent developments. The state that must not be destroyed but which can be taken over and turned to one's own ends, the military-bureaucratic machine that is not to be dismantled but transferred 'from one hand to another', is already embryonically a state 'indifferent' in class nature: it is a technical or 'neutral' instrument, a mere means that can do good or ill, according to who controls it and uses it.

Hence the theory of the simple seizure, without at the same time the destruction-transformation of power, contains the germ of an *interclass* theory of the state. Or rather it is a perennial oscillation between two extreme poles: a reckless subjectivism that sees the essence of the revolution and socialism in the promotion to power of particular *political personnel*, who are, as we know, the party bureaucracy; and an inter-class conception of the state. The first pole gives the so-called Rakosi-type regime: the 'dictatorship of the proletariat' *by decree,* which can then in due time evolve towards the conception of . . . the 'State of the whole people'. The second pole gives the mandarins of social-democratic bureaucracy: the Scheidemanns, Léon Blums, Mollets, Wilsons, who – while serving the bourgeois state, and precisely because they are serving the bourgeois state – believe that they are thereby serving the interests of the *whole* society, the 'general' and 'common' interest.

The aim of our political struggle, wrote Kautsky, is 'the conquest of state power by winning a majority in parliament, and by raising parliament to the rank of master of the government'.[7] Parliament – evidently – has existed hitherto, will continue to exist hereafter, indeed must always exist. Not only is it independent of classes, but even of historical epochs. This is the acme of inter-classism. Kautsky's formula (and that of his present-day imitators) does not suggest even as a hypothesis that the parliamentary regime might be linked in some way to the class structure of bourgeois society. This formula makes *tabula rasa* of the whole of Marx's critique of the modern representative state. Furthermore, in so far as it is prepared to concede that the parliamentary regime has any class character whatsoever, it identifies this not in the regime itself *as such* but in its abuses: electoral frauds, *trasformismo*, 'pork-barrelling', *sottogoverno*, etc.[8] It stresses these 'anomalies' all the more willingly in that they allow it to invoke the 'true parliament', 'true mirror of the nation', which Togliatti, too, foretold: the only utopianism which the 'old foxes' can envisage.

To win a parliamentary majority and convert parliament into the master of the government. The essential question for Kautsky is who is in control in parliament; simply a change, even if a radical one, in the government's political personnel. That it is possible and necessary to go further, that the essential point is precisely to destroy the distinction between governors and governed – Kautsky cannot even imagine such a thing. His formula is parliament as 'master of the government'; Lenin's is the people as 'masters of the parliament' – i.e. the suppression of parliament as such.

We must make sure that we understand properly this Leninist critique of the parliamentary system. It is not a primitive and sectarian critique, the impotent critique of Bordiga, the denunciation of parliament as a 'fraud', of political democracy as a 'fraud', etc. This latter is the critique that has prevailed historically in the Communist tradition. It is an elementary critique which, failing to give a class analysis of liberal democracy or to grasp the organic way in which its growth is linked to that of the capitalist socio-economic order, denounces parliament and the modern representative state in subjectivist terms as if it were an institution consciously 'invented' by the ruling class to fool the people (rather as, according to Voltaire, religion is an invention of the priests). The superficiality and impotence of this critique emerges clearly when we remember that from it has descended precisely the nihilistic contempt for the problem of *democracy* and of the *power structure* in a socialist society that has permeated the whole experience of Stalinist and post-Stalinist political circles to this day. In *State and Revolution*, on the contrary, Lenin's critique of parliament succeeds for the first time – and, note, for the first time within Lenin's own thought (hence the crucial importance of this text, which is far and away his greatest contribution to political theory) – in restoring some of the basic lines of Marx's critique of the modern representative state. So much so that, just as on the level of political practice *State and Revolution* coincides with Lenin's first real penetration and discovery of the significance of the soviet (which had first emerged much earlier, during the 1905 Revolution, but which he had long failed to understand), so on the level of political theory *State and Revolution* coincides with his discovery that the 'dictatorship of the proletariat' is not the dictatorship of the party but the Paris Commune, the very same Commune that, even as late as the early months of 1917, Lenin had still regarded as only a form, though an extreme one, of 'bourgeois democratism'.

The difference between the two viewpoints is so radical that whereas in the first case the critique of parliament becomes a critique of *democracy*, in Lenin's case, on the contrary, the critique of parliament, i.e. of *liberal* or *bourgeois* democracy, is a critique of the *anti-democratic* nature of parliament – a critique made in the name of that infinitely 'fuller' (and hence qualitatively different) democracy, the democracy of the soviets, the only democracy that deserves the name of socialist democracy.

Marxist literature since Marx knows nothing that could even remotely compete with the seriousness of the critique of parliament contained in *State and Revolution*; nor, at the same time, anything pervaded with such a profound democratic inspiration as that which animates Lenin's text from beginning to end. The 'imperative mandate', the permanent and constant revocability of representatives by those they represent, the demand for a legislative power which would be 'a working, *not* a parliamentary body, executive and legislative at the same time' and in which, hence, the representatives 'have to work, have to execute their own laws, have themselves to test their results in real life, and to account directly to their constituents'.⁹ All this is no 'reform' of parliament (as imagined in the extremist folklore of some tiny sects, prey to party bureaucracy, but 'implacable' in their denunciations of Lenin's parliamentarianism!); it is rather the *suppression* of parliament, and its replacement by representative organs of a 'council' or 'soviet' type: to refer again to Lenin's own words, it is 'a gigantic replacement of certain institutions by other institutions of a fundamentally different order'.

Hence the destruction of the state and its replacement by institutions of 'proletarian democracy', i.e. by the self-government of the mass of producers. Lenin's line of thought is so rigorous that he does not hesitate to draw the most extreme conclusions from this: the socialist state itself – in so far as socialism (i.e. the first phase of communist society) still has need of a state – is a remnant of the bourgeois state.

> The state withers away in so far as there are no longer any capitalists, any classes, and, consequently, no *class* can be *suppressed*. But the state has not yet completely withered away, since there still remains the safe-guarding of 'bourgeois right' [i.e. of the principle of 'to each according to his labour' rather than according to his needs] which consecrates actual inequality.¹⁰

Hence 'in its first phase . . . communism *cannot* as yet be fully mature economically and entirely free from traditions or traces of capitalism. Hence the interesting phenomenon that communism in its first phase retains "the narrow horizon of bourgeois right".' And since 'bourgeois right in regard to the distribution of *consumer* goods inevitably presupposes the existence of the *bourgeois state*, for right is nothing without an apparatus capable of *enforcing* the observance of the standards of right. It follows,' concludes Lenin, 'that under communism there remains for a time not only bourgeois right, but even the bourgeois state without the bourgeoisie!'¹¹

As we see, the level of development of socialism is here measured by the level of development of democracy. The further the withering away of the state has advanced and the self-government of the masses has been extended, the more progress has been made in the transition from socialism to communism. Communism is not the Volga-Don Canal plus the state. It is not 'swathes of forest windbreaks' plus the police, concentration camps and bureaucratic omnipotence. Lenin has a different idea. But precisely because this idea is still today only an *idea*, we should reject all taboos and speak frankly.

State and Revolution was written in August and September 1917 at the height of the revolutionary process. None of Lenin's writings have a 'contemplative' character. This is less than ever the case with *State and Revolution*. Lenin embarked upon it so as to decide what to do in the on-going revolution. He was a realist who did not trust to 'inspiration', to the political improvisation of the moment, but aspired to act with a full consciousness of what he was doing. This was the moment and this the man of which *State and Revolution* was born. And yet we only have to look around today to see that the relation between this *idea* of socialism and socialism as it exists is not much different from the relationship between the Sermon on the Mount and the Vatican.

The answer we must accept – but which we should give thoughtfully and calmly, without dramatization – is the answer we all know: the countries we call socialist are only socialist metaphorically. They are countries which are no longer capitalist. They are countries where all the principal means of production have been nationalized and are state-owned – but not *socialized*, which is quite different. They are those 'links' in the world imperialist chain that have broken (and so far this chain has broken at its weakest links). This is true of China, of the 'people's democracies', not to speak of the Soviet Union. None of these countries is really socialist, nor could they be. Socialism is not a national process but a world process. This tremendous process – which today is above all the disintegration of the world capitalist system – is precisely the process we are living and which, simply in terms of its totally unprecedented proportions, obviously cannot reach harbour in a single day. The process is visible to everybody. Only the purblind 'concreteness' of Social-Democracy, convinced that it will be in the saddle for all time, can grant itself the luxury of ignoring it. This social-democratic illusion is the fate of anyone who thinks the idea of *State and Revolution* is outdated. There are few writings more timely or more relevant. Lenin is not outdated. National socialism, the 'construction of socialism in one country', these are outdated. Communism, said

Marx, cannot exist as a 'local event': 'The proletariat can thus only exist on the *world-historical* plane, just as communism, its activity, can only have a world-historical existence.'[12]

Notes

1. Lenin, *State and Revolution*, in *Selected Works*, op. cit., vol. II, p. 355.
2. ibid., pp. 333–4.
3. ibid., pp. 293–4.
4. ibid., p. 295.
5. ibid., p. 298.
6. ibid., p. 357.
7. ibid., p. 358.
8. *Trasformismo* is the process whereby opposition forces, or their leaders, are absorbed into the ruling elites. *Sottogoverno* is the practice prevalent in Italy, whereby the party in power bypasses sections of the State administration by setting up parallel bureaucratic organizations directly dependent upon itself.
9. ibid., pp. 301–2.
10. ibid., p. 339.
11. ibid., pp. 342–3.
12. Marx and Engels, *The German Ideology*, London and Moscow, 1965, pp. 46–7.

The Leninist Theory of Organization

ERNEST MANDEL

(Reprinted from *International Socialist Review*, 31, 1970)

A serious discussion of the historical importance and current relevance of the Leninist theory of organization is possible only if one determines the exact position of this theory in the history of Marxism – or to be more precise, in the historical process of the unfolding and development of Marxism. This, like any process, must be reduced to its internal contradictions through the intimate interrelation between the development of theory and the development of the actual proletarian class struggle.

Approached in this way, the Leninist theory of organization appears as a dialectical unity of three elements: a theory of the actuality of revolution for the underdeveloped countries in the imperialist epoch (which was later expanded to apply to the entire world in the epoch of the general crisis of capitalism); a theory of the discontinuous and contradictory development of proletarian class consciousness and of its most important stages, which should be differentiated from one another; and a theory of the essence of Marxist theory and its specific relationship to science on the one hand and to proletarian class struggle on the other.

Looking more closely, one discovers that these three theories form, so to speak, the 'social foundation' of the Leninist concept of organization, without which it would appear arbitrary, non-materialist and unscientific. The Leninist concept of the party is not the only possible one. It is, however, the only possible concept of the party which assigns to the vanguard party the historic role of leading a revolution which is considered, in an intermediate or long-range sense, to be inevitable. The Leninist concept of the party cannot be separated from a specific analysis of proletarian class consciousness, i.e., from the understanding that *political* class consciousness – as opposed to mere 'trade union' or 'craft' consciousness – grows neither spontaneously nor automatically out of the objective developments of the proletarian class struggle.[1] And the Leninist concept of the party is based upon the premise of a *certain degree of autonomy of scientific analysis*, and especially of Marxist theory. This theory, though conditioned by the unfolding of the proletarian class struggle and the first embryonic beginnings of the proletarian revolution, should not be seen as the mechanically inevitable product of the class struggle but as the result of a theoretical practice (or 'theoretical production') which is able to link up and unite with the class struggle only through a prolonged struggle. The history of the worldwide socialist revolution in the twentieth century is the history of this prolonged process.

These three propositions actually represent a deepening of Marxism, i.e., either of themes that were only indicated but not elaborated upon by Marx and Engels, or of elements of Marxist theory which were scarcely noticed due to the delayed and interrupted publication of Marx's writings in the years 1880–1905.[2] It therefore involves a further deepening of Marxist theory brought about because of gaps (and in part contradictions) in Marx's analysis itself, or at least in the generally accepted interpretation of it in the first quarter century after Marx's death.

What is peculiar about this deepening of Marx's teachings is that, setting out from different places, it proceeds towards the same central point, namely, to a determination of the specific character of the proletarian or socialist revolution.

In contrast to all previous revolutions – not only bourgeois revolutions, whose laws of motion have been studied in great detail (in the first place by Marx and Engels themselves), but also those revolutions which have hitherto been far less subjected to a systematic, generalized analysis (such as the peasant revolutions and those of the urban petty bourgeoisie against feudalism; the uprisings of slaves and the revolts of clan societies against slaveholding society; the peasant revolutions that occurred as the old Asiatic mode of production periodically disintegrated, etc.) – the proletarian revolution of the twentieth century is distinguished by four particular features. These give it a specific character, but also, as Marx foresaw,[3] make it an especially difficult undertaking.

1. The proletarian revolution is the first successful revolution in the history of mankind to be carried out by the lowest social class. This class disposes of a potentially huge, but actually extremely limited, economic power and is by and large excluded from any share in the social wealth (as opposed to the mere possession of consumer goods which are continuously used up). Its situation is quite different from the bourgeoisie and the

feudal nobility, who seized political power when they already held in their hands the actual economic power of society, as well as from the slaves, who were unable to carry through a successful revolution.

2. The proletarian revolution is the first revolution in the history of humanity aimed at a consciously planned overthrow of existing society, i.e., which does not seek to restore a previous state of affairs (as did the slave and peasant revolutions of the past), or simply to legalize a transfer of power already achieved on the economic field, but rather to bring into being a completely new process, one which has never before existed and which has been anticipated only as a 'theory' or a 'programme'.[4]

3. Just like every other social revolution in history, the proletarian revolution grows out of the internal class antagonisms and the class struggle they inevitably produce within the existing society. But while revolutions in the past could by and large be satisfied with pushing this class struggle forward until a culminating point was reached – because for them it was not a question of creating completely new and consciously planned social relations – the proletarian revolution can become a reality only if the proletarian class struggle culminates in a gigantic process, stretching out over years and decades. This process is one of systematically and consciously overturning all human relations, and of generalizing first the independent activity of the proletariat, and later (on the threshold of the classless society) that of all members of society. While the triumph of the bourgeois revolution makes the bourgeoisie into a conservative class (which is still able to achieve revolutionary transformations in the technical and industrial fields, and which plays an objectively progressive role in history for a rather long period of time, but which pulls back from an active transformation of social life, since in that sphere its mounting collisions with the proletariat it exploits make it increasingly reactionary), the conquest of power by the proletariat is *not the end but the beginning* of the activity of the modern working class in revolutionizing society. This activity can end only when it liquidates itself as a class, along with all other classes.[5]

4. In contrast to all previous social revolutions, which by and large have taken place within a national or an even more limited regional framework, the proletarian revolution is by nature international and can reach its conclusion only in the world-wide construction of a classless society. Although it certainly can

achieve victory at first within a national framework alone, this victory will constantly be endangered and provisional so long as the class struggle on an international scale has not inflicted a decisive defeat upon capital. The proletarian revolution, then, is a world revolutionary process, which is carried out neither in a linear fashion nor with uniformity. The imperialist chain breaks first at its weakest links, and the discontinuous ebb and flow of the revolution occurs in conformity with the law of uneven and combined development. (This is true not only for the economy but also for the relationship of forces between classes; the two by no means automatically coincide.)

The Leninist theory of organization takes into account all these peculiarities of the proletarian revolution. It takes into consideration the peculiarities of this revolution in light of, among other things, the peculiarities and contradictions in the formation of proletarian-class consciousness. Above all, it expresses openly what Marx only intimated, and which his epigones scarcely understood at all, namely, that there can be neither an 'automatic' overthrow of the capitalist social order nor a 'spontaneous' or 'organic' disintegration of this social order through the construction of a socialist one. Precisely because of the uniquely conscious character of the proletarian revolution, it requires not only a maturity of 'objective' factors (a deep-going social crisis which expresses the fact that the capitalist mode of production has fulfilled its historic mission), but also a maturity of so-called subjective factors (maturity of proletarian class consciousness and of its leadership). If these 'subjective' factors are either not present, or are present to an insufficient extent, the proletarian revolution will not be victorious at that point, and *from its very defeat* will result the economic and social possibilities for a temporary consolidation of capitalism.[6]

The Leninist theory of organization represents, then, broadly speaking, the deepening of Marxism, applied to the basic problems of the social superstructure (the state, class consciousness, ideology, the party). Together with the parallel contributions of Rosa Luxemburg and Trotsky (and, in a more limited sense of Lukacs and Gramsci), it constitutes the *Marxist science of the subjective factor*.

Bourgeois ideology and proletarian-class consciousness

The Marxian proposition that 'the dominant ideology of every society is the ideology of the dominant class' appears at first glance to conflict with the character of the proletarian revolution as the *conscious* overturning of society by the proletariat, as a product of the conscious, independent activity of the wage-earning masses. A superficial interpretation of this proposition might lead to the conclusion that it is utopian to expect the masses who, under capitalism, are manipulated and exposed to the constant onslaught of bourgeois and petty-bourgeois ideas, to be capable of carrying out a revolutionary class struggle against this society, let alone a social revolution. Herbert Marcuse, who draws this conclusion, is (for the time being) simply the latest in a long series of theoreticians who, taking as their point of departure the Marxian definition of the ruling class, finish by calling into question the revolutionary potential of the working class.

The problem can be solved by replacing the formalistic and static point of view with a dialectical one. The Marxian proposition simply needs to be made more 'dynamic'. The dominant ideology of every society is the ideology of the dominant class in the sense that the latter has control over the means of ideological production which society has at its disposal (the Church, schools, mass media, etc.), and uses these means in its own class interests. As long as class rule is on the upswing, stable and hence hardly questioned, the ideology of the dominant class will also dominate the consciousness of the oppressed class. Moreover, the exploited will, as a rule, tend to formulate the *first phases* of the class struggle in terms of the formulas, ideal and ideologies of the exploiters.[7]

However, the more the stability of the existing society is brought into question, and the more the class struggle intensifies, and the more the class rule of the exploiters itself begins to waver in practice, the more will at least sections of the oppressed class begin to free themselves from the control of the ideas of those in power. Prior to, and along with, the struggle for the social revolution, a struggle goes on between the ideology of the rulers and the new ideals of the revolutionary class. This struggle in turn intensifies and accelerates the concrete class struggle out of which it arose by lifting the revolutionary class to an awareness of its historical tasks and of the immediate goals of its struggle. Class consciousness on the part of the revolutionary class can therefore develop out of the class struggle in spite of and in opposition to the ideology of the ruling class.[8]

But it is only in the revolution itself that the majority of the oppressed can liberate themselves from the ideology of the ruling class.[9] For this control is exerted not only, nor even primarily, through purely ideological *manipulation* and the mass assimilation of the ruling class's ideological production, but above all through the actual day-to-day workings of the existing economy and society and their effect on the consciousness of the oppressed. (This is especially true in bourgeois society, although parallel phenomena can be seen in all class societies.)

In capitalist society this control is exerted through the internalization of commodity relations, which is closely tied to the reification of human relations and which results from the generalized extension of commodity production and the transformation of labour power into a commodity, and from the generalized extension of the social division of labour under conditions of commodity production. It is also accomplished through the fatigue and brutalization of the producers through exploitation and the alienated nature of labour, as well as through a lack of leisure time, not only in a quantitative but also in a qualitative sense, etc. Only when the workings of this imprisonment are blown apart by a revolution, i.e., by a sudden, intense increase in *mass activity outside of the confines of alienated labour* – only then can the mystifying influence of this very imprisonment upon mass consciousness rapidly recede.

The Leninist theory of organization therefore attempts to come to grips with the inner dialectic of this formation of political class consciousness, which can develop fully only *during* the revolution itself, yet only on the condition that it has already begun to develop *before* the revolution.[10] The theory does this by means of three operative categories: the category of the working class in itself (the mass of workers); the category of that part of the working class that is already engaging in more than sporadic struggles and has already reached a first level of organization (the proletarian vanguard in the broad sense of the word);[11] and the category of the revolutionary organization, which consists of workers and intellectuals who participate in revolutionary activities and are at least partially educated in Marxism.

The category of 'the class in itself' is linked to the objective class concept in the sociology of Marx, where a social layer is determined by its objective position in the process of production *independent* of its state of consciousness. (It is well known that the young Marx – in the *Communist Manifesto* and in his political writings of 1850–2, for instance – had put forward a subjective concept of the class according to which the working class becomes a class only through its struggle, i.e. by reaching a minimum degree of class consciousness. Bukharin, in connection with a formula from *The Poverty of Philosophy*, calls this concept the concept of 'the class for itself', as opposed to the concept of the 'class in itself'.)[12] This objective concept of the class remains fundamental for Lenin's ideas on organization, as it did for Engels and the German Social Democracy under the influence of Engels, Bebel and Kautsky.[13]

It is only because there exists an objectively revolutionary class that can, and is periodically obliged to, conduct an actual revolutionary-class struggle, and it is only in relation to such an actual class struggle, that the concept of a revolutionary vanguard party (including that of professional revolutionaries) has any scientific meaning at all, as Lenin himself explicitly observed.[14] All revolutionary activity not related to this class struggle leads at best to a party *nucleus*, but not to a party. This runs the risk of degenerating into sectarian, subjective dilettantism. According to Lenin's concept of organization, there is no self-proclaimed vanguard. Rather, the vanguard must win recognition as a vanguard (i.e., the historical right to act as a vanguard) through its attempts to establish revolutionary ties with the advanced part of the class and its actual struggle.

The category of 'advanced workers' stems from the objectively inevitable stratification of the working class. It is a function of their distinct historical origin, as well as their distinct position in the social process of production and their distinct class consciousness.

The formation of the working class as an objective category is itself an historical process. Some sections of the working class are the children, grandchildren and great-grandchildren of urban wage labourers; others are the children and grandchildren of agricultural labourers and landless peasants. Still others are only first or second generation descendants of a petty bourgeoisie that owned some means of production (peasants, artisans, etc.). Part of the working class work in large factories where both the economic and the social relations give rise to at least an elementary class consciousness (consciousness that 'social questions' can be solved only through collective activity and organization). Another part work in small or medium-sized factories in industry or in the so-called service sectors, where economic self-confidence as well as an understanding of the necessity for broad mass actions flow much less easily from the objective situation than in the large industrial plant. Some sections of the working class have been living in big cities for a long time. They have been literate for a long time and have several generations of trade-union organization and political and cultural education behind them (through youth organizations, the workers' press, labour education, etc.). Still others live in small towns or even in the countryside. (This was true into the late 1930s, for instance, for a significant number of European miners.) These workers have little or no collective social life, scarcely any trade-union experience, and have received no political or cultural education at all in the organized workers' movement. Some sectors of the working class are born from nations which were independent for a thousand years, and whose ruling class oppressed for long periods other nations. Other workers are born from nations which fought for decades or centuries for their national freedom – or who lived in slavery or serfdom no more than one hundred years ago. The working class is still deeply marked by the traditional division of labour between the sexes and women workers usually constitute a specially oppressed layer of the working class.

If one adds to all these historical and structural differences the various personal abilities of each wage worker – not just differences in intelligence and ability to generalize from immediate experiences, but differences in the amount of energy, strength of character, combativity and self-assurance too – then one understands that the stratification of the working class into various layers, depending on the degree of class consciousness, is an inevitable phenomenon in the history of the working class itself. *It is this historical process of becoming a class which, at a given point in time, is reflected in the various degrees of consciousness within the class.*

The category of the revolutionary party stems from the fact that Marxian socialism is a *science* which, in the final analysis, can be completely assimilated only in an individual and not in a collective manner. Marxism constitutes the culmination (and in part also the dissolution) of at least three classical social sciences: classical German philosophy, classical political economy, and classical French political science (French socialism and historiography). Its assimilation presupposes at least an understanding

of the materialist dialectic, historical materialism, Marxian
economic theory and the critical history of modern revolutions
and of the modern labour movement. Such an assimilation is
necessary if it is to be able to function, in its totality, as an
instrument for analysing social reality and as the compilation of
the experiences of a century of proletarian class struggle. The
notion that this colossal sum of knowledge and information
could somehow 'spontaneously' flow from working at a lathe or a
calculating machine is absurd.[15]

The fact that as a science Marxism is an expression of the
highest degree in the development of proletarian class consciousness means simply that it is only through an *individual* process of
selection that the best, most experienced, the most intelligent
and the most combative members of the proletariat are able to
directly and independently acquire this class consciousness in its
most potent form. To the extent that this acquisition is an
individual one, it also becomes accessible to other social classes
and layers (above all, the revolutionary intelligentsia and the
students).[16] Any other approach can lead only to an idealization
of the working class – and ultimately of capitalism itself.

Of course it must always be remembered that Marxism could
not arise independently of the actual development of bourgeois
society and of the class struggle that was inevitably unfolding
within it. There is an inextricable tie between the collective,
historical experience of the working class in struggle and its
scientific working out of Marxism as collective, historical class
consciousness in its most potent form. But to maintain that
scientific socialism is an historical product of the proletarian
class struggle is not to say that all or even most members of this
class can, with greater or lesser ease, reproduce this knowledge.
Marxism is not an automatic product of the class struggle and
class experience but a result of scientific, theoretical production.
Such an assimilation is made possible only through participation
in that process of production; and this process is by definition
an *individual* one, even though it is only made possible through
the development of the social forces of production and class
contradictions under capitalism.

Proletarian-class struggle and proletarian-class consciousness

The process whereby the proletarian mass, the proletarian
vanguard and the revolutionary party are united depends on the

elementary proletarian class struggle growing over into *revolutionary* class struggle – the proletarian revolution – and on the effects this has on the wage-earning masses. Class struggle has taken place for thousands of years without those who struggled being aware of what they were doing. Proletarian class struggle was conducted long before there was a socialist movement, let alone scientific socialism. Elementary class struggle – strikes, work stoppages around wage demands or for shorter working hours and other improvements in working conditions – leads to elementary forms of class organization (mutual aid funds, embryonic trade unions), even if these are short-lived. (It also gives rise to a general socialist ideal among *many* workers.) Elementary class struggle, elementary class organization and elementary class consciousness are born, then, *directly out of action*, and only the experience arising out of that action is able to develop and accelerate consciousness. It is a general law of history that only through action are *broad masses* able to elevate their consciousness.

But even in its most elementary form, the spontaneous class struggle of the wage earners under capitalism leaves behind a residue in the form of a *consciousness crystallized in a process of continuous organization*. Most of the mass is active only during the struggle; after the struggle it will sooner or later retreat into private life (i.e., 'into the struggle for existence'). What distinguishes the workers' vanguard from this mass is the fact that even during a lull in the struggle it does not abandon the front lines of the class struggle but continues the war, so to speak, 'by other means'. It attempts to solidify the resistance funds generated in the struggle into ongoing resistance funds – i.e., into unions.[17] By publishing workers' newspapers and organizing educational groups for workers, it attempts to crystallize and heighten the elementary class consciousness generated in the struggle. It thus helps give form to a factor of continuity, as opposed to the necessarily discontinuous action of the mass,[18] and to a factor of consciousness, as opposed to the spontaneity of the mass movement in and of itself.

However, advanced workers are driven to continuous organization and growing class consciousness less by theory, science, or an intellectual grasp of the social whole than by the practical knowledge acquired in struggle. Since the struggle shows[19] that the dissolving of the resistance funds after each strike damages the effectiveness of the strike and the working sums in hand, attempts are made to go over to the permanent strike fund. Since experience shows an occasional leaflet to have less effect than a regular newspaper, the workers' press is born. Consciousness arising directly out of the practical experience of struggle is *empirical and pragmatic consciousness*, which can enrich action to a certain extent, but which is far inferior to the effectiveness of a *scientifically global* consciousness, i.e., of theoretical understanding.

Based on its general theoretical understanding the revolutionary vanguard organization can consolidate and enrich this higher consciousness, provided it is able to establish ties to the class struggle, i.e., provided it does not shrink from the hard test of verifying theory in practice, of reuniting theory and practice. From the point of view of mature Marxism – as well as that of Marx himself and Lenin – a 'true' theory divorced from practice is as much an absurdity as a 'revolutionary practice' that is not founded on a scientific theory. This in no way diminishes the decisive importance and absolute necessity for theoretical production. It simply emphasizes the fact that wage-earning masses and revolutionary individuals, proceeding from different starting points and with a different dynamic, can bring about the unity of theory and practice.

This process can be summarized in the following diagram:

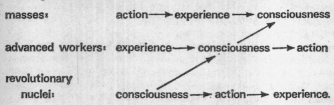

If we rearrange this diagram so that certain conclusions can be drawn from it, we get the following:

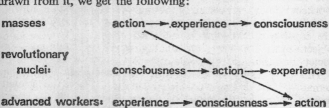

This formal diagram reveals a series of conclusions about the dynamics of class consciousness which were already anticipated in the analysis but which only now obtain their full value. The collective action of the advanced workers (the 'natural leaders' of the working class in the shops) is, relatively speaking, more difficult to attain because it can be aroused neither through pure conviction (as with the revolutionary nuclei) nor through purely spontaneous explosiveness (as with the broad masses). It is precisely the struggle *experience* – the important motivating factor in the actions of the advanced workers – that makes them much more careful and cautious before they undertake action on a broad scale. They have already digested the lessons of past actions and know that an explosion is not at all sufficient for them to be able to reach their goal. They have fewer illusions about the strength of the enemy (not to mention his 'generosity') and about the durability of the mass movement. The greatest 'temptation' of economism can be traced to this very point.

To summarize: the building of the revolutionary class party is the merging of the consciousness of the revolutionary nuclei with that of the advanced workers. The ripening of a pre-revolutionary situation (of potentially revolutionary explosion) is the merging of action by the broad masses with that of the advanced workers. A revolutionary situation – i.e., the possibility of a revolutionary conquest of power – arises when a merging of *actions* by the vanguard and the masses with the *consciousness* of the vanguard and revolutionary layers has been accomplished.[20] For the broad masses, the elementary class struggle arising from the contradictions of the capitalist mode of production is always kindled only by matters of immediate concern. The same is true for all mass actions, even political ones. Thus the problem of the broad mass struggle growing over into a revolutionary one depends not only on a quantitative factor, but also on a qualitative one. This requires the existence of sufficiently advanced workers within the masses or the mass movement who, on the basis of the stage of consciousness they have already reached, are capable of sweeping broader masses into action around objectives that challenge the continued existence of bourgeois society and the capitalist mode of production.

This also highlights the central importance of transitional demands,[21] the strategic position of advanced workers already trained in propagating these transitional demands, and the historical importance of the revolutionary organization, which alone is capable of working out a comprehensive programme of transitional demands corresponding to the objective historical conditions, as well as to the subjective needs, of the broadest layers of the mass. *A successful proletarian revolution is only possible if all these factors are successfully combined.*

We have already stated that Lenin's theory of organization is, in fact, above all a theory of revolution. To have misunderstood this is the great weakness of Rosa Luxemburg's polemic against Lenin in 1903–4. It is characteristic that the concept of centralization which is attacked in the essay 'Organizational Question of Social Democracy' is – and this is clear if it is read attentively – a purely organizational one. (Yet while it is attacked, it is also confirmed. On this point modern 'Luxemburgists' ought to read their 'Rosa' more carefully and more thoroughly!) Lenin is accused of advocating an 'ultracentralist' line, of dictating the composition of local party committees, and of wishing to stymie any initiative by lower party units.[22]

When we turn to the Leninist theory of organization as developed by Lenin himself, however, we see that the emphasis is by no means upon the formal, organizational side of centralization but upon its *political and social function*. At the heart of *What is to Be Done?* is the concept of the transformation of proletarian class consciousness into political class consciousness *by means of a comprehensive political activity* that raises and, from a Marxist point of view, answers all questions of internal and external class relations:

'In reality, it is possible to "raise the activity of the working masses" *only* when this activity *is not restricted* to "political agitation on an economic basis." A basic condition for the necessary expansion of political agitation is the organization of *comprehensive* political exposure. *In no way* except by means of such exposures *can* the masses be trained in political consciousness and revolutionary activity.'

And further:

The consciousness of the working masses cannot be genuine class consciousness, unless the workers learn, from concrete, and above all from topical, political facts and events to observe *every* other social class in *all* the manifestations of its intellectual, ethical, and political life; unless they learn to apply in practice the materialist analysis and the materialist estimate of all aspects of the life and activity of *all* classes, strata, and groups of the population. Those who concentrate the attention, observation, and consciousness of the working class exclusively, or even mainly, upon itself alone are not Social Democrats; for the self-knowledge of the working class is indissolubly bound up, not solely with a fully clear theoretical understanding – it would be even truer to say, not so much with the theoretical, as with the practical, understanding – of the relationships between *all* the various classes of modern society, acquired through the experiences of political life.[23]

And it is for the same reason that Lenin emphasizes so strongly the absolute necessity for the revolutionary party to make *all* progressive demands and movements of *all* oppressed social layers and classes its own – even 'purely democratic' ones. The central strategic plan advanced by Lenin in *What is to Be Done?*[24] is therefore one of party agitation that unites all elementary, spontaneous, dispersed and 'merely' local or sectional protests, revolts and movements of resistance. The emphasis of centralization clearly lies in the political and not in the formal, organizational sphere. The aim of formal organizational centralization is only to make possible the realization of this strategic plan.

Although she does not recognize this essence of Lenin's 'centralism', Luxemburg is compelled in her polemic to indirectly counterpose to it another conception of the formation of political class consciousness and the preparation of revolutionary situations. Her doing so emphasizes even more poignantly how utterly wrong she was in this debate. Luxemburg's concept that 'the proletarian army is recruited and becomes aware of its objectives in the course of the struggle itself'[25] has been completely refuted by history. In even the broadest, longest and most vigorous of workers' struggles, the working masses have *not* gained a clear understanding of the tasks of the struggle, or did so only to an insufficient degree. (One need only recall the French general strikes of 1936 and 1968, the struggles of the German workers from 1918 to 1923, the great struggles of the Italian workers in 1920, 1948 and 1969, as well as the prodigious class struggles in Spain from 1931 to 1937, to mention only these four European countries.)

Experience in struggle is by no means sufficient for clarity on the tasks of a broad pre-revolutionary, or even a revolutionary, mass struggle to be attained. Not only, of course, are these tasks connected to the immediate motives that set off the struggle, but they can be grasped only by means of a comprehensive analysis of the overall social development, of the historical position achieved by the capitalist mode of production and its internal contradictions, and of the national and international relationship of forces between classes. Without protracted and consistent preparation, without the education of hundreds and thousands of advanced workers in the spirit of a revolutionary programme, and without the practical experience accumulated over the years by these advanced workers through attempting to bring this programme to the broad masses, it would be absolutely illusory to assume that suddenly, overnight so to speak, with the mere aid of mass *actions*, a consciousness equal to the demands of the historical situation could be created among these broad masses.

Actually, one could turn Luxemburg's proposition around and say that the proletarian army will *never* reach its historic objectives if the necessary education, schooling and testing of a proletarian vanguard in the working out and agitational application of the revolutionary programme in struggle has not taken place *before* the outbreak of the broadest mass struggles, which by themselves create only the *possibility* of the broad masses attaining revolutionary consciousness. That is the tragic lesson of the German revolution after the First World War, which was crushed precisely because of the lack of such a trained vanguard.

The objective of Lenin's strategic plan is to create such a vanguard through an organic union of individual revolutionary nuclei with the vanguard of the proletariat. Such a fusion is impossible without a comprehensive *political* activity that takes the advanced workers beyond the confines of a horizon limited to the trade union or the factory. Empirical data available to us today confirm that Lenin's party, before and during the revolution of 1905 and after the mass movement began to pick up again in 1912, was in fact such a party.[26]

To fully grasp the profoundly revolutionary nature of Lenin's strategic plan, it must be approached from yet another point of view. Any concept based on the probability, if not the inevitability, of a *revolution* occurring in the not-too-distant future, must inevitably deal with the question of a direct collision with state power, i.e., the question of the conquest of political power. As soon as this difficulty is built into the concept, however, the result is one more argument in favour of centralization. Lenin and Luxemburg agreed that capitalism itself and the bourgeois state exert a powerful centralizing influence on modern society,[27] and that it is in turn absolutely illusory to think that this centralized state power can be gradually dismantled, as for instance a wall can be taken apart brick by brick.

In the final analysis, the ideological essence of the reformism and revisionism rejected by Luxemburg and Lenin with equal passion[28] was rooted in the illusion that this could be done. Once the question of the conquest of state power is no longer placed far off in the distance, however, but is recognized to be an objective for the near or not-too-distant future, the revolutionary is immediately confronted with the question of the means necessary for achieving the revolutionary conquest of power. Here again Luxemburg misconstrued the *import* of Lenin's purely polemical use of the notion of 'Jacobins inseparably linked to the organization of the class-conscious proletariat.' What Lenin meant with this idea was certainly *not* a brand of Blanquist conspirators but *an advanced group oriented, like the Jacobins, towards an unremitting attempt to carry out the revolutionary tasks*, one that does not permit itself to be diverted from concentrating on *these* tasks by the inevitable conjunctural ebb and flow of the mass movement.

Yet to do justice to Luxemburg it must be added that, in the first place, she took up – in fact *had* to take up – this question from a different historical viewpoint since, by 1904, she was already influenced more by German than by Russian or Polish reality; and second, that she completely drew the necessary conclusions in the Leninist sense as soon as it became clear that in Germany too the coming of the revolution was an immediate possibility.[29]

The young Trotsky likewise made a serious error in his polemic against Lenin when he reproached him for this 'substitutionism', i.e., the replacement of the initiative of the working class with that of the party alone.[30] If we remove the core of this reproach from its polemical shell, we find here too an idealistic, inadequate conception of the evolution of the class consciousness of the proletariat: 'Marxism teaches that the interests of the proletariat are determined by its objective conditions of life. These interests are so powerful and so unavoidable that they eventually [!] compel the proletariat to bring them into the scope of its consciousness, i.e., to make the realization of its *objective* interests into its *subjective* interest.'[31] Today it is easy to see what a naïvely fatalistic optimism was concealed in this inadequate analysis. Immediate interests are here put on the same level with historical interests, i.e., with the unravelling of the most complex questions of political tactics and strategy. The hope that the proletariat will 'eventually' recognize its historical interests seems rather shallow when compared to the historical catastrophes that have arisen because, in the absence of an adequate revolutionary leadership, the proletariat was not even able to accomplish the revolutionary tasks of the here and now.

The same naïve optimism is even more strikingly manifested in the following passage from the same polemic:

> The revolutionary social democrat is convinced not only of the inevitable [!] growth of the political party of the proletariat, but also of the inevitable [!] victory of the ideas of *revolutionary* socialism within this party. The first proof lies in the fact that the development of bourgeois society spontaneously leads the proletariat to politically demarcate itself; the second in the fact that the objective tendencies and the tactical problems of this demarcation find their best, fullest and deepest expression in revolutionary socialism, i.e., Marxism.[32]

This quotation makes clear that what the young Trotsky was championing in his polemic against Lenin was the 'old, tested tactic' and the naïve 'belief in the inevitability of progress' à la Bebel and Kautsky which prevailed in international Social Democracy from the time of Marx's death until the First World War. Lenin's concept of class consciousness was incomparably richer, more contradictory and more dialectical precisely because it was based on a keen grasp of the relevance of the revolution for the present (not 'finally some day', but in the coming years).

To round out the historical development it must be added that following the outbreak of the Russian revolution in 1917, Trotsky fully adopted Lenin's analysis of the formation of proletarian class consciousness and hence also Lenin's theory of organization, and until his death he stubbornly defended them against all sceptics and arch-pessimists (who claimed to detect in them the 'embryo' of Stalinism). Thus he wrote in his last, unfinished manuscript:

A colossal factor in the maturity of the Russian proletariat in February or March 1917 was Lenin. He did not fall from the skies. He personified the revolutionary tradition of the working class. For Lenin's slogans to find their way to the masses, there had to exist cadres, even though numerically small at the beginning; there had to exist the confidence of the cadre in the leadership, a confidence based upon the entire experience of the past. To cancel these elements from one's calculations is simply to ignore the living revolution, to substitute for it an abstraction, the 'relationship of forces', because the development of the revolution precisely consists of this, that the relationship of forces keeps incessantly and rapidly changing under the impact of the changes in the consciousness of the proletariat, the attraction of backward layers to the advanced, the growing assurance of the class in its own strength. The vital mainspring in this process is the party, just as the vital mainspring in the mechanism of the party is its leadership.[33]

The revolutionary vanguard and spontaneous mass action

It would be a great injustice to Lenin to characterize his life's work as a systematic 'underestimation' of the importance of spontaneous mass actions as opposed to their 'appreciation' by Luxemburg or Trotsky. Apart from polemical passages, which can only be understood when seen in context, Lenin welcomed huge, spontaneous outbreaks of mass strikes and demonstrations just as enthusiastically and just as explicitly as Rosa Luxemburg and Trotsky.[34] Only the Stalinist bureaucracy falsified Leninism with its increasing distrust of spontaneous mass movements – which after all is characteristic of any bureaucracy.

Luxemburg is completely correct to say that the outbreak of a proletarian revolution cannot be 'predetermined' by the calendar, and nothing to the contrary will ever be found in Lenin. Lenin, like Luxemburg, was convinced that these elemental mass explosions, without which a revolution is unthinkable, can neither be 'organized' according to rules nor 'commanded' by a row of disciplined non-commissioned officers. Lenin, like Luxemburg, was convinced of the mighty arsenal of creative energy, resourcefulness and initiative that a truly broad mass action unfurls and will always unfurl.

The difference between the Leninist theory of organization and the so-called theory of spontaneity – which can be attributed to Luxemburg only with important reservations – is thus to be found *not in an underestimation of mass initiative but in an understanding of its limitations*. Mass initiative is capable of many magnificent accomplishments. But by itself it is not able to draft, in the course of the struggle, a complete, comprehensive programme for a socialist revolution touching upon all social questions (not to mention socialist reconstruction); nor is it alone capable of bringing about a sufficient centralization of forces to make possible the downfall of a centralized state power with its repressive apparatus resting on a full utilization of the advantages of its 'inside lines' of communication. In other words, the limitations of mass spontaneity begin with the understanding that a victorious socialist revolution *cannot be improvised*. And 'pure' mass spontaneity always boils down to improvisation.

What is more, 'pure' spontaneity exists only in books containing fairy tales about the workers' movement – but not in its real history. What is understood by 'spontaneity of the masses' are movements that have not been planned out in detail ahead of time by some central authority. What is *not* to be understood by 'spontaneity of the masses' are movements that take place without 'political influence from the outside'. Scratch off the blue coat of an ostensibly 'spontaneous movement' and you will find the unmistakable residue of a bright red veneer. Here a member of a 'vanguard' group who set off a 'spontaneous' strike. There a former member of another 'left-deviationist' affiliation, who has long since left it but who received sufficient mental equipment to be able, in an explosive situation, to react with lightning speed while the anonymous mass was still hesitating.

In one case, we will be able to detect in 'spontaneous' action the fruits of years of 'underground activity' by a trade-union opposition, or a rank-and-file group; in another case, the result of contacts that, for a rather long period of time, have patiently – and without apparent success – been nurtured by militants in a neighbouring city (or a neighbouring factory) where the 'left-wingers' are stronger. In the class struggle too there is no such thing as a goose 'spontaneously' falling from heaven already cooked.

Thus, what differentiates 'spontaneous' actions from the 'intervention of the vanguard', is not at all that in the former everyone in the struggle has reached the same level of consciousness, whereas in the latter 'the vanguard' is distinct from 'the mass'. What differentiates the two forms of action is also not that in 'spontaneous' actions no solutions have been carried into the proletariat from 'outside', while an organized vanguard relates to the elementary demands of the mass 'in an elitist fashion', 'imposing' a programme upon it. Never have there been 'spontaneous' actions without some kind of influence from vanguard elements. The difference between 'spontaneous' actions and those in which 'the revolutionary vanguard intervenes' is essentially that in 'spontaneous' actions *the nature of the intervention of the vanguard elements is unorganized, improvised, intermittent and unplanned* (occurring by chance in this plant, that district, or that city), while the existence of a revolutionary organization makes it possible to co-ordinate, plan, consciously synchronize, and continuously shape this intervention of the vanguard elements in the 'spontaneous' mass struggle. Nearly all the requirements of Leninist 'supercentralism' are based on this and this alone.

Only an incorrigible fatalist (i.e., a mechanical determinist) could be convinced that all mass explosions *had* to take place on a given day just because they broke out on that day, and that, conversely, in all cases where mass explosions did not occur it was because they were not possible. Such a fatalistic attitude (common to the Kautsky-Bauer school of thought) is in reality a caricature of the Leninist theory of organization. In any case, it is characteristic that many opponents of Leninism, who in opposing Lenin have so much to say about 'mass spontaneity', at the same time fall into this vulgar, mechanical determinism without realizing how much it contradicts their 'high esteem' for 'mass spontaneity'.

If, on the other hand, one proceeds from the inevitability of periodic spontaneous mass explosions (which occur when socio-economic contradictions have ripened to the point where the capitalist mode of production in fact *has* to periodically produce such pre-revolutionary crises), then one has to understand that it is impossible to determine the exact moment when this will happen since thousands of minor incidents, partial conflicts and accidental occurrences could play an important role in determining it. For this reason, a revolutionary vanguard which at decisive moments is able to concentrate its own forces on the 'weakest link', is incomparably more effective than the diffuse performance of large numbers of advanced workers who lack this ability to concentrate their forces.[35]

The two greatest workers' struggles to take place in the West – the French, May 1968 and the Italian, autumn 1969 – entirely confirmed these views. Both began with 'spontaneous' struggles prepared neither by the trade unions nor by the big social-democratic or 'communist' parties. In both cases individual, radical workers and students or revolutionary nuclei played a decisive role in here or there triggering a first explosion and providing the working masses with the opportunity to learn from an 'exemplary experience'. In both cases millions upon millions came into the struggle – up to ten million wage earners in France, up to fifteen million in Italy. This is more than ever before seen – even during the greatest class struggles following the First World War.

In both cases the spontaneous tendency demonstrated by the workers went way beyond the 'economism' of a purely economic strike. In France this was attested to by the factory occupations and numerous partial initiatives, in Italy not only by huge street demonstrations and the raising of political demands, but also by the embryonic manifestation of a tendency towards self-organization at the point of production, i.e., by the attempt to take the first step towards establishing dual power: the election of *delegati di reparto*. (In this sense, the vanguard of the Italian working class was more advanced than the French, and it drew the first important historical lessons from the French May.[36]) But in neither case did these powerful, spontaneous mass actions succeed in overthrowing the bourgeois state apparatus and the capitalist mode of production, or even in advancing a mass understanding of the objectives that would have made such an overthrow possible within a short period of time.

To recall Trotsky's metaphor from *The History of the Russian Revolution*: the powerful steam evaporated for lack of a piston that would have compressed it at the decisive moment.[37] Certainly, in the final analysis, the driving force is the steam, i.e., the energy of mass mobilization and mass struggle, and not the piston itself. Without this steam the piston remains a hollow shell. Yet without this piston even the most intense steam is wasted and accomplishes nothing. This is the quintessence of the Leninist theory of organization.

Organization, bureaucracy and revolutionary action

There is a difficulty in this connection, however, which Lenin, during the years of the most heated disputes with the Mensheviks, recognized either not at all (1903–5) or only to an insufficient degree (1908–14). And it is here that the full value of the historic work of Trotsky and Rosa Luxemburg becomes clear in facilitating an understanding of the dialectical formula 'working class – advanced workers – workers' party'.

A vanguard party and a certain *separation* between the party and the mass are made necessary precisely because of the inevitably inadequate level of class consciousness on the part of broad working masses. As Lenin repeatedly stressed, this is a complex dialectical relationship – a unity of separation and integration – which totally conforms to the historical peculiarities of the revolutionary struggle for a socialist revolution.

This separate party, however, originates within *bourgeois* society which, with its inherent features of a universal division of labour and commodity production, tends to bring about a reification of *all* human relations.[38] This means that the building of a party apparatus separated from the working masses involves the danger of this apparatus becoming autonomous. When this danger develops beyond an embryonic stage, the tendency arises for the self-preservation of the apparatus to become an end in itself, rather than a means to an end (successful proletarian-class struggle).

This is the root of the degeneration of both the Second and the Third Internationals, i.e., the subordination of the mass social-democratic as well as the communist parties of western Europe to conservative, reformist bureaucracies which, in their day-to-day practice, have become part of the status quo.[39]

Bureaucracy in workers' organizations is a product of the social division of labour, i.e., of the inability of the working masses, who are largely excluded from the cultural and theoretical process of production under capitalism, to themselves regularly take care of all the tasks which must be dealt with within the framework of their organization. Attempts to do this anyway, as was often done at the onset of the workers' movement, provide no solution because this division of labour completely corresponds to *material conditions* and is in no way invented by wicked careerists. If these conditions are overlooked, primitivism, ignorance and the brawling it produces will place the same limitations on the movement as would otherwise be set by the bureaucracy. Having taken a different point of departure here – that of organizational *technique* instead of the level of consciousness – we have run up against the same problem which we had already cleared up earlier: namely, that it would be giving the capitalist mode of production too much credit to assume it to be a perfect school for preparing the proletariat for independent activity, or that it automatically creates the ability of the working masses to spontaneously recognize and achieve all the objectives and organizational forms of their own liberation.

Lenin, in his first debate with the Mensheviks, very much underestimated the danger of the apparatus becoming autonomous and of the bureaucratization of the workers' parties. He proceeded from the assumption that the danger of opportunism in the modern labour movement was a threat coming mainly from petty-bourgeois academicians and petty-bourgeois 'pure trade unionists'. He made fun of the struggle of many of his comrades against the danger of 'bureaucratism'. Actually, history showed that the greatest source of opportunism in the Social Democracy before the First World War came from neither the academicians nor the 'pure trade unionists', but *from the social-democratic party bureaucracy itself*, i.e., from a practice of 'legalism' limited on the one hand to electoral and parliamentary activity, and on the other to a struggle for immediate reforms of an economic and trade union nature. (To merely describe this practice is to confirm how much it resembles that of today's West European Communist parties!)

Trotsky and Luxemburg recognized this danger more accurately and earlier than Lenin. As early as 1904 Luxemburg expressed the thought that a 'difference between the eager attack of the mass and the [overly] prudent position of the Social Democracy' was possible.[40] The thought is hardly expressed before it is discarded; the only possible validity it might have would be in the imaginary case of an 'overcentralization' of the party along Leninist lines. Two years later Trotsky already expresses this with more precision:

The European Socialist parties, particularly the largest of them, the German Social-Democratic Party, have developed their conservatism in proportion as the masses have embraced socialism and the more these masses have become organized and disciplined. As a consequence of this, Social Democracy as an organization embodying the political experience of the proletariat may at a certain moment become a direct obstacle to open conflict between the workers and bourgeois reaction. In other words, the propagandist-socialist conservatism of the proletarian parties may at a certain moment hold back the direct struggle of the proletariat for power.[41]

This prognosis has been tragically confirmed by history. Lenin did not yet see this until the eve of the First World War, whereas the German left had long before shed its illusions about the social-democratic party administration.[42]

Organizational theory, revolutionary programme, revolutionary practice

After the traumatic shock suffered by Lenin on 4 August 1914, however, he too made a decisive step forward on this question. *From then on, the question of organization became one not only of function but also of content.* It is no longer simply a question of contrasting 'the organization' in general to 'spontaneity' in general, as Lenin frequently does in *What is to Be Done?* and in *One Step Forward, Two Steps Backward.* Now it is a question of carefully distinguishing between an objectively conservative organization and an objectively revolutionary one. This distinction is made according to *objective* criteria (revolutionary programme, bringing this programme to the masses, revolutionary practice, etc.), and the spontaneous combativity of the masses is consciously preferred to the actions or even the existence of conservative reformist mass organizations. 'Naïve' organizational fetishists might claim that after 1914 Lenin went over to the Luxemburgist view of 'spontaneism' when, in conflicts between 'unorganized masses' and the social-democratic organization, he systematically defends the former against the latter, or accuses the latter of betraying the former.[43] Lenin now even regards the destruction of conservatized organizations as an inescapable prerequisite for the emancipation of the proletariat.[44]

Yet the correction, or better yet completion, of his theory of organization, which Lenin undertook after 1914, was not a step backwards to the worship of 'pure' spontaneity, but rather a step forward towards distinguishing between the *revolutionary* party and organization in general. Now, instead of saying that

the purpose of the party is to develop the political-class consciousness of the working class, the formula becomes much
more precise: the function of the revolutionary vanguard consists in developing *revolutionary consciousness* in the vanguard of
the working class. The building of the revolutionary class party
is the process whereby the programme of the socialist revolution
is fused with the experience the majority of the advanced workers
have acquired in struggle.[45]

This elaboration and expansion of the Leninist theory of
organization following the outbreak of the First World War
goes hand in hand with an expansion of the Leninist concept
of the relevance of revolution to the present. Although before
the year 1914 this was for Lenin limited by and large to Russia,
after 1914 it was extended to all of Europe. (After the Russian
revolution of 1905, Lenin had already recognized the immediate
potential for revolution in the colonies and semi-colonies.)

Consequently, the validity of the Leninist 'strategic plan' for
the imperialist countries of western Europe today is closely tied
to the question of the nature of the historical epoch in which we
live. From the standpoint of historical materialism, one is justified in deriving a conception of the party from the 'present
potential for revolution' only if one proceeds from the assumption
– correct and provable, in our estimation – that beginning with
the First World War, and no later than the Russian October
revolution, the worldwide capitalist system entered an epoch of
historic structural crisis[46] which *must* periodically lead to revolutionary situations. If, on the other hand, one assumes that we
are still in an ascending stage of capitalism as a world system,
then such a conception would have to be rejected as being
completely 'voluntaristic'. For what is decisive in the Leninist
strategic plan is certainly not revolutionary *propaganda* – which,
of course, revolutionaries have to carry out even in non-revolu-
tionary periods – but its focus on revolutionary *actions* breaking
out in the near or not distant future. Even in the ascending
epoch of capitalism such actions were possible (cf. the Paris
Commune), but only as unsuccessful exceptions. Under such
conditions, building a party by concentrating efforts on preparing
to effectively participate in such actions would hardly make
sense.

The difference between a 'workers' party' in general (referring to
its membership or even its electoral supporters) and a revolu-

tionary workers' party (or the nucleus of such a party) is to be found not only in programme or objective social functions (which is to promote, not pacify, all objectively revolutionary mass actions, or all challenges and forms of action that attack and call into question the essence of the capitalist mode of production and the bourgeois state), but also in its ability to find a suitable pedagogical method enabling it to bring this programme to an ever-growing number of workers.

One can go further, however, and formulate the question more sharply: Is the danger of the apparatus becoming autonomous limited only to opportunist and reformist 'workers'' organizations, or does it threaten *any* organization, including one with a revolutionary programme and a revolutionary practice? Is not a developing bureaucracy the *unavoidable* consequence of *any* division of labour, including that between 'leadership' and 'membership', and even in a revolutionary group? And is not, therefore, every revolutionary organization, once it has spread beyond a small milieu, condemned at a certain point in its development and in the development of mass struggles to become a brake on the struggle of the proletarian masses for emancipation?

If this line of argument were accepted as correct, it could lead to only one conclusion: that the socialist emancipation of the working class and of humanity is impossible – because the supposedly inevitable 'autonomization' and degeneration of any organization must be seen *as one part of a dilemma*, the other part of which is represented by the tendency for all unorganized workers, all intellectuals only partially involved in action, and all persons caught up in universal commodity production to sink into a petty-bourgeois 'false consciousness'. Only a comprehensive, revolutionary practice, aiming at total consciousness and enriching theory, makes it possible to avoid the penetration of the 'ideology of the ruling class' into even the ranks of individual revolutionaries. This can only be a collective and organized practice. If the above argument were correct, one would have to conclude that, with or without an organization, advanced workers would be condemned either not to reach political class consciousness or to rapidly lose it.

In reality, this line of argument is false since it equates the beginning of a process with its end result. Thus, from the existence of a *danger* that even revolutionary organizations will become autonomous, it deduces, in a static and fatalistic fashion, that this autonomy is *inevitable*. This is neither empirically nor theoretically demonstrable. For the extent of the danger of bureaucratic degeneration of a revolutionary vanguard organization – and even more of a revolutionary party – depends not only on the *tendency* towards autonomy, which in fact afflicts all institutions in bourgeois society, but also upon existing *counter-tendencies*. Among these are the integration of the revolutionary organization into an international movement which is independent of 'national' organizations and which constantly keeps a theoretical eye on them (not through an apparatus but through political criticism); a close involvement in the actual class struggle and actual revolutionary struggles that make possible a continuous selection of cadres in practice; a systematic attempt to do away with the division of labour by ensuring a continuous rotation of personnel between factory, university and full-time party functionaries; institutional guarantees (limitations on the income of full-timers, defence of the organizational norms of internal democracy and the freedom to form tendencies and factions, etc.).

The outcome of these contradictory tendencies depends on *the struggle between them*, which, in turn, is ultimately determined by *two social factors*:[47] on the one hand, the degree of *special social interests* set loose by the 'autonomous organization', and on the other hand, the extent of the *political activity* of the vanguard of the working class. Only when the latter decisively diminishes can the former decisively break out into the open. Thus, the entire argument amounts to a tedious tautology: during a period of *increasing passivity* the working class cannot be actively struggling for its liberation. It does not at all prove that during a period of *increasing activity* on the part of advanced workers, revolutionary organizations are not an effective instrument for bringing about liberation, though their 'arbitrariness' can and must be circumscribed by the independent activity of the class (or of its advanced sections). The revolutionary organization is an instrument for making revolutions. And, without the increasing political activity of broad masses of workers, proletarian revolutions are simply not possible.

Organizational theory, democratic centralism and soviet democracy

The objection was made to Lenin's theory of organization that through its exaggerated centralization it would prevent the development of internal party democracy. But this objection is a confused one, for in as much as the Leninist principles of organization restrict the organization to active members *operating under a collective control*, they actually expand rather than reduce the scope of party democracy.

Once a workers' organization surpasses a certain numerical size there are basically only two possible organizational models: that of the dues-paying electoral club (or territorial organization), which corresponds today to the organizational forms of the Social-Democratic party of Germany and of the French Communist party; or that of a combat unit based on the selection of only active and conscious members. To be sure, the first model in theory permits a certain latitude for grumblers and opponents to fool around in, but only where matters of secondary importance are involved. *Otherwise, the great mass of the apolitical and passive membership provides the apparatus with a voting base that can always be mobilized*, and which has nothing to do with class consciousness. (A not insignificant number of these members are even materially dependent on the apparatus – the bulk of the municipal and administrative workers and employees, the employees of the workers' organization itself, etc.)

In the combat organization, however, which is composed of members who have to exhibit a minimum of consciousness simply to become members, the possibility of finding independent thinking is actually much greater. Neither 'pure apparatchiks' nor pure careerists can take over as easily as in an ordinary electoral club. So differences of opinion will be resolved less in terms of material dependency or abstract 'loyalty' than according to actual substance. To be sure, the mere fact that the organization is composed in this fashion is no automatic guarantee against bureaucratization of the organization. But at least it provides an essential condition for preventing it.[48]

The relation between the revolutionary organization (a party nucleus or a party) and the mass of workers abruptly changes as soon as an actual revolutionary explosion occurs. At that point the seeds sown over the years by revolutionary and consciously socialist elements start sprouting. Broad masses are able to achieve revolutionary-class consciousness at once. The revolutionary initiatives of broad masses can far out-distance that of many revolutionary groupings.

In his *History of the Russian Revolution*, Trotsky emphasized in several instances that at certain conjunctures in the revolution the Russian working masses were even ahead of the Bolshevik party.[49] Nevertheless, one should not generalize from this fact, and above all, it must not be separated from the fact that, prior to Lenin's April Theses, the Bolshevik party's strategic conception of the nature and goal of the Russian revolution was insufficiently worked out.[50] It ran the risk of having to pay for this until Lenin took decisive action with his April Theses. He was able to do so with such ease, however, because the masses of educated worker-Bolsheviks were pushing him in that very direction and were themselves a reflection of the powerful radicalization of the Russian working class.

An objective, i.e., comprehensive, view of the role of the Bolshevik party organization in the Russian revolution would no doubt have to be formulated somewhat differently. While the leading cadre of the party proved several times to be a conservative block preventing the party from going over to Trotsky's position on the struggle for the dictatorship of the proletariat (soviet power), at the same time it became evident that the crystallization of a revolutionary workers' cadre schooled in two decades of revolutionary organization and revolutionary activity was instrumental in making this decisive strategic turn a success. Should one wish to construct a correlation between the Stalinist bureaucracy and the 'Leninist concept of the party', one would at least have to make allowances for this decisive element of intervention. *Stalin's victory was not the result of the Leninist 'theory of organization' but the result of the disappearance of a decisive component of this concept: the presence of a broad layer of worker cadres, schooled in revolution and maintaining a high degree of activity, with a close relationship to the masses.* Moreover, Lenin himself would have in no way denied that in the absence of this factor the Leninist concept of the party could turn into its opposite.[51]

The soviet system is the only universal answer discovered thus far by the working class to the question of how to organize its independent activity during and following the revolution.[52] It allows all of the forces within the class – and all the labouring and progressive layers of society in general – to be brought together in a simultaneous, open confrontation between the various tendencies existing within the class itself. Every true soviet system – i.e., one that is actually elected by the mass of the workers and has not been imposed upon them by one or another selective power apparatus – will for that reason only be able to reflect the social and ideological diversity of the proletarian layers emphasized above. A workers' council is in reality a united front of the most diverse political tendencies that are in agreement on one central point: the common defence of the revolution against the class enemy. (In the same way, a strike committee reflects the most widely differing tendencies among the workers, yet with one exception: it includes only those tendencies that are participating in the strike. Scabs have no place in a strike committee.)

There is no contradiction whatever between the existence of a revolutionary organization of the Leninist type and genuine soviet democracy, or soviet power. On the contrary, without the systematic organizational work of a revolutionary vanguard, a soviet system will either be quickly throttled by reformist and semi-reformist bureaucracies (cf. the German soviet system from 1918–19), or it loses its political effectiveness due to its inability to solve the central political tasks (cf. the Spanish revolutionary committees between July 1936 and spring 1937).

The hypothesis that a soviet system makes parties superfluous has one of two sources. Either it proceeds from the naïve assumption that the introduction of soviets homogenizes the working class overnight, dissolves all differences of ideology and interest, and automatically and spontaneously suggests to the entire working class 'the revolutionary solution' to *all* the strategic and tactical problems of the revolution. Or, it is merely a pretext for giving to a small group of self-appointed 'leaders' the opportunity to manipulate a rather broad, inarticulate mass in that this mass is deprived of any possibility of systematically coming to grips with these strategic and tactical questions of the revolution, i.e., *of freely discussing and politically differentiating itself.* (This is obviously the case, for example, with the Yugoslav system of so-called self-management.)

The revolutionary organization *can*, therefore, guarantee the working masses in the soviet system a greater degree of independent activity and self-awareness, and thereby of revolutionary-class consciousness, than could an undifferentiated system of representation. But of course to this end it must stimulate and not hold back the independent action of the working masses. It is precisely this independent initiative of the masses which reaches its fullest development in the soviet system. Again we reach a similar conclusion: the Leninist concept of organization, built upon a correct revolutionary strategy (i.e., on a correct assessment of the objective historical process), is simply the collective co-ordinator of the activity of the masses, the collective memory and digested experience of the masses, in place of a constantly repetitive and expanding discontinuity in time, space and consciousness.

History has also shown in this connection that there is a substantial difference between a party *calling* itself a revolutionary party and actually *being* a revolutionary party. When a group of functionaries not only opposes the initiative and activity of the masses but seeks to frustrate them by any means, including military force (one thinks of Hungary in October-November 1956 or Czechoslovakia since August 1968), when this group not only finds no common language with a soviet system springing spontaneously from mass struggles, but throttles and destroys this system behind a pretext of defending 'the leading role of the party'[53] – then we are obviously no longer dealing with a revolutionary party of the proletariat but with an apparatus that represents the special interests of a privileged layer deeply hostile to the independent activity of the masses: the bureaucracy. The fact that a revolutionary party *can* degenerate into a party of bureaucracy is, however, no more an argument against the Leninist concept of organization than the fact that doctors have killed, not cured, many patients represents an argument against medical science. Any step away from this concept towards 'pure' mass spontaneity would be comparable to reverting from medical science to quackery.

Sociology of Economism, bureaucratism and spontaneism

When we emphasized that Lenin's concept of organization in reality represents a concept of the current potential for proletarian revolution, we already touched upon the central factor in the Leninist theory of proletarian-class consciousness: the problem of the definition of the revolutionary subject under capitalism.

For Marx and Lenin (as well as for Luxemburg and Trotsky, although they did not draw all the necessary conclusions from this fact until some time before 1914), the revolutionary subject is *the only potentially, only periodically revolutionary working class* as it works, thinks and lives under capitalism, i.e., in the totality of its social existence.[54] The Leninist theory of organization proceeds directly from this assessment of the position of th revolutionary subject, for it is self-evident that a subject, thus defined, can only be a *contradictory* one. On the one hand it is exposed to wage slavery, alienated labour, the reification of all human relations, and the influence of bourgeois and petty-bourgeois ideology. On the other hand, at periodic intervals it passes over into a radicalizing class struggle, and even into open revolutionary battle against the capitalist mode of production and the bourgeois state apparatus. It is in this periodic fluctuation that the history of the *real* class struggle of the last one hundred and fifty years is expressed. It is absolutely impossible to sum up the history of, say, the French or the German labour movements of the past hundred years with either the formula 'increasing passivity' or 'uninterrupted revolutionary activity'. It is obviously a unity of *both* elements with an alternating emphasis on one or the other.

As ideological tendencies, opportunism and sectarianism have their deepest theoretical roots in an undialectical definition of the revolutionary subject. For the opportunists, this revolutionary subject is the *everyday worker*. They tend to imitate the attitude of this worker in everything and 'to idolize his backward side', as Plekhanov so well put it. If the workers are concerned only with questions limited to the shops, then they are 'pure trade unionists'. If the workers are caught up in a wave of patriotic jingoism, then they become social-patriots or social-imperialists. If the workers submit to cold-war propaganda, they become cold-warriors: 'The masses are always right.' The latest and the most wretched expression of such opportunism consists of determining the programme – let it be an electoral programme – no longer through an objective scientific analysis of society but with the aid of . . . opinion polls.

But this opportunism leads to an insoluble contradiction. Fortunately, the moods of the masses do not stand still but can change dramatically in a rather short period of time. Today the workers are concerned only with internal shop questions, but tomorrow they will throng the streets in a political demonstration. Today they are 'for' the defence of the imperialist fatherland against the 'external enemy', but tomorrow they will be fed up with the war and again recognize their own ruling class as the main enemy. Today they passively accept collaboration with the bosses, but tomorrow they will move against it through a wildcat strike. The logic of opportunism leads – once the adaptation to bourgeois society has been excused through references to the attitude of the 'masses' – to resistance *to these very masses* as soon as they begin in a sudden reversal, to move into action against bourgeois society.

Sectarians simplify the revolutionary subject just as much as opportunists, but in the opposite sense. If only the everyday worker counts for the opportunists – i.e., the worker who is assimilating and adapting to bourgeois relations – for the sectarians it is only the 'ideal' proletarian, one who acts like a revolutionary, who counts. If the worker does not behave in a revolutionary fashion, he has ceased to be a revolutionary subject: he is demoted to being 'bourgeois'. Extreme sectarians – such as certain ultra-left 'spontaneists', certain Stalinists, and certain Maoists – will even go so far as to equate the working *class* with the capitalist *class* if it hesitates to completely accept the particular sectarian ideology in question.[55]

Extreme objectivism on the one hand ('everything the workers do is revolutionary'), and extreme subjectivism on the other hand ('only those who accept our doctrine are revolutionary or proletarian'), join hands in the final analysis when they deny the objectively revolutionary character of huge mass struggles led by masses with a contradictory consciousness. For the opportunist objectivists these struggles are not revolutionary because 'next month the majority will still go ahead and vote for the SPD (West German Social Democrats) or De Gaulle'. For the sectarian subjectivists they have nothing to do with revolution 'because the (i.e., our) revolutionary group is still too weak'.

The social nature of these two tendencies can be ascertained without difficulty. It corresponds to the petty-bourgeois intelligentsia: the opportunists for the most part represent the intelligentsia tied to the labour bureaucracy in mass organizations or in the bourgeois state apparatus, while the sectarians represent an intelligentsia that is either declassed or merely watches things from the sidelines, remaining outside of the real movement. In both cases, the forced separation between the objective and subjective factors at work in the contradictory but undivided revolutionary subject corresponds to a divorce between practice and theory which can lead only to an opportunist practice and to an idealizing 'theory' embodying 'false consciousness'.

It is characteristic, however, for many opportunists (among others, trade-union bureaucrats), as well as many sectarian literati, to accuse precisely the revolutionary Marxists of being petty-bourgeois intellectuals who would like to 'subjugate' the working class.[56] This question also plays a certain role in the discussions within the revolutionary student movement. Therefore, it is necessary to analyse more closely the problem of the sociology of the bureaucracy, of economism, and of spontaneism (or, of the 'handicraftsman's approach' to the question of organization).

The mediation between manual and mental labour, production and accumulation, occurs at several points in bourgeois society, though at different levels, for example, in the factory. What is meant by the general concept of 'intelligentsia', or 'intellectual petty bourgeoisie' or 'technical intelligentsia' corresponds in reality to many diverse activities of such mediation whose relation to the actual class struggle is quite distinct. One could essentially distinguish the following categories (which in no way do we claim constitute a complete analysis):

1. The genuine intermediaries between capital and labour in the process of production, i.e., the secondary officers of capital: foremen, timekeepers and other cadre personnel in the factories, among whose tasks is the maintenance, in the interest of capital, of labour discipline within the factory.

2. The intermediaries between science and technique, or between technique and production: laboratory assistants, scientific researchers, inventors, technologists, planners, project engineers, draughtsmen, etc. In contrast to category 1, these layers are not accomplices in the process of extracting surplus value from the producer. They take part in the material process of production itself and for that reason are not exploiters but producers of surplus value.

3. The intermediaries between production and realization of surplus value: advertising managers and offices, market research institutes, cadres and scientists occupied in the distribution sector, marketing specialists, etc.

4. The intermediaries between buyers and sellers of the commodity labour power: Above all, these are the trade-union functionaries and, in a wider sense, all functionaries of the bureaucratized mass organizations of the labour movement.

5. The intermediaries between capital and labour in the sphere of the superstructure, the ideological producers (i.e., those who are occupied with producing ideology): a section of the bourgeois

politicians ('public opinion makers'), the bourgeois professors of the so-called humanities, journalists, some artists, etc.

6. The intermediaries between science and the working class, the theoretical producers, who have not been professionally incorporated into the ideological production of the ruling class and are relatively able, being free from material dependency on this production, to engage in criticism of bourgeois relations.

One could add a seventh group, which is partially included in the fifth, and partially in the sixth. In classical, stable bourgeois society, teaching as a profession falls into category 5, both because of the unlimited predominance of bourgeois ideology and because of the generally abstract and ideological character of all professional teaching. With the growing structural crisis in the neocapitalist high schools and universities, however, a change in its objective standards takes place. On the one hand, the general crisis of capitalism precipitates a general crisis in neo-capitalist ideology, which is increasingly called into question. On the other hand, teaching serves less as abstract, ideological indoctrination and more as the direct technocratic preparation for the future intellectual workers (of categories 2 and 3) to be incorporated into the process of production. This makes it possible for the content of such teaching to be increasingly tied to a regained awareness of individual alienation, as well as to social criticism in related fields (and even to social criticism in general).

It now becomes clear which part of the intelligentsia will exert a negative influence upon the developing class consciousness of the proletariat: it is above all groups 3, 4 and 5. (We need say nothing about group 1 because in general it keeps its distance from the workers' organizations anyway.) What is most dangerous for the initiative and self-assurance of the working class is a symbiosis or fusion of groups 4 and 5, as has occurred on a broad scale since the First World War in the social-democratic and today already partially in the Moscow-orientated Communist mass organizations in the West.

Groups 2 and 6, on the other hand, can only enhance the impact of the working-class and revolutionary organizations *because they equip them with the knowledge that is indispensable for a relentless critique of bourgeois society and for the successful overthrow of this society, and even more for the successful taking over of the means of production by the associated producers.*

Those who rail against the growing union of workers' organizations with groups 2 and 6 of the intelligentsia objectively assist groups 3, 4 and 5 in exerting their negative influence on the working class. For never in history has there been a class struggle that has not been accompanied by an ideological struggle.[57] It boils down to a question of determining *which* ideology can sink roots in the working class; or, to phrase it better, whether bourgeois and petty-bourgeois ideology or Marxist scientific theory will develop among the workers. Whoever opposes 'every outside intellectual influence' within the working class in struggle either forgets or pushes aside the fact that the influence which groups 1, 3, 4 and 5 exert on this working class is *permanently and unremittingly* at work upon the proletariat through the entire mechanism of bourgeois society and capitalist economy, and that the ultra-left 'spontaneists' have no panacea at their disposal for putting an end to this process. To thunder against the influence of Marxist intellectuals within the working class means simply to allow the influence of the bourgeois intelligentsia to spread without opposition.[58]

Still worse. By resisting the formation of a revolutionary organization and the education of professional proletarian revolutionaries, Mensheviks and 'spontaneists' are objectively forced to help perpetuate the division between manual and intellectual labour, i.e., the spiritual subjugation of the workers to the intellectuals and the rather rapid bureaucratization of the workers' organizations. For, a worker who continuously remains within the capitalist process of production will most often not be in a position to globally assimilate theory, and will thereby remain dependent upon 'petty-bourgeois specialists'. For that reason, a decisive step can be taken within the revolutionary organization towards the intellectual emancipation of at least the most advanced workers and towards an initial victory over the division of labour within the workers' movement itself through the intermittent removal of workers from the factories.

This is not yet the final word on the sociology of spontaneism. We must ask ourselves: in which layers of the working class will the 'antipathy' and 'distrust' towards intellectuals have the most influence? Obviously in those layers whose social and economic existence *most sharply exposes them to an actual conflict with intellectual labour*. By and large, these are the workers of the small and medium-sized factories threatened by technological progress; self-taught workers who, through personal effort, have differentiated themselves from the mass; workers who have scrambled to the top of bureaucratic organizations; workers who, because of their low educational and cultural level, are the furthest removed from intellectual labour – and therefore also regard it with the greatest mistrust and hostility. In other words, the social basis of economism, spontaneism, the 'handicraftsman's approach' to the question of organization and hostility towards science within the working class is the craft layer of this class.

On the other hand, among the workers of the large factories and cities, of the extensive branches of industry in the forefront of technological progress, the thirst for knowledge, the greater familiarity with technical and scientific processes, and the greater audacity in projecting the conquest of power in both the factory and the state make it much easier to understand the objectively necessary role of revolutionary theoreticians and of the revolutionary organization.

The spontaneous tendencies in the labour movement often, if not always, correspond exactly to this social basis. This was especially true for anarcho-syndicalism in the Latin countries before the First World War. This was also true for Menshevism, which was thoroughly defeated by Bolshevism in the large metropolitan factories, but which found its most important proletarian base in the typically small-town mining and oil-field districts of southern Russia.[59] Attempts today, in the era of the third industrial revolution, to revive this craftsman caste approach under the pretext of guaranteeing 'workers' autonomy' could only have the same result as in the past – namely, to dissipate the forces of the advanced and potentially revolutionary working class and to give a boost to the semi-craft, bureaucratized sections of the movement that are under the constant influence of bourgeois ideology.

Scientific intelligentsia, social science and proletarian class consciousness

The massive reintroduction of intellectual labour into the process of production brought about by the third industrial revolution, which was foreseen by Marx and whose foundations were already laid in the second industrial revolution,[60] has created the prerequisite for a much broader layer of the scientific intelligentsia to regain the awareness of alienation which it had lost through its removal from the process of direct production of surplus value and its transformation into a direct or indirect consumer of surplus value. For it, too, is overcome by alienation in bourgeois society. This is the material basis not only for the student revolt in the imperialist countries but also for the possibility of involving increasing numbers of scientists and technicians in the revolutionary movement.

The participation of the intelligentsia in the classical socialist movement before the First World War generally tended to decline. Though it was considerable at the start of the movement, it became smaller and smaller as the organized mass movement of the working class became stronger. In a little-known polemic against Max Adler in 1910, Trotsky revealed the causes of this process to be on the whole materialistic: the intelligentsia's social dependency on the big bourgeoisie and the bourgeois state; an ideological identification with the class interests it thereby serves; and the inability of the workers' movement, organized as a 'counter-society', to compete with its counterpart. Trotsky predicted that this would probably change very quickly, in a revolutionary epoch, on the eve of the proletarian revolution.[61]

From these correct premises, however, he drew what were already incorrect tactical conclusions, when for instance he failed to see the great importance which in 1908–9 Lenin accorded the student movement (which was re-emerging in the middle of the victorious counter-revolution), considering it an albatross for the subsequent, new rise in the revolutionary mass movement (that was to begin in 1912).

He even went so far as to maintain that it was the 'fault' of the leading revolutionary intelligentsia in the Russian Social-Democracy if it was able to spread 'its overall social characteristics: a spirit of sectarianism, an individualism typical of intellectuals, and ideological fetishism'.[62] As Trotsky later admitted, he at that time underestimated the *political and social significance* of the faction fight between the Bolsheviks and the Liquidators, which was only an extension of the earlier struggle between Bolsheviks and Mensheviks. History was to show that this struggle had nothing to do with a product of 'intellectual sectarianism', but with the separation of socialist, revolutionary consciousness from petty-bourgeois, reformist consciousness.[63]

It is correct, however, that the participation of the Russian revolutionary intelligentsia in the building of the revolutionary-class party of the Russian proletariat was still a pure product of individual selection without any social roots. And since the

October revolution, this has inevitably turned against the *proletarian* revolution, for the masses of the technical intelligentsia were not *able* to go over to the camp of the revolution. At first they sabotaged economic production and the methods of social organization on the broadest scale; then their co-operation had to be 'bought' through high salaries; and finally they were transformed into the driving force behind the bureaucratization and degeneration of this revolution.

In as much as the position of the technical intelligentsia (especially category 2 above) in the material process of production has today decisively changed, and since this technical intelligentsia is gradually being transformed into a section of the wage-earning class, the possibility of its massive participation in the revolutionary process and in the reorganization of society stands on much firmer ground than in the past. Frederick Engels had already pointed to the historically decisive role this intelligentsia could play in the construction of the socialist society.

> In order to take over and put into operation the means of production, we need people, and in large numbers, who are technically trained. We do not have them . . . I foresee us in the next eight to ten years recruiting enough young technicians, doctors, lawyers and teachers to be in a position to let party comrades administer the factories and essential goods for the nation. Then our accession to power will be quite natural and will work itself out relatively smoothly. If, on the other hand, we prematurely come to power through a war, the technicians will be our main opponents, and will deceive and betray us whenever possible. We will have to use terror against them and still they will shit all over us.[64]

Of course, it must be added that in the course of this third industrial revolution the working class itself, which is much better qualified than in 1890, exhibits a much greater ability to directly manage the factories than in Engels's time. But in the final analysis, it is technical abilities that are required for the broad masses to be able to exert political and social control over the 'specialists' (a matter about which Lenin had so many illusions in 1918). A growing union between the technical intelligentsia and the industrial proletariat, and the growing participation of revolutionary intellectuals in the revolutionary party, can only facilitate that control.

As the contradiction between the objective socialization of production and labour on the one hand, and private appropriation on the other, intensifies (i.e., as the crisis of the capitalist relations of production sharpens) – and today we are experiencing a new and sharper form of this contradiction, which underlay the May 1968 events in France and the mass struggles in Italy in 1969 – and as neocapitalism seeks to win a new lease of life by raising the working-class's level of consumption, science will increasingly become for the masses a revolutionary, productive force in two regards: with automation and the growing mountain of commodities, it produces not only a growing crisis in the production and distribution process of capital, which is based upon generalized commodity production; it also produces revolutionary consciousness in growing masses of people by allowing the myths and masks of the capitalist routine to be torn away, and by making it possible for the worker, reconquering the consciousness of being alienated, to put an end to that alienation. As the decisive barrier which today holds back the working class from acquiring political-class consciousness is found to reside less in the misery of the masses or the extreme narrowness of their surroundings than in the constant influence of petty-bourgeois and bourgeois ideological consumption and mystification, it is precisely then that the eye-opening function of critical social science can play a truly revolutionary role in the new awakening of the class consciousness among the masses.

Of course, this makes necessary the existence of concrete ties with the working masses – a requirement that can only be met by the advanced workers on the one hand and the revolutionary organization on the other. And this also requires the revolutionary, scientific intelligentsia not to 'go to the people' with the modest populist masochism that restricts it to humbly supporting struggles for higher wages but to bring the awakened and critical layers of the working class what they are unable to achieve by themselves, due to their fragmented state of consciousness: the scientific knowledge and awareness that will make it possible for them to recognize the scandal of concealed exploitation and disguised oppression for what it is.

Historical pedagogy and communication of class consciousness

Once it is understood that the Leninist theory of organization tries to answer the problems of the current potential for revolution and of the revolutionary subject, this theory then leads directly to the question of historical pedagogy, i.e., the problem of *transforming* potential class consciousness into actual class consciousness, and trade-unionist consciousness into political, revolutionary consciousness. This problem can only be resolved in the light of the classification of the working class delineated above – into the mass of the workers, advanced workers, and organized revolutionary cadre. To assimilate its growing class consciousness, each layer requires its own methods of instruction, goes through its own learning process and needs to have a special form of communication with the class as a whole and with the realm of theoretical production. The historical role of the revolutionary vanguard party Lenin had in mind can be summed up as that of jointly expressing these three forms of pedagogy.

The broad masses learn only through action. To hope to 'impart' to them revolutionary consciousness through propaganda is an endeavour worthy of Sisyphus – and as fruitless. Yet although the masses learn only through action, all actions do not necessarily lead to a mass acquisition of *revolutionary* class consciousness. Actions around immediately realizable economic and political goals that can be completely achieved within the framework of the capitalist social order do not produce revolutionary-class consciousness. This was one of the great illusions of the 'optimistic' Social-Democrats at the end of the nineteenth century and the beginning of the twentieth (including Engels) who believed that there was a straight line leading from partial successes in electoral struggles and strikes to revolutionary consciousness and to an increase in the proletariat's revolutionary combativity.[65]

This has proven to be historically incorrect. These partial successes certainly played a significant and positive role in strengthening the self-confidence and combativity of the proletarian masses in general. (The anarchists were wrong to reject these partial struggles out of hand.) Yet they did not prepare the working masses for revolutionary struggle. The German working class's lack of experience in revolutionary struggles on the one hand, and the existence, on the other hand, of such experience in the Russian working class, was the most important difference in consciousness between the two classes on the eve of the First World War. It decisively contributed to the dissimilar outcome of the revolutions of 1917–19 in Germany and in Russia.

Since the goal of mass actions is generally the satisfaction of immediate needs, it becomes an important aspect of revolutionary strategy to link to these needs demands that objectively cannot be achieved or co-opted within the framework of the capitalist social order, and which produce an objectively revolutionary dynamic that has to lead to a test of strength between the two decisive social classes over the question of power. This is the strategy of transitional demands which, through the efforts of Lenin, was incorporated into the programme of the Communist International at its fourth congress, and which was later elaborated by Trotsky into the main body of the programme of the Fourth International.[66]

The development of revolutionary class consciousness among the broad masses is possible only if they accumulate experiences of *struggles* that are not only limited to the winning of partial demands within the framework of capitalism. The gradual injection of these demands into mass struggles can come about only through the efforts of a broad layer of advanced workers who are closely linked to the masses and who disseminate and publicize these demands (which normally do *not* spontaneously grow out of the day-to-day experiences of the class) in the factories, experimenting with them in various skirmishes, and spreading them through agitation, until a point is reached where favourable objective and subjective conditions converge, making the realization of these demands the actual objective of great strikes, demonstrations, agitational campaigns, etc.

Although revolutionary class consciousness among the broad masses develops only out of the experience of *objectively revolutionary struggle*, among advanced workers it flows from the experience of life, work and struggle in general. These experiences do not necessarily *need* to be revolutionary at all. From the daily experiences of class conflict, these advanced workers draw the elementary conclusions about the need for class solidarity, class action and class organization. The programmatic and organizational forms through which this action and organization are to be led will differ greatly depending upon objective conditions and concrete experiences. But the advanced workers' experience of life, work and struggle leads them to the threshold of understanding the inadequacy of activity which seeks merely to reform the existing society rather than abolish it.

The activity of the revolutionary vanguard can make it possible for the class consciousness of the advanced workers to cross over this threshold. It can fulfil this role of catalyst neither automatically nor without regard for objective conditions. It can only fulfil it when it is itself equal to the task, i.e., if the content of its theoretical, propagandistic and literary activity corresponds to the needs of the advanced workers, and if the form of this activity does not trample underfoot the laws of pedagogy (avoiding ultimatistic formulations). At the same time, this kind of activity must be linked to *activity of a practical nature* and to a *political perspective*, thus enhancing the credibility of both the revolutionary strategy and the organization putting it forward.

In periods of abating class struggles, of a temporary decline in the self-confidence of the working class, during which the stability of the class enemy appears temporarily assured, the revolutionary vanguard will not be able to achieve its objectives even if its activity is completely equal to the task of catalysing revolutionary class consciousness among the broadest layer of advanced workers. The belief that a mere defence of 'the correct tactic' or 'the correct line' is sufficient to miraculously generate a growing revolutionary force, even in periods of declining class struggle, is an illusion stemming from bourgeois rationalism, not from the materialist dialectic. This illusion, incidentally, is the cause of most splits within the revolutionary movement because the organizational sectarianism of the splitters is based on the naïve view that the 'application of the correct tactic' can win over more people in the as yet untouched periphery than it can among revolutionaries who are already organized. As long as the objective conditions remain unfavourable, these splits for that reason usually result in grouplets that are even weaker than those whose 'false tactics' made them seem so worthy of condemnation in the first place.

This does not mean, however, that the work of the revolutionary vanguard among the advanced workers remains useless or ineffectual during unfavourable objective circumstances. It produces no great *immediate* successes, yet it is a tremendously important, and even decisive, *preparation* for that turning-point when class struggles once again begin to mount!

For just as broad masses with no experience of revolutionary struggle cannot develop revolutionary class consciousness, advanced workers who have never heard of transitional demands cannot introduce them into the next wave of class struggle. The patient, persistent preparation carried out, with constant attention to detail, by the revolutionary vanguard organization, sometimes over a period of years, pays off in rich dividends the day the 'natural leaders of the class', still hesitating and not yet completely free from hostile influences, suddenly, during a big strike or demonstration, take up the demand for workers' control and thrust it to the forefront of the struggle.[67]

To be in a position, however, to convince a country's advanced workers and radical intelligentsia of the need to extend broad mass struggles beyond the level of immediate demands to that of transitional demands, it is not enough for the revolutionary vanguard organization to learn by heart a list of such demands culled from Lenin and Trotsky. It must acquire a twofold knowledge and a two-sided method of learning. On the one hand, it must assimilate the body of the experiences of the international proletariat over more than a century of revolutionary class struggle. On the other hand, it must carry on a continuous, serious analysis of the present overall social reality, national as well as international. This alone makes it possible to apply the lessons of history to the reality at hand. It is clear that on the basis of the Marxist theory of knowledge, only practice can ultimately provide the criterion for measuring the actual theoretical assimilation of present-day reality. For that reason, international practice is an absolute prerequisite for a Marxist international analysis, and an international organization is an absolute prerequisite for such a practice.

Without a serious assimilation of the entire historical experience of the international workers' movement from the revolution of 1848 to the present, it is impossible to determine with scientific precision either the contradictions of present neo-capitalist society – on a world scale as well as in individual countries – or the concrete contradiction accompanying the formation of proletarian class consciousness, or the kind of struggles that could lead to a pre-revolutionary situation. History is the only laboratory for the social sciences. Without assimilating the lessons of history, a pseudo-revolutionary Marxist today would be no better than a 'medical student' who refused to set foot inside the dissecting laboratory.

It should be pointed out in this connection that all attempts to keep the newly emerging revolutionary movement 'aloof from the splits of the past' demonstrate a complete failure to understand the socio-political nature of this differentiation within the international workers' movement. If one puts aside the inevitable personal and incidental factors involved in these differentiations, one has to come to the conclusion that the great disputes in the international workers' movement since the foundation of the First International (the disputes between Marxism and anarchism; between Marxism and revisionism; between Bolshevism and Menshevism; between internationalism and social-patriotism; between defenders of the dictatorship of the proletariat and defenders of bourgeois democracy; between Trotskyism and Stalinism; between Maoism and Khrushchevism) touch upon fundamental questions relating to the proletarian revolution and to the strategy and tactics of revolutionary class struggle. *These basic questions are products of the very nature of capitalism, the proletariat and revolutionary struggle.* They will therefore remain pressing questions as long as the problem of creating a classless society on a world scale has not been solved in practical terms. No 'tactfulness', no matter how artful, and no 'conciliationism', no matter how magnanimous, can in the long run prevent these questions rising out of practice itself to confront each new generation of revolutionaries. All that is accomplished by attempting to avoid a discussion of these problems is that instead of raising, analysing and solving them in a methodical and scientific fashion, this is done unsystematically, at random, without plan, and without sufficient training and knowledge.

However, while the assimilation of the historical substance of Marxist theory is necessary, it is nevertheless in and of itself an insufficient prerequisite for conveying revolutionary-class consciousness to the advanced workers and the radical intelligentsia. In addition, a systematic analysis of the present is required without which theory cannot furnish the means for disclosing either the immediate capacity of the working class for struggle or the 'weak links' in the neocapitalist mode of production and bourgeois society; nor can it furnish the means for formulating the appropriate transitional demands (as well as the proper pedagogical approach to raising them). Only the combination of a serious, complete social and critical analysis of the present and the assimilation of the lessons of the history of the workers' movement can create an effective instrument for the theoretical accomplishment of the task of a revolutionary vanguard.[68]

Without the experience of revolutionary struggle by broad masses, there can be no revolutionary class consciousness among these masses. Without the conscious intervention of advanced workers, who inject transitional demands into workers' struggles, there can hardly be experiences of revolutionary struggle on the part of the broad masses. Without the spreading of transitional demands by a revolutionary vanguard, there can be no possibility of advanced workers influencing mass struggles, in a truly anti-capitalist sense. Without a revolutionary programme, without a thorough study of the history of the revolutionary workers' movement, without an application of this study to the present, and without practical proof of the ability of the revolutionary vanguard to successfully play a leading role in at least a few sectors and situations, there can be no possibility of convincing the advanced workers of the need for the revolutionary organization and therefore no possibility (or only an unlikely one) that the appropriate transitional demands for the objective situation can be worked out by the advanced workers. In this way the various factors in the formation of class consciousness intertwine and underpin the timeliness of the Leninist conception of organization.

The process of building a revolutionary party acquires its unified character through jointly expressing the learning of the masses in action, the learning of the advanced workers in practical experience, and the learning of the revolutionary cadre in the transmission of revolutionary theory and practice. There is a constant inter-relationship between learning and teaching, even among the revolutionary cadre, who have to achieve the ability to shed any arrogance resulting from their theoretical knowledge. *This ability proceeds from the understanding that theory proves its right to exist only through its connection to the real class struggle and by its capacity to transform potentially revolutionary class consciousness into the actual revolutionary class consciousness of broad layers of workers.* The famous observation by Marx that the educators must themselves be educated[69] means exactly what it says. It does not mean that a consciously revolutionary transformation of society is possible without a revolutionary pedagogy. And it is given a more complete expression in the Marxist proposition that 'In revolutionary activity the changing of oneself coincides with the changing of circumstances.'[70]

Notes

1. This concept was by no means invented by Lenin but corresponds to a tradition leading from Engels, through Kautsky, to the classical doctrines of the international Social Democracy between 1880 and 1905. The Hainfeld Programme of the Austrian Social Democracy, drafted in 1888–9, explicitly states: 'Socialist consciousness is something that is brought into the proletarian class struggle from outside, not something that organically develops out of the class struggle.' In 1901, Kautsky published his article 'Akademiker und Proletarier' in *Neue Zeit* (19th year, vol. 2, April 17, 1901) in which the same thought is expressed (p. 89) in a form that directly inspired Lenin's *What is to Be Done?*

It is well known that Marx had developed no uniform concept of the party. But while he sometimes totally rejected the idea of a vanguard organization, he also formulated a conception which very closely approaches that of 'introducing revolutionary-socialist consciousness' into the working class. Note the following passage from a letter, written by him on January 1, 1870, from the executive board of the First International to the federal committee of Romanic Switzerland:

'The English possess all the necessary *material prerequisites* for a social revolution. What they lack is a *spirit of generalization and revolutionary passion*. That the executive board alone can remedy, and in doing so, hasten the development of a truly revolutionary movement in this country, and hence *everywhere*. The great successes that we have already achieved in this regard are being attested to by the wisest and most distinguished newspapers of the ruling class . . . not to mention the so-called radical members of the House of Commons and the House of Lords, who only a short time ago had quite a bit of influence on the leaders of the English workers. They are publicly accusing us of having poisoned and almost suffocated the *English spirit* of the working class, and of having driven it to revolutionary socialism.' Marx/Engels, *Werke*, Berlin: 1964, vol. 16, pp. 386–7.

The concept of the 'actuality of revolution' in Lenin was first formulated by Georg Lukacs, as is well known, in *History and Class Consciousness* and particularly in his *Lenin*.

2. This is especially true for the crucial Marxian category of *revolutionary practice*, which was developed in the then unknown *German Ideology*.

3. It is in this sense that, among others, the famous statement by Marx at the beginning of *The Eighteenth Brumaire of Louis Bonaparte* must be understood, in which he stresses the constant self-critical nature of the proletarian revolution and its tendency to come back to things that appeared to have already been accomplished. In this connection, Marx speaks also of the proletariat as being hypnotized by the 'undefined magnitude of its own objectives'.

4. In the *Communist Manifesto* Marx and Engels state that communists 'do not set up any special principles of their own, by which to shape and mould the proletarian movement'. In the English edition of 1888, Engels substituted the word 'sectarian' for the word 'special'. In doing so, he expresses the fact that scientific socialism certainly does try to advance 'special' principles in the labour movement, but only those objectively resulting from the general course of the proletarian class struggle, i.e., from

contemporary history, and not those peculiar only to the creed of a particular sect, i.e., to a purely incidental aspect of the proletarian class struggle.

5. This thought is poignantly expressed by Trotsky in the introduction to the first Russian edition of his book, *The Permanent Revolution*, New York: 1969. Mao Tse-tung too has more than once called attention to this thought. In sharp contrast to it is the notion of a 'socialist mode of production' or even of a 'developed social system of socialism' in which the first stage of communism is regarded as something fixed and not as simply a transitional phase in the permanent revolutionary development from capitalism to communism.

6. Note Lenin's well-known statement that there are no 'inextricable economic situations' for the imperialist bourgeoisie.

7. Thus the rising bourgeois class consciousness, and even the rising plebeian or semiproletarian class consciousness in the sixteenth and seventeenth centuries, were expressed within a completely religious framework, finding the way to overt materialism only with the full-blown decadence of the feudal absolutist order in the second half of the eighteenth century.

8. Gramsci's 'concept of political and ethical hegemony,' which an oppressed social class must establish within society before it can take political power, expresses this possibility especially well. cf. *Il Materialismo Storico e la Filosofia di Benedetto Croce*, Milan, 1964, p. 236; and also *Note sul Machiavelli*, Milan, 1964, pp. 29–37, 41–50 ff. This hegemony concept has been criticized or modified by numerous Marxist theoreticians. See, for example, Nicos Poulantzas, *Political Power and Social Class*, London 1973. Concerning the significance of overall social *consensus* with the material and moral foundations of bourgeois class rule, see Jose Ramon Recalde, *Integracion y lucha de clases en el neo-capitalismo*, Madrid 1968, pp. 152–7.

9. This is expressed by Marx and Engels in the proposition in *The German Ideology* that 'this revolution is necessary therefore, not only because the *ruling* class cannot be overthrown in any other way, but also because the class *overthrowing* it can only in a revolution succeed in ridding itself of all the muck of ages and become fitted to found society anew'. Karl Marx and Frederick Engels, *The German Ideology*, Moscow 1968, p. 87.

10. Note Lenin: 'Our wiseacre fails to see that it is precisely during the revolution that we shall stand in need of the results of our [pre-revolutionary – E. M.] theoretical battles with the Critics in order to be able resolutely to combat their *practical* positions!' *What is to Be Done?* Moscow 1964, p. 163. How tragically this came true seventeen years later in the German revolution.

11. In this connection in *What is to Be Done?* Lenin speaks of the 'social-democratic' and 'revolutionary' workers in contrast to the 'backward' workers.

12. N. Bukharin, *Theorie des Historischen Materialismus*, (published by the Communist International, 1922), pp. 343–5.

'Economic conditions had first transformed the mass of the people of the country into workers. The combination of capital has created for this mass a common situation, common interests. This mass is thus already a class as against capital, but not yet for itself. In the struggle, of which we have noted only a few phases, this mass becomes united, and constitutes itself as a class for itself.' Karl Marx, *The Poverty of Philosophy*, New York 1963, p. 173.

13. cf. the section of the SPD's 'Erfurt Program' that was not criticized by Engels, in which the proletarians are described as simpy the class of wageworkers separated from the means of production and condemned to sell their labour power, and in which the class struggle is described as the objective struggle between exploiters and exploited in modern society (i.e., without relation to the degree of organization or consciousness of the wage earners). Following this objective fact, which is established in the first four sections, comes the following addition to the conclusion of the general body of the programme: 'The task of the social-democratic party is to mould this struggle of the working class into a conscious and homogeneous one and to point out what is by nature its essential goal.' This once again explicitly confirms that there can be classes and class struggle in capitalist society without the struggling working class being conscious of its class interests. Further on, in the eighth section, the programme speaks of the 'class-conscious workers of all countries', and Engels proposes a change which again underlines the fact that he made a definitive distinction between the 'objective' and the 'subjective' concept of class: 'Instead of "class conscious", which for us is an easily understandable abbreviation, I would say (in the interests of general understanding and translation into foreign languages) "workers permeated with the consciousness of their class situation", or something like that.' Engels, 'Zur Kritik des sozial-demokratischen Programmentwurfs 1891' in Marx/Engels, *Werke*, Band 22, Berlin 1963, p. 232.

14. Lenin: 'The basic prerequisite for this success [in consolidating the party – E. M.] was, of course, the fact that the working class, whose elite has built the Social Democracy, differs, for objective economic reasons, from all other classes in capitalist society in its capacity for organization. Without this prerequisite, the organization of professional revolutionaries would only be a game, an adventure . . .' Lenine, *Oeuvres Complètes*, Tome 12, Paris 1969, p. 74.

15. To counter this view, many critics of the Leninist concept of organization (beginning with Plekhanov's article, 'Centralism or Bonapartism' in *Iskra*, No. 70 [Summer, 1904]), refer to a passage in *The Holy Family*. The passage states: 'When socialist writers ascribe this historic role to the proletariat, it is not, as Critical Criticism pretends to think, because they consider the proletarians as *gods*. Rather the contrary. Since the abstraction of all humanity, even of the *semblance* of humanity, is practically complete in the full-grown proletariat; since the conditions of life of the proletariat sum up all the conditions of life of society today in all their inhuman acuity; since man has lost himself in the proletariat, yet at the same time has not only gained theoretical consciousness of that loss, but through urgent, no longer disguisable, absolutely imperative *need* – that practical expression of *necessity* – is driven to revolt against that inhumanity; it follows that the proletariat can and must free itself. But it cannot free itself without abolishing the conditions of its own life. It cannot abolish the conditions of its own life without abolishing *all* the inhuman conditions of life of society today which are summed up in its own situation. Not in vain does it go through the stern but steeling school of *labour*. The question is not what this or that proletarian, or even the whole of the proletariat, at the moment *considers* as its aim. The question is *what the proletariat is*, and what, consequent on that *being*, it will be compelled to do. Its aim and historical action is irrevocably and obviously demonstrated in its own life situation as well as in the whole organization of bourgeois society today. There is

no need to dwell here upon the fact that a large part of the English and French proletariat is already *conscious* of its historic task and is constantly working to develop that consciousness into complete clarity.' Karl Marx and Frederick Engels, *The Holy Family*, Moscow 1956, pp. 52–3.

Aside from the fact that Marx and Engels were hardly in a position in 1844–5 to produce a mature theory of proletarian class consciousness and proletarian organization (to become aware of this, one need only compare the last sentence of the above quotation with what Engels wrote forty years later about the English working class), these lines say the very opposite of what Plekhanov reads into them. They say only that the social *situation* of the proletariat prepares it for radical, revolutionary *action*, and that the determination of the general socialist objective (the abolition of private property) is 'prescribed' by its conditions of life. In no way do they indicate, however, that the proletariat's 'inhuman conditions of life' will somehow mysteriously enable it to 'spontaneously' assimilate all the social sciences. Quite the opposite! (Concerning Plekhanov's article, see Samuel H. Baron's *Plekhanov*, Stanford 1963, pp. 248–53.

16. Today it is almost forgotten that the Russian socialist movement too was founded largely by students and intellectuals, and that around three-quarters of a century ago they were faced with a problem similar to that of the revolutionary intelligentsia today. Similar, but of course not identical: today there is an additional obstacle (the reformist, revisionist mass organizations of the working class), as well as an additional strength (historical experience, including the experience of great victory which the revolutionary movement has accumulated since then).

In *What is to Be Done?* Lenin speaks explicitly of the capacity of intellectuals to assimilate 'political knowledge', i.e., scientific Marxism.

17. cf. Karl Marx, *The Poverty of Philosophy*. An absorbing description of the various early forms of trade unions and of workers' resistance funds can be found in E. P. Thompson's *The Making of the English Working Class*, London 1968.

18. The necessarily discontinuous nature of mass action is explained by the class condition of the proletariat itself. As long as a mass action does not succeed in toppling the capitalist mode of production, its duration will be limited by the financial, physical and mental ability of the workers to withstand the loss of wages. It is obvious that this ability is not unlimited. To deny this would be to deny the material conditions of the proletariat's existence, which compel it, as a class, to sell its labour power.

19. See a few examples from the first years of the metal workers' union of Germany: *Fünfundsiebzig Jahre Industriegewerkschaft Metall*, Frankfurt 1966, pp. 72–8.

20. We cannot describe in detail here the differences between a pre-revolutionary and a revolutionary situation. Simplifying the matter, we would differentiate a revolutionary from a pre-revolutionary situation in this way: While a pre-revolutionary situation is characterized by such extensive mass struggles that the continued existence of the social order is *objectively* threatened, in a revolutionary situation this threat takes the form, organizationally, of the proletariat establishing organs of dual power (i.e., potential organs for the exercising of power by the working class), and *subjectively* of the masses raising directly *revolutionary* demands that the ruling class is unable to either repulse or co-opt.

21. See below the Leninist origins of this strategy.

22. Rosa Luxemburg, 'Organizational Question of Social Democracy'

in Mary-Alice Waters, ed., *Rosa Luxemburg Speaks*, New York 1970, pp. 112–30.

23. Lenin, *What is to Be Done?* op. cit., p. 66.

24. For a relating of this plan directly to revolution, see *What is to Be Done?*, op. cit., pp. 165–6. It is true that there are also *organizational* rules for centralization in *What is to Be Done?*, but they are determined exclusively *by the conditions* imposed by illegality. Lenin recommends the broadest 'democratism' for 'legal' revolutionary parties: 'The general control (in the literal sense of the term) exercised over every act of a party man in the political field brings into existence an automatically operating mechanism which produces what in biology is called the "survival of the fittest". "Natural selection" by full publicity, election and general control provides the assurance that, in the last analysis, every political figure will be "in his proper place", do the work for which he is best fitted by his powers and abilities, feel the effects of his mistakes on himself, and prove before all the world his ability to recognize mistakes and to avoid them.' ibid., p. 130.

Within her Polish party, which was also defined by highly conspiratorial restrictions, Luxemburg, for her part, practised (or accepted) a centralism that was no less stringent than that of the Bolsheviks (cf. the conflict with the Radek faction in Warsaw and the serious charges made against it).

25. *Rosa Luxemburg Speaks*, op. cit., p. 118.

26. For this see David Lane, *The Roots of Russian Communism*, Assen 1969. Lane has attempted to analyse the social composition of the membership of the Russian Social Democracy and of the Bolshevik and Menshevik factions between 1897 and 1907 on the basis of empirical data. He comes to the conclusion that the Bolsheviks had more worker members and activists than the Mensheviks (pp. 50–1).

27. 'Generally speaking it is undeniable that a strong tendency towards centralization is inherent in the social-democratic movement. This tendency springs from the economic make-up of capitalism which is essentially a centralizing factor. The social-democratic movement carries on its activity inside the large bourgeois city. Its mission is to represent, within the boundaries of the national state, the class interests of the proletariat, and to oppose those common interests to all local and group interests.

'Therefore, the social democracy is, as a rule, hostile to any manifestations of localism or federalism. It strives to unite all workers and all worker organizations in a single party, no matter what national, religious, or occupational differences may exist among them.' *Rosa Luxemburg Speaks*, op. cit., p. 116.

28. cf. the thesis put forward by Andre Gorz, according to which a new party can be created only 'from the bottom up' once the network of factory and rank-and-file groups 'stretches out over the entire national territory' 'Ni-Trade-Unionists, ni Bolcheviks,' *Les Temps Modernes*, October, 1969. Gorz has not understood that the crisis of the bourgeois state and the capitalist mode of production does not develop gradually 'from the periphery towards the centre,' but that it is a discontinuous process which tends towards a decisive test of strength once it reaches a definite turning-point. If the centralization of revolutionary groups and combatants does not take place in time, attempts by the reformist bureaucracy to steer the movement back into acceptable channels will only be facilitated – as quickly happened in Italy, in fact while Gorz was writing his article. This

in turn quickly led to a set-back for the 'rank-and-file' groups. It did not at all lead to their spread throughout the whole country.

29. cf. Rosa Luxemburg's article on the founding of the Communist Party of Germany entitled 'The First Convention': 'The revolutionary shock troops of the German proletariat have joined together into an independent political party.' (*The Founding Convention of the Communist Party of Germany*, Frankfurt 1969, p. 301). 'From now on it is a question of everywhere replacing revolutionary moods with unflinching revolutionary convictions, the spontaneous with the systematic.' (p. 303). See also (on p. 301) the passage from the pamphlet written by Luxemburg, *What Does the Spartacus League Want?*: 'The Spartacus League is not a party that seeks to come to power over or with the help of the working masses. *The Spartacus League is only that part of the proletariat that is conscious of its goal.* It is that part which, at each step, points the working-class masses as a whole towards their historic task, which, at each separate stage of the revolution, represents the ultimate socialist objective and, in all national questions, the interests of the proletarian world revolution.' (Emphasis added.) In 1904 Luxemburg had not yet understood the essence of Bolshevism – that 'that part of the proletariat that is conscious of its goal' must be organized *separately* from the 'broad mass'.

It is a complete confirmation of our thesis that as soon as Luxemburg adopted the concept of the vanguard party, she too was then accused by Social Democrats ('left' Social Democrats at that) of wanting 'the dictatorship over the proletariat'. (Max Adler, 'Karl Liebknecht und Rosa Luxemburg', *Der Kampf*, vol. xii, No. 2 [February, 1919], p. 75.)

30. Leon Trotsky, *Nos Tâches Politiques*, Paris 1970, pp. 123–9.

31. ibid., p. 125.

32. ibid., p. 186.

33. Leon Trotsky, 'The Class, the Party and the Leadership', *Fourth International* [predecessor of the *International Socialist Review*], vol. i, No. 7 (December, 1940), p. 193.

34. Numerous examples of this could be mentioned. See, among others, Lenin, *Collected Works*, vol. 18, Moscow 1963, pp. 471–7; vol. 23, pp. 236–53; vol. 10, pp. 277–8.

35. The impossibility of 'spontaneous' concentration of the revolutionary vanguard elements on a national scale was demonstrated with particular clarity in the French general strike of May 1968.

36. Yet here too these initial forms of independent organization were unable, in the absence of an organized revolutionary vanguard, which would have carried out the necessary preparatory work, to neutralize for long, let alone to smash, the conservative centralization of the trade-union and state apparatuses, and of the entrepreneurs.

37. Leon Trotsky, *The History of the Russian Revolution*, Ann Arbor 1957, p. xix.

38. See among others Georg Lukacs, *History and Class Consciousness*, London 1971.

39. The defence of the political and material special interests of these bureaucracies is nevertheless the social substructure upon which the superstructure of this autonomy and its ideological sediment are able to arise.

40. *Rosa Luxemburg Speaks*, op. cit., p. 121.

41. Leon Trotsky, 'Results and Prospects' in *The Permanent Revolution*, op. cit., p. 114.

42. cf., for instance, Clara Zetkin's biting scorn for the SPD executive

committee (as well as Kautsky's lack of character), which she expressed in her correspondence concerning the party leadership's censorship in 1909 of the publication of Kautsky's *The Road to Power*, K. Kautsky, *Le Chemin de Pouvoir*, Paris 1969, pp. 177–212. Contrast this with the respect shown by Lenin for Kautsky in the same year.

43. Lenin, 'Der Zusammenbruch der II Internationale' in Lenin and Zinoviev, *Gegen den Strom* (published by the Communist International, 1921), p. 164.

44. ibid., p. 165.

45. Lenin, ' "Left Wing" Communism, an Infantile Disorder' in *Collected Works*, vol. 31, Moscow 1966, pp. 17–118.

See also the above-mentioned passage from the pamphlet *What Does the Spartacus League Want?*, written by Rosa Luxemburg.

This conclusion was superior to that of Trotsky in 1906 or Luxemburg in 1904. In the face of a growing conservatism on the part of the social-democratic apparatus, they had illusions about the ability of the masses to solve the problem of the seizure of power with the aid of their revolutionary ardour alone. In 'The Mass Strike, the Political Party and the Trade Unions,' (in *Rosa Luxemburg Speaks*, op. cit., pp. 153–219). Luxemburg even shifts the problem temporarily on to the 'unorganized', i.e., the poorest, section of the proletariat that for the first time attains consciousness during a mass strike. In his writings after 1914, Lenin too explicitly contrasts these masses to the 'labour aristocracy', in a somewhat oversimplified manner, in my opinion. At that time the workers in the large steel and metal processing plants, among others, belonged to the unorganized sectors of the German proletariat, and while they turned to the left *en masse* after 1918, they did not at all belong to the 'poorest' layers.

46. This so-called general crisis of capitalism, i.e., the onset of the historical epoch of the decline of capitalism, should not be confused with conjunctural crises, i.e., periodic economic crises. These have occurred during the period of rising, as well as declining, capitalism. For Lenin, the epoch beginning with the First World War is the 'era of beginning social revolution'. See, among others, *Gegen den Strom*, op. cit., p. 393.

47. Herein undoubtedly lies the greatest weakness of this fatalistic theory. Out of the tendency towards growing autonomy, it automatically deduces a *social danger*, without including in its analysis the transmission of potential social power and specific social interests. The tendency for doormen and cashiers to develop their own interests does not give them power over banks and large firms – except for the 'power' of robbery, which is effective only under very specific conditions. If the analysis of this tendency towards autonomy is to have any social content, therefore, it must be accompanied by a definition of these conditions.

48. The formal rules of democratic centralism are, of course, part of these prerequisites. These rules include the right of all members to be completely informed about differences of opinion in the leadership; the right to form tendencies and to present contradictory points of view to the membership before leadership elections and conventions; the regular convening of conventions; the right to periodically revise majority decisions in the light of subsequent experiences, i.e., the right of minorities to periodically attempt to reverse decisions made by the majority; the right of political initiative by minorities and members at conventions, etc.

These Leninist norms of democratic centralism were rather strikingly formulated in the new party statutes drawn up before August 1968 in preparation for the fourteenth convention of the Czechoslovakian CP. The Moscow defenders of bureaucratic centralism reacted with the invasion. In fact, this proposed return to Leninist norms of democratic centralism was one of the most important 'thorns' in the side of the Soviet bureaucracy as far as the developments in Czechoslovakia were concerned.

49. Leon Trotsky, *The History of the Russian Revolution*, op. cit.

50. Between 1905 and 1917 the Bolshevik party was educated in the spirit of achieving the 'democratic dictatorship of the workers and peasants', i.e., in the spirit of a formula with its eye on the possibility of a coalition between a workers' party and a peasant party within the framework of capitalism – foreseeing, in other words, a *capitalist* development of Russian agriculture and industry. Lenin clung to this possibility until late 1916. Only in 1917 did he realize that Trotsky had been correct back in 1905 when he predicted that the agrarian question could only be solved by the dictatorship of the proletariat and the socialization of the Russian economy.

Hartmut Mehringer ('Introduction historique' in Trotsky, *Nos Tâches Politiques*, op. cit., pp. 17–18, 34 ff.) is completely wrong to link Lenin's theory of organization with his specific strategy in the Russian revolution, to explain it in terms of the 'subordinate' role (?) of the working class in this struggle, and to trace Trotsky's theory of the gradual extension of class consciousness to the entire working class to the theory of the permanent revolution. Aside from the fact that Mehringer gives an inadequate outline of Lenin's revolutionary strategy (Lenin was for the *absolute independence* of the Russian working class in opposing the Russian bourgeoisie, and was completely in favour of this class playing a leading role in the revolution); and aside from the fact that, like Lenin, Luxemburg rejected as premature any attempt to establish the proletarian dictatorship in Russia and assigned the revolutionary struggle of the Russian proletariat the mere goal of carrying out the historical tasks of the bourgeois revolution (while at the same time she fought against Lenin's theory of organization), it appears obvious to us that the very theory of permanent revolution (i.e., the task of establishing the proletarian dictatorship in an underdeveloped country) can be grasped with a minimum of realism only through the utmost concentration on the revolutionary tasks in general. Thus it leads not away from Lenin's theory of organization but straight to it. See in this regard also the excellent pamphlet by Demise Avenas, *Économie et politique dans la pensée de Trotsky*, Paris: 'Cahiers Rouges', 1970.

51. Lenine, *Oeuvres Complètes*, Tome 12, Paris 1969, p. 74.
'The pamphlet *What is to Be Done?* repeatedly emphasizes that the organization of professional revolutionaries which it proposes makes sense only insofar as it is connected to the "truly revolutionary class irresistibly rising up in struggle". ' Lenin underlines the fact that the sickness of small group existence can only be overcome through 'the ability of the party, through its open mass work, to reach out to proletarian elements. (ibid., p. 75.)

52. Maspero in Paris will soon publish an anthology by us entitled 'Workers' Control, Workers' Councils and Workers' Self-Management', which attempts to prove this thesis. Europaischer Verlaganstalt has announced plans to publish a German edition in 1971.

53. For Lenin the 'leading role of the party' in the soviet system is a political one, not one of substitution. It is a question not of substituting

itself for the majority in the soviet, but of convincing them of the correctness of the communist policy. The 'leading role of the party' is not even
mentioned in his basic work on soviets, *State and Revolution*. And if, in
times of the greatest confusion and civil war, he sometimes made sharp
sallies on tactical questions, arguments can be found in his writings against
'soviets without communists', but no arguments in favour of 'communists
without soviets'.

54. Georg Lukacs in *History and Class Consciousness*, is wrong to think
that he discovers one of the roots of Luxemburg's 'theory of spontaneity'
in 'the illusion of a purely proletarian revolution'. Even in countries where
the numerical and social importance of the proletariat is so overwhelming
that the question of 'allies' becomes insignificant, the separate organization
of the vanguard remains absolutely necessary in a 'purely proletarian
revolution' because of the internal stratification of the proletariat.

55. A striking example of this are the Chinese Maoists, for whom one
wing of their own party (including the majority of the central committee
that led the Chinese revolution to victory) is said to be made up of 'defenders
of the capitalist line' – and even 'capitalists' pure and simple.

For the Italian Bordigists, the general strike of 14 July, 1948, had nothing
to do with proletarian class struggle because the workers were striking in
defence of the 'revisionist' leader of the CP, Togliatti.

Cf., also the lovely formulation of the French spontaneist Denis Anthier:
'When the proletariat is not revolutionary, it does not exist, and revolutionaries cannot do anything with it. It is not they who, by assuming the
role of educators of the people, will be able to create the historical situation
in which the proletariat will become what it is; this can only be done by the
development of modern society itself'. Preface to Leon Trotsky, 'Rapport
de la delegation siberienne', Paris: *Spartacus*, 1970, p. 12. This quote also
shows how clearly extreme subjectivism and extreme objectivism are
related. And how is it explained that despite huge struggles the proletariat
does not achieve victory? 'Circumstances are to blame, the objective
conditions were not ripe.' Behind the ultraleft mask one can see those well-
known 'spontaneists' Karl Kautsky and Otto Bauer eagerly nodding their
wise heads. The ridiculous conclusions to which this extreme fatalism and
mechanical determinism lead become clear as soon as the 'development of
modern society itself' is expected to explain to us in concrete terms just
why at a given moment the majority of factory A and city B (but not of
factory C or city D) come out in favour of the dictatorship of the proletariat and against reformism. Yet for better or for worse, the outcome of
the revolution depends upon the answer to this question. As long as the
'development of modern society itself' does not drop *all* factories and *all*
cities like ripe fruit into the lap of the revolution, the 'educators of the
people', according to Anthier, should presumably refrain from doing
violence to 'objective conditions', by seeking to win over the workers of
C and D.

56. This reproach against Lenin and the Leninists was made by the
Russian 'Economists', and now today's spontaneists have rediscovered
it.

57. Cf., on this subject Nicos Poulantzas, *Political Power and Social Class*,
op. cit.

58. It is interesting to confirm that after the split in the Russian Social
Democracy there were many more intellectuals, including professional
revolutionary intellectuals, with the Mensheviks than with the Bolsheviks.

See in this connection David Lane, *The Roots of Russian Communism*, op. cit., pp. 47, 50.

59. David Lane too emphasizes the preponderance of the Bolsheviks in the cities with large factories and an old, stabilized working class. (ibid., pp. 212–13.)

60. In his last work ('Zum allgemeinen Verhaltnis von wissenschaftlicher Intelligenz und proletarischen Klassenbewusstsein,' *SDS-Info*, No. 26–27 [Dec. 22, 1969]), Hans-Jurgen Krahl brought out 'the' Marx quotation on this question which we are reprinting here. (It comes from the unincorporated section 'Sechstes Kapitel, Resultate des unmittelbarn Produktionsprozesses' in the draft of Chapter Six of Book One of the first volume of *Capital*, which was published for the first time, in the 'Marx/Engels Archives' in 1933.) We should like to dedicate this article, which was intended to promote discussion and understanding with him, to this young friend who so tragically passed away.

'With the development of a real subsuming of labour under capital (or in the specifically capitalist mode of production), the real functionary in the overall labour process is not the individual worker, but increasingly a combined social capacity for work, and the various capacities for work, which are in competition with one another and constitute the entire productive machine, participate in very different ways in the direct process of creating commodities – or, more accurately in this sense, products – (one works more with his hands, another more with his head, one as a manager, an engineer, a technician, etc., another as a supervisor, and a third as a simple manual labourer, or even a helper). As a result of this, the functions of labour capacity will increasingly tend to be classified by the direct concept of productive labour, while those who possess that capacity will be classified under the concept of productive workers, directly exploited by capital and subordinated to its process of consumption and production.' (Karl Marx, *Resultate* [Frankfurt 1969], p. 66.)

61. Leon Trotsky, *The Intelligentsia and Socialism*, London 1966.

62. Leon Trotsky, 'Die Entwicklungstendenzen der russischen Sozialdemkratie,' in *Die Neue Zeit*, vol. XXVIII, No. 2 (1910), p. 862.

63. Already in his first polemical book against Lenin (*Nos Tâches Politiques*, op. cit., pp. 68–71, for example), Trotsky had undertaken an effort to represent the entire Leninist polemic against 'Economism' and the 'handicraftsman's approach to organization' in *What is to Be Done?* as a pure discussion between intellectuals, or at best an attempt to win over the best forces of the petty-bourgeois intelligentsia to the revolutionary Social Democracy. He did not understand that it was a question of repelling the petty-bourgeois, revisionist influence *upon the working class*. His polemic against Lenin from 1903 to 1914 was characterized by an underappreciation of the catastrophic consequences of opportunism for the working class and the labour movement. Only in 1917 did he overcome this underappreciation once and for all.

64. August Bebel, *Briefwechsel mit Friedrich Engels*, The Hague 1965, p. 465.

65. The sole difficulty for the revolution seemed to them to lie in a necessary reaction to any possible repeal of universal suffrage, as might happen in case of war. In contrast, Luxemburg had, in dealing with the question of the mass strike, undertaken a conscious attempt to develop the proletariat's forms of struggle by going beyond electoral and wage struggles and closely following the example of the Russian revolution of 1905.

Even today, Lelio Basso, in an interesting analysis of *Rosa Luxemburg's Dialektik der Revolution*, Frankfurt 1969, pp. 82–3, attempts to present as the quintessence of Luxemburg's strategy a centrist reconciliation between day-to-day struggles and ultimate objectives which is limited to 'sharpening the contradictions' of objective development. The fact that the deeper meaning of the mass strike strategy escapes him as a result of this error does not need to be dwelt on here in detail.

66. See the discussion of programme at the fourth congress of the Communist International (*Protokoll des Vierten Kongresses der Kommunistischen Internationale* [published by the Communist International, 1923], pp. 404–48). It provisionally concluded with the following declaration of the Russian delegation, signed by Lenin, Trotsky, Zinoviev, Radek and Bukharin: 'The dispute over how the transitional demands should be formulated and in which section of the programme they should be included had awakened a completely erroneous impression that there exists a principled difference. In light of this, the Russian delegation unanimously confirms that the drawing up of transitional slogans in the programmes of the national sections and their general formulation and theoretical motivation in the general section of the programme cannot be interpreted as opportunism.' (ibid., p. 542). Trotsky seemed to foresee such a strategy already in 1904 when he wrote: 'The party stands on the proletariat's *given lack of consciousness* . . . and attempts to implant itself in the proletariat by *raising* this level . . .' (*Nos Tâches Politiques*, op. cit., p. 126).

67. Georg Lukacs, *Lenin*, London 1970, p. 31, is completely correct when he concludes from similar considerations that the Leninist revolutionary party cannot 'make' a revolution, but can accelerate the tendencies that will lead to one. Such a party is *both* producer and product of the revolution – which amounts to a resolution of the antithetical positions of Kautsky ('The new party must prepare the way for the revolution') and Luxemburg ('The new party will be created by the revolutionary action of the masses').

68. Hans-Jurgen Krahl (op. cit., p. 13 ff.) is quite correct when he reproaches Lukacs for his 'idealizing' concept of the totality of proletarian class consciousness, and when he accuses him of an inability to combine empirical knowledge and abstract theory – itself based on an inability to transmit revolutionary theory to the working masses. He should have been able to conclude from our essay, however, that such a transmission can be completely achieved on the basis of the Leninist concept of organization – that it, in fact, lies at the very heart of this concept. Since he makes a sharp distinction between 'alienated lot in life' and alienated process of production, however, he is predisposed by the Marcusian tendency to see the 'alienation of the consumer' as the central problem, and as a result to regard the 'civilized satisfaction of needs', which the neocapitalist system ostensibly makes possible for the working class, as an obstacle on its way towards acquiring proletarian class consciousness. Yet the Achilles heel of the capitalist mode of production must more than ever be sought in the sphere of alienation in the production process; there alone can a truly revolutionary rebellion begin, as the events in France and Italy have demonstrated. With that we are brought back to the process, which we described, of formulating and conveying class consciousness. In describing it, we, like Krahl (and, we are convinced, like Lenin and Trotsky), in no way substitute the naive concept of the 'omniscient party' for that of the

evolution of revolutionary theory *as a specific and permanent ongoing process of production.*

69. Karl Marx, 'Theses on Feuerbach', third thesis: 'The materialist doctrine concerning the changing of circumstances and upbringing forgets that circumstances are changed by men and that it is essential to educate the educators themselves.' (Marx/Engels, *The German Ideology*, op. cit., p. 660.)

70. ibid., p. 234.

Marxism and the National Question

MICHAEL LÖWY

(Reprinted from *New Left Review*, 96, 1976)

The aim of this article is to isolate certain key theoretical and methodological aspects of the classic Marxist debate on the national question: a debate which had its starting-point in the relatively imprecise positions developed by Marx and Engels themselves in their writings, and which was carried on vigorously in the Second International before the First World War, culminating in Lenin's formulation of a realistic revolutionary theory of the right of nations to self-determination.

Marx and Engels: nationality and internationalism

Marx offered neither a systematic theory of the national question, a precise definition of the concept of a 'nation', nor a general political strategy for the proletariat in this domain. His articles on the subject were, for the most part, concrete political statements relating to specific cases. As far as 'theoretical' texts proper are concerned, the best-known and most influential are undoubtedly the rather cryptic passages in the *Manifesto* concerning communists and the nation. These passages have the historical value of proclaiming in a bold and uncompromising way the internationalist nature of the proletarian movement, but they are not always free from a certain economism and a surprising amount of Free Tradist optimism. This can be seen particularly in the suggestion that the victorious proletariat will merely carry on the task of abolishing national antagonisms which was begun by 'the development of the bourgeoisie, Free Trade, the world market', etc. This idea, however, is contradicted in other texts from the same period, in which Marx stressed that 'while the bourgeoisie of each nation still retained separate national interests, big industry created a class, which in all nations has the same interest and with which nationality is already dead'.[1] In his later writings (particularly those on the question of Ireland), Marx showed that not only does the bourgeoisie tend to foster national antagonisms, but it actually tends to increase them, since: 1. the struggle to control markets creates conflicts between the capitalist powers; 2. the exploitation of one nation by another produces national hostility; 3. chauvinism is one of the ideological tools which enables the bourgeoisie to maintain its domination over the proletariat.

Marx was on firm ground in stressing the internationalization of the economy by the capitalist mode of production: the emergence of the world market which 'has destroyed industry's national base' by creating 'the universal interdependence of nations'. However, there was a tendency towards economism in his idea that the 'standardization of industrial production and corresponding living conditions' helps to dissolve national barriers (*Absonderungen*) and antagonisms, as though national differences could be equated simply with differences in the production process.

As for Marx's famous ironical and provocative statement that 'the proletariat has no country', this must be interpreted first and foremost in the sense that the proletariat of all nations have the *same interests*, a fact that Marx considered as being tendentially equivalent to the abolition of nationality (see the passage from *The German Ideology* quoted above): for the proletariat, the nation is merely the immediate political framework for the seizure of power. But Marx's anti-patriotism had a deeper significance: 1. for proletarian humanism, the whole of humanity is the meaningful totality, the supreme value, the final goal; 2. for historical materialism, communism can only be established on a world scale, due to the immense development of productive forces which surpass the narrow framework of nation states.

While the *Communist Manifesto* did lay the basis for proletarian internationalism, it gave hardly any indication of a concrete political strategy in relation to the national question. Such a strategy was only developed later, particularly in Marx's writings on Poland and Ireland (as well as in the struggle he waged in the International against the liberal-democratic nationalism of Mazzini and the national nihilism of the Proudhonists). Support for Poland's struggle for national emancipation was a tradition in the democratic workers' movement of the nineteenth century. Although they belonged to this tradition, Marx and Engels supported Poland less in the name of the general democratic principle of self-determination of nations than because of the struggle of the Poles against Tsarist Russia, the main bastion of reaction in Europe and the *bête noire* of the founding fathers of scientific socialism. This approach contained a certain ambiguity: if Poland was only to be supported because her national struggle was also an anti-Tsarist struggle, did this mean that pro-Russian Slavs (like the Czechs) did not have the right to self-determination? This was precisely the problem with which Engels was grappling in 1848–9.

The writings on Ireland, on the other hand, have a far wider application and state, implicitly, some general principles on the question of oppressed nations. In an early phase, Marx was in favour of Ireland having autonomy within a union with Britain and believed that the solution to the oppression of the Irish (by the big English landlords) would come through a working-class (Chartist) victory in England. In the sixties, on the other hand, he saw the liberation of Ireland as the condition for the liberation of the English proletariat. His writings on Ireland in this period elaborated three themes which were to be important for the future development of the Marxist theory of national self-determination, in its dialectical relationship with proletarian internationalism: 1. only the national liberation of the oppressed nation enables national divisions and antagonisms to be overcome, and permits the working class of both nations to unite against their common enemy, the capitalists; 2. the oppression of another nation helps to reinforce the ideological hegemony of the bourgeoisie over workers in the oppressing nation: 'Any nation that oppresses another forges its own chains'; 3. the emancipation of the oppressed nation weakens the economic, political, military and ideological bases of the dominating classes in the oppressor nation and this contributes to the revolutionary struggle of the working class of that nation.

Engels

Engels's positions on Poland and Ireland were broadly similar to those of Marx. However, in his writings one finds a curious theoretical concept, the doctrine of 'non-historic nations', which – although in my view fundamentally foreign to Marxism[2] – is well worth examining as an extreme example of the mistakes which can be made on the national question, even when one bases oneself on a revolutionary socialist, democratic position.

In 1848–9, analysing the failure of the democratic revolution in central Europe, Engels attributed it to the counter-revolutionary role played by the south Slav nations (Czechs, Slovaks, Croats, Serbs, Rumanians, Slovenes, Dalmatians, Moravians,

Ruthenians, etc.), who enlisted *en masse* in the Imperial Austrian and Russian armies and were used by the forces of reaction to crush the liberal revolution in Hungary, Poland, Austria and Italy.

In fact, the Imperial Austrian army consisted of peasants, both Slavs and German/Austrians. The victory of the counter-revolution was made possible by one important factor: the bourgeois-liberal leadership of the revolution was too hesitant, too 'moderate', too fearful, to spark off a national agrarian revolution. Consequently, it was unable to win the mass of the peasants and national minorities to its side and prevent them from becoming the blind instrument of reaction. The 1848 revolution is the classic example of a revolution which failed because it did not provide a radical solution to the agrarian question and the national question (precisely what made the 1917 October revolution successful!). This failure resulted from the narrow social base of its leadership: the central European liberal bourgeoisie was, by the nineteenth century, no longer a significant revolutionary class.

Because he failed to grasp the true *class* reasons for the failure of 1848–9, Engels tried to explain it with a metaphysical ideology: the theory of inherently counter-revolutionary 'non-historic nations' – a category in which he includes, pell-mell, southern Slavs, Bretons, Scots and Basques. According to Engels, these 'remnants of a nation, mercilessly crushed, as Hegel said, by the course of history, this *national refuse*, is always the fanatical representative of counter-revolution and remains so until it is completely exterminated or de-nationalized, as its whole existence is in itself a protest against a great historical revolution'.[3] Hegel, the originator of the theory, had argued that nations which have not succeeded in creating a state, or whose state has long since been destroyed, are 'non-historic' and condemned to disappear. As examples, he mentioned precisely the southern Slavs – the Bulgarians, Serbs, etc. Engels developed this pseudo-historical metaphysical argument in an article in 1855, which stated that 'Pan-Slavism is a movement which is attempting to wipe out what a thousand years of history have created, a movement which cannot achieve its aims without sweeping Turkey, Hungary and half of Germany off the map of Europe . . .'[4] There is no need to add that such an argument owed more to the conservative principles of the historical school of law (Savigny, etc.) than to the revolutionary ideas of historical materialism!

Paradoxically, the same Engels, in an article from the same period (1853), had stressed that the Turkish empire was destined to disintegrate as a result of the liberation of the Balkan nations, a fact which in no way surprised him since, as a good dialectician, he admired in history 'the eternal changes in human destiny . . . where nothing is stable except instability, nothing is immovable, except movement'.[5]

An 1866 series of articles on Poland[6] demonstrated the ideological consistency of Engels, who persisted in contrasting the 'great historical nations of Europe' (Italy, Poland, Hungary, Germany), whose right to national unity and independence was accepted, and the 'many traces of nations' of no 'European importance' and with no 'national vitality' (Rumanians, Serbs, Croats, Czechs, Slovaks, etc.) which were instruments in the hands of the Tsar and Napoleon III. However, we might claim in Engels's defence that these were newspaper articles, lacking the rigorous character of a scientific work, and thus having a different status from his theoretical writings proper. Moreover, the basis of Engels's position was democratic and revolutionary: how to defeat Tsarism and the Austrian empire. He was in no way motivated by any kind of Slavophobia. In an article written before the 1848 revolution, he had called for the defeat of the Austrian empire in order to 'clear all obstacles from the road to the liberation of the Italians and Slavs'.[7] Neither was Engels prey to German chauvinism, as is proved by his attacks on the German minority in Hungary (Siebenburger Sachsen), who 'persist in retaining an absurd nationality in the middle of a foreign country'.[8]

The Radical Left Against National Separatism

The 'radical left' current (Linksradikale) represented by Luxemburg, Pannekoek, Trotsky (before 1917) and Strasser was characterized, to varying degrees and sometimes in very different forms, by its opposition to national separatism, in the name of the principle of proletarian internationalism. Moreover, its stance on the national question was one of the principal differences between this current and Lenin, to whom it was close in its Marxist and revolutionary approach.

Rosa Luxemburg

In 1893 Rosa Luxemburg founded the Social-Democratic Party of the Kingdom of Poland (SDKP), with a Marxist and inter-nationalist programme, as a counter to the Polish Socialist Party (PPS), whose aim was to fight for the independence of Poland. Denouncing the PPS (with some justification) as a social-patriotic party, Rosa and her comrades of the SDKP were resolutely opposed to the slogan of independence for Poland and stressed, on the contrary, the close link between the Russian and Polish proletariats and their common destiny. The 'Kingdom of Poland' (part of Poland annexed to the Tsarist empire), they said, should proceed towards territorial *autonomy*, not towards independence, within the framework of a future Russian democratic republic.

In 1896 Luxemburg represented the SDKP at the Congress of the Second International. The positions for which she argued in her intervention were set out in a subsequent article:[9] the liberation of Poland is as utopian as the liberation of Czecho-slovakia, Ireland or Alsace-Lorraine . . . The unifying political struggle of the proletariat should not be supplanted by a 'series of sterile national struggles'. The theoretical bases for this position were to be provided by the research she did for her doctoral thesis, 'The Industrial Development of Poland' (1898).[10] The central theme of this work was that, from the economic point of view, Poland was already integrated into Russia. The industrial growth of Poland was being achieved thanks to Russian markets and, consequently, the Polish economy could no longer exist in isolation from the Russian economy. Polish independence was the aspiration of the feudal Polish nobility; now industrial development had undermined the basis of this aspiration. Neither the Polish bourgeoisie, whose economic future depended on the Russian economy, nor the Polish proletariat, whose historic interests lay in a revolutionary alliance with the Russian proletariat, was nationalist. Only the petty bourgeoisie and the pre-capitalist layers still cherished the utopian dream of a united, independent Poland. In this respect, Luxemburg considered her book to be the Polish equivalent of Lenin's 'The Development of Capitalism in Russia',[11] which was directed against the utopian and retrogressive aspirations of the Russian populists.

Her most controversial statement on the national question

(which Lenin, in particular, attacked) was the 1908 series of articles published under the title 'The National Question and Autonomy' in the journal of the Polish social-democratic party (which had become the SDKPL, after a Lithuanian Marxist group had joined). The main – and most debatable – ideas put forward in these articles were the following: 1. the right of self-determination is an *abstract* and metaphysical right such as the so-called 'right to work' advocated by the nineteenth century utopians, or the laughable 'right of every man to eat from gold plates' proclaimed by the writer Chernichevsky; 2. support for the right of secession of each nation implies in reality support for *bourgeois* nationalism: the nation as a uniform and homogenous entity does not exist – each class in the nation has conflicting interests and 'rights'; 3. the independence of small nations in general, and Poland in particular, is utopian from the economic point of view and condemned by the laws of history. For Luxemburg, there was only one exception to this rule: the Balkan nations of the Turkish empire (Greeks, Serbs, Bulgarians, Armenians). These nations had reached a degree of economic, social and cultural development superior to Turkey, a decadent empire whose dead weight oppressed them. From 1896 (following a Greek national uprising on the island of Crete) Luxemburg considered – in contrast to the position defended by Marx at the time of the Crimean War – that the Turkish empire was not viable, and that its decomposition into nation states was necessary for historical progress.

To back up her views on the lack of future for small nations, Luxemburg used Engels's articles on 'non-historic nations' (though she attributed them to Marx: their true authorship was in fact only established in 1913, with the discovery of unpublished Marx/Engels letters). In particular, she used the article of January 1849 on the Hungarian struggle, quoting the passage we have already mentioned on 'remnants of a nation mercilessly crushed by the course of history'. She recognized that Engels's views on the southern Slavs were mistaken, but she believed his method was correct and praised his 'sober realism, free from all sentimentality' as well as his contempt for the metaphysical ideology of the rights of nations.[12]

As is well known, in 1914 Luxemburg was one of the few leaders of the Second International who did not succumb to the great wave of social-patriotism which engulfed Europe with the advent of war. Imprisoned by the German authorities for her internationalist and anti-militarist propaganda, in 1915 she wrote and smuggled out of prison her famous Junius Pamphlet. In this text Luxemburg to some extent adopted the principle of self-determination: 'socialism gives to every people the right of independence and the freedom of independent control of its own destinies'.[13] However, for her this self-determination could not be exercised within existing capitalist states, particularly colonialist states. How could one speak of 'free choice' in relation to imperialist states like France, Turkey or Tsarist Russia? In the age of imperialism the struggle for the 'national interest' is a mystification, not only in relation to the large colonial powers, but also for the small nations which are 'only the pawns on the imperialist chessboard of the great powers'.[14]

Luxemburg's theories on the national question, developed between 1893 and 1917, are based on four fundamental theoretical, methodological and political errors.

1. Particularly before 1914, she adopted an economist approach to the problem: Poland is economically dependent on Russia, therefore cannot be politically independent – an argument which tends to ignore the specificity and the relative individuality of each political situation. This determinist-economist method is particularly striking in her doctoral thesis and her early writings on the Polish question: the industrial development of Poland, linked to the Russian market, determines 'with the iron strength of historical necessity' (an expression which Luxemburg frequently used at this time, together with another of the same type: 'with the inevitability of natural law') on one hand, the utopian nature of Polish independence and, on the other hand, the unity between the Russian and Polish proletariats. A characteristic example of this unmediated assimilation of politics to economics occurs in an article she wrote in 1902 on social-patriotism, which stressed that the economic tendency – 'and therefore' the political tendency – in Poland was for union with Russia; the phrase 'and therefore' was an expression of this lack of mediation, which was not demonstrated but simply assumed to be self-evident.[15] However, this type of argument began to disappear as Luxemburg increasingly succeeded in avoiding the economist trap, i.e. particularly after 1914, when she coined the phrase 'socialism or barbarism' (Junius Pamphlet), which represented a fundamental methodological break with fatalistic, Kautsky-type economism. Her arguments on the national question in the Junius Pamphlet

were essentially political and not based on any mechanistic preconception.

2. For Luxemburg the nation was essentially a cultural pheno-menon. Again, this tends to play down its political dimension, which cannot be equated simply with economy or ideology and whose concrete form is the independent nation state (or the struggle to establish it). This is why Luxemburg was in favour of abolishing national oppression and allowing 'free cultural development', but refused to countenance separatism or the right to political independence. She did not understand that the denial of the right to form an independent nation state is precisely one of the main forms of national oppression.

3. Luxemburg saw only the anachronistic, petty-bourgeois and reactionary aspects of national liberation movements and did not grasp their revolutionary potential against Tsarism (and later, in another context, against imperialism and colonialism). In other words, she did not understand the complex and con-tradictory dialectic of the *dual nature* of these nationalist move-ments. With regard to Russia, in general she underestimated the revolutionary role of the non-proletarian allies of the working class: the peasantry, the oppressed nations. She saw the Russian revolution as *purely* working class, and not – like Lenin – as *led* by the proletariat.[16]

4. She failed to understand that the national liberation of oppressed nations is not only a demand of the 'utopian', 'reac-tionary' and 'pre-capitalist' petty bourgeoisie, but also of *the masses as a whole*, including the proletariat; and that, therefore, the recognition by the Russian proletariat of the right of nations to self-determination was an *indispensable condition* of its solidarity with the proletariat of oppressed nations.

What was the source of these mistakes, inconsistencies and shortcomings? It would be wrong to think that they were logically linked to Luxemburg's method (apart from pre-1914 economism) or to her political positions as a whole (e.g. on the party, demo-cracy, etc.). In fact, these theories on the national question were not peculiar to Luxemburg, but were shared by the other leaders of the SDKPL, even those who, like Dzerzhinsky, supported Bolshevism. It is most likely that Luxemburg's one-sided position was, in the last analysis, an ideological by-product of the continual, intense and bitter ideological struggle of the SDKPL against the PPS.[17]

The difference between Lenin and Luxemburg was, therefore,

to a certain extent (at least as regards Poland), a result of the different standpoints of the Russian internationalists (struggling to defeat Great Russian chauvinism) and the Polish internationalists (combating Polish social-patriotism). Lenin at one time seemed to recognize a certain 'division of labour' between Russian and Polish Marxists on this question. Having said this, his major criticism of Luxemburg was that she tried to generalize from a certain specific situation (Poland at a particular point in history) and therefore to deny not just Polish independence, but that of all other small oppressed nations.

However, in one article Luxemburg stated the problem in terms very similar to Lenin's: the 1905 Introduction to the collection *The Polish Question and the Socialist Movement*.[18] In this essay, Luxemburg made a careful distinction between the undeniable *right* of every nation to independence ('which stems from the elementary principles of Socialism'), which she recognized, and the *desirability* of this independence for Poland, which she denied. This is also one of the few texts in which she recognized the importance, depth and even justification of national feelings (though treating them as merely a 'cultural' phenomenon), and stressed that national oppression is the 'most intolerable oppression in its barbarity' and can only arouse 'hostility and rebellion'. This work, together with certain passages in the Junius Pamphlet, shows that Luxemburg's thought was too realistic, in the revolutionary sense of the word, simply to present a linear coherence, of a metaphysical and rigid kind.

Trotsky

Trotsky's writings on the national question prior to 1917 can be defined as 'eclectic' (the word Lenin used to criticize them), occupying a half-way position between Luxemburg and Lenin. It was in particular after 1914 that Trotsky became interested in the national question. He took it up in his pamphlet *The War and the International* (1914) – a polemical work directed against social-patriotism – from two different – if not contradictory – standpoints.

1. *A historical/economic approach.* The world war was a product of the contradiction between the productive forces, which tend towards a world economy, and the restrictive framework of the nation state. Trotsky therefore heralded 'the destruction of the

nation state *as an independent economic entity*' – which, from the strictly economic point of view, was a totally justifiable proposition. However, he concluded from this premise the 'collapse' (*Zusammenbruch*) and the 'destruction' (*Zertrummerung*) of the nation state *altogether*; the nation state as such, the very concept of the nation, would only be able to exist in the future as a 'cultural, ideological and psychological phenomenon'. Of course, the conclusion does not at all follow from the premises. The ending of the economic independence of a nation state is in no way synonymous with the disappearance of the nation state as a political entity. Like Luxemburg, Trotsky tended to reduce the nation either to economics or to culture, and thus lost sight of the specifically political aspect of the problem: the nation state as a political phenomenon, distinct from the economic or ideological spheres (though, of course, having mediated relations with both).

2. *A concrete political approach.* Unlike Luxemburg, Trotsky explicitly proclaimed the right of nations to self-determination as one of the conditions for 'peace between nations', which he contrasted with 'the peace of the diplomats'. Moreover, he supported the perspective of an independent and united Poland (i.e., free from Tsarist, Austrian and German domination) as well as the independence of Hungary, Rumania, Bulgaria, Serbia, Bohemia, etc. It was in the liberation of these nations and their association in a Balkan federation that he saw the best barrier to Tsarism in Europe. Furthermore, with remarkable perception Trotsky demonstrated the dialectical relationship between proletarian internationalism and national rights: the destruction of the International by the social-patriots was a crime not just against socialism, but against the 'national interest, in its widest and correct sense', since it dissolved the only force capable of reconstructing Europe on the basis of democratic principles and the right of nations to self-determination.[19]

In a series of articles in 1915 ('Nation and Economy'[20]), Trotsky tried to define the national question in a more precise way, but not without a certain ambiguity. The contradictory lines of his argument were indicative of a thought which had not yet crystallized. He began with a polemic against the social-imperialists, who justified their political position by the need to expand markets and productive forces. This polemic, from the methodological point of view, seemed to reject economism: yes, Marxists are in favour of the greatest possible expansion in the economic sphere, but not at the expense of dividing, disorganizing and weakening the workers' movement. Trotsky's argument was somewhat confused, in that he wrote of the workers' movement as 'the most important productive force in modern society'; nevertheless, what he did was to affirm the overriding importance of a *political* criterion. However, throughout both articles he returned to the 'centralizing needs of economic development', which call for the destruction of the nation state as a hindrance to the expansion of productive forces. How could these 'needs' be reconciled with the right of nations to self-determination, which Trotsky also recognized? He escaped this dilemma by means of a theoretical somersault which led him back into economism: 'the state is essentially an economic organization, it will be forced to adapt to the needs of economic development'. Therefore, the nation state would be dissolved into the 'Republican United States of Europe', while the nation, divorced from the economy and freed from the old framework of the state, would have the right to self-determination . . . in the sphere of 'cultural development'.

In 1917 Trotsky abandoned these 'eclectic' positions and adopted the Leninist conception of the national question, which he brilliantly defended at Brest-Litovsk in his capacity as People's Commissar for Foreign Affairs.[21]

Pannekoek and Strasser

Pannekoek's *Class Struggle and Nation* and Strasser's *Worker and Nation* were both published in 1912 at Reichenberg (Bohemia), as an internationalist response to the theses of Otto Bauer.[22] The common central idea of both writers was the superiority of class interest over national interest; the practical conclusion was the unity of the Austrian social-democratic party and the refusal to divide it into separate or autonomous national sections. Both compared the nation with religion, as an ideology destined to disappear with the advent of socialism, and rejected as a-historical, idealist and national-opportunist Bauer's doctrine on the national question.

For Pannekoek, the 'national phenomenon is a bourgeois ideological phenomenon'. Bauer's belief that this ideology can be an independent force was characteristic of a Kantian and not a materialist method. However, the interesting thing is that both Pannekoek and Strasser accepted in its essentials the national programme of Bauer and Austrian social-democracy: national autonomy, within the framework of the multi-national Austro-Hungarian state. Pannekoek further stressed that this was an autonomy founded on the personal principle and not the territorial principle, which was consistent with his conception of the national phenomenon as purely ideological and cultural. It is true that Pannekoek and Strasser, in contrast to Bauer, did not consider the programme could be realized within the framework of capitalism, but attributed to it a purely propagandist and educative value.

Economism was indirectly present in the common basic premise of the two writers: the priority of class interest over national interest was due to the economic origins of the former. In a very amusing passage of his pamphlet, Strasser explained that the good German-Austrian patriot would still do his shopping in Czech-owned shops if they were cheaper than their German equivalents. But is this really sufficient to allow one to say, as Strasser did, that when national and economic interests come into conflict, economic interests will triumph? Pannekoek's and Strasser's polemic against Bauer was inserted in a revolutionary perspective, but it was incomplete, to the extent that it confined itself to contrasting internationalism with Austro-Marxist national-reformism, without laying down an alternative concrete political approach in the actual sphere of the national problem and particularly the struggle of oppressed nations.

The Austro-Marxist Centre and Cultural Autonomy

The main idea of the Austro-Marxists was cultural autonomy within the framework of a multi-national state, by means of the arrangement of nationalities into public juridical corporations, with a whole series of cultural, administrative and legal powers. With regard to the national question, as all political questions, their doctrine was marked by 'centrism', half-way between reform and revolution, nationalism and internationalism. They wished both to recognize the rights of national minorities and at the same time to maintain the unity of the Austro-Hungarian state. Although, like the radical left, they tended to reject separatism as a solution to the national question, the Austro-Marxists did so not just for different reasons, but from an almost diametrically opposite standpoint.

Karl Renner

Prior to 1917, the future Chancellor of Austria (1918–20) published several studies on the national question, of which the first and best known is *The State and the Nation* (1899). His method was basically legal/constitutionalist and his conception of the state had more in common with Lassalle than with Marx (as was correctly pointed out by Mehring, Kautsky and the bourgeois lawyer, Hans Kelsen). The influence of Lassalle's statism was implicit even in his early writings, but became much more obvious after 1914, for example in his work *Marxism, the War and the International* (1917), which contained the following ideas (their relationship to Marxism is somewhat problematical): 1. 'The economy serves the capitalist class more and more exclusively; on the other hand the state increasingly serves the proletariat.' 2. 'The germ of socialism is to be found today in all the institutions of the capitalist state.'[23]

It is in the light of this 'social-statism' that Renner's positions on the national question must be understood; his essential aim was to stop the 'disintegration of the Empire' and the 'dissolution of Austria', i.e. to save the 'historic Austrian state'. The Austro-Hungarian Imperial state therefore appeared as the basic framework of Renner's political thought, a framework which had to be preserved, through a certain number of democratic reforms and concessions (cultural, legal, etc.) to national minorities. Paradoxically, it was because of this statism that Renner tried to de-politicize the national question, to reduce it to an administrative and constitutional question,[24] to transform it into a legal problem. He sought to neutralize the danger of political separatism and the break-up of the multi-national state by means of a subtle and complex juridical-institutional apparatus: national corporations based on the principle of personality, a 'national register' listing all people having chosen a nationality, separate electoral rolls for each national minority, territorial and/or national bodies with administrative autonomy, etc. In reality, Renner's positions, which lacked any class perspective or revolutionary direction, despite their author's claims, lay largely outside the political and theoretical sphere of Marxism.

Otto Bauer

Bauer's great work *The National Question and Social Democracy* (1907) had considerably more theoretical weight and influence than Renner's writings. However, Bauer shared with Renner the fundamental premise of Austro-Marxism: the preservation of the multi-national state. Bauer saw the solution to the national question in reformist terms ('national evolution' was the phrase he used to describe his strategy), as the progressive manipulation of the institutions of the Austro-Hungarian state: 'It is hardly likely that national autonomy could be the result of a momentous decision, or a bold action. In a long process of evolution, in difficult struggles . . . Austria will journey step by step towards national autonomy. The new Constitution will not be created by a great legislative act, but by a series of provincial and local laws.'[25]

What was peculiar to Bauer's analysis was the psycho-cultural nature of his theory of the national question, which was constructed on the basis of the vague and mysterious concept of 'national characteristics', defined in psychological terms: 'diversity of purpose, the fact that the same stimulus can provoke different movements and that the same external situation can lead to different decisions'. In fact, this concept was purely metaphysical, of neo-Kantian origin. It was hardly surprising that it was severely criticized by Bauer's Marxist opponents (Kautsky, Pannekoek, Strasser, etc.).

The second key concept in Bauer's theoretical edifice was, of course, national culture, the basis for his entire strategy of national autonomy. Placing the analysis on the level of culture naturally leads one to ignore the political problem: self-determination through the creation of nation states. In this sense, Bauer's 'culturalism' played the same methodological role as Renner's 'juridicism'; it de-politicized the national question.

What is more, Bauer almost completely excluded classes and the class struggle from the sphere of national culture. His programme aimed to give the working class access to 'cultural advantages' and to 'the national cultural community' from which they were excluded by capitalism. He therefore seemed to consider 'cultural values' to be absolutely *neutral* and devoid of class content. He thus made the reverse mistake to the devotees of 'Proletkult', who ignored the relative autonomy of the cultural world and wished to reduce it directly to its social base ('proletarian culture' versus 'bourgeois culture'). It was thus easy for Pannekoek to stress in his polemic against Bauer that the proletariat reads very different things into Goethe and Schiller (or Freiligrath and Heine) than the bourgeoisie. The complex relationship of the proletariat to the bourgeois cultural heritage, a dialectical relationship of *Aufhebung* (conservation/negation/transcendence), was reduced by Bauer to a simple act of appropriation, or rather passive acceptance. Obviously Bauer was correct to stress the decisive importance of culture in defining the national question, but his theory resulted in a real fetishization of national culture, the most striking expression of which was the idea that socialism leads to a *growth in cultural differentiation* between nations.[26]

Because of his tendency to 'nationalize' socialism and the workers' movement, his rejection of what he called the 'naïve cosmopolitanism' of the proletariat in its infancy, and his inability to conceive of an international socialist culture, Bauer's theory was to some degree contaminated by the nationalist ideology it was seeking to defeat. It is thus not surprising that it became the doctrine of 'nationalist/cultural' currents in the workers' movement, not just in Austria-Hungary but also in the Russian empire (Bund, Caucasian social-democrats, etc.) and elsewhere. However, despite these limitations, Bauer's work had an undeniable theoretical value, particularly with regard to the *historicist* nature of its method. In defining the nation as the product of a common historical destiny (the material basis of which is man's struggle against nature), as the 'never-finished outcome of a constant process', as a crystallization of past events, a 'frozen piece of history', Bauer stood firmly on the ground of historical materialism and in outright opposition to bourgeois national conservatism, the reactionary myths of the 'eternal nation' and racist ideology. This historical approach gave Bauer's book a real methodological superiority, not just over Renner, but over most Marxist writers of the period, whose writings on the national question often had an abstract and rigid character. In so far as Bauer's method entailed not only a historical explanation for existing national structures, but a conception of the nation as a process, a movement in perpetual transformation, he was able to avoid Engels's mistake in 1848–9: the fact that a nation (like the Czechs) 'has had no history' does not necessarily mean that it will have no future. The development of capitalism in central Europe and the Balkans leads not to the assimilation but to the *awakening* of 'non-historic' nations.[27]

Lenin and the Right of Self-determination

The national question is one of the fields in which Lenin greatly developed Marxist theory, by spelling out (on the basis of Marx's writings, but going far beyond them) a coherent, revolutionary strategy for the workers' movement, based on the fundamental slogan of national self-determination. In its coherence and realism, the Leninist doctrine was far in advance of the positions of other Marxists of the period, even those closest to Lenin on this question: Kautsky and Stalin.

Kautsky's position prior to 1914 was similar to Lenin's, but was distinguished by its unilateral and almost exclusive concentration on language as the basis of the nation, and by a lack of clarity and boldness in the formulation of the right of nations to secession. After 1914, the ambiguous and contradictory positions of Kautsky on the rights of nations in the context of the war were violently denounced by Lenin as 'hypocritical' and 'opportunist'.

Stalin

As for the famous article by Stalin 'Marxism and the National Question',[28] it is true that it was Lenin who sent Stalin to Vienna to write this, and that in a letter to Gorky in February 1913 he spoke of the 'marvellous Georgian who has sat down to write a big article'.[29] But once the article was finished, it does not appear (contrary to a popular myth) that Lenin was particularly enthusiastic about it, as he does not mention it in any of his numerous writings on the national question, apart from a brief, parenthetical reference in passing in an article dated 28 December 1913. It is obvious that the main ideas in Stalin's work were those of the Bolshevik party and Lenin. Having said this, Trotsky's suggestion that the article was inspired, supervised and corrected 'line by line' by Lenin seems rather questionable.[30] On the contrary, on a certain number of fairly important points Stalin's work implicitly and explicitly differs from, and even contradicts, Lenin's writings.

1. The concept of 'national character', of 'common psychological make-up, or 'psychological particularity' of nations *is not at all*

Leninist. This problematic is a legacy from Bauer, whom Lenin explicitly criticized for his 'psychological theory'.[31] In fact, the idea of a national psychology has more in common with certain superficial and pre-scientific folklore than with a Marxist analysis of the national question.

2. By baldly stating that 'it is only when all these characteristics [common language, territory, economic life and "psychic formation"] are present together that we have a nation', Stalin gave his theory a dogmatic, restrictive and rigid character which one never finds in Lenin. The Stalinist conception of a nation was a real ideological Procrustean bed. According to Stalin, Georgia before the second half of the nineteenth century was not a nation, because it had no 'common economic life', being divided into economically independent principalities. There is no need to add that on this criterion Germany, prior to the Customs Union, would not have been a nation either . . . Nowhere in Lenin's writings do we find such an ultimatist, rigid and arbitrary 'definition' of a nation.

3. Stalin explicitly refused to allow the possibility of the unity or association of national groups scattered within a multi-national state: 'The question arises: is it possible to unite into a single national union groups that have grown so distinct? . . . Is it conceivable, that, for instance, the Germans of the Baltic Provinces and the Germans of Trans-caucasia can be "united into a single nation"?' The answer given, of course, was that all this was 'not conceivable', 'not possible' and 'utopian'.[32] Lenin, by contrast, vigorously defended the '*freedom* of association, including the association of any communities no matter what their nationality, in any given State', citing as an example precisely the Germans of the Caucasus, the Baltic and the Petrograd area. He added that freedom of association of every kind between members of the nation, scattered in different parts of the country or even the globe, was 'indisputable, and can be argued against only from the hidebound, bureaucratic point of view'.[33]

4. Stalin made no distinction between Great-Russian Tsarist oppressive nationalism and the nationalism of oppressed nations. In a very revealing paragraph in his article, he rejected in one breath the 'warlike and repressive' nationalism of the Tsars 'from above' and the 'wave of nationalism from below which sometimes turns into crass chauvinism' of the Poles, Jews, Tatars, Georgians, Ukrainians, etc. Not only did he fail to make any distinction between nationalism 'from above' and 'from

below', but he aimed his most severe criticisms at social-democrats in oppressed countries who had not 'stood firm' in the face of the nationalist movement. Lenin, on the other hand, not only considered the difference between the nationalism of the oppressor and the oppressed nation to be absolutely decisive, but always attacked most bitterly those who capitulated, consciously or unconsciously, to Great-Russian national chauvinism. It is no accident that one of the main targets of his polemic were the Marxist social-democrats of an oppressed nation, Poland, who by their 'firm' stand against Polish nationalism ended up by denying Poland's right to secede from the Russian empire. This difference between Lenin and Stalin was highly significant, and already contained the germ of the later violent conflict between them on the national question in Georgia (December 1922) – Lenin's famous 'last fight'.

Lenin

Lenin's starting-point in working out a strategy on the national question was the same as for Luxemburg, Trotsky and Pannekoek: proletarian internationalism. However, Lenin understood better than his comrades of the revolutionary Left the dialectical relationship between internationalism and the right of national self-determination. He understood, firstly, that only the *freedom* to secede makes possible *free* and voluntary union, association, co-operation and, in the long term, fusion between nations. Secondly, that only the recognition by the workers' movement in the oppressor nation of the right of the oppressed nation to self-determination can help to eliminate the hostility and suspicion of the oppressed, and unite the proletariat of both nations in the international struggle against the bourgeoisie.

Similarly, Lenin grasped the dialectical relationship between national-democratic struggles and the socialist revolution and showed that the popular masses (not just the proletariat, but also the peasantry and petty bourgeoisie) of the oppressed nation were the allies of the conscious proletariat: a proletariat whose task it would be to *lead* the struggle of this 'disparate, discordant and heterogenous mass', containing elements of the petty bourgeoisie and backward workers with their 'preconceptions, reactionary fantasies, weaknesses and errors', against capitalism and the bourgeois state.[34] It is true, however, that in relation to Russia it was only really after April 1917, when Lenin adopted the strategy of permanent revolution, that he began to see the national liberation struggle of oppressed nations within the Russian empire not only as a *democratic* movement, but as an ally of the proletariat in the Soviet *socialist* revolution.

From the methodological point of view, Lenin's principal superiority over most of his contemporaries was his capacity to 'put politics in command', i.e. his obstinate, inflexible, constant and unflinching tendency to grasp and highlight the *political* aspect of every problem and every contradiction. This tendency stood out in his polemic against the Economists on the question of the party in 1902–3; in his discussion with the Mensheviks on the question of the democratic revolution in 1905; in the originality of his writings on Imperialism in 1916; in the inspired turn which the April Theses represented in 1917; in the whole of his most important work *State and Revolution* and, of course, in his writings on the national question. It is this methodological aspect which explains (amongst other things) the striking *actuality* of Lenin's ideas in the twentieth century, an age of imperialism, which has seen the political level become increasingly *dominant* (even though, in the last analysis, it is of course *determined* by the economic).

On the national question, while most other Marxist writers saw only the economic, cultural or 'psychological' dimension of the problem, Lenin stated clearly that the question of self-determination 'belongs wholly and exclusively to the sphere of political democracy',[35] i.e. to the realm of the right of *political* secession and the establishment of an independent nation state. What is more, Lenin was perfectly conscious of the methodological foundation of the differences: 'An "autonomous" nation does not enjoy rights equal to those of a "sovereign" nation; our Polish comrades could not have failed to notice this had they not (like our old Economists) obstinately avoided making an analysis of *political* concepts and categories.'[36] Thanks to Lenin's understanding of the relative autonomy of the political process, he was able to avoid both subjectivism and economism in his analysis of the national question.[37]

Needless to say, the political aspect of the national question for Lenin was not at all that with which chancelleries, diplomats and armies concern themselves. He was totally indifferent to whether this or that nation had an independent state or what the frontiers were between two states. His aim was *democracy* and the *internationalist unity* of the proletariat, which both require the recognition of the right of nations to self-determination. What is more, precisely because it concentrates on the political aspect, his theory of self-determination makes absolutely no concession to nationalism. It is situated solely in the sphere of the democratic struggle and the proletarian revolution.

It is true that these two aims did not have equal importance in Lenin's eyes; democratic demands must always be subordinated to the overriding interests of the revolutionary-class struggle of the world proletariat. For example, according to Lenin, if the republican movement turns out, in a particular case, to be an instrument of reaction (Cambodia 1971!), Marxists will not support it. This does not mean that the working-class movement must strike out republicanism from its programme. The same goes, *mutatis mutandis*, for self-determination. Even though there are some exceptions, the general rule is the right of secession for each nation. In fact, Lenin's analysis that the recognition of the right to self-determination is of primary importance in creating the conditions for internationalist unity among workers tends implicitly to exclude even the possibility of 'exceptions', i.e. of a contradiction between the interests of the proletariat and the democratic rights of nations.

Conclusion: The Lesson of History

Some of the specific debates among Marxists on aspects of the national question have been settled by history. The multi-national state of Austria-Hungary broke up into several nation states after the First World War. The Basques, 'an essentially reactionary nation' according to Engels, are today at the peak of revolutionary struggle in Spain. The reunification of Poland, which Luxemburg referred to as petty-bourgeois utopianism, became a reality in 1918. The 'non-historic' Czech nation, which was destined to disappear because of its lack of 'national vitality' (Engels), did set up a state, through voluntary federation with the Slovak nation.

The experience of post-1917 history also shows us that the nation is not simply a collection of abstract, external criteria. The subjective element, i.e. the consciousness of a national identity, a national political movement, are no less important. Obviously these 'subjective factors' do not come out of the blue; they are the result of certain historical conditions – persecution, oppression, etc. But this means that self-determination must have a wider application; it must relate not just to secession, but to the 'national entity' itself. It is not a doctrinaire 'expert' armed with a list of 'objective criteria' (of the Stalin type) who will determine whether a community constitutes a nation or not, but *the community itself*.[38]

On the other hand, ever since Woodrow Wilson, the nationalism of the great powers has re-stocked its ideological arsenal by appropriating the slogans of democracy, equality of nations and the right of self-determination. These principles are now proclaimed by bourgeois statesmen everywhere. Lyndon Johnson, when President of the United States, declared solemnly in 1966: 'We are fighting to uphold the principle of self-determination, so that the people of South Vietnam may be free to choose their own future.'[39] Truly, the policy of the great powers in relation to small nations has changed out of all recognition since the nineteenth century, when Treitschke wrote, on the occasion of an uprising in Africa: 'It is pure mockery to apply normal principles of war in wars with savages. A negro tribe must be chastized by setting its villages on fire, because this is the only kind of remedy that is effective.'[40]

The real threat today to the political health of the workers' movement is not the infantile disorder which Luxemburg's generous errors represented, but pathological phenomena of a far more dangerous kind: the viruses of great-power chauvinism and opportunist capitulation to bourgeois nationalism which are spread abroad by the Russian and Chinese bureaucracies and their disciples internationally. Indeed, 'ultra-leftism' on the national question hardly survives today. Only in certain sectors of the revolutionary Left does one still sometimes find a distant echo of Luxemburg's theses, in the form of an abstract opposition to national liberation movements, in the name of 'working-class unity' and internationalism. The same is true with respect to Engels's notion of 'reactionary nations'. Thus, if one looks at certain of the national questions of today, complex questions where national, colonial, religious and ethnic aspects combine and interlace – for example, the Arab-Israeli conflict or the struggle between catholics and protestants in Northern Ireland – one can see that there are two contrary temptations which haunt the revolutionary Left. The first temptation is to deny the legitimacy of the national movement of Palestinians or catholics in Ulster: to condemn these movements as 'petty-bourgeois' and divisive of the working class, and to proclaim abstractly against them the principle of the necessary unity between proletarians of all nationalities, races or religions. The second temptation is to espouse uncritically the nationalist ideology of these movements and condemn the dominant nations (Israeli Jews or Northern Irish protestants) en bloc, without distinction of class, as 'reactionary nations' – nations to which the right of self-determination is denied.

The task facing revolutionary Marxists is to avoid these twin reefs and discover – through a concrete analysis of each concrete situation – an authentically internationalist course, which draws its inspiration from the nationalities policy of the Comintern when it was led by Lenin and Trotsky (1919–23) and from the famous resolution of the Second International's 1896 Congress whose rare privilege it was to be approved by both Lenin and Luxemburg: 'The Congress proclaims the full right to self-determination of all nations; and it expresses its sympathy to the workers of all countries at present suffering beneath the yoke of military, national or any other kind of absolutism; the Congress calls on the workers of these countries to join the ranks of the conscious workers of the whole world, in order to struggle beside them to defeat international capitalism and attain the goals of international social-democracy.'

Notes

1. Karl Marx, *The German Ideology*, Moscow 1964, p. 76. cf. Friedrich Engels, 'Das Fest der Nationen in London' (1846), in Marx, Engels, Lassalle, *Aus dem literarische Nachlass*, Stuttgart 1902, vol. 2, p. 408: 'The dreams of a European Republic, of a lasting peace under political organization, have become as grotesque as phrases about the unity of nations under the aegis of universal freedom of commerce . . . In each country the bourgeoisie has its own particular interests and cannot transcend nationality . . . But in every country the proletariat has a sole and common interest, a sole and common enemy, a sole and common struggle. Only the proletariat can abolish nationality, only the vigilant proletariat can make the brotherhood of nations possible . . .'
2. See on this question the remarkable essay of the Polish Marxist, Roman Rosdolsky, 'Friedrich Engels und das Problem der "geschichtlosen Völker" ', *Archiv für Sozialgeschichte* IV, 1964.
3. Engels, 'The Magyar Struggle', in Marx, *The Revolutions of 1848*, London 1973, pp. 221–2.
4. Engels, 'Deutschland und der Panslawismus', (*Neue Oder Zeitung* 1855), Marx/Engels XI, cited in Rosdolsky, op. cit., p. 174.
5. Engels, 'What is to Become of Turkey in Europe?' (*New York Daily Tribune* 1853), Werke IX, cited in Rosdolsky, op. cit., p. 174.
6. Engels, 'What Have the Working Classes to Do with Poland?', in

Marx, *The First International and After*, London 1974, pp. 378–88.

7. Engels, 'Anfang des Endes in Österreich' (1847), Werke IV, p. 510.

8. Engels, 'The Magyar Struggle', op. cit., p. 219.

9. Rosa Luxemburg, 'Sozial-patriotische Programakrobatik', *Internationalismus und Klassenkampf*.

10. See Paul Frölich, *Rosa Luxemburg*, Paris 1965.

11. V. I. Lenin, *Collected Works*, vol. 3.

12. Luxemburg, 'Nationalität und Autonomie' (1908), in *Internationalismus und Klassenkampf*, Neuwied 1971, pp. 236, 239.

13. Luxemburg, 'The Junius Pamphlet', in Mary-Alice Waters (ed.), *Rosa Luxemburg Speaks*, New York 1970, p. 304.

14. Luxemburg, 'Theses on the Tasks of International Social Democracy', ibid., p. 329.

15. Luxemburg, 'Sozial-patriotische Programakrobatik', in *Internationalismus und Klassenkampf*, op. cit.

16. cf. Georg Lukács, 'Critical Observations on Rosa Luxemburg's "Critique of the Russian Revolution" ', in *History and Class Consciousness*, London 1971, pp. 272–95.

17. cf. Lenin, 'On the Right of Nations to Self-determination', *Collected Works*, vol. 20, p. 430: 'It is quite understandable that in their zeal (sometimes a little excessive, perhaps) to combat the nationalistically blinded petty bourgeoisie of Poland the Polish Social Democrats should overdo things.'

18. Luxemburg, 'Vorwort zu dem Sammelband "Die polnische Frage und die sozialistische Bewegung" ', in *Internationalismus und Klassenkampf*, op. cit.

19. Leon Trotsky, *The Bolsheviki and World Peace*, New York 1918, pp. 21, 230–1, etc.

20. *Nashe Slovo* 130, 135 (3 and 9 July 1915), reprinted in vol. 9 (1927) of Trotsky's *Collected Works* in Russian.

21. cf. Trotsky, *History of the Russian Revolution*, London 1967, vol. 3, p. 62: 'Whatever may be the further destiny of the Soviet Union . . . the national policy of Lenin will find its place among the eternal treasures of mankind.'

22. Anton Pannekoek, *Klassenkampf und Nation*, Reichenberg 1912; Josef Strasser, *Der Arbeiter und die Nation*, Reichenberg 1912.

23. Karl Renner, *Marxismus, Krieg und Internationale*, Stuttgart 1917, p. 26.

24. cf. Arduino Agnelli, *Questione nazionale e socialismo: K. Renner e O. Bauer*, Bologna 1969, p. 109.

25. Otto Bauer, *Die Nationalitätenfrage und die Sozialdemokratie*, Vienna 1924, p. 404.

26. ibid., pp. 105–8.

27. ibid., pp. 239–72. It should be added that Bauer's programme of cultural autonomy had some value as a *complement* – not an alternative – to a policy based on recognition of the right to self-determination. Indeed, the first constitution of the Soviet Union in a sense incorporated the principle of cultural autonomy of national minorities.

28. Joseph Stalin, 'Marxism and the National Question', in *Works*, Moscow 1953, vol. 2, pp. 300–81.

29. Lenin, *Collected Works*, vol. 35, p. 84.

30. cf. Trotsky, *Stalin*, London 1969, vol. I, p. 233.

31. Lenin, 'The Right of Nations to Self-determination', in *Collected*

Works, vol. 20, p. 398.

32. Stalin, op. cit., pp. 306–7, 309, 305 and 339.

33. Lenin, 'The National Programme of the RSDLP', *Collected Works*, vol. 19, p. 543 and 'Critical Remarks on the National Question', in *Collected Works*, vol. 20, pp. 39, 50.

34. On this question, Lenin's analysis of the 1916 Rising in Ireland is a model of revolutionary realism: see 'The Discussion of Self-determination Summed Up', *Collected Works*, vol. 22, pp. 353–8.

35. Lenin, 'The Socialist Revolution and the Right of Nations to Self-determination', *Collected Works*, vol. 22, p. 145.

36. Lenin, 'The Discussion on Self-determination Summed Up', op. cit., p. 344.

37. As A. S. Naïr and C. Scalabrino stressed in their excellent article, 'La question nationale dans la théorie marxiste révolutionnaire', *Partisans* 59–60, May–August 1971.

38. cf. Trotsky on the Blacks in the United States: 'An abstract criterion is not decisive in this case: much more decisive are historical consciousness, feelings and emotions.' *Trotsky on Black Nationalism and Self-determination*, New York 1967, p. 16.

39. Quoted in A. Schlesinger jnr, *The Bitter Heritage*, Boston 1967, p. 108.

40. Heinrich von Treitschke, *Politics*, London 1916, vol. 2, p. 614.

PART TWO
The Course of Revolution

The failure of the revolutionary movement in the advanced countries after the First World War was to isolate the first socialist revolution in the backward and war-devastated territory of the Soviet Union. The Civil War utterly disrupted Russian industry, with a whole series of baneful consequences: it destroyed or displaced the major sections of the working class and undermined the basis of economic exchange with the peasantry in the countryside. The young Soviet state saved itself from extinction at the hands of the White Guards and the intervention of the various imperialist powers, but at the terrible price of stifling the vital proletarian democracy which had been the mainspring of the revolution. The soviets became mere rubber stamp bodies subordinate to the party leadership. The forms of workers' control in the factories were swept aside. Moreover the Bolshevik Party itself, which retained a vigorous internal life during the Civil War, eventually succumbed to the bureaucratic gangrene which afflicted all Soviet institutions. In March 1921 the formation of factions within the Bolshevik Party was banned, and shortly before this all opposition parties outlawed. The conditions which prevailed in the aftermath of the Civil War set the scene for the triumph of Stalin in the internal struggle within the Bolshevik Party.

This section opens with a study by Lucio Colletti of the original Marxist strategy in Russia and of the cruel travesty of it which Stalin's rule was to produce. Despite all Stalin's crimes and blunders, the Soviet Union did become a major economic power and played the main role in defeating Nazi Germany in the Second World War. But Stalin's policies ensured that these successes – made possible by the political and social transformation inaugurated in 1917 – were only achieved at maximum cost to the Soviet people. Colletti argues that there were no redeeming features to Stalin's terroristic dictatorship, even if he was not able to entirely cancel out the legacy of October.

Only Communist Parties which in practice broke with Stalin's international policy proved capable of making a socialist revolution in the aftermath of the Second World War. In Yugoslavia, China and Vietnam – all predominantly peasant societies – occupation by a foreign power undermined the local ruling class and state machine. In these conditions a Communist Party, having initially developed among workers and students, was able to strike deep roots among the rural masses and mobilize them against the existing order. This permitted a path to socialist revolution which substituted a Red Army, based on the peasants, for the workers' soviets that had made the revolution possible in Russia. Whereas soviets had for a time involved a fully developed revolutionary democracy, the peasant armies remained subordinate to the Communist Party leadership. Since the Communists had made themselves the bearers of national liberation and social revolution they could successfully enlist peasant support. Because their ultimate control of the peasant masses was bureaucratic they could press through a socialist revolution which went beyond the aims of the peasant small-holders. The resulting revolutions have dealt hard blows at imperialism and represent a gigantic social advance for the countries concerned. But they have not been based on the proletarian democracy that will be required to defeat bourgeois power in countries where it is more strongly entrenched. In a historical survey Isaac Deutscher traces the strategy adopted by the leaders of Chinese Communism, exploring their relation both to Leninism and to Stalinism.

Jiří Pelikan was a leader of the reform movement in Czechoslovakia in 1967–8. In the interview printed here he gives a personal account of the long travail of Czechoslovak socialism from 1938 to 1968: it has been somewhat shortened for inclusion in the Reader. He describes the post-war Stalinization and the obstacles it encountered in a relatively developed country with a strong working-class movement. The reform movement of the sixties was an expression of the deep crisis of the Stalinist system and of the need to find some way out of the bureaucratic stagnation to which it led. Pelikan pin-points what he sees as the crucial errors made by the reform movement, both before and after the Russian invasion of 1968. The Czechoslovak experience suggests that left to themselves the reforming Communist leaders can never successfully challenge the Stalinist system and that the assertion of an uninhibited workers' power from below will be essential for any definitive settling of accounts with the bureaucratic regime.

In the concluding essay Ernest Mandel surveys more than half a century of revolutionary struggles from the perspective of their impact on the relationship of forces in world politics. In this study he examines the contradictory dynamic of the Soviet Union's role in international affairs. The Soviet leaders are preoccupied by advancing the interests of their bureaucratic regime and defending their military domination of much of eastern Europe. On occasion this has led them to play an openly counter-revolutionary role, and at best it means that they give fitful and inconsistent support to revolutionary movements. The weak social base of the Soviet and eastern European regimes makes them normally anxious to placate the major imperialist states. However the alternating cycle of adventurism and appeasement in Soviet foreign policy is, as Ernest Mandel shows, highly dangerous both for the Soviet Union itself and for the interests of the world revolution. Mandel argues that the real danger of a devastating nuclear conflict cannot be averted by appeasing the belligerence of the imperialist states, but only by a consistent revolutionary policy which avoids both adventures and capitulations, and appeals over the heads of the bourgeois statesmen directly to the mass of the population in the imperialist countries.

The Question of Stalin

LUCIO COLLETTI

(Reprinted from *New Left Review*, 61, 1970)

When in November 1917 the Bolshevik party unleashed an insurrection and took power, Lenin and his comrades were convinced that this was the first act in a world revolution. The process was started in Russia, not because Russia was considered internally ripe for a socialist revolution, but because the immense carnage of the First World War, military defeat, hunger and the deep misery of the masses had precipitated a social and political crisis in Russia before any other country. The collapse of Tsarism in February 1917 thus produced an uncertain and vacillating bourgeois-democratic republic, incapable of remedying the disasters of Russian society, or providing the basic necessities of life for the popular masses. The Bolsheviks, in other words, believed that their party could take power and begin the socialist revolution even in Russia, despite its secular backwardness. For the World War had confirmed once again what had already been revealed in 1905. Not merely in spite, but precisely because of its backwardness, and the sum of old and new contradictions that were interlaced within it, Russia represented both the most explosive point in the chain of world imperialism and the 'weakest link'. This link, once broken, would carry with it the entire chain, accelerating the revolutionary process in the more developed industrialized countries of Europe, starting above all with Germany.

The premises of Bolshevism

Their objective was therefore not simply to achieve the revolution in one particular country, even a country of such gigantic proportions as the Tsarist empire, spread over two continents. Their objective was world revolution. The revolution which the Bolsheviks accomplished in Russia was not conceived essentially as a Russian revolution, but as the first step in a European and world revolution; as an exclusively Russian phenomenon, it had no significance for them, no validity and no possibility of survival.

Hence the country in which the revolutionary process began

did not interest the Bolsheviks for its own sake, its special characteristics or its national destiny, but as a platform from which an international upheaval could be launched. In these years Europe was – or seemed to be – the pivot of the world. If the revolution could spread from vast and backward Russia to triumph in Germany, Austro-Hungary, Italy, the axis of the whole globe would be shifted.

What is striking today in retracing this experience, is the intense travail and inflexible determination with which the Bolsheviks, in a relatively short period of time, distilled and selected this strategic vision. The most impressive fact here is the rigid intransigence of their refusal to make any concessions to nationalism. In the concluding years of the nineteenth century, Marxism had penetrated Russia not only as a foreign ideology, historically and culturally developed in western Europe, but as an open denial of any special mission peculiar to Russia, any privileged path for reaching socialism. It is enough to recall the implacable polemics of Lenin and Plekhanov against populism. In opposition to Slavophile tendencies, which were deeply rooted in Russian culture and often took up combative revolutionary positions at the political level, the first Marxist nuclei of what was later to become the Russian Social-Democratic Labour Party did not hesitate to advocate the path of *Westernization*. The economic and social development of the country was not to be entrusted to the primordial virtues of Mother Russia. Development meant industrialization, the advance of capitalism. The only cure for the ills arising from the 'Asiatic backwardness' of Tsarist Russia was Western science and technology, capitalist industrial development, which would itself engender a modern factory proletariat.

The importance of this ideological emphasis and the extent to which the entire first generation of Russian Marxists were committed to it, are documented in Lenin's monumental research dedicated to *The Development of Capitalism in Russia*. In the last decade of the century the Russian Marxists thus occupied the difficult position (which was naturally exploited polemically by the Populists) of advocating, though with radically divergent goals and perspectives, the same process of rapid industrialization that was supported by the liberal bourgeoisie.

The basic idea governing this position was that which forms the very core and nucleus of the whole of Marx's thought. The socialist revolution is a revolution made and led by the working class, a class which grows with the development of industrial capitalism itself. The socialist revolution is a complete human emancipation, but this emancipation presupposes certain historical and material conditions: not only the 'socialization of labour' or formation of the 'collective worker', not only a vertiginous increase in the productivity of labour, but also the dissolution of local and corporative limits, which can only be achieved in the framework of modern industrial production and the world market created by capitalism. In the absence of these last two decisive preconditions, Marx's whole theory itself remains in the air. For they provide both a worldwide revolutionary theatre in which the unification of all humanity, international communism, can be realized, and a revolutionary agency linked to *scientific* and *rational* work processes – the modern worker and technician.

In the first years of this century, however, Russian Marxists soon began to graft a series of specifications, and at times even modifications, on to this basic system of premises. They had to correct their sights for the specific social and political terrain in which they had to operate, contemporary Russian society, in order to make a deep impact on it and act effectively as a revolutionary force.

The central contradiction

The first and one of the most important of these specifications was, of course, the 'Jacobin' conception of the party introduced by Lenin. In this conception, the party became a 'party of cadres' or 'professional revolutionaries', in other words a highly centralized vanguard. It is not difficult to discern the pressure, indeed necessity, exercised on Russian Marxism here by the special conditions of *illegality* in which the party was obliged to operate under the Tsarist autocracy.

A second specification, or rather in this case alteration, was critical discussion of the classic Marxist schema, or at least that which had hitherto been attributed to Marx, of two epochs or phases of revolution – bourgeois-democratic and socialist – as distinct stages located in successive historical eras. The problem encountered here derived even more from the specificity of Russian conditions. However the sheer scale of the problem in this case was such that it profoundly affected the whole strategy and future of the workers' party. Given the autocratic character of the Tsarist regime and the complete absence of any form of liberal constitutionalism – not to speak of the still somewhat feeble development of industrial capitalism – the Marxist party had to operate in an environment where it was universally acknowledged that a bourgeois revolution would in any event have to take place before the socialist revolution. The problem then was: what position should a Marxist party take towards this bourgeois revolution, which both promotes the further development of capitalism, and reinforces and organizes the working class?

Until about 1905, the Russian Marxists were broadly content to accept the thesis according to which socialist revolution was not possible in an economically backward country like Russia, where the industrial proletariat was a tiny minority and where no bourgeois revolution had yet taken place. In Russia, they argued, the revolution could only be bourgeois; the task of Russian social-democrats could only be that of supporting the bourgeoisie and not therefore that of carrying out their own revolution.

After 1905, however, only the Mensheviks continued to maintain this thesis. The Menshevik line, which implied either support for the liberal bourgeoisie in accomplishing the bourgeois revolution or abstention by the social-democratic party to 'keep its hands clean', was opposed by two other strategic perspectives within the Russian workers' movement during the 1905 revolution. These two alternative perspectives were themselves counterposed: Lenin's 'revolutionary-democratic dictatorship of the proletariat and the peasantry' and Trotsky's 'permanent revolution'.

Common to both these positions, as against the Mensheviks, was their assignation of a positive and leading role to the social-democrats during the bourgeois-democratic revolution itself. The differences between them, however, were great enough to make them antithetical in other respects. Lenin thought that the party should promote a revolutionary worker-peasant coalition which would accomplish the bourgeois revolution and thereby prepare the ground for the socialist revolution; yet this process would nevertheless remain for a whole historical period a purely *bourgeois* revolution, given the preponderance of the peasantry. Trotsky, on the other hand, maintained that while the Russian proletariat ought to win the peasants and lead them in the bourgeois revolution, it would not be able to halt the process at that point. The completion of the bourgeois revolution would necessarily oblige the proletariat to initiate its own revolution in an uninterrupted process.

It is important to grasp one point: both these lines, born precisely as responses to the specific problem of revolution *in Russia*, nonetheless presuppose more or less explicitly an integration, support and completion at the international level. Removed from this global context and enclosed within the limits of Russian society at that period, they would clearly have been arbitrary and impracticable. Lenin's line would have meant summoning the proletariat to take a leading role, through the bourgeois-democratic revolution, in the establishment of a regime in which it could itself only suffer the generalized reign of wage labour and capitalist exploitation. Trotsky's line, on the other hand, would have meant advocating the uninterrupted transition from a bourgeois to a socialist revolution in a country in which the industrial proletariat represented a mere island surrounded by a limitless sea of peasants.

Nevertheless, despite their differences and limits, particularly in their 1905 versions, the force and originality of these two theses lies in the fact that they both resolutely posed the real, central *contradiction* in which the Russian party found itself: it was a party of socialist revolution in a country profoundly immature for such a revolution, yet a party born for this destination on such apparently mistaken terrain not by chance but for deep historical reasons.

In grappling with this central contradiction, these two positions already implicitly contained new elements of analysis which only came to light and were adequately explained several years later, in the Leninist theory of *imperialism*. The first of these was the conviction that a revolutionary bourgeoisie could no longer exist in the twentieth century: hence the inevitability of the proletariat itself leading the bourgeois-democratic revolution, where this had still to take place. This idea reclaimed and developed Marx's earlier analysis of the history of modern Germany, in which he discussed the weakness and inability of the German bourgeoisie to confront the problem of its own revolution and to break its pact with Prussian *Junkertum*. The second novel element, yet more original than the first, lay in the incipient hypothesis that the socialist revolution was not necessarily bound to break out initially in the Western heartland of advanced capitalism, but could be set in motion from the backward East or even from zones peripheral to the metropolitan countries themselves and the nerve centres of the system. This thesis to some extent prefigured Lenin's later analysis of imperialism. It prepared the ground for what he was to call the law of 'uneven development', according to which the most explosive point in the world system is not necessarily the most 'developed', but can on the contrary be the 'weakest' link from the standpoint of capitalist industry; for despite its weakness, this link may be rich in revolutionary potential and volcanic forces, precisely because it cumulates both old and new contradictions.

Lenin's internationalism

It has often been noted that both these theses considerably modified Marx's original conception in certain ways; the Mensheviks were only the first to point this out. However, a more considered and objective appraisal, from the vantage-point of historical distance, would suggest that despite the changes they introduced, the positions of Lenin and Trotsky not only preserved the essentials of Marx's analysis, but would be quite inconceivable apart from it. For while both of them confronted the challenge presented by history, to think through the revolutionary tasks of a Marxist workers' party in a relatively backward country, their common characteristic was a clear awareness that the upheaval which was ripening, wherever it might actually begin, could only be an *international* revolutionary upheaval – the sole adequate response to the world imperialist order. Both, moreover, emphasized that the decisive terrain on which the battle would ultimately be lost or won could only be the central countries of metropolitan capitalism – at that period this meant, above all, Germany – and its principal protagonist could only be the modern factory proletariat, which was the historical subject of the revolution for Marx.

It is crucially important to situate these points correctly and clearly, for they correspond to a historical reality – the conception which underlay the Bolshevik seizure of power in 1917 and the theory and practice of the party leadership at least until 1924. Indeed, only the Bolsheviks' conscious reference to the basic content of Marx's analysis can explain what was undoubtedly the most salient feature that characterized most of them: their intense and consistent consciousness of the 'exceptional' and in a certain sense *contradictory* nature of the tasks posed to the Russian party, as the instrument of socialist revolution in a country that was not yet ripe for it.

In this connection there is a particularly illuminating passage from Engels's *Peasant War in Germany*, which may help us to express what we have in mind: 'The worst thing that can befall a leader of an extreme party is to be compelled to take over a government in an epoch when the movement is not yet ripe for the comination of the class which he represents, and for the realization of the measures which that domination implies. What he *can* do depends not upon his will but upon the level of development of the material means of existence, of the conditions of production and commerce . . . What he *ought* to do, what his party demands of him, again depends not upon him . . . He is bound to the doctrines and demands hitherto propounded . . . Thus, he necessarily finds himself in an unsolvable dilemma. What he *can* do contradicts all the previous actions, principles and immediate interests of his party, and what he *ought* to do cannot be done. In a word, he is compelled to represent not his party or his class, but the class for whose domination the movement is then ripe. In the interests of the movement he is compelled to advance the interests of an alien class, and to feed his own class with phrases and promises, and with the asseveration that the interests of that alien class are their own interests. Whoever is put into this awkward position is irrevocably lost.'[1]

None of the Bolshevik leadership and least of all Lenin would ever have accepted the idea that their prospects were hopeless. But it is nevertheless striking that the Bolsheviks again and again showed such a clear awareness of the *contradiction* imposed on them by history and by the development of imperialism, that – in order to master rather than suffer it – they took the only possible correct course: namely, not to ignore or conceal it, but to assume its consequences openly in their own strategy. This is the clue that explains, for example, the first acts of the Bolshevik party in power, such as the decrees distributing land to the peasants or granting nationalities the right of self-determination, including the right to secede from the ex-Tsarist empire: both measures attacked by critics, notably Rosa Luxemburg, as bourgeois-democratic and counter-productive, serving only to create future obstacles to the building of socialism. The same awareness lies behind the travail of Lenin's thought on the nature of the October revolution and the question of its socialist character, not only immediately after the seizure of power but also later in 1919 or 1921. This travail is supremely reflected in the very title bestowed on the new regime: 'Workers' and peasants' government'. Here the omission of Russia underlines the internationalist nature of the revolution, while a second class, never anticipated in the original theory of the dictatorship of the proletariat, appears alongside the working class – the peasantry. His awareness of this contradiction in fact underlies virtually all of Lenin's political actions and changes of course, from the beginning to the end of his career.

The limits of backwardness

Today there seems to be a need, which I would not wish to dispute, for an impartial re-examination of several key points in the thought and work of Lenin. The objects of greatest contemporary concern lie, firstly, in his conception of the party and, secondly, in the delay with which he came to appreciate the role and meaning of the Soviets, which had already emerged in the 1905 revolution. These interrogations naturally arise in the light of developments in Russia after Lenin's death. Here we discover the prophetic meaning of Rosa Luxemburg's celebrated warning in her pamphlet on the Russian revolution: 'With the repression of political life in the land as a whole, life in the soviets must also become more and more crippled. Without general elections, without unrestricted freedom of press and assembly, without a free struggle of opinion, life dies out in every public institution, becomes a mere semblance of life, in which only the bureaucracy remains as the active element. Public life gradually falls asleep, a few dozen party leaders of inexhaustible energy and boundless experience direct and rule. Among them, in reality only a dozen outstanding heads do the leading and an elite of the working class is invited from time to time to meetings where they are to applaud the speeches of the leaders, and to approve resolutions unanimously – at bottom, then, a clique affair – a dictatorship, to be sure, not the dictatorship of the proletariat, however, but only the dictatorship of a handful of politicians, that is a dictatorship in the bourgeois sense, in the sense of the rule of the Jacobins.'[2]

It is of course true, as Lenin himself fully acknowledged, that the form of political regime realized by the October revolution in Russia was never, even at the beginning, a dictatorship of the proletariat; it was rather a *dictatorship of the party* exercised on behalf of the proletariat. Because of the existing 'low cultural level of the working masses', Lenin wrote as early as 1919, 'the soviets, which according to their programme are organs of direct administration *by the workers*, are instead organs of administration *for the workers*, led by the proletarian vanguard, not by the working masses'. In the same year, he affirmed, no less explicitly, that the dictatorship of the party was to be considered the effective form of the dictatorship of the proletariat, and he specified that 'the dictatorship of the working class is realized by the Bolshevik party, which since at least 1905 has been united with the whole revolutionary proletariat'.

However much we may be aware of these problems, it is essential to emphasize two points: 1. These 'contradictions' in Lenin's and the Bolsheviks' policies were not something marginal or fortuitous which they encountered *after* taking power. On the contrary, they represented one aspect of the basic contradiction I have already outlined: the contradiction of a party as the instrument of socialist revolution in a country as yet unripe for it. Clearly, we cannot lightly attribute this contradiction to Lenin, without simultaneously reproaching him, like the Mensheviks, for making the revolution instead of leaving Kerensky in power in the first place. 2. The brief passages cited above show that this contradiction was (almost) always *avowed* in Lenin's writings and the most lucid party texts, in complete consciousness, openly subjected to analysis and debate. This is not, as one might imagine, merely a question of form, but also a matter of content and substance: the very act of making the problem explicit simultaneously posed the question of the means by which it could be, if not solved, at least contained and mitigated. (One only has to think, for example, of Moshe Lewin's account of *Lenin's Last Struggle*.)

It seems likely that Lenin's fault lay in having too often made a virtue of necessity, adopting the means necessary for action in the *Russian* context, without always making explicit the historical and political limits, in terms of which these means were imposed and derived their validity. This could, for instance, be the case with the strongly centralized character of the party, adapted to conditions of illegality. In my view it does not, however, apply to another aspect of this theory, namely the bringing of 'political consciousness' to the working class 'from outside', which produces such scandal today among intellectual currents of ouvrièrism and spontaneism.

In short, no amount of sophism can escape the essential point: given that Russia was not ripe for socialist revolution, the

Bolshevik party – small, cohesive, yet permeated with a dialectical political life to an extent not even imagined today – represented the indispensable tool for operating under *these* conditions. While it is not easy to be sure from the evidence, it must nonetheless be emphasized that the 'isolation' of the Bolshevik vanguard from the masses was never a 'choice' made by Lenin, nor even an 'effect' of his political line: it was dictated by the objective situation. One could object that in spite of general backwardness, Russia did contain several industrial centres. Deutscher has indeed observed that these industries were in certain sectors among the most modern in the world, that their 'coefficient of concentration was even higher than that of American industry at the time'. This is of course true and helps to explain why the October revolution – unlike the Chinese revolution which was essentially peasant in character – was a workers' revolution, which spread from the city to the countryside and not vice versa. But we must not forget the artificial origins of this industrial concentration, its implantation 'from above', its recent development, and finally, the fact that Russia remained in the last analysis a country with a vast peasant majority.

To fail to see this situation clearly means to preclude from the outset any understanding of Lenin's life and work. The Bolshevik party, at least in the years immediately before 1917, was the expression of highly concentrated nuclei of the working class, endowed with all the qualities of discipline, organization and vanguard consciousness proper to the modern 'collective worker'; it nonetheless remained, in relation to the whole country, without a firm class base. This state of affairs, not unlike that referred to by Engels in the passage quoted, implicitly contained an objective danger, the awareness of which dominated Lenin's thought and practice. For the party, precisely in so far as it was adequate to the task of carrying out the socialist revolution, was condemned to isolation from the broad masses of backward Russian society. Hence the impulse to close itself off, to become concentrated, to make itself not only a vanguard but the depository of a political goal, relatively inaccessible because premature. On the other hand, the party had to escape from this dilemma if it was really to act as a *revolutionary force*, mobilizing the masses, rather than as a simple putschist organization.

This poses a problem that has not been sufficiently studied for some time, but which had a vital, central importance for Lenin:

the problem of *consensus* – that is, the necessity for the party to operate in accordance with the fundamental aspirations of the broad masses. A casual glance at his writings, especially those of 1917, is sufficient to reveal his continual insistence on this theme. 'The party of the proletariat cannot assume the task of introducing socialism in a country of small peasants, until the vast majority of the population has become conscious of the need for socialist revolution.' Or: 'We are not Blanquists, we do not advocate the seizure of power by a minority. We are Marxists.' 'The Commune (the Soviet of Workers' and Peasants' Deputies) does not and must not intend to introduce *any* reform that is not fully warranted both by economic reality and by the consciousness of the vast majority of the people. To the extent that the organizing experience of the Russian people is weak, we must all the more firmly build up our organizations through the work of the *masses themselves.*'

Each of the problems raised here deserves a chapter to itself which the reader must try to formulate. To start with, what I have called the problem of *consensus* is at the same time the question, essential to Leninism, of the attention bestowed on the peasantry and relations with the petty bourgeoisie as a whole. 'Russia', Lenin wrote in 1917, 'is a country of petty-bourgeois. The vast majority of the population belong to this class.' It also raises the problem of nationalities, and that of exploited colonial peoples. Finally, it bears upon the most important problem of all, precisely the one nowadays most obscured: namely, the need for the class struggle to be structured and articulated as a *political struggle*, which, in so far as it surpasses the limits of mere ouvrièrism, cannot avoid coming to terms with the problem of *alliances*. Marx had already said as much in 1844: if the socialist revolution is 'a political revolution with a social essence', this essence or content is itself insufficient because it needs a *political form*, if only because 'revolution in general is a *political act*' and 'without the revolution socialism cannot be realized.'

The meaning of Lenin's oscillations

The attention given to winning the consent of the masses, combined with the objective gulf that isolated the party from the vast backward strata of Russian society, explains the continuous oscillations and adjustments of Lenin's political line. This was always prey to two contradictory exigencies. On the one hand, there was the need to *adhere* to the Russian situation, which meant not only that the party had to defer genuinely socialist objectives, but also that in the meantime it had to represent the only future agent and depository of these objectives. On the other hand, since Russia was also only the point of departure and temporary platform for a European or world revolution, there was a permanent need to *anticipate* a world beyond the existing state of affairs, prefiguring not only the transition to socialism but even communism itself.

This helps us to understand the ideal projection or 'leap' represented by *State and Revolution* – both a 'utopian' work from the standpoint of the time and place in which it was written, and also an indispensable statement of the goals and finality of any authentic socialist revolution. Alternatively, it helps to situate Lenin's perplexity and doubts, almost at the very moment of the revolution, as to its nature and significance. Here we gain a measure of the dramatic seriousness of Lenin's Marxism, which distinguishes him from all the others – from Zinoviev, Kamenev, Stalin, Bukharin and perhaps even from Trotsky: by his very uncertainty, he emerged as the most conscious protagonist of them all. In August 1921, he wrote that the revolution from November 1917 to January 1918 had been bourgeois-democratic, that the socialist stage had only begun with the establishment of proletarian democracy. But then he proposed a different periodization; the socialist stage was only reached with the class struggle of the committees of poor peasants against the kulaks. This oscillation never ceased. Two months later, in October 1921, a further periodization emerges: this time the bourgeois-democratic stage of the revolution was only completed in 1921, at the very moment when he was writing.

Behind these oscillations lay precisely the development that had been least foreseen. The decisive presupposition upon which the Bolsheviks had based their seizure of power, which would itself have more than compensated for the difficulties arising from Russia's backwardness, was slow to materialize. The revolution in western Europe did not occur, or rather had occurred and been temporarily defeated. From the delay attending the second wave, Lenin was forced to confront the truth that he, more than anyone else, had always known: that the economic and social foundations essential for the realization of the goals of Soviet power in Russia were almost totally lacking and therefore the dictatorship of the party was suspended in a void. With the Bolsheviks in power, the old contradiction with which the party had struggled since its birth was presented much more acutely: while Russia now had the most advanced political regime in the world, she had not even a minimally adequate economic structure to correspond to this regime. The terms of the classic formula of historical materialism on the relationship between structure and super-structure were now turned upside-down to its most stern devotees. The Mensheviks, already defeated on the battleground of historical struggle, could now brandish these very formulae against Lenin. The seizure of power in the absence of an adequate economic base; the dictatorship of the proletariat in the near absence of a proletariat, and moreover by a party in which this element was in a minority; the reintroduction of capitalism after the revolution with NEP; the preponderance of a vast bureaucratic state machine; all these added up to a body of evidence that flew in the face of doctrine as well as common sense. Scarcely two years after *State and Revolution*, in which he had theorized the 'destruction of the state machine', Lenin had to admit with his usual frankness that not only was this machine still intact, but it remained largely in the hands of its original personnel. 'We have an indeterminate quantity of our militants at the higher levels – at the least a few thousands, at most ten thousand. However, at the base of the hierarchy hundreds of thousands of ex-function-aries whom we inherited from the Tsar and the bourgeoisie are working, partly consciously and partly unconsciously, against us.'

If we add to this the civil war and armed intervention of foreign powers, the enormous difficulties faced by the Bolshevik leadership begin to emerge concretely. Within months of taking power, the party found itself commanding an armed fortress, starved of food and besieged on all sides and even from within. To resist, it had continually to resort to ever greater centralization. The masses who had supported the Bolsheviks in the first phase now fell back, decimated and scattered. The workers' battalions deserted the semi-ruined factories to march to the front.

It is scarcely possible to paint the picture too sombrely; Russian society, already badly shaken by the First World War, now seemed to totter on the brink of destruction under the combined effects of physical decimation and industrial paralysis. The surviving nuclei of workers fled from famine into the countryside. The history of human progress which has always proceeded from the countryside to the city, now seemed violently to reverse itself. From 1917 to 1920, it has been observed, the urban population of European Russia decreased by 35.2 per cent. Petrograd, with a population of 2,400,000 in 1916, by 1920 had no more than 740,000, while that of Moscow fell in the same period from 1,900,000 to 1,120,000.

In this situation, the revolutionary impetus reached the limits of its endurance; NEP represented an inevitable retreat. After October and the tremendous exertions of the Civil War, Old Russia, until then regarded as merely the outpost of international revolution, threw the whole weight of her backwardness into the scales. The party, suspended between an exhausted working class, a mere shadow of its past, and a peasantry anxious to profit at last from the lands granted them in the revolution, now had to face the task of bringing a bleeding and paralysed society, wholly preoccupied with food, clothing and heating, back to life. The great revolutionary goals were laid aside; political programmes gave way to everyday routine, subversive theory to traditional practice. The party was now forced to take on an omnipresent role, not only political, but administrative, social and economic. It was thus obliged to swell its ranks, not with agitators or political militants but rather with administrators who could control, manage, manoeuvre and supervise: the men demanded by this new situation.

The genesis of Stalin

This was the moment of the greatest cleavage between the vanguard and the class which it ought to have represented. The very results of 1917 seemed on the point of vanishing. With freedom of commerce, NEP introduced measures to facilitate the revival of businessmen, merchants, capitalists. While it benefited the peasantry, more especially rich and middle peasants, it necessarily disappointed the demands of the proletariat which had hitherto had to carry the heaviest burdens of the revolution. The most important element which defined the new situation, already emerging during the NEP period, was the definitive abandonment of the strategy upon which the revolution had been carried out. The last hope of revolution in Europe collapsed. The bourgeois order in Germany, three times on the point of its breakdown, resisted. Its victory both carried within it the seeds of Nazism and contributed to the definitive isolation of the USSR, reinforcing the trend towards retrenchment and post-revolutionary involution.

178 *Lucio Colletti*

The rise of Stalin to leadership, first within the party and then within the state, must be seen in this perspective. His importance begins to emerge with the growing bureaucratization of party and state. But the bureaucracy in its turn developed and expanded because of Russia's extreme backwardness and isolation; it was the product of a revolution in retreat, pinned down within the frontiers of a poverty-striken economy, dependent on an enormous mass of primitive peasants.

The change which occurred in these years, preceding and immediately following Lenin's death, proved decisive for the whole subsequent course of world history. The failure of the western revolution destroyed the strategy which had hitherto underpinned the practice of the Bolsheviks. The possibility of gradually bridging the gulf between Russian backwardness and a socialist programme, through the industrial and cultural support afforded by the resources of a socialist Europe, was now unpredictably severed. Almost at once the party found itself no longer on solid ground.

The first result of this new situation was the internal struggle within the Bolshevik leadership after Lenin's death. The rapid defeat to which the Left Opposition was fated was not the defeat of revolutionary romanticism; it was the immediate repercussion of the aborted European revolution within the USSR. Indeed it is not possible to reduce the conflict between Stalin and the Left Opposition to a series of mere struggles for power, in which Stalin, cautious and slow, used his cunning against an adversary who had shown in the revolution and civil war great capacity for manoeuvre, but had now mysteriously become too proud, clumsy, sure of himself. The premises of this struggle must be sought elsewhere. The first rung of the ladder which was to carry Stalin to power was supplied by the Social-Democratic leaders who in January 1919 murdered Rosa Luxemburg and Karl Liebknecht; their absence weighed heavily in the defeats of 1921 and 1923 in Germany. The remaining rungs were supplied by the reactionary wave which subsequently swept Europe, conjuring forth Mussolini, Primo de Rivera, Horthy and so many others.

Isolated and enclosed within the 'Asiatic backwardness' of Russia, the party underwent more than a mere change in strategy. The weight and inertia of the Russian historical legacy now reasserted itself over every force of change and revolutionary rupture. The re-emergent features of the old order were manifested not only in the rebirth of former ideological and institutional structures, but also, as Carr has shown, in a *national restoration*. The social forces which now re-emerged from their previous defeat to make their compromise with the new revolutionary order and insensibly to influence its course, were above all forces which reaffirmed the validity of an autochthonous tradition against foreign influences.

The cause of Russia and the cause of Bolshevism were now fused into an undifferentiated unity. This was a truly hybrid amalgam; within it the old Slavophile, anti-enlightenment tendencies soon gained an unexpected new lease of life. A complete reversal of origins now occurred. Communism, which had entered Russia with a programme of Westernization (industry, science, modern working class, critical and experimental outlook), condensed in Lenin's formula 'Electrification + Soviets', which itself contains the whole message of Marxism to the modern world, now began to be impregnated with the corrupt humours of the autocratic Great-Russian mentality.

'On his departure from us, Comrade Lenin commanded us to revere and maintain the purity of the name of party member. We swear, Comrade Lenin, that we will faithfully carry out this command! . . . On his departure from us, Comrade Lenin commanded us to safeguard, like the pupil of our eyes, the unity of our party. We swear, Comrade Lenin, that we will faithfully carry out this command!'

These lines from Stalin's famous speech at the 11th Congress of the Soviets (January 26th, 1924) measure the abyss of centuries – centuries which had witnessed Galileo, Newton, Voltaire and Kant – separating this language and mentality from that of Marx and Lenin. The tone of this 'oath', laden with liturgical solemnity, in which Stalin poses as the earthly vicar and executor of the last testament of a defunct god, allows us more easily to understand certain connections than would any amount of analysis. Above all, the links between Stalin and his bureaucratic apparatus, with its proliferation of obscure functionaries extraneous to the history of Bolshevism and the revolution (Poskrebyshev, Smitten, Yezhov, Pospelov, Bauman, Mekhlis, Uritsky, Varga, Malenkov, and others) on the one hand, and on the other the mass party membership, which through the 'Lenin levy', the incipient purges, the massive entry of Mensheviks and remnants of the old regime, increasingly became an opaque and enfeebled body, already largely composed of devoted cyphers or straightforward political illiterates.

It is crucial to bear all this in mind in order to understand the real meaning of the banner under which Stalin was victorious, 'Socialism in One Country'. This slogan does not mean, as the legend has it, that Stalin alone, in the midst of a bewildered and confused leadership, had the courage and foresight to indicate a solution in the conditions of isolation which followed the failure of revolution in the West. In fact, there is no programme or political strategy if this is what we mean by 'solution', which bears Stalin's name. Ideas, for Stalin, were always means, or rather mere pretexts. Zinoviev and Kamenev provided him with the themes with which to combat Trotsky. Bukharin's advocacy of 'Socialism at a Snail's Pace' provided him with the basis for 'Socialism in One Country', and for his struggle against the United Opposition. Finally, the industrialization programme, conceived by the Opposition, provided him with the platform from which to destroy Bukharin, after the Opposition had already been expelled from the party.

What constituted Stalin's specific characteristic, or, if this is what one is expected to say, the element of his 'greatness', which enabled him as an individual to assume a Hegelian 'world-historical' role? It was his ability to interpret the isolation forced upon Russia – which from a revolutionary Marxist position, could only be regarded as a negative event, to be surmounted as soon as possible – as a fortunate opportunity from the standpoint of Russia's destiny as a state. This does not mean that one can simply speak of chauvinism, or even nationalism in the common sense of the term, as early as 1925 or 1926. The process was more complex. It had its roots, as Carr has acutely observed, in a certain sense of pride in the fact that the revolution had, after all, succeeded, that it had been a Russian achievement, that Russia had succeeded where other, supposedly more advanced countries had failed. For those who felt this new 'nationalist-revolutionary' pride, it was an immense pleasure to be told that Russia would lead the world, not only in making the revolution but in constructing a new economy. It was precisely his instinctive ability to interpret and represent this 'force', obscure yet palpable like all elements of so-called 'national spirit', that enabled Stalin to establish and fortify his power. 'Socialism in One Country' was above all a declaration of independence from the West, a proclamation which re-echoed some of the old Slavophile Russian tradition. It did not represent an economic analysis, programme, or a long-term political strategy. For this Stalin's intellectual qualities were quite inadequate, as were those of his advisers: Molotov, Kaganovitch, Ordjhonokidze, Kirov, Yaroslavsky, Yagoda, and later Beria, Zhdanov and so on. This declaration was something else: something for which the Marxism of most of the Bolshevik leadership, with its high intellectual level and profoundly international education, rendered them quite incapable. It was, in short, a declaration of faith in the virtue and destiny of the Russian people.

According to Carr, who is in many respects so favourable towards Stalin, it was the fusion of two characteristic elements of his personality that enabled him to express an objective process at work in the years following Lenin's death. These were: firstly, a 'reaction against the prevalent "European" model in terms of which the revolution had hitherto been conducted', in favour of 'a conscious or unconscious return to national Russian traditions'; and secondly, the abandonment of an intellectual and theoretical framework developed in the whole period when Lenin led the party, for 'a decided re-evaluation of practical and administrative tasks'.

Stalin alone, among the Bolshevik leaders, had never lived in Europe, nor had he ever read or spoken a Western language. From this standpoint his rise to power represented something that far surpassed his own personality, namely the replacement of an entire political group within the leading ranks of the party, concomitant with the adoption of 'Socialism in One Country'. Trotsky, Radek, Rakovsky, Preobrazhensky, Zinoviev, Kamenev, Piatakov, Bukharin and others were gradually removed; they were replaced by a radically different type of personnel, whose most striking features were fundamental indifference towards Marxist theory and a purely 'administrative' attitude towards major questions of political analysis and strategy. Molotov, Kirov, Kaganovitch, Voroshilov, or Kuibyshev, the men who were subsequently closest to Stalin, were like himself totally lacking in Western culture or any internationalist outlook whatever.

Carr writes:

All the original Bolshevik leaders, except Stalin, were in a sense the heirs or products of the Russian intelligentsia and took for granted the premisses of nineteenth-century Western rationalism. Stalin alone was reared in an educational tradition which was not only indifferent to Western ways of life and thought, but consciously rejected them. The Marxism of the older Bolsheviks included an unconscious assimilation of the Western cultural foundations on which Marxism had first arisen. The fundamental assumptions of the enlightenment were never questioned; a basis of rational argument was always presupposed. Stalin's Marxism was imposed on a background totally alien to it, and acquired the character of a formalistic creed rather than of an intellectual conviction.'[3]

The arrival on the scene of this new political elite, which in most cases expressed a 'national-socialist' rather than international outlook, explains the new direction imposed by Stalin on the Third International – which he soon came to call 'the shop'. In the years when the Comintern was still a vital organism, involving Lenin, Trotsky and Zinoviev in feverish activity, he showed no interest in it. He began to concern himself with it only after 1924, when it had already ceased to serve the needs of world revolution and had become a bureaucratic machine and an instrument for the promotion of Russian policy, or merely of his own personal designs. Henceforward, the abandonment of any internationalist perspective was complete. International prospects and goals were replaced by unscrupulous diplomatic manoeuvres with various capitalist states; the world working-class movement and its Communist parties were definitively and totally subordinated to the interests of the Soviet state. Within this state, Stalin not only showed himself to be the most 'Russian' of all the Bolshevik leaders of the older generation but violently subjugated all the other nationalities of the ex-Tsarist empire (starting with his native Georgia).

The consequences of Stalin

It would be useless to dwell upon these points any further; subsequent events have made them all too limpidly evident. The distortion and instrumentalization of the Communist International is writ large on the mediocre bureaucrats who were progressively promoted within it, while the leaderships of the various national sections were destroyed. In the post-war period these personalities appear in the satellite states at the head of the so-called 'People's Democracies'; the Beiruts, Rakosis, Anna Paukers and Georghiu Dejs, the Gottwalds, Novotnys and Ulbrichts – often pursued by popular hatred beyond the grave, or if they survived, no longer daring to set foot in their native countries. Great Russian corruption and chauvinism was sealed in Stalin's Pact with Hitler, to mention no more: even if a declaration of non-aggression was dictated by necessity, the 'pact of friendship', containing secret clauses by which the Soviet Union obtained and later kept the Baltic republics (Latvia, Lithuania, Estonia, part of Poland and Bessarabia), was not. Here we well and truly have a direct reply to Lenin's text on the right of nations to self-determination, written less than thirty years before, and the first example of 'socialist policy' at the service of state expansion and territorial annexation.

For the rest, we can grasp the general sense of the political outlook and aims with which Stalin presided over what should have been the 'Union of Soviet Socialist Republics' from actions and signs which, though ostensibly trivial, are nonetheless richly eloquent. In 1944 he dissolved the Comintern as a pledge and guarantee to the USA and Britain. In the same year, the *Internationale* was replaced by a new *national* anthem, the text of which sings his glory and greatness. In March 1946, he rebaptized the Council of People's Commissars as the Council of Ministers, a title which Lenin had always abhorred. On 25 February 1947, he changed the name 'Red Army of the Workers and Peasants' into that of 'Armed Forces of the USSR'. At the Nineteenth Congress of the party he suppressed the qualification 'Bolshevik' which had hitherto designated it. He was so concerned to break any connection, even of a formal kind, which linked the post-war USSR to the October revolution that in his speech of 9 February 1946, speaking of those outside the party and militants within the party, he declared: 'The only difference between them consists in the fact that the latter are members, the former are not. But this is only a formal difference.'

This was an official sanction for the death of the party as such. For some time already the party had been only one instrument of absolute rule among others, alongside the various secret police organizations. A compact and congealed layer of functionaries, police, informers, flatterers and bureaucrats covered and suffocated the entire country and society. 'To flatter them Stalin gave distinctions to the small and large bureaucrats upon whom his power depended': on 28 May 1943, the personnel of the Foreign

Ministry were assigned ranks 'indicated by epaulettes trimmed with silver thread with old insignia representing two interwoven palms'.[4] Distinctions and uniforms elegantly ranked all the other civil servants. In their turn, the endless swarm of petty and large functionaries, academics, pseudo-scientists and sinister bards of the regime, in order to merit these marks of favour, put in the form of verse or 'scientific memoranda', what Tacitus simply called *ruere in servitium*: 'J. V. Stalin and Linguistics', 'J. V. Stalin and Chemistry', 'J. V. Stalin and Physics' ad infinitum. *Pravda*, which had once carried the incisive and sarcastic prose of Lenin now sang lullabies to the masses in the form of stanzas like: 'O Stalin, Great Leader of all Peoples,/ You have given birth to Man,/ You fertilize the Earth,/ You rejuvenate the Centuries,/ You are one and the same with Spring,/ You make the Lyre sing . . .,/ You are the flower of my Springtime,/ a Sun reflected in thousands of human hearts.' . . .

The change which had occurred in Russia since Lenin is demonstrated quite unequivocally by the forces and values called upon by the state during the Second World War. The spiritual energies of the country were not mobilized in the name or defence of Communism but in that of 'Russian Patriotism'. In his speech in Red Square at the moment when the Nazi armies were approaching Moscow (7 November 1941), Stalin appealed to the founders of the Russian Fatherland and to the great Tsarist generals: 'In this war let us be inspired by the glorious example of our great ancestors, Alexander Nevsky, Dimitri Donskoi, Kuzma Minin, Dimitri Poyarsky, Alexander Suvorov, Mikhail Kutuzov!' In October 1942 he abolished the political commissars of the Red Army and several weeks later created for officers the orders of Suvorov, Kutuzov and Alexander Nevsky. In the beginning of 1943, he issued a regulation defining the privileges of the officer caste, reintroducing several aspects of Tsarist etiquette. For the Ukrainians he created the order of Bogdan-Chmelnitsky, after the name of the (historic) Ukrainian Ataman, a specialist in Jewish pogroms.[5] Finally the new national unity was sealed by a *rapprochement* with the Russian Orthodox Church. Stalin crowned the Patriarch of Moscow, permitted the re-establishment of the Holy Synod, and received the three metropolitans of the Russian Church, Sergius, Alexis and Nicolai, who greeted him as 'Father of us All, Joseph Vissarionovitch'.

From this time onwards the World War was officially designated in Russia the 'Great Patriotic War'. Under this name it ended. On the day of the Japanese surrender, Stalin addressed a message to the Soviet people: 'We have for forty years been waiting for this day . . .'. He was of course, alluding to revenge for the Tsarist defeat in the Russo-Japanese war, a defeat that had led to the revolution of 1905 and was at that time greeted as a victory by all revolutionaries. The political past of the Stalinist USSR was not, therefore, that of Bolshevism, but that of Tsarist Russia.

The significance of all these aspects of Stalin's work became explicit in the climate at the moment of his death, in mysterious circumstances, in 1953. Lenin's Russia, the first bastion of the socialist transformation of the world, was now no more than a distant memory. At the moment of Stalin's death the country was a prey to the furies of obscurantism. From Moscow, there no longer resounded the summons: 'Workers of the World Unite!', but rather a call to anti-semitic persecution (the 'Doctors Plot') and the struggle to death against so-called 'cosmopolitanism'.

What need is there here to re-evoke the Moscow Trials or to speak of the systematic destruction of all the old Bolshevik cadres and militants? To record the toll of the 'purges', of the mass liquidations, of the concentration camps and deportations? Since moral indignation and horror are not effective, we must harness our hatred and trust ourselves to the power of reasoning. This cold and despotic man, whom we have attempted to describe, had more Communists on his conscience than had hitherto been exterminated by the entire world bourgeoisie; he calculated impassively the ruin of whole populations; far from the masses, under his regime the soviets born in 1917 ended as dependencies of the Ministry of the Interior. Nonetheless this man was in his own way endowed with a 'greatness' that we must in some way attempt to define, more to understand what he produced than what he was himself. The liberal English historian Carr has written: 'Stalin is the most impersonal of the great historical figures.'[6] Through industrialization, 'he Westernized Russia, but through a revolt, partly conscious, partly unconscious, against Western influence and authority and a reversion to familiar national attitudes and traditions. The goal to be attained and the methods adopted or proposed to attain it often seemed in flagrant contradiction . . . Stalin's ambiguous record was an expression of this dilemma. He was an emancipator and a tyrant; a man devoted to a cause, yet a personal dictator; and he consistently displayed a ruthless vigour which issued, on the one hand, in extreme boldness and determination and, on the other, in extreme brutality and indifference to human suffering. The key to these ambiguities cannot be found in the man himself. The initial verdict of those who failed to find in Stalin any notable distinguishing marks had some justification. Few great men have been so conspicuously as Stalin the product of the time and place in which they lived.'[7]

It is obvious that this judgement could have no foundation if it were not for the fact that the Stalin period also included industrialization and the great Five Year plans. Through this process Russia became the second industrial power in the world; it is undeniable that this transformation contained within it not only potentially but in real terms a liberatory content. Enormous masses of men were brought into contact with modern productive processes, technology and scientific rationality. Illiteracy was wiped out. The nationalities of central Asia were dragged out of their nomadic past and in some sense involved in the circuit of modern life: their elementary cultural and material needs were satisfied. The mechanization of agriculture began the transformation of the *muzhik* into a worker.

The criticisms levelled at the manner in which collectivization of the countryside was achieved are both well-known and well-justified. Brutality and violence, no attempt to win consent, millions and millions of victims. Even if these criticisms had never been made, the results of this collectivization would speak for themselves: the permanent crisis of Soviet agriculture, the low productivity of labour, the still high percentage of those employed in the countryside, and Russia's import of grain supplies.

However at the root of these criticisms, there may also be a certain tendency to underestimate the 'irrationality' or at least the exceptional character of the problem which the Bolshevik party was obliged to confront and which several other Communist parties, on taking power, were later to encounter. The problem was that of the transition towards socialism in a country in which the process of *accumulation* had not yet taken place, that accumulation which in Europe was the work of capitalism and its industrial revolution.

Workers' Democracy and Accumulation

To build a socialist society means to establish *socialist relations of production*. However one interprets it, this construction is inseparable from the development of *socialist democracy*, soviet power or the self-government of the producers, in the real and not metaphorical sense of the word. On the other hand, and on the contrary, *accumulation* implies saving an extremely high quota of the national product for investment in industrial development; this means violently repressing mass consumption, violently restraining the needs of the population. It presupposes the precise opposite of democracy and of soviets: a coercive apparatus, charismatic power and the *utilization* rather than the self-regulation of the masses.

This is the problem with which Stalin was faced, or rather in the face of which the 'situation' selected Stalin. It is also substantially the problem which, *mutatis mutandis*, confronts Mao and the Chinese leadership today, whatever so many intellectuals in their naïveté may suppose. Why is industrial accumulation necessary? Why is it not possible to construct socialism on the basis of small peasant production or more simply by changing men's souls, appealing to altruism, converting everyone from cormorants into doves? Why is it not possible to abolish, here and now, the 'division of labour'? The innocence with which these questions are asked by so many intellectuals today is a witness of the radical destruction which theoretical Marxism has undergone in recent decades.

It is, of course, true that the reply to these questions is not contained at any particular point in Marx's work. It is only to be found on every page that he ever wrote, from first to last, starting naturally with the 1848 *Manifesto of the Communist Party* (what, the party already in Marx?). The self-government of the masses presupposes: a high productivity of labour, the possibility of a drastic reduction in the working day, the progressive combination of intellectual and industrial work in the category of the worker-technician, masses conscious and capable of making society function at a higher historical level. In short, the self-government of the masses, the rule of the proletariat, presupposes the modern *collective worker*. These conditions can only arise on the basis of large-scale industry, and not of agricultural communes or production with the wooden plough.

Let us return to the thread of the discussion. Stalin's 'greatness' lay in his construction of a great state (the state which Lenin had hoped would rapidly wither away) and a Great Power. He was great in the same sense as Peter the Great. His importance belongs less to the history of the international workers' move-

ment than to its 'pre-history', which is still being prolonged beyond
all our anticipations: a history not of human emancipation but
of great powers dividing the world, of *raison d'état*, of races
confronting one another and displacing class divisions, history
governed by geopolitics.

In face of the enormous scale of what he built, Stalin has
impressed many admirers for his realism. What do principles
matter? What does it matter how people live? Does it count or
decide anything? What counts is millions of tons of steel, missiles,
nuclear power. Admiration for 'realism' of this kind has often
led to the conclusion that 'Stalin constructed socialism' and that
'Russia is the first socialist country'!

In reality, what Stalin produced is inseparable from *the way*
in which it was produced. Seventeen years after his death (an
entire historical epoch!) Russia is still, more than ever, gripped
by the same contradictions as in 1953. As the passage of time
reveals, this is a society which cannot be reformed peacefully.
Yet, unable to reform itself, it is destined for deep convulsions.

How then can we characterize Soviet society? The strategic
sector of the means of production is owned by the state. But state
ownership is certainly not the same as the *socialization* of the
means of production. Nonetheless it allows for a *planning policy*
which, whatever its defects, is not only quite different from so-
called 'programming' of the West, but in so far as it reduces and
maintains control over the mechanisms of the market, makes it
impossible to speak for the time being of a real capitalist restoration. On the other hand, to attribute to this society a so-called
basis of socialism is equally impossible, for if the words have any
meaning this 'basis' must be the socialist relations of production
and exchange themselves, which clearly do not exist in Russia. A
provisional conclusion – certainly not sufficient but perhaps the
least unacceptable of those suggested – is provided by the
formula 'society of transition', but not in the classic, original
sense, in which the society of 'transition' is already a 'socialist'
one. The formula in this case refers to a society half-way between
capitalism and socialism and capable, therefore, of advancing
or regressing. We must, moreover, qualify this definition with
the proviso that in the present degree of degeneration of the
Soviet state, the general laws of transition from capitalism to
socialism are not expressed; instead, an exceptional and temporary refraction of these laws obtains in a country which developed
from a profound backwardness, and which has for so many

decades now been oppressed and stifled by a bureaucracy which often combines habits and mores of autocratic absolutism with methods of fascist extraction.

The long stagnation

To conclude, Stalinist and post-Stalinist Russia constitutes a long *stagnation* in the process of transformation of bourgeois society into socialist society; a repugnant stagnation which *could* be the preamble and inception of a new exploitative society. Amidst this chaos of problems, completely unforeseen by theory, in which at times everyone must feel lost and despairing, one thing at least is clear. The epoch of 'Socialism in One Country' is over; this epoch which saw the triumph of Realpolitik over 'utopia' has in the end revealed the unrealistic side of this 'realism'. Not only has Russia emerged from the hands of Stalin afflicted with the gravest ailments, but the whole edifice of which it was for years the keystone is collapsing into fragments. The so-called 'socialist camp' is partly falling apart, partly held together by military violence and police coercion. The danger of war today does not run along the frontiers of the USSR and the imperialist world, but along the border between the USSR and People's China.

Revolutionary thought has often paid dearly for its recourse to utopias. But in the long run Realpolitik has itself – though for opposite reasons – been revealed as a utopia; the idea that 'moral energies' count for nothing in History, that force is everything, that force is enough to subject peoples, has been conclusively exposed. For, today this Realpolitik has failed. The policy of 'Socialism in One Country' is now shown to be completely unequal to the tasks posed by the problems arising from any 'socialist camp', that is, a community of peoples engaged in a common task of building socialism. Stripped naked, it is revealed for what it has in the meantime become: a crude disguise for the old *raison d'état*, a theory of 'limited sovereignty', limited, that is, for the weaker states, unlimited for the chauvinism of the most powerful state. This historical defeat of Stalinism, in all its forms, has only one positive outcome. It restores to the internationalist theory of Marx and Lenin a sense of truth and actuality. For this theory, the socialist transformation of the world was unthinkable without the determinant contribution of revolution in the West, that is in the heart of capitalism itself.

Yet it must also be said that – even though the time of society is not that of individuals – theoretical Marxism today confronts a test: it is for us to decide whether it is to be merely a chiliasm, or the forceps capable of giving birth to history.

Notes

1. F. Engels *The Peasant War in Germany*, Moscow 1956.
2. R. Luxemburg, *The Russian Revolution*, Michigan 1961, pp. 71–2.
3. E. H. Carr, *Socialism in One Country*, Harmondsworth 1970, p. 196.
4. J. J. Marie, *Staline*, Paris 1967.
5. ibid.
6. E. H. Carr *Socialism in One Country*, p. 192.
7. ibid., pp. 201–2.

Maoism: Its Origins and Outlook [1]

ISAAC DEUTSCHER

(Reprinted from *Ironies of History*, London and New York 1966)

I

What does Maoism stand for? What does it represent as a political idea and as a current in contemporary communism? The need to clarify these questions has become all the more urgent because Maoism is now openly competing with other communist schools of thought for international recognition. Yet before entering this competition Maoism had existed as a current, and then as the dominant trend of Chinese communism for thirty to thirty-five years. It is under its banner that the main forces of the Chinese revolution waged the most protracted civil war in modern history, and won their victory in 1949, making the greatest single breach in world capitalism since the October revolution, and freeing the Soviet Union from isolation. It is hardly surprising that Maoism should at last advance politically beyond its national boundaries and claim world-wide attention to its ideas. What is surprising is that it has not done so earlier and that it has for so long remained closed within the confines of its national experience.

Maoism presents in this respect a striking contrast with Leninism. The latter also existed at first as a purely Russian school of thought; but not for long. In 1915, after the collapse of the Second International, Lenin was already the central figure in the movement for the Third International, its initiator and inspirer – Bolshevism, as a faction in the Russian Social-Democratic party, was not much older then than a decade. Before that the Bolsheviks, like other Russian socialists, had lived intensely with all the problems of international Marxism, absorbed all its experience, participated in all its controversies, and felt bound to it with unbreakable ties of intellectual, moral, and political solidarity. Maoism was from the outset Bolshevism's equal in revolutionary vitality and dynamism, but differed from it in a relative narrowness of horizon and a lack of any direct contact with critical developments in contemporary Marxism. One hesitates to say it, yet it is true that the Chinese revolution which in its scope is the greatest of all revolutions in history, was led by the most provincial-minded and 'insular' of revolutionary parties. This paradox throws into all the sharper relief the inherent power of the revolution itself.

What accounts for the paradox? An historian notes first of all the total absence of any Socialist-Marxist influence in China prior to 1917.[2] Ever since the middle of the nineteenth century, from the Opium Wars and the Taiping Rebellion, through the Boxer Rising and till the overthrow of the Manchu dynasty in 1911, China had been seething with anti-imperialism and agrarian revolt; but the movements and secret societies involved in the risings and revolts were all traditional in character and based on ancient religious cults. Even bourgeois Liberalism and radicalism had not penetrated beyond the Great Wall till the beginning of this century: Sun Yat-sen formulated his republican programme only in 1905. By that time the Japanese Labour movement, of which Sen Katayama was the famous spokesman in the Socialist International, had officially embraced Marxism. In Russia the invasion of Western socialist ideas had begun by the middle of the nineteenth century; and ever since Marxism had gripped the minds of all revolutionaries, Populists and Social-Democrats. As Lenin put it, Bolshevism stood on the shoulders of many generations of Russian revolutionaries who had breathed the air of European philosophy and socialism. Chinese communism has had no such ancestry. The archaic structure of Chinese society and the deeply ingrained self-sufficiency of its cultural tradition were impermeable to European ideological ferments. Western imperialism managed to sap that structure and tradition, but was unable to fructify the mind of China with any vital liberating idea. Only the revolutionary explosion in neighbouring, yet remote, Russia shook the immense nation from its inertia. Marxism found a way to China via Russia. The lightning speed with which it did so after 1917, and the firmness with which it then struck roots in China's soil are the most stupendous illustration of the 'law of combined development': here we see the most archaic of nations avidly absorbing the most modern of revolutionary doctrines, the last word in revolution, and translating it into action. Lacking any native Marxist ancestry, Chinese communism descends straight from Bolshevism. Mao stands on Lenin's shoulders.[3]

That Marxism should have reached China so late and in the form of Bolshevism was the result of two factors: the First World War, exposing and aggravating to the utmost the inner contradictions of Western imperialism, discredited it in the eyes of the East, intensified socio-political ferments in China, made China 'mature' for revolution and extraordinarily receptive to revolutionary ideas; while Leninism, with its original, vigorous emphasis on anti-imperialism and the agrarian problem, rendered Marxism, for the first time in history, directly and urgently relevant to the needs and strivings of the colonial and semi-colonial peoples. In a sense, China had to 'jump over' the pre-Bolshevik phase of Marxism in order to be able to respond to Marxism at all.

Yet the impact of undiluted Leninism on China was very brief. It lasted only through the early 1920s till the opening of the 'national' revolution in 1925. Only a very small elite of the radical intelligentsia acquainted itself with the programme of Leninism and adopted it. At the foundation Congress of the Chinese Communist party in 1921 only twelve delegates were present – Mao Tse-tung was one of them – representing a total membership of fifty-seven! At the second Congress, in the following year, the same apostolic number of delegates spoke for a membership of 123. There were still no more than 900 party members in the whole of China at the beginning of 1925, shortly before the communists were to find themselves at the head of insurgent millions.[4] On these first communist propaganda circles the basic ideas of Leninism left a deep impression. No matter how much the Stalinized Comintern did later to confound the mind of Chinese communism, the germ of Leninism survived, grew, and became transformed into Maoism.

Leninism offered its Chinese adepts a few great and simple truths rather than any clear-cut strategy or precise tactical prescriptions. It taught them that China could achieve emancipation only through revolution from below, for which they must work as tirelessly, indomitably, and hopefully as the Bolsheviks had worked for their revolution; that they ought to distrust any bourgeois reformism and hope for no accommodation with any of the Powers that held China in subjection; that against those Powers they ought to join hands with patriotic elements of the Chinese bourgeoisie, but that they must distrust any temporary bourgeois allies and be ever ready for their treachery; that Chinese communism must look for support to the destitute masses of the peasantry and unfailingly be on their side in their struggles against war-lords, landlords and money-lenders; that China's small urban working class was the sole consistently revolutionary and potentially the most dynamic force in society, the only force capable of exercising leadership ('hegemony') in the nation's struggle for emancipation; that China's 'bourgeois-democratic' revolution was part of an 'uninterrupted', or 'permanent', revolution, part of a global upheaval in which socialism was bound to overcome imperialism, capitalism, feudalism, and every form of archaic Asian society; that the oppressed peoples of the East should rely on the solidarity with them of the Soviet Union and the Western working classes; that the Communist party, acting as the vanguard of the movement, must never lose touch with the mass of workers and peasants, but should always be ahead of them; and, finally, that they must guard jealously the party's total independence in policy and organization *vis-à-vis* all other parties.[5] This was the quintessence of Leninism which the few pioneers of Chinese communism had absorbed before the revolution of 1925–7.

As far as Maoism is concerned, these were still the years of its 'pre-history'. It was only during the revolution that Maoism began to announce itself; and only in consequence of the revolution's defeat did it form a special trend in communism. The 'pre-historical' period is nevertheless of obvious importance, because some of the lessons Maoism had learned in the school of Leninism, although they were to be overlaid by other ideological elements, entered firmly into its political make-up.

2

The next formative influences were the revolution itself and the traumatic shock of its defeat. The years 1925–7 brought to eruption all the national and international contradictions by which China had been torn; and the eruption was astounding in suddenness, scale and force. All social classes – and all the Powers involved – behaved as Leninism had predicted they would. But the most outstanding feature of the events – a feature that was not to be found in the next Chinese revolution and is therefore easily forgotten or ignored – was the revelation of the extraordinary political dynamism of China's small working class.[6] The main centres of the revolution were in the industrial and commercial cities of coastal China, especially Canton and Shanghai. The most active organizations were the trade unions (which had almost overnight become a great mass movement). General strikes, huge street demonstrations and workers' insurrections were the main events and turning-points of the revolution, as long as the revolution was on the ascendant. The agrarian upheaval in the background, widespread and deep, was far slower in the take-off, scattered over immense areas, and uneven in tempo and intensity. It gave a nationwide resonance to the action of the urban proletariat but could not affect the events as directly and dramatically as that action did. It cannot be emphasized too strongly that in 1925–7 China's working class displayed quite the same energy, political initiative, and capacity for leadership that Russia's workers had shown in the revolution of 1905. For China these years were what the years 1905–6 had been for Russia – a general rehearsal for revolution, with this difference, however, that in China the party of the revolution drew from the rehearsal conclusions very different from those that had been drawn in Russia. This fact, in combination with other, objective factors, discussed later, was to be reflected in the differences between the socio-political alignments in the China of 1949 and the Russia of 1917.

At the time of the Chinese 'rehearsal', official Moscow was already reacting against its own high hopes and international-revolutionary aspirations of the Lenin era – it had just pro-claimed Socialism in One Country as its doctrine. The Stalinist and Bukharinist factions, which still jointly exercised power, were sceptical of the chances of Chinese communism, afraid of international 'complications', and resolved to play for safety. To avoid challenging the Western Powers and antagonizing the Chinese bourgeoisie, Stalin and Bukharin acknowledged the Kuomintang as the legitimate leader of the revolution, cultivated 'friendship' with Chiang Kai-shek, proclaimed the necessity of a 'bloc of four classes' in China, and instructed the Communist party to enter the Kuomintang and submit to its guidance and discipline. Ideologically, this policy was being justified on the ground that the Chinese revolution was bourgeois in character, and must be kept within the limits of a bourgeois revolution. No proletarian dictatorship was therefore on the order of the day – only 'a democratic dictatorship of the workers and peasants', a vague and self-contradictory slogan which Lenin had advanced in 1905, when he still held that the Russian revolution would be only 'bourgeois democratic'.

To follow this course, the Chinese communists had to give up almost every principle Moscow had inculcated in them quite recently. They had, as a party, to resign their independence and freedom of movement. They had to give up, in deeds if not words, the aspiration of proletarian leadership and accept bourgeois leadership instead. They had to trust their bourgeois allies. In order to bring about and keep in being the 'bloc of the four classes', they had to curb the militancy of the urban workers and the rebelliousness of the peasantry, which constantly threatened to explode that bloc. They had to abandon the idea of continuous (or permanent) revolution, for they had to 'interrupt' the revolution whenever it tended to overlap the safety margins of a bourgeois order, which it constantly tended to do. They had to break the proletarian-socialist momentum of the movement – or else Moscow would denounce them as adherents of Trotskyism. Socialism in One Country, in the USSR, meant no socialism in China.[7]

At this point Chinese communism fell a prey to its own weaknesses as well as Moscow's opportunism and national egoism. Having no Marxist tradition of their own to fall back upon, being dependent on Moscow for inspiration, ideas, and the sinews of their activity, finding themselves raised by events of dizzy suddenness from the obscurity of a tiny propaganda circle to the leadership of millions in revolt, lacking political experience and self-confidence, bombarded by an endless stream of categorical orders, instructions and remonstrances from Moscow, subjected to persuasion, threats and political blackmail by Stalin's and the Comintern's envoys on the spot, bewildered and confounded, the pioneers of Chinese communism gave in. Having learned all their Leninism from Moscow, they could not bring themselves to say, or even think, that Moscow was wrong in urging them to unlearn it. In the best circumstances they would have found it very hard to rise to their task and would have needed firm, clear, absolutely unequivocal advice. The advice they got from Moscow was unequivocal only in prompting them to equivocate, to shirk their responsibilities, and to abdicate. They did not know that the Trotskyist Opposition was defying Stalin's and Bukharin's 'General Line'; and that Trotsky himself opposed the idea that the Chinese party must enter the Kuomintang and accept its dictates. (They had no contact with the Opposition and Trotsky was criticizing Stalin's and Bukharin's 'friendship' with Chiang Kai-shek in the privacy of the Politbureau.) To the Chinese therefore Stalin and Bukharin spoke with the voice of Bolshevism at large.

It was at that moment, the moment of the surrender to the

Kuomintang, that Mao first registered his dissent. His expression of dissent was only oblique; but within its terms it was firm and categorical. In the second half of 1925 and at the beginning of 1926 Mao spent much time in his native Province of Hunan, organizing peasant revolts, and participated in communist activity in Canton and Shanghai, representing the party within some of the leading bodies of the Kuomintang. His experience led him to assess the social alignments, especially the class struggle in the countryside, in two essays (*The Classes of Chinese Society*, written in March 1926, and *A Study of the Peasant Movement in the Hunan Province*, March 1927). He did not attempt to analyse China's social structure in depth or to criticize the party line in general; but he made his assessment in terms that conflicted implicitly and irreconcilably with every premiss of the party's and the Comintern's policy.

'. . . There has not been a single revolution in history,' he wrote in March 1926, 'that has not suffered defeat when its party guided it along the wrong road. To gain confidence that we shall not lead the revolution along the wrong road . . . we must take care to rally our genuine friends and strike at our genuine enemies . . . [we must be able] to tell our genuine friends from our genuine enemies . . .' The 'genuine friends' of the revolutionary proletariat were the poor peasants and the semi-proletarian elements in the villages; the 'genuine enemies' – the landlords, the wealthy peasants, the bourgeoisie, the Right wing of the Kuomintang. He characterized the behaviour of all these classes and groups with such total lack of illusion and such clarity and determination that, in the light of what he said, the 'bloc of the four classes', the party's submission to the Kuomintang, and the idea of a containment of the revolution within bourgeois limits appeared as so many absurdities, suicidal for the party and the revolution. He was not yet turning his eyes from the town to the country, as he was to do presently, although he already responded far more sensitively and fully to what the peasants were feeling and doing than to the workers' movement. But he still insisted, in good Leninist style, on the workers' primacy in the revolution; and his emphasis on this reflected the actual relationship of workers and peasants in the events of that period.

By this time in the Soviet Union only the Trotskyists and Zinovievists still spoke such language;[8] Mao was something of a 'Trotskyist' Jourdain unaware of what kind of prose he was using. His role in the party was not prominent enough for the Comintern to notice his heresy; but already in 1926 he was at loggerheads with the Chinese Central Committee and Chen Tu-hsiu, the party's undisputed leader and his own erstwhile intellectual and political guide. In the *Study of the Hunan Peasant Movement*, written shortly before Chiang Kai-shek's *coup d'état*, Mao vented his indignation at those Kuomintang leaders and those 'comrades within the Communist party', who sought to tame the peasantry and halt the agrarian revolution. 'Quite obviously,' he castigated them,

> this is a reasoning worthy of the landlord class . . . a counter-revolutionary reasoning. Not a single comrade should repeat this nonsense. If you are holding definite revolutionary views and happen to be in the country even for a while, you can only rejoice at seeing how the many millions of enslaved peasants are settling accounts with their worst enemies . . . All comrades should understand that our national revolution requires a great upheaval in the country . . . and all should support that upheaval – otherwise they will find themselves in the camp of counter-revolution.

This attitude cost Mao his seat on the Central Committee. He was to regain it a year later; but the streak of radicalism or of 'pristine Leninism' was to survive in him, even underneath many later accretions, and was to bring upon him the charge of Trotskyism . . . thirty-six years later.

3

It was, however, from the defeat of the revolution that Maoism took its proper origin, and that it acquired those features that distinguished it from all other currents in communism and from – Leninism.

The defeat caused much heart-searching among the Chinese communists, especially after they had learned the truth about the struggle over China that had gone on in the Russian Politbureau. There were several conflicting reactions to what had happened. Chen Tu-hsiu ruefully acknowledged that he had misguided his party but pleaded that he himself (and the Central Committee) had been misguided by Moscow. Exposing dramatically the inner story of the revolution, relating the many acts of pressure and blackmail to which Moscow had subjected him, he acknowl-edged that Trotsky had all along been right over China. He was for this expelled from the party, slandered and persecuted by both the Kuomintang and the Comintern.[9] Chen Tu-hsiu and his few friends, arguing from an analogy with the Russian revolution (and accepting Trotsky's guidance), saw ahead of them a period of political stagnation, an interval between two revolutions; and they proposed to act as the Bolsheviks had acted during the interval between 1907 and 1917: retreat, dig in, and hold out primarily among the industrial workers; regain and build up strongholds in the cities which would be the main centres of the next revolution; combine clandestine work with open propaganda and agitation; struggle for 'partial demands', wage claims and democratic freedoms; press for the unification of China and call for a National Constituent Assembly; support the peasantry's struggles; use all discontents against Chiang Kai-shek's dictatorship and so gather strength for the next revolution, which would at last be the uninterrupted revolution Lenin and Trotsky had preached.

This was, theoretically at least, a comprehensive prospect and a coherent programme of action. What the Comintern, through its nominees, Li Li-san and Wang Ming, offered was an utterly incoherent combination of basic opportunism and ultra-left tactics, designed to justify the policy of 1925–7 and to save Stalin's face. The canon was upheld that the next revolution would also be only 'bourgeois democratic' – the canon could be used in future to justify a renewal of a pro-Kuomintang policy and a new 'bloc of the four classes'. (Stalin always held that policy in reserve, even during his wildest ultra-left zigzags.) Meanwhile the Comintern, denying that the Chinese revolution had suffered any defeat, encouraged the Chinese party to stage hopeless coups and armed risings. These tactics, initiated with the armed Canton insurrection in December 1927, fitted in well with the Comintern's new 'General Line', which consisted in a forecast of imminent revolution in East and West alike, a call for 'direct struggle for power', rejection of any socialist-com-munist united front in Europe, refusal to defend democratic freedoms, slogans about social-fascism, etc. In Germany this policy led to the disaster of 1933. In China the hopeless risings, coups, and other mad adventures demoralized and disorganized what had been left of the Chinese labour movement after the 1927 defeat.

It was against this background that Maoism made its entry.
Although its official historians (and Mao himself) never admit it,
Mao shared Chen Tu-hsiu's view that the revolution was in
decline and that a political lull was ahead. He rejected the
Comintern's ultra-left tactics, beginning with the Canton rising
and ending with the various versions of 'Li-Li-sanism'. He held,
however, that communism would for a long time to come have
no chance at all of re-entrenching itself in the cities and regaining
footholds in the working class – so deep, as he saw it, was the
moral débâcle that followed the surrenders of 1925–7. He did
not as yet give up the hope that eventually the urban proletariat
would rise again; but he turned his eyes wholly to the peasantry,
which had not ceased to struggle and rise up in revolts. What was
supposed to be merely the agrarian 'accompaniment' of the
revolution in the cities could still be heard, loud and stormy,
after the cities had been reduced to silence. Was it possible, Mao
wondered, that this was no mere 'accompaniment'? Were
perhaps the revolts of the peasants not just the backwash of a
receding wave of revolution, but the beginning of another revolution of which rural China would be the main theatre?

A historian of Maoism may follow the subtle gradations by
which Mao arrived at the affirmative answer to this question.
Here it will be enough to recall that late in 1927, after his quarrel
with the Central Committee, he retired to his native Hunan;
then after the defeat of the Autumn Harvest Rising he withdrew
at the head of small armed bands into the mountains on the
Hunan-Kiangsi border; and from there he urged the Central
Committee to 'remove the party as a whole', its headquarters
and cadres, 'from the cities to the countryside'. Official Chinese
textbooks now credit Mao with having conceived already then,
in 1927–8, the far-sighted strategy that was to bring victory
twenty years later. Mao's contemporary writings suggest that at
first he thought of the 'withdrawal into the countryside' as a
temporary expedient and possibly a gamble, but not as desperate
a gamble as were the party's attempts to stir the urban workers
back into insurrectionist action. Again and again he argued that
the 'Red Base' he and Chu Teh had formed in the Hunan-
Kiangsi mountains was only a 'temporary refuge' for the forces
of the revolution.[10] Yet this temporary and provisional expedient did already point to the later Maoist strategy. The party
leaders, 'opportunists' and 'ultra-radicals' alike, rejected Mao's
advice, holding that it amounted to a break with Leninism. And,

indeed, who could imagine Lenin, after the 1905 defeat, 'withdrawing the party' from Petersburg and Moscow and going at the head of small armed bands into the wilderness of the Caucasus, the Urals, or Siberia? The Marxist tradition, in which the idea of the supremacy of the town in modern revolution held a central place, was too deeply ingrained in Russian socialism for any Russian socialist group to embark upon such a venture. Nothing like it occurred even to the Social Revolutionaries, the descendants of the Narodniks, Populists and agrarian socialists.

4

Mao gradually became aware of the implications of his move and in justifying the 'withdrawal from the cities', he recognized more and more explicitly the peasantry as the sole *active* force of the revolution, until, to all intents and purposes, he turned his back upon the urban working class. He treated his new 'road to socialism' as a 'uniquely Chinese phenomenon', possible only in a country which was neither independent nor ruled by a single imperialist Power, which was the object of an intense rivalry between several Powers, each with its own zone of influence, and its own war-lords, *compradores*, and puppets. That rivalry, he argued, made it impossible for China to achieve national integration; the Kuomintang would no more be able to achieve it, and to set up a cohesive national administration, than previous governments had been. Chiang Kai-shek could smash with a few military blows the concentrated strength of the urban workers, but would not be able to deal likewise with the peasantry, which, being dispersed, was less vulnerable to the white terror and could fight on for many years. There should therefore always exist 'pockets' in rural China where forces of the revolution could survive, grow, and gather strength. Renouncing the prospects of a revolutionary revival in the towns, Maoism banked on the permanence of the agrarian revolution.

Mao assumed in effect a prolonged stalemate between the defeated urban revolution and a paralytic counter-revolution, a prolonged and unstable equilibrium between the divided imperialisms, the impotent Kuomintang bourgeoisie, and the apathetic working class. The stalemate would allow the peasantry to display its revolutionary energies, and to support the communists and their Red Bases as scattered islands of a new regime. From this assumption he drew (in 1930) this broad generalization about the international prospects of communism:

> If . . . the subjective forces of the Chinese revolution are weak
> at present, so are also the reactionary ruling classes and their
> organization . . . based on a backward and unstable socio-
> economic system . . . In western Europe . . . the subjective
> forces of the revolution may at present be stronger than they
> are in China; but the revolution cannot immediately assert
> itself there, because in Europe the forces of the reactionary
> ruling classes are many times stronger than they are in China
> . . . *The revolution will undoubtedly rise in China earlier than
> in western Europe* (my italics).[11]

This assumption, so characteristic of Maoism, was not
altogether original – it had appeared fleetingly in some of Lenin's,
Trotsky's, Zinoviev's, and Stalin's reasonings a decade earlier.[12]
But Mao made of it the cornerstone of his strategy, at a time
when no other communist school of thought was prepared to
do so. In retrospect, the events have amply justified him. Yet if
the Maoist orientation and action are judged not retrospectively,
but against the background of the late 1920s, and early 1930s,
they may not appear as faultless as they seem now. It may be
argued that the superiority of the 'reactionary ruling classes' in
western Europe would not have been so overwhelming, and that
it might even have crumbled, if the Stalinist and Social-Democratic self-defeating policies (passivity *vis-à-vis* rising Nazism,
and the shams of the Popular Fronts) had not worked to preserve
and enhance it. One may further argue that the Maoist road of
the Chinese revolution was not necessarily predetermined by the
objective alignment of social forces, that the Chinese working
class might have reasserted itself politically, if the Comintern
had not recklessly wasted its strength and if the Chinese party
had not 'withdrawn from the cities', and so deserted the workers,
at a time when they needed its guidance more than ever. As so
often in history so here, the objective and subjective factors are
so enmeshed and intertwined after the events that it is impossible
to disentangle them and determine their relative importance.

It should further be noted that the period of the middle 1930s
was extremely critical for Maoism; its major premisses were
brought under question and nearly refuted by the events. In the
south of China, the area to which Mao's action had been con-

fined till 1935, the peasantry was utterly exhausted by its many revolts and was crushed by Chiang Kai-shek's punitive expeditions. The Red Bases of Hunan and Kiangsi, having held out against Chiang's 'extermination drives' for seven years, were succumbing to blockade and attrition. Mao and Chu Teh just managed to lead the Partisans out of the trap and start on the Long March. They thereby acknowledged their defeat in that part of China which had been the main theatre of their operations. It looked as if the counter-revolution, far from being impotent in the countryside, had demonstrated its superior strength there and gained a decisive advantage. In the meantime, the workers of Shanghai and other coastal cities had shown a new defiance and staged turbulent strikes and demonstrations. But, lacking competent leadership and organization, they were defeated again and again. Maoist historians cast a veil of obscurity over this chapter of the movement in the cities, precisely because it raises the question whether under effective guidance those struggles of the urban workers might not have opened up a new revolutionary situation much earlier than it could be opened up from the country. Was it inevitable that the interval between the two revolutions should last not ten years, as it lasted in Russia, but more than twice as long? Or had the Maoist withdrawal from the cities something to do with it? Whatever the truth of the matter – the historian can pose the question but not answer it – around 1935 the Maoist strategy was on the point of collapse and nearly bankrupt. These facts are recalled here not for any polemical purpose, but because they lead to a conclusion of some topical relevance, namely, that Maoism as a strategy of revolution owes its ultimate vindication to an extraordinarily complex and largely unpredictable set of circumstances.

In 1935 Mao fought his way out of the impasse by means of the Long March, which has since become the heroic legend of Chinese communism. Yet at the end of the Long March Mao had under his orders only one-tenth of the force he had before the March – 30,000 out of 300,000 Partisans.[13] What saved Maoism and decisively contributed to its further evolution were, apart from its own heroic determination to survive, two major events or series of events: the Japanese invasion, and the deliberate de-industrialization of coastal China by the invader. The Japanese conquest deepened the contradictions between the imperialist Powers and interrupted the unification of China under the Kuomintang. It thus reproduced that impotence of the reactionary ruling class on which Mao had based his calculations. Northern China was in turmoil; the Kuomintang was unable to assert its military control there and to prevent the emergence and consolidation of the northern 'Soviets'. Maoism derived fresh strength from the Kuomintang's inability to secure the nation's independence and from its own revolutionary–patriotic, 'Jacobin', stand against Japan. On the other hand, with the systematic de-industrialization of coastal China, the small working class was removed from the scene. As the Japanese dismantled industrial plant in Shanghai and other cities, the workers dispersed, became *déclassés*, or vanished in the country.[14] From this fact Maoism obtains a kind of retroactive vindication. Henceforth no one could hope for the rise of a new 'proletarian wave' in the cities. The class alignments of 1925–7 could not be expected to reappear in the next revolution. The Marxist-Leninist scheme of class struggle became inapplicable to China. The peasants were the sole force struggling to subvert the old order; and Mao's party focused and armed all their rebellious energies. It was now, in the late 1930s, that Mao finally formulated the main and most original principle of his strategy: The Chinese revolution, unlike other revolutions, will have to be carried from country to town.[15]

5

The relationship between Maoism and Stalinism was ambiguous from the beginning. The motives which had led Maoism to take on the protective colour of Stalinist orthodoxy are obvious enough. In the late 1930s, Mao and his colleagues were aware of the weight of the influence on Chinese affairs that Stalin's government would exercise in consequence of the Second World War; and they feared that it might exercise it in a narrowly self-interested manner, and as opportunistically as in 1925–7. They knew their dependence on Moscow's goodwill; but they were determined *not* to allow Moscow to use them as it had used Chen Tu-hsiu, Li Li-san, and Wang Ming. They were determined to prevent another abortion of the Chinese revolution. They played, therefore, a most intricate game, pursuing their independent strategy without arousing Stalin's suspicion and wrath. Stalin could not have been quite unaware of this. Yet the Comintern neither sanctioned nor condemned Mao's 'un-Marxist' and 'un-Leninist' strategy. Stalin would not have tolerated anything like the Maoist heresy in any Communist party situated in a sphere of world politics which he considered more vital to his interests. But Maoism had started upon its career on what looked to Stalin like a remote periphery; and Mao behaved as some heretics had once behaved in the Catholic Church who, defying their local bishop or cardinal, strenuously avoided any collision with the Pope himself. Later, when Maoism moved closer to the centre of Chinese politics, it was already too strongly entrenched – yet was outwardly still submissive enough – for Stalin to conclude that to excommunicate Mao was both risky and unnecessary. He did not himself believe, not even as late as 1948, that Mao's Partisans would ever be able to conquer the whole of China and carry out a revolution; he was willing to use them as bargaining counter or instruments of pressure on Chiang Kai-shek, whom he again considered his chief ally in Asia.

In the Comintern the years after 1935 were again a period of 'moderation', the period of Popular Fronts. Translated into Chinese terms, the policy of the Popular Fronts meant the re-establishment of the 'bloc of the four classes' and of the 'friend-ship' between the Kuomintang and the communists, this time in a united front against the Japanese invader. The old, never abandoned and now emphatically reasserted canon about the exclusively bourgeois-democratic character of the Chinese revolution served as the 'ideological' justification of this turn of policy. For Maoism, engaged as it was in civil war against the Kuomintang, the Comintern's new demands were a severe trial. Only the show of an unreserved acceptance of the Comintern's line could prove that Mao and his comrades remained loyal to Stalinism. And so Mao 'moderated' his Yenan regime and his propaganda and agitation; he appealed to the Kuomintang for patriotic solidarity and joint action against Japan; and he even used his influence to save Chiang Kai-shek's position and probably even his life during the Sian incident. Yet the Partisans never yielded to the Kuomintang even as much as an inch of their territory and power.

Mao's Stalinism was in some respects, however, more than sheer mimicry. The persistence with which Mao asserted and reasserted the purely bourgeois character of the Chinese revolu-tion accorded well with the complete identification of his Parti-sans with the peasantry. To the great mass of the peasantry the perspective of an 'uninterrupted revolution', that is of a revolution solving the land problem, unifying China and also *opening up a socialist upheaval*, was either meaningless or unacceptable. In the primitive pre-industrial society of Shensi and Ninghsia – where Mao's writ ran during the Yenan period – there was no room for the application of any measures of socialism. It was only after its conquest of the cities in 1949 that Maoism was to run up against the inevitability of the uninterrupted (permanent) revolution and obey its dictates.

6

From the theoretical Marxist viewpoint the central question posed by all these events is how a party, which had for so long based itself only on the peasantry and acted without any industrial working class behind it, was after all able to go beyond the 'bourgeois'-agrarian upheaval and initiate the socialist phase of the revolution. Communist writers have so far avoided discussing this embarrassing question frankly and have allowed anti-communist 'Marxologists' to monopolize it. Has not the course of events in China, the latter argue, refuted once and for all the Marxist and the Leninist conceptions of revolution and socialism? Surely, the idea of proletarian revolution in China belongs to the sphere of mythology – and, surely, the Chinese experience shows up the Russian revolution too to have been the work of a ('power hungry', 'totalitarian') intelligentsia which used the workers and their allegedly socialist aspirations only as the ideological cover for its own ambitions. All that both these revolutions have achieved, M. Raymond Aron, for instance, is quick to point out, is merely to change the ruling elites, which is nothing surprising to anyone who has learned his lessons from Pareto and Max Weber. (Even a writer like the late C. Wright Mills, convinced of the relevance of Marxism to the problems of our age, concluded that not the working class but the revolutionary intelligentsia is the real historic 'agency' of socialism.) Ex-Marxists, who have found out that socialism has been 'the illusion of our age', and that the reality behind it is state capitalism or bureaucratic collectivism, invoke the old Marxist dictum that 'socialism will be the work of the workers or it will not be at all'. How then, they ask, is it possible to speak of a revolution in which the workers have played no part as being socialist in any degree whatsoever? In a different context and on a different level of argument, the question arises whether the famous

Russian controversy between Narodniks and Marxists over the relative roles of workers and peasants in modern revolution has in fact been as irrevocably resolved as it seemed to have been until recently. Even if the Marxists were right in Russia, are the Narodniks not vindicated in China? Has not the peasantry there turned out to be the sole revolutionary class, the decisive agent of socialism?

There is no question that the record of Maoism compels a critical review of some habitual Marxist assumptions and reasonings. How this is necessary is illustrated *inter alia* by the assessment of Maoism which Trotsky gave in the 1930s. Grasping all the intensity of the agrarian upheaval in China, but apprehensive about the Maoist withdrawal from the cities, Trotsky bluntly ruled out the possibility of the consummation of the Chinese revolution without a previous revival of the revolutionary movement among the urban workers. He feared that Maoism, despite its communist origin, *might* become so completely assimilated with the peasantry as to become nothing but its mouthpiece, that is the champion of the small rural proprietors. If this were to happen, Trotsky went on, Mao's Partisans, on entering the cities, might clash in hostility with the urban proletariat and become a factor of counter-revolution, especially at that critical turn when the revolution would tend to pass from the bourgeois into the socialist phase. Trotsky's analysis, reverberating unmistakably with decades of the Russian Marxist-Narodnik controversy and the experience of the Russian revolution, was reduced *ad absurdum* by some of his Chinese disciples who denounced the victory of Maoism in 1949 as a 'bourgeois and Stalinist counter-revolution'.[16]

The phenomenon of a modern socialist (or be it even 'bureaucratic collectivist') revolution of which the working class had not been the chief driving force stood indeed without precedent in history. What drove the Chinese revolution beyond the bourgeois phase? The peasantry was interested in the redistribution of land, the abolition or reduction of rents and debts, the overthrow of the power of the landlords and money-lenders, in a word in the 'bourgeois'-agrarian upheaval. It could not give the revolution a socialist impulse; and Maoism, as long as it operated only within the peasantry, could not have been more reticent than it was about the prospects of socialism in China. This changed with the conquest of the cities and the consolidation of Maoist control over them. Yet the cities were almost dead politically, even if a galvanized remnant of the old labour movement stirred here and there.

We are confronted here, on a gigantic scale, with the phenomenon of 'substitutism', i.e. the action of a party or a group of leaders which represents, or stands in the stead of, an absent, or inactive, social class. The problem is familiar from the history of the Russian revolution, but it presents itself there in quite a different form. In Russia the working class could not have been more conspicuous as the driving force of the revolution than it was in 1917. Yet, after the civil war, amid utter economic ruin and industrial collapse, the working class shrank, disintegrated, and dispersed. The Bolshevik party set itself up as its *locum tenens*, and as trustee and guardian of the revolution. If the Bolshevik party assumed this role only some years *after* the revolution, Maoism assumed it long *before* the revolution and during it. (And Mao and his followers did this without any of the scruples, compunction, and *crises de conscience* that had troubled Lenin's party.)

Liberal or 'radical' Paretists, who see in this yet another proof that all that revolutions achieve is a change of ruling elites, have still to explain why the Maoist elite was determined to give the revolution a socialist (or collectivist) turn, instead of keeping it within bourgeois limits. Why has the Chinese communist elite behaved so differently from the Kuomintang elite? This was not even the case of a 'young' elite replacing an old and 'exhausted' one, for both elites were contemporaries and had entered the political stage almost simultaneously. Why then have Mao and his comrades given China a new social structure, while Chiang Kai-shek and his friends floundered hopelessly in the wreckage of the old? And what accounts for the stern puritanical morale of Maoism and for the notorious corruption of the Kuomintang? The answer surely is that Chiang Kai-shek and his men identified themselves with the classes that had been privileged under the old order, while Mao and his followers embraced the cause of those that had been oppressed under it. Behind the change of the elites there was a profound transformation in the basic social relationships of China, the decline of one social class and the rise of another. No one doubts the extent to which the peasantry backed the Partisans during the twenty-two years of their armed struggle – without that support they would not have been able to hold out, to make the Long March, to shift their bases from one end of China to the other, to keep the Kuomintang's greatly superior military strength engaged all the time, to repulse so many 'annihilation drives', etc. So strong and intimate were the ties between the Partisans and the peasantry that at one time Mao appeared to many, to friend and foe alike, as the commander of a gigantic Jacquerie rather than as the leader of a Communist party – as a kind of Chinese Pugachev.

Yet this Chinese Pugachev, or super-Pugachev, had gone through the school of Leninism; and no matter how far he deviated from it in his methods of action, some general ideas of Leninism continued to govern his thought and action. He did not abandon his commitment to socialism (or collectivism) in favour of the peasants' individualism and attachment to private property, even while he was doing his best to satisfy that individualism and unfold its bourgeois-revolutionary potentialities. Nor should it be forgotten that revolutionary agrarian movements have always produced their utopian communists, their Münzers and Anabaptists. Of the peasants' 'two souls' – the expression is Lenin's – one is craving property, while the other dreams of equality and has visions of a rural community, the members of which own and till their land in common. It might be said that Maoism expressed both 'souls' of the peasantry, had it not been for the fact that it never was just the peasantry's mouthpiece. It always looked upon itself as the legatee of the defeated revolution of 1925–7, of which the industrial workers had been the driving force. Identifying itself ideally with those workers, Maoism continued to echo their socialist aspirations. Was this arrogance or usurpation? But what else could a party, committed to the communist programme, do after the dispersal of the urban working class and the political decline of the cities?

In carrying the revolution beyond the bourgeois phase Maoism was actuated not merely by ideological commitments but also by a vital national interest. It was determined to turn China into an integrated and modern nation. All the experience of the Kuomintang was there to prove that this could not be achieved on the basis of a belated, and largely imported, capitalism, superimposed upon patriarchal landlordism. National ownership of industry, transport and banking, and a planned economy were the essential preconditions for any even half-way rational deployment of China's resources and for any social advance. To secure these pre-conditions meant to initiate a socialist revolution. Maoism did precisely that. This is not to say that it has turned China into a socialist society. But it has used every ounce of the nation's energy to set up the socio-economic framework indispensable for socialism and to bring into being, develop, and educate the working class, which alone can make of socialism a reality eventually.

International factors, in the first instance the relationship between China and the USSR, co-determined the course and outcome of the revolution. That relationship has been much wider and more positive than the ambiguous connection between Maoism and Stalinism. Whatever the mutations of the political regime of the USSR, the Chinese revolution could not – and cannot – be dissociated from the Russian. Although the Partisan armies had received little or no Soviet support and had overthrown the rule of the Kuomintang in the teeth of Stalin's obstruction, Red China, born into a world split into two Power blocs, and herself confronted by American hostility and intervention, could not but align herself with the USSR. In this alignment, Maoism found another potent motive for carrying the revolution beyond the bourgeois phase. The ultimate guarantee of the solidity of that alignment lay in the collectivist structure of the Chinese economy. As I have pointed out elsewhere,

> the revolutionary hegemony of the Soviet Union achieved [despite Stalin's initial obstruction] what otherwise only Chinese workers could have achieved – it impelled the Chinese revolution into an anti-bourgeois and socialist direction. With the Chinese proletariat almost dispersed or absent from the political stage, the gravitational pull of the Soviet Union turned Mao's peasant armies into agents of collectivism.[17]

No Marxist textbook has or could have foreseen so original a concatenation of national and international factors in a revolution: Maoism does not fit into any preconceived theoretical scheme. Does this refute the Marxist analysis of society and conception of socialism? When Marx and Engels spoke of the working class as *the* agency of socialism, they obviously presupposed the presence of that class. Their idea had no relevance to a pre-industrial society in which such a class did not exist. It should be recalled that they themselves pointed this out more than once; and that they even made allowance for the possibility of a revolution like the Chinese. They did this in the exchanges of views they had with the Russian Narodniks in the 1870s and

1880s. The Narodniks, we know, saw Russia's basic revolutionary force in the peasantry – no industrial working class existed as yet in their country. They hoped that by preserving the *obshchina*, the rural commune, the Russia of the *muzhiks* could find her own way to socialism and avoid capitalist development. Marx and Engels did not dismiss these hopes as groundless. On the contrary, in a well-known letter addressed, in 1877, to *Otechestvennye Zapiski* Marx declared that Russia had 'the finest chance [to escape capitalism] ever offered by history to any nation'; and that even as a pre-industrial agrarian society she could start moving towards socialism. For this, as he saw it, one condition was necessary, namely that western Europe should make its socialist revolution before Russia had succumbed to capitalism. Russia would then be carried forward by the gravitational pull of Europe's advanced, socialist economy. Marx repeated this view some years later in an argument with Vera Zasulich, pointing out that his scheme of social development and revolution, as he had expounded it in *Das Kapital* and elsewhere, applied to western Europe; and that Russia might well evolve in a different manner. Engels expressed himself in the same sense even after Marx's death.[18]

All this has been well known and many times discussed. What have been less clear are the implications of this argument. How did Marx view the social alignments in that hypothetical Russian revolution which he anticipated? Evidently he did not see the industrial working class as its chief driving force. The revolution could find its broad base only in the peasantry. Its leaders had to be men like the Narodniks, members of the intelligentsia, who had learned something in the Marxist school of thought, had embraced the socialist ideal, and considered themselves to be the trustees of all the oppressed classes of Russian society. The Narodniks were, of course, the classical *zamestiteli*, the arch-substitutists, who acted as the *locum tenens* for an absent working class and a passive peasantry (the *muzhiks* did not even support them) and who championed what they considered to be the progressive interest of society at large. Yet Marx and Engels encouraged them to act as they did and trusted that their action would be fruitful for socialism, if revolution in more advanced countries transformed the whole international outlook early enough.

True, Marx's prospect failed to materialize in Russia because, as Engels pointed out much later, the western European working classes had been 'far too slow' in making their revolution and in the meantime Russia had succumbed to capitalism. But on an incomparably larger scale, and against a changed international background, that prospect has materialized in China. It should be noted that the Maoists were far more broadly based on the peasantry than the Narodniks had ever been, that their socialist consciousness was far more mature – they engaged in mass action not in individual terrorism; and that, on assuming power, they could lean on the advanced collectivist structure of the USSR, which even as an economic Power was rising to the second place in the world. In proclaiming that socialism can be the work only of the workers, Marxism did not preclude the inception of socialist revolution in backward pre-industrial nations. But even in such nations the working class remains the chief 'agency' of socialism in the sense that fully fledged socialism cannot be attained without industrialization, without the growth of the working class and its self-assertion against any post-revolutionary bureaucracy, in a word, without the real, social and political ascendancy of the 'proletariat' in post-capitalist society.

7

The present outlook of Maoism has crystallized in the post-revolutionary period, which has now lasted nearly fifteen years. Yet the seizure of power was not for the Chinese communists the sharp and decisive turn in their fortunes it had been for the Bolsheviks: even as Partisans they had controlled considerable areas of their country; their leaders and cadres had been half-rulers and half-outlaws before they became full rulers. On gaining national victory, the party had to 'urbanize' itself and to cope with a wide range of new tasks. But it was less dependent on the old bureaucracy for the business of government than the Bolsheviks had been and therefore probably less exposed to infiltration by socially and ideologically alien elements.

It is unfortunately impossible to be categorical or precise about these questions, because the Maoists do not provide us with enough information. Such is their secretiveness that we know incomparably less of the 'inner story' of the fifteen years of their rule than we know from official Bolshevik sources about the early periods of the Bolshevik regime. However, a comparison between Maoism and Bolshevism, viewed at approximately the same remove from the moment of the revolution, a comparison between the China of 1963–4 and the Soviet Union of the early 1930s, based only on the generally established facts, brings out certain crucial similarities, differences, and contrasts which may help to illumine the picture of Maoism in the post-revolutionary era.

It is a truism that the Chinese revolution has occurred in a socio-economic environment far more backward than that in which the Russian revolution had taken place. China's industrial output had never been more than a fraction of the Russian, an infinitesimal fraction in relation to the needs of a far larger population. The predominance of the archaic rural structure of society was almost absolute. The Chinese peasantry was even more primitive than the Russian (although, unlike the latter, it had not been subjected to centuries of serfdom, a fact which may show to some advantage in its character – in the greater independence, sobriety, and industriousness of the Chinese peasants). Age-old economic, technological, and social immobility, rigid survivals of tribalism, despotic ancestral cults, immutable millenary religious practices – all these have made the task of the Chinese revolution even more difficult and have affected Maoism itself, its methods of government and ideological outlook. Bent on industrializing China, Maoism has had to initiate primitive socialist accumulation on a level far lower than that on which accumulation had proceeded in Russia. The extraordinary scarcity of all material and cultural resources has necessitated an unequal distribution of goods, the formation of privileged groups, and the rise of a new bureaucracy. National history, custom, and tradition (including the deep philosophical influences of Confucianism and Taoism) have been reflected in the patriarchal character of the Maoist government, the hieratic style of its work and propaganda among the masses, and the magic aura surrounding the leader. Like Stalinism (and partly under its influence), Maoism allows no open discussion or criticism of its high priest and hierarchy. And the fact that for two decades before its rise to power the party had existed as a military organization has favoured the perpetuation of unquestioning discipline and blind obedience in its ranks.

Yet encumbered as it is by the greater backwardness of its environment, the Chinese revolution has in some respects been more advanced than the Russian, if only because it has come after it. It has never experienced the fearful isolation that has cramped and crippled the mind and the character of Bolshevism.

It has come into the world as a member of the 'socialist camp', with the USSR as its powerful, though difficult, ally and protector; even the exposed flanks of Red China have to some extent been protected by the high tide of anti-imperialist revolt that has swept Asia. Despite American hostility, Mao's China did not have to beat off anything like the 'Crusade of fourteen nations' that the Russia of Lenin and Trotsky had to repulse. In embarking upon primitive socialist accumulation China was not wholly reduced to her own meagre resources: Russian assistance, limited though it was, helped her in priming the pump of industrialization. More important than the material aid was the Russian experience from which the Maoists could learn: China did not have to pay the terrible price for pioneering in socialization and economic planning Russia had had to pay. Her industrialization, despite the partial failure of the Great Leap, has proceeded more smoothly than Russia's did in the early stages. And, despite a long sequence of natural calamities and bad harvests, Red China has not known any of the terrible famines that the Soviet Union suffered in 1922 and 1930–2, when millions of people starved to death.

Altogether, the social tensions have not been even remotely as acute and dangerous in China as they had been in the Soviet Union. Nor has the post-revolutionary conflict between the rulers and the ruled been as severe and tragic. Maoism in power has enjoyed the peasants' confidence to a degree which Bolshevism has never attained. The Chinese have been far less reckless and brutal in collectivizing farming; and for a long time far more successful. Even the rural communes do not seem to have antagonized the peasants as disastrously as Stalin's collectivization did.

The fact that the Chinese peasantry has not been driven into a mortal enmity towards the regime has influenced the behaviour of all other social classes of the workers who, recruited from the peasantry, are bound to reflect its moods; and of that section of the intelligentsia which has its roots in the country. Nor has the Chinese bourgeoisie been as hostile and aggressive towards the new regime as the Russian bourgeoisie, feeling the peasantry's backing, was in its time; and Mao's government has treated the bourgeoisie more prudently than Lenin's government did; wherever possible it has preferred to buy off the entrepreneurs and merchants rather than expropriate them.

Yet another vital difference in the starting points of the two revolutions has decisively contributed to making the social climate in China milder than in the Soviet Union. In Russia the civil war was waged *after* the revolution, whereas in China it had been fought *before* the revolution. The question whether communists enter the civil war as a ruling party or as a party of opposition is of the greatest consequence for their subsequent relationship with all classes of society. If, like the Bolsheviks, they have to fight as a ruling party, they bear in the eyes of the people the odium of the devastation, suffering, and misery caused by civil war – as a rule the people's despair and fury at the conditions of their existence turn against those in office. In 1921–2 the Bolsheviks had wielded power for four or five years, during which they could do nothing to improve the lot of the workers and peasants, or rather to prevent its disastrous worsening. 'Is this what we have made the revolution for? Is this how the Bolsheviks keep their promises?' – these were the angry questions the Russian workers and peasants asked. A gulf was already fixed between the rulers and the ruled; a gulf which it was impossible to bridge; a gulf to which the Bolsheviks reacted with a self-defensive, panicky distrust of society and which they perpetuated and deepened thereby until there was no escape from it; a gulf which yawns ominously through the whole record of Stalinism.

In China, by contrast, the people blamed Chiang Kai-shek's government for all the devastation and misery of the civil war. The revolution came as the conclusion, not the opening of hostilities. The communists, having seized power, could at once give their undivided attention to their economic problems and use at once all available resources constructively, so that very soon the lot of the people began to improve and went on improving steadily. And so the first years of the new regime, far from producing disillusionment, were characterized by rising popular confidence. If the Bolsheviks set out to industrialize Russia after they had nearly exhausted their political credit with the masses, the Maoists were able to draw on an immense and growing credit. They had far less need to use coercion in the realization of their ambitious programme. They did not have to resort to the inhuman labour discipline Stalin had imposed on the workers; or to send punitive expeditions to the villages in order to extract grain, to deport huge masses of peasants, etc. Lenin once said that it had been easy to make the revolution in Russia, but far more difficult to build socialism; and that in other countries it would be far more difficult to overthrow the bourgeoisie, but much easier to cope with the constructive tasks of the revolution. Lenin made this prediction with an eye to western Europe, but to some extent it has come true even in China. Although the material resources of the Chinese revolution were so much poorer than those of the Russian, its moral resources were larger; and in revolution as in war the Napoleonic rule holds good that the moral factors are to the material ones as three to one.

Maoism has therefore been far less hag-ridden with fear than Stalinism had been. As in the nation at large so within the ruling party the tensions have been less explosive and destructive. Here, paradoxically, Maoism benefits from certain advantages of backwardness, whereas Bolshevism suffered from progressiveness. The establishment of the single party system in China was not the painful and dramatic crisis it had been in Russia, for the Chinese had never had the taste of any genuine multi-party system. No Social-Democratic reformism had struck roots in Chinese soil. Maoism has never had to contend with opponents as influential as those that had defied Bolshevism: there were no Chinese Mensheviks or Social Revolutionaries. And, lacking Marxist tradition, and the habits of inner party freedom, the habits of open debate and criticism, Maoism was never in the throes of a deep conflict with its own past, such as troubled the Bolshevik mind when it was being forced into the monolithic mould. Maoism had so much less to suppress both within itself and in society that it did not have to give to suppression (and self-suppression) the prodigious mental and physical energy the Soviet Communist party had to waste on that job.

Nor has the Chinese party become the ruthless promoter of inequality and the champion of the new privileged strata that the Soviet party had become. While in China too, amid all the prevailing want and poverty, the recrudescence of inequality has been inevitable, this has *not* so far been accompanied by anything like Stalin's frantic and shameless drives against egalitarianism. This circumstance throws fresh light on the problem of inequality in post-revolutionary society. Although the 'general want and poverty' are, according to Marx, the objective causes for the recrudescence of inequality, the intensity of the process depends on subjective human factors such as the character of the ruling group, the degree of its identification with the new privileged strata, and the viciousness (or the lack of it) with which it is prepared to foster inequality. The fact that Mao and his colleagues have spent the best part of their lives in the midst of the poorest peasants, hiding with their Partisans in the mountains, sleeping in the caves, fighting, marching and starving together, allowing no estrangement between officers and men, and no differences in food rations and uniforms – this extraordinary experience of the Maoists, an experience of over two decades, no other ruling group has gone through, may have left its imprint on their character and in some measure shielded them from the worst corruption of power. Characteristically, the Chinese party insists that its brain workers and dignitaries should periodically descend from their high offices to the factories and farms and, for about a month every year, perform manual labour, so as not to lose touch with the workers and peasants. Such practices, sometimes bizarre in form, cannot overcome the contradictions between the rulers and the ruled and between brain workers and manual labourers; but they may help to keep these contradictions within certain limits, and they indicate that the egalitarian conscience is not dead even in the ruling group. (On the other hand, Chinese officialdom, like the Russian, refuses to disclose just how wide are the discrepancies between high and low wages and salaries, which suggests that it is afraid of disclosing the real scope of the existing inequality.)

Against these features which distinguish so favourably Maoism from Stalinism must again and again be set the marks of its backwardness, which make for its affinity with Stalinism. The Chinese party is strictly monolithic, far more so than the Soviet party is now, in the post-Stalin era. Having had no proletarian background and no Marxist, socialist-democratic traditions of its own – having formed itself at a time when the whole Communist International was already Stalinized – Maoism was born into the monolithic mould and has lived, grown, and moved within it, as the snail moves within its shell. Except for one pregnant moment (when the Hundred Flowers were to blossom all over China), Maoism has taken its monolithic outlook for granted. The Leader's infallibility is at least as firmly established as it had ever been in Russia, with this difference that for about twenty-five years no one has seriously challenged it. The Chinese party has not so far been involved in any convulsions as terrible as those that once shook the Russian party. It has had its important and obscure purges, one of which resulted in the 'liquidation' of Kao Kang in 1955; but the composition of the ruling group has not significantly changed since the days of the revolution or even of the Partisan struggle. Mao has not had to contend against a Trotsky, a Bukharin, or a Zinoviev. But neither do the assemblies and conferences of the Chinese party resound with the abject recantations of defeated Opposition leaders that had poisoned Soviet political life by 1932, and were to end in the Moscow trials.

8

The Maoist challenge to Moscow's 'leadership' of the Communist movement is partly a result of the consolidation of the Chinese revolution – the Maoists would not have risked such a conflict with Moscow earlier; and consolidation and growth of strength and confidence are expressed in a 'shift to the left' and in the Maoist ambition to speak for all the militant elements of world communism.

Here again, a comparison with the Soviet Union of the early 1930s lights up a signal contrast. The prevalent mood in the Soviet Union at that time was one of moral-political weariness and of a reaction against the high revolutionary internationalism of the Lenin era. In the name of Socialism in One Country, the ruling group had initiated ideological 'retrenchment', and was seeking to disengage the Soviet Union from its commitment to world revolution – Stalin was already then practising the revisionism of which Mao is now accusing Khrushchev. The fact that at a comparable remove from the revolution, opportunism, and national egoism ruled supreme in the Soviet party, while the Chinese party proclaims its radicalism and proletarian internationalism is of immense historic and political consequence.

We have seen how the radical Leninist streak, now submerged and now coming into the open, has run through every phase of Maoism, and in decisive moments did not allow it to yield or surrender, under Stalinist pressure, to the Kuomintang and abandon the road of revolution. It is this, the Leninist element in Maoism that is at present asserting itself more strongly than ever and that seems to be transforming the outlook of Chinese communism. If Bolshevism after some years in power was morally declining, its enthusiasm withering and its ideas shrinking, Maoism is on the ascendant, discovers new horizons, and enlarges its ideas. The débâcle of official Bolshevism was epitomized in its vehement and venomous repudiations of permanent (continuous) revolution, which was not merely Trotskyist doctrine but the principle Lenin's party had deeply and passionately held in the heroic years of the Russian revolution. Maoism, on the contrary, had long and stubbornly dwelt on the limited bourgeois character of the Chinese revolution; yet now it is solemnly proclaiming that permanent revolution is the principle by which it lives, the *raison d'être* of international communism. At the close of his career, Mao appears once again as the Trotskyist Jourdain he was at its beginning. Like Trotsky, though without the latter's deep roots in classical Marxism yet with all the resources of power at his command, Mao is calling communism to return to its source, to the irreconcilable class struggle Marx and Lenin had preached.[19]

Part of the explanation for this shift to the left lies certainly in the West's attitude towards Red China, in the continuing American blockade, in the fact that so many Western Powers have not yet recognized the Peking government and have barred it from the United Nations. It should not be forgotten that the first great wave of opportunism came over the Soviet Union in the years 1923–5, after Clemenceau's and Churchill's *cordon sanitaire* had broken down, when most Western governments established diplomatic relations with Moscow. Beneficial in so many respects, this change in the international position of the Soviet Union had its adverse side: it encouraged the ruling group to practise *Realpolitik*, to take distance from the oppressed classes and peoples of the world, and to make far-reaching concessions of principle to the 'class enemy'. China's ruling group has not so far been exposed to such temptations. On the contrary, events constantly remind it that to capitalism's unabated hostility it has one reply only – its own unflagging defiance. Moreover, the ideological retreat of the Russian party was also a reaction to the many defeats the revolution had suffered in Germany and in the rest of Europe between 1918 and 1923; whereas Maoist militancy has drawn nourishment from the upsurge of anti-imperialism in Asia, Africa, and Latin America. Here too, China is benefiting from the fact that she has not been the first country to embark upon the road of socialism. It is proving much more difficult for the capitalist world to tame or intimidate the second major revolution of the century than it was to contain, if not to 'roll back', the first.

Of course, grave dangers may be lurking behind the breach

between the USSR and China. How will Maoism react to isolation from the Soviet Union, if the isolation deepens and hardens? How will it be affected by a relative stabilization of the 'national bourgeois' regimes in most of the formerly colonial or semi-colonial countries? And if some Western Powers were to try to play China against the Soviet Union, instead of playing the latter against the former – might Peking not succumb to the temptation? The prospect would be clearer than it is if one could be sure that Maoist professions of revolutionary internationalism are not merely a response to Western provocation but that they genuinely reflect the frame of mind of the Chinese masses. But we know far too little, next to nothing, about that aspect of the problem.

The credibility and effectiveness of the Chinese call for a restoration of Leninist principles would be far greater if Maoism did not seek to rescue the myths of Stalinism from the discredit into which they have deservedly fallen. In this Maoism is acting from motives of self-defence: it has to vindicate its own record, its past commitments, and its rigidly ritualistic party canon which, like every such canon, requires that its formalistic continuity be unalterably upheld. The infallible leader could not have been in error on any of those past occasions on which he extolled the Stalinist orthodoxy. The obeisance Mao paid to the living Stalin compels him to pay obeisance to the dead as well. Maoism's affinity with Stalinism lies precisely in this need to uphold established cults and magic rituals designed to impress primitive and illiterate minds. No doubt, one day China will grow out of these crude forms of ritualistic ideology, as the USSR is growing out of them; but that day has not yet come. Meanwhile, the conservative element in Maoism, its backwardness, is at logger-heads with its dynamic element, especially with its revolutionary internationalism. In a similar way, elements of backwardness and advance, differently assorted, have been in constant collision within the Soviet party after Stalin. The prospects would be infinitely more hopeful if it were possible for the diverse progressive urges in the two great Communist parties to release themselves from the grip of retrograde factors, and to coalesce – if the Chinese fervour for Leninist internationalism went hand-in-hand with a zeal for a genuine and consistent de-Stalinization of the Communist movement. The impossibility of disentangling progress from backwardness is the price that not only Russia and China but mankind as a whole is paying for the confinement of the revolution to the underdeveloped countries. But this is the way history has turned; and now nothing can force its pace.

London 1964

Notes

1. Written for *Socialist Register* and *Les Temps Modernes* in 1964.
2. The first Chinese translation of the *Communist Manifesto* appeared only in 1920; it was then that Mao, at the age of twenty-seven, read the *Manifesto* for the first time. The year before he still went on a pilgrimage to the grave of Confucius, although he was not a believer.
3. A parallel may be drawn here between the fortunes of Marxism and revolution in Europe and Asia. Just as in Europe Marxism first exercised a wide influence in industrial Germany, so in Asia it found its first important following in industrial Japan, the 'Prussia of the Far East'. But in neither of these two 'advanced' countries did Marxism go beyond propaganda and agitation. On both continents it fell to the great 'backward' nations to accomplish the revolution.
4. Ho Kan-chih, *A History of the Modern Chinese Revolution*, Peking 1959, pp. 40, 45, 63, 84.
5. The Second Congress of the Communist International occupied itself, in 1920, especially with the problems of the colonial and semi-colonial countries; and Lenin was the prime mover of the theses and resolutions on this subject. See Lenin, *Sochineniya*, Moscow 1963, vol. 41.
6. Mao gives the number of Chinese industrial workers, employed in large-scale enterprises as two million. There were about ten million coolies, rikshas, etc. Mao Tse-tung, *Izbrannye proizvedeniya*, Moscow 1952, vol. I, pp. 24–5.

Mao explains the decisive role of the workers in the revolution by the high degree of their concentration in big factories, their extraordinarily oppressive conditions, and exceptional militancy. Russia had no more than three million workers employed in modern industry about the time of the revolution; and Trotsky explains their decisive role in much the same way.

7. See my account of these events in *The Prophet Unarmed*, pp. 316–38.
8. A comparison of the documents contained in Trotsky's *Problems of the Chinese Revolution* with Mao's writings of 1926–7 shows the complete identity of their views on these points. Ho Kan-chih in op. cit. (which is the official Maoist account of the Chinese revolution) unwittingly gives many other illustrations of that identity. Thus, he relates that early in 1926 Mao protested against the Chinese party's decision to vote for the election of Chiang Kai-shek to the Executive Committee of the Kuomintang and to back his candidature to the post of Commander-in-Chief of the Armed Forces. About the same time Trotsky protested in Moscow against Chiang's election as an Honorary Member of the Executive of the Comintern. The Maoist historian blames only Chen Tu-hsiu for the 'opportunist' policy, pretending not to know that Chen behaved as he did on Moscow's orders and that Chiang was Stalin's candidate to the post of the Commander-in-Chief. The fact that Chiang was Honorary Member of the Comintern's Executive is not even mentioned in the Maoist *History*.

9. Chen Tu-hsiu's fate – denounced as 'traitor' by the Comintern, he was imprisoned and tortured by the Kuomintang police – was a terrible warning to Mao who henceforth avoided any *open* breach with Stalinist orthodoxy, even while he was at loggerheads with its successive Chinese guardians. Mao was never to risk a conflict with both Stalin and Chiang Kai-shek. His cautious, ambiguous attitude towards Stalinism reflected something of the sense of weakness and ultimate dependence on Soviet backing which had caused Chen Tu-hsiu to accept Stalin's and Bukharin's dictates in 1925–7. But unlike Chen, Mao, for all his outward deference to Stalin, was never to give up his own judgement on Chinese affairs and swerve from his own course of action.

10. Mao, op. cit., vol. I, pp. 99–110 and 117 ff. and passim.

11. Mao, ibid., p. 196.

12. See *The Prophet Armed*, pp. 456–7 and *The Prophet Outcast*, p. 61.

13. Ho Kan-chih, op. cit., p. 270. The author blames the recklessness of the 'ultra-lefts' in the party and army for these disastrous losses.

14. A most instructive description of this process and of its political effects is to be found in Chen Tu-hsiu's correspondence with Trotsky (The Trotsky Archives), quoted in *The Prophet Outcast*, pp. 423–4.

15. From what has been said it is clear that the validity of the Maoist method of revolution is of necessity limited. Mao himself, in the early days of Partisan warfare, used to underline this – he spoke of the 'unique Chinese character' of the conditions in which his method could be applied. Only in primitive countries, where the body politic has not achieved national integration (or where it has disintegrated) and where there does not exist any bourgeoisie capable of exercising national leadership, can Partisans enjoying the peasantry's support carry revolution from the country to the towns; and then it depends on the revolutionaries' 'ideology' and international connections whether they can impart a socialist impulse to their revolution. An analysis of the social alignments in the Cuban and Algerian revolutions, and in other Afro-Asian upheavals, may show to what extent, and with what variations, the 'Chinese' conditions have or have not been reproduced in those countries. Victorious leaders of a Partisan movement are, of course, inclined to claim for their experience wider validity than it inherently possesses. Thus Che Guevara, in his essay on guerrilla warfare, recommends the Castroist strategy to revolutionaries all over Latin America. In those Latin American countries, however, where the bourgeois regime is more broadly based, integrated, and centralized than it was in Cuba under Batista, Che Guevara's recommendation, if acted upon, may lead to abortive coups.

We may mention here as a grotesque curiosity that the leaders of the French counter-revolution in Algeria, the OAS colonels, also tried to 'apply some lessons of Maoism'. Mao is undoubtedly a great authority on the military aspects of Partisan warfare. But the main secret of the success of his strategy lies in its close combination with agrarian revolution. It is impossible to apply his military prescriptions without his social strategy, as the leaders of the OAS have learned to their detriment.

16. See the controversy over this among the Chinese Trotskyists, reproduced in several issues of the *International Information Bulletin* of the Socialist Workers' Party (New York), for the year 1952. Trotsky's articles on the Chinese Partisans had appeared in the *Byulleten Oppozitsii*.

17. *The Prophet Outcast*, p. 520.

18. *Perepiska K. Marksa i F. Engelsa s russkimi politicheskimi deyatelyami,*

pp. 177–9, 241–2 and passim.

19. Mao's view of class antagonisms in post-revolutionary society is also far closer to Trotsky's than to Stalin's. Recently Maoist theorists have written about what Trotsky called the Thermidorian spirit of the Soviet bureaucracy very much along the lines of his argumentation. And several decades after Trotsky, they hint at the 'danger of capitalist restoration' in the USSR.

Bibliographical note

The article by Isaac Deutscher reprinted here was written before the Cultural Revolution: for his initial assessment of this latter event see the equally prescient interview, Isaac Deutscher, *China's Cultural Revolution*, (Bertrand Russell Peace Foundation, 1967). The text, of Trotsky to which Deutscher refers are now available in *Leon Trotsky on China*, (New York, 1976). For the recent evolution of Chinese communism see, in particular, Livio Maitan, *Party, Army, Masses in China* (London, 1976) and Fred Halliday, 'Marxist Analysis of China', *New Left Review*, 100, December, 1976 – February 1977.

R.B.

The Struggle for Socialism in Czechoslovakia

INTERVIEW WITH JIŘI PELIKAN

(Reprinted from *New Left Review*, 71, 1972)

We would like to begin by asking something about the period in which you first became politically active, just before World War Two. We understand that you joined an anti-fascist organization in 1937, while still at school, and became a member of the Czech Communist party in 1939. Could you tell us how you experienced the major events of those years, the Nazi occupation of Czechoslovakia in 1938 and 1939, the German/Russian pact in the summer of 1939, the invasion of the Soviet Union in 1941 and the Czechoslovak resistance movement?

My case is typical of many people of my generation who entered the political arena as secondary school students in the late thirties. The Spanish Civil War was in progress and the danger of a German invasion already hung over Czechoslovakia. We were, of course, very excited about the fight of the Spanish people against fascism, and saw the important role of the communists in that struggle – though without any real understanding of the problems involved. Then we saw that the communists were the most resolute opponents of fascism in Czechoslovakia and internationally, and this brought us into sympathy with the Communist party. It is most important to understand that Czechoslovakia, unlike the other east European countries subsequently liberated by the Red army, had always had a legal Communist party before the war. During the twenty years of bourgeois parliamentary government between 1918 and 1938, there had been real guarantees for democratic freedom. The fact that Czechoslovakia was an industrialized country, and had a working class with long revolutionary and democratic traditions, was the basis for the subsequent success of the Communist party.

When the invasion of Czechoslovakia proper started in 1939, we saw the Communist party as the only force which opposed it – although there were, in fact, other patriotic groups which did so too. It was at this time that I joined the Communist party and became a part of its underground network. I helped to produce and distribute leaflets and newspapers, organize students and so on, until 1940 when I was arrested.

The Nazi/Soviet pact, of course, came as a great shock to us. But right from the moment of the invasion, when the resistance started, Russian policy had dismayed us. For example, I remember clearly a friend's case. He was much older, had been a Communist since his university studies in 1933 and was one of the leading members of the party in our city in Moravia. When he received instructions from the Comintern after the Nazi occupation he was extremely shaken. Even messages signed by Gottwald himself stated that the German soldiers who had invaded Czechoslovakia were, in fact, proletarians in soldiers' uniforms and therefore in no way class enemies! The real enemies were the Czech bourgeoisie headed by Beneš, and the American and British plutocrats. This was the Comintern line at the time. I remember my friend refused to transmit these instructions to the members of the party. They would have meant that instead of fighting against the occupiers we would be fighting against our own people. In fact the party throughout the country modified these instructions, saying firstly that the comrades in Moscow were not well informed about the situation and secondly that the instructions were completely out of touch with reality. When the German/Russian pact was signed at the end of August, this was a further shock. We had received a lot of explanations of how the Soviet Union had been obliged to do this, because of the refusal of the Western powers to conclude a military treaty and in order to buy time. Despite our feelings, we could appreciate rationally that the pact probably was necessary. But what we did not understand at all were the positive articles which we started to read in the German newspapers about the Soviet Union and the broadcasts we heard from Radio Moscow at the time: instead of working to build up the Resistance, they began toning down all anti-fascist propaganda and just putting out items about how many pigs there were on some kolkhoz or other and how many tons of such and such a product the Soviet Union had produced. I remember the comrades were very angry when they saw that what was involved was not just a pact of non-aggression with a fascist country, but rather some sort of political agreement. Another thing which dismayed us was Molotov's speech after the collapse of Poland, in which he spoke of Poland as an artificial state from its creation, now destroyed for ever by the common action of the German and Soviet armies.

But all these hesitations came to an end in June 1941, when the war between the Soviet Union and Germany started. After that, of course, the situation changed completely; the Moscow party leaders now gave full support to the Resistance and co-operation with other anti-fascist forces began.

Yet the Communist party had not lost its position as the main force of resistance in Czechoslovakia during the period from March 1939 to June 1941?

I would not say that the Communist party was the main force. In fact we claimed after the war that we were the main force, but it is difficult to assess. There certainly were other groups – though not so well organized as the Communist party. I think the claim that the Communist party was the only, or the main, force in the Resistance was a sectarian one.

Could you say something about the development of the party during the war? For example what were the relations between the leadership in Moscow and the new leaders in the Resistance? Were there differences destined to be important later on?

To answer that, one must go back to the history of the Communist party of Czechoslovakia. I have mentioned that the party was always a legal one, unlike in the other eastern European countries. It was founded in 1921 as the result of a break with the Social Democratic party. Again, in contrast to other central and eastern European countries, it was from the very beginning a real mass party. The leader at that time, Šmeral, developed some sort of conception of a Czechoslovakian path to socialism, which brought him into conflict with the Comintern and with the twenty-one points laid down by it. The mass base of the Communist party in Czechoslovakia which was the sign of its real success was very adversely affected by the Fifth Congress in 1929, when Gottwald took over the leadership. This Congress, officially called the Congress of Bolshevization, was in fact a congress of subjugation of the Communist party of Czechoslovakia to the Soviet leadership. It accepted the crushing of the Soviet opposition and Stalin's conception of building Socialism in One Country, and acknowledged the Soviet Union as the single monopolistic centre of the international revolutionary movement. The acceptance of this line led to the elimination of many outstanding leaders from the party, which lost about seventy per cent of its membership during this period. Later on it won a lot of them back through its fight against fascism, starting in 1934–5 with the new line of the Comintern – the Popular Front. It was in this period between 1929 and 1939 that a new leading nucleus of the party was developed – Gottwald, Slánský, Kopecký and others. They were educated to a complete subordination to the Soviet party and to Stalin. It was, in fact, this leadership which was in the Soviet Union during the war, and which came back unchanged to take power after the liberation. The people who were inside the country were never, in fact, integrated into the leading positions of the party and they were always viewed with a certain suspicion. Take, for example, Smrkovský. Smrkovský was one of the leaders of the Prague uprising and a central figure in the underground committee of the party at the end of the war. He became vice-president of the Czech National Council in 1945. But the very fact that he organized the popular uprising was held against him. For Gottwald's aim had been that the country should be liberated by the Soviet army, not by a popular uprising, whereas the whole strategy of the 'internal' party had been directed towards a popular uprising, towards partisan struggle. Of course during the war the contradictions were not apparent, because even Gottwald appealed for an uprising and for armed struggle. But as we learnt later, the Soviet Union insisted categorically that Czechoslovakia should be liberated by the Soviet army and this fact was of decisive importance. Consequently, in all ideological work and propaganda the role played by the Resistance movement at home was played down and sometimes even portrayed as hostile. It was in this context that when the political trials started in 1949, Smrkovský was accused of being an agent of the Gestapo, put in prison and condemned, together with many other leaders of the Resistance movement. Since they drew their political strength from the popular movement, they were considered insufficiently disciplined or loyal to the Soviet leadership, and for this reason they were viewed with a certain suspicion.

What was your personal involvement in these events? What happened after you were arrested by the Gestapo in 1940?

My personal role was a very small one because I was a young student. When I was arrested I was seventeen years old; I spent about one year in prison, then I was released on parole because I was under eighteen. I was on the point of being arrested again when the German/Soviet war began, but I escaped from where I had been assigned to stay while on parole. I spent the remaining four years of the war underground, with a false name, in various regions of Czechoslovakia. Since I was being looked for by the Gestapo, my parents were taken as hostages, and my mother was killed by the Germans. My brother had been arrested with me in 1940, but he remained in prison for the whole five years the war lasted. I spent the last two and a half years of the war in a small village called Koronec near Boskovice in Moravia. I was the secretary of the local village administration, under my false name of course – and was able to continue my underground work at the same time. There was a partisan movement in the area; there were a lot of Soviet prisoners of war who had joined us and we were able to help our people.

When did partisan struggle begin, and what was its extent?

It began in 1944 and was, of course, strongest in the mountainous part of the country. It was strongest of all in Slovakia, after that in eastern and central Moravia where I was, and it was weakest in Bohemia, which is much more densely populated and industrialized, lies on a plain and was more tightly controlled by the Germans.

What happened when the Red army liberated Czechoslovakia? Could you tell us how the new administration was established, and about the workers' councils which sprang up in 1945, especially in Bohemia?

During the last years of the war, there was an attempt to create underground *Národní vybory* or National Committees as popular organs for the future, local society. In the factories there were also to be *Závodní vybory* or factory committees formed by the workers and technicians. There were some factories, I would not say that there were many, where such underground committees actually existed; where they did exist they organized the rising of 5 May 1945 – above all in Prague. This insurrection, we know today, was launched against the will of the Soviet leadership. The same was true of the uprising in Slovakia in August 1944. Stalin wanted this uprising to start only when the Red army had already surrounded the frontiers of Slovakia as far as Katowice.

But the uprising broke out spontaneously and although the Soviet army tried to give it support, it was suppressed. It was a tragedy like that of the risings in Warsaw and elsewhere. I would not say myself that the Russians did not want to help it, but I would say that they did not view with enthusiasm a popular uprising without clear political control from Moscow.

Was there any resistance to the imposition of the Moscow leadership and Gottwald immediately after the liberation?

No, I don't think there was any real resistance, because the war was a victorious one. Everybody knew after Stalingrad that the Soviet Union had played a decisive role in it, and I think that Gottwald was accepted as the acknowledged leader of the Communist party, and hence also of the resistance movement as a whole. It was argued, I think in *Rude Pravo*, that the liberation of Prague by the Soviet army was some sort of confirmation of the correctness of the line of Gottwald.

What was the situation of the bourgeoisie in Czechoslovakia at the time of liberation? What was the relationship of class forces between the working class and its allies and the bourgeoisie?

I think that the bourgeoisie was discredited. First of all by the defeat of the First Republic in 1938, secondly by the collaboration of part of it with the Germans – although it must be acknowledged that part of the national bourgeoisie also participated in the resistance movement. At all events, the formula of the 'national and democratic revolution', as it was called at the time, allowed the party the occasion to undermine all the economic and political power of the bourgeoisie in 1945. The four parties which were permitted to exist – the Communist party, the Social Democratic party, the National Socialist party and the Catholic party (there were other parties in Slovakia) – all agreed to put through the programme of the National Front which had directed the resistance. It was a programme for national and democratic revolution, but it already went beyond the programme of any bourgeois government. It was, in fact, the programme of a 'People's Democracy'. It involved the nationalization of big industry, the banks, all external trade, etc., agrarian reform; the establishment of national committees as the legislative and executive organs of power; a single union federation, and so on. The bourgeoisie lost any real power and the balance of forces was completely in favour of the working class. The peasants supported the workers because they wanted the agrarian reform. Of course, there were still some remnants of the reactionary forces left, and when they had got over the first shock of defeat, they started to oppose the new course and tried to sabotage the realization of the National Front programme. This is what led to the crisis in February 1948.

What was the character of this crisis? It appeared as an attempt to push the social revolution through a further stage, but it also appeared as an episode in the Cold War. How did this seem to you as a Czech Communist at the time?

I think there were both internal and international aspects of the Czechoslovakian crisis of 1948. Inside Czechoslovakia, tension was growing. Although the other political parties supported the programme of the National Front and collaborated with the communists, the rightist forces which I mentioned had stabilized certain positions of strength within these parties, and even had some support among the population at large – as a result of dissatisfaction with the country's economic development, the difficulties, hardship, shortages, etc. As a counter-offensive the Communist party launched proposals to extend nationalization even to small industries, to confiscate all personal fortunes exceeding one million crowns, and to carry out a further distribution of land. From this point of view, the 1948 crisis did represent a sharpening of the class struggle. But at the same time, from an international point of view, it was clear from the time of the Informburo meeting in Poland in 1947 that the Soviet Union saw itself not as a base for the revolutionary movements of the world, but increasingly as a great power essentially concerned with the distribution of zones of influence. Moscow wanted to consolidate its influence and power over Czechoslovakia, since these had not been clearly established at Yalta. At Yalta there had been no discussion about Czechoslovakia as such – at least as far as we know. Of course, nobody knows exactly what was discussed, but from all the evidence and documents published it emerges that there was a lot of discussion about Poland, Yugoslavia and Greece, but the Czechoslovakian problem was never discussed at all. Perhaps this was because it was then the only government recognized by everybody. However, I would say that the 1948 crisis was not just a putsch launched by the Soviet Union or by Stalin; it was an internal clash between the progressive and reactionary forces in which the latter were defeated by the tactics of Gottwald, who emerged as the leader of the country.

You mean that neither the Russians nor Gottwald had been restraining class struggle in 1945–6? You have no impression that the workers perhaps wanted to strike some more decisive blows for socialism than had been achieved?

This problem, of course, existed. I remember, for example, I think it was in about 1946, a meeting of the party activists in Prague to which Gottwald was invited and where he was obliged to defend the strategy of the party against heavy criticism. A lot of the delegates, particularly those from factories, were saying: 'What are we doing and where are we going? It is all very well talking about the national and democratic revolution, but we want socialism and the party does not speak about socialism.' Gottwald was trying to explain that, of course, the final aim of the party was socialism, but at the present stage to propagate socialism too much might create problems amongst certain sections of the population, and the party should not go beyond this stage of the national and democratic revolution. I remember that some people were not very much convinced by this, saying that this sort of practice could, of course, be valid if the party publicly declared that its aim was to build a socialist society, but as it was being carried out it appeared that the aim was to deceive the people and confront them with a *fait accompli*. Then again, I was a student at that time, and I remember there was a lot of critical discussion of party strategy among the students. It was felt that the party had no clear strategy or perspective, but was too much involved in day-to-day political problems. Of course, these criticisms were superseded in 1948 when people thought that the way to socialism was open.

What was your personal experience of the internal life of the party in the period between 1945 and 1948? What sort of things were discussed in party circles?

Discussion was quite free. There were none of the limitations which appeared later on, when the party took over power. The leadership wanted discussion to be concentrated mainly on economic problems and on how the communists could contribute to the building of a new Czechoslovakian state. Gottwald's slogan was 'the better we work, the more we shall be accepted as a leading force'. This line of course implied avoiding real ideological discussion. But the arguments used by other parties against the Communist party were inevitably reflected within the latter, especially in intellectual and student bodies. There was also frequent discussion about the Czechoslovak road to socialism – about the aim of the whole development. But there was never any clear explanation from the leadership, from the representatives of the Central Committee, on this question.

Another subject of great discussion in 1947 was Zhdanov's speech on proletarian culture, and the measures taken against Akhmatova, Kachaturian and Shostakovich. An exhibition of Soviet painters was put on in Prague at which the so-called socialist realism made its first appearance. There was a violent clash between the party and the communist intellectuals, because the latter were for the most part people who were communists before the war, when to be a communist artist meant to be an *avant garde* artist. Many of them were, for example, surrealists. They recognized in Soviet socialist realism the reactionary realism of the bourgeoisie of the First Republic, and they refused to accept this kind of art as real socialist art. The leadership tried to resolve this conflict by explaining that 'socialist realism' was due to the historical development of the Soviet Union, and that at all events in Czechoslovakia there would not be any such imposition of a single style on the artists. Nevertheless, this was a big topic of discussion.

What about the question of workers' power in Czechoslovakia? Were there people who felt that the workers did not get real state power in Czechoslovakia in 1948?

No, I don't think that this view was expressed at all in 1948. The official line in Czechoslovakia in this respect was typical of all the eastern European countries. Once the Communist party takes power, the Communist party which represents the working class, once it has a leading role in the state, the parliament, and the trade unions, then this leading role of the Communist party is seen as identical to the leading role and to the power of the workers. The workers themselves have nothing to do except follow the instructions of the party. I think this was the original source of the crisis which appeared later. The working class, which had been rather active before the war, during the war and after the war, was systematically being de-politicized by the party's leadership. Party slogans claimed that since the working class was in power, the role of the workers was to work to increase productivity, to compete in Stakhanovite fashion; this would be the best contribution the working class could make towards the building of socialism. Of course, some of the best working-class cadres were taken from the factory floor and made into directors, or given posts in the diplomatic service. The universities were opened to the children of the working class. This was real progress and was also necessary to ensure the stability of the new regime. But we were to realize later that this was an inadequate conception of workers' power. The workers soon discovered that they were in almost the same situation as in a capitalist country. They had to work, they received a money wage and, what is more, they could not buy what they needed even with this wage because of the shortage of goods. However, I do not think that the problem of workers' power was really posed at this time – except by Kalandra, a communist poet and writer, a Trotskyist, who was arrested in 1948 and executed. A lot of other people whom we did not even know, people who had criticized the Moscow trials in 1936–8, were the first victims after the victory of the Communist party. Then, of course, after the Informburo resolution on Yugoslavia, the real clash came on the question of the specificity of roads to socialism. The conflict with Yugoslavia was reflected in Czechoslovakia, Poland and elsewhere. I do not think that this conflict broke out because Yugoslavia was the most liberal of all the east European countries. Czechoslovakia, for example, was probably more so. But Yugoslavia was the only country in the Soviet zone in eastern Europe which had effectively liberated itself. True, it did so in the overall context of the Soviet army's defeat of Germany, but nevertheless Yugoslavia had a real partisan army, whereas the other countries' resistance was on an altogether smaller scale. For this reason the Yugoslavs did not want to accept the monopoly role of the Soviet Union. In Czechoslovakia, the Yugoslav issue was used as a pretext to break all potential opponents capable of thinking independently or contesting (I don't say they did any real contesting) the leading role of Moscow. If you take the people who were arrested among the communists, it was the old communists, those who had been in the Spanish Civil War, those who had been in the resistance movement abroad, people of Jewish origin who had been in exile in the West, the best economists, in short, all the people who were able to think for themselves. The victims were, in fact, themselves Stalinists at the time, but the blow was directed against potential enemies. I should say that I only realized the full significance of the repression of 1949–54 years later. It was after the events in Poland and Hungary in 1956 and there was a meeting of the Central Committee, in 1957 I think, when they were discussed. Kopecky, who at that time was a member of the Politbureau, said that the reason such events did not occur in Czechoslovakia was that Kadar and Gomulka had been arrested, but not liquidated physically, while we had liquidated all our political opponents physically. Thus we were able to overcome this crisis because there was no alternative leadership in Czechoslovakia. At all events, the political trials put an end to all attempts at specific national paths of development and initiated the imposition of the Soviet model of socialism in all the eastern European countries.

I wonder if we could now turn to a somewhat later period. You, of course, in the 1950s and early 1960s became very prominent in the International Union of Students?

From 1953 I was General Secretary and from 1955 the President of the IUS.

What was your experience of working within that organization? Was there any contradiction between its subordination to Russian interests and the presence within it of many student unions which were genuine, militant anti-imperialist organizations?

First of all I must say that personally I was very pleased to be able to leave domestic politics; like many other communists, I did not feel very happy about the way things were going. In the IUS, I found again the genuinely revolutionary, extremely free atmosphere of the student movement. At that time, of course, I had no doubts about the sincerity of Soviet policy. It seemed to me that this policy was basically correct because it was directed against imperialism. Don't forget, it was still the period of the Korean War. There was even felt to be a danger of world conflict, and it was a period when a great number of African and Asian countries were still colonies. So the IUS at the time played a very positive role in mobilizing students against colonialism, and in that respect there was no basic contradiction with Soviet policy, which supported the anti-colonial revolutions. Later, of course, after the Twentieth Congress and Khrushchev's speech, we had our first doubts. But Khrushchev's policy initially seemed positive – broader contacts, a rejection of sectarianism, which we felt had been a great failing of the IUS in the period of the Cold War. We welcomed the opportunity to extend the common front to organizations which, although not communist, were generally anti-imperialist and anti-colonialist.

But the policy of peaceful coexistence as it was in fact carried out created the first and real problems inside the IUS. There was on occasion a conflict between its anti-imperialist and anti-colonialist mission and the way in which the Russians applied the policy of peaceful coexistence. For example, we were very much involved in organizing support for the national liberation struggle in Algeria. But when Khrushchev went to France, the Soviet representatives became reluctant to vote for IUS resolutions in favour of Algeria, because to do so would create problems with the French government. Other conflicts of interest arose. With regard to the Cuban revolution and the Latin American movement as a whole; whereas the communist parties were unenthusiastic the student organizations were very revolutionary, very progressive. Differences also emerged on the question of peace. The great discussion in the IUS between 1956 and 1960 was about the connection between the fight for peace and that for national independence. On the one hand, the tendency of the Soviet Union was to concentrate solely on the fight for peace. On the other, the majority of students in the colonial or newly independent countries felt that the main problem for them was the fight against colonialism, neo-colonialism and imperialism; they were therefore not in favour of this policy of peaceful coexistence. Further contradictions arose on the question of atomic weapons, since the Soviet Union was always trying to impose its tactical policy of the moment on the organization. For example, the IUS urged a campaign for stopping all nuclear tests, and then, just as the Congress of the IUS was taking place in Leningrad, I think it was in 1961 after the Youth Festival, there was a nuclear explosion in the Soviet Union. The Japanese delegation proposed that it should be condemned, in line with IUS policy, and there were very heated discussions on the subject; many delegates were frustrated by the fact that the IUS could condemn US nuclear tests but was not allowed to condemn Soviet ones. We tried to explain to Soviet comrades that this was a mistake, because we were convinced that it was due only to their failure to understand the mentality of students. But, of course, it became increasingly clear that they saw the IUS and similar organizations merely as unofficial instruments of Soviet foreign policy.

A further type of contradiction reflected within the IUS derived from the internal conflicts of the international communist movement – for example, the Sino-Soviet dispute, which had its first impact on the IUS as early as 1957.

What was your own reaction to the eruption of the dispute between China and the Soviet Union? Were you fully convinced by the Soviet case at that time?

First of all we did not realize that it was a real and deep disagreement. We thought of it as mainly due to the difference in mentality of the two parties and two peoples; also to a clash of personalities between Khrushchev and Mao Tse-tung. When Khrushchev visited Mao in Peking in August 1958, I had the opportunity of observing them both, and realized what different personalities they had. I must confess frankly that at that time the majority of us sympathized more with the Soviet point of view that war should be avoided through agreements and negotiations, whereas we felt that the Chinese view at the time was rather crude. The slogan which they proposed at the IUS congress was that we should not be afraid of war. This was not very well understood. Although I can see now that the Chinese side was not able at the time to explain its attitude to this conflict, there was another thing which disturbed us. Everybody was quoting Lenin and Marx, but the Chinese made constant references to Stalin too. In eastern Europe, of course, Stalin was the symbol of all the deformations of socialist society. All in all, we were very distressed by this conflict, but hoped that it would not lead to a real split. But both sides were hiding the real reasons for the dispute, and it was very difficult to realize its true dimensions.

Czechoslovakia was the country in eastern Europe where an unreconstructed Stalinist system seemed to be strongest and to survive longest – up to 1966–7 in fact. How then was it possible for a movement of change and renewal to emerge in the Czech party in 1966–7, a movement which culminated in the Prague Spring of 1968?

This does appear strange on the face of things, but it can be understood if one looks back at the development of Czechoslovakia before and after the war. It was in Czechoslovakia that there were the most favourable conditions for socialism in the whole of eastern Europe; because of the industrialization of the country, because of the developed working class, because of the role and prestige of the Communist party and because of the friendship of the people for the Soviet Union. From this point of view it would seem strange that the greatest purge in any Communist party was that which took place in Czechoslovakia in 1949–54. I think it was precisely because Czechoslovakia had the most favourable conditions that it seemed likely to be the most independent in seeking its own path of development. This did not at all suit the Soviet leadership. They wanted to monopolize eastern Europe, and to impose the Soviet model. For this reason they were obliged to strike hardest against the Czechoslovakian Communist party. Parties like the Polish, Hungarian or Bulgarian were just small groups who had been underground for twenty to thirty years; it was not so difficult for them to accept Soviet hegemony. But in Czechoslovakia, although the party was subjectively willing to accept that hegemony, it was nevertheless seen by the Russians as a potential heretic. Naturally, it appeared paradoxical and shocking to us that the number of the victims of repression should be highest in Czechoslovakia, despite all our democratic traditions. Nothing comparable in scale occurred elsewhere in eastern Europe. Fourteen people were assassinated in the Slánský Trial, several hundred people, as the Piller Report revealed, were condemned to death. In Poland it was possible for Bierut to save Gomulka's life, even though he had been politically disgraced. The same was true for Kadar in Hungary. In the DDR, Bulgaria and Russia, too, the repression was on a lesser scale. In Czechoslovakia there was both the greatest degree of repression and also the deepest crisis as a result of that repression, precisely because of the contradiction between the former favourable conditions for a democratic road to socialism and the complete destruction of the country's democratic tradition. Furthermore, since this political terror created a kind of moral crisis, the Novotny leadership later tried, as far as possible, to avoid any real rehabilitation and hide the truth about the trials.

This was the reason why Stalin's system was maintained for a long time in Czechoslovakia. I would not agree with you that Czechoslovakia was the most Stalinist country up to 1966–7. That was the general impression given in the Western press. But I would say that the crisis in Czechoslovakia goes back to the Twentieth Congress. It is true that it was halted for a time, as a result of the events in Hungary, but it recommenced in 1963, after the report of the so-called Kolder Commission to the Central Committee, when a great part of the truth about the political trials, though not all of it, was revealed. I think the process of liberation began when Novotny, under pressure from various sides, was obliged to make concessions. Pressure was coming from the youth, a section of which had lost all faith in socialism and was creating a lot of problems. There was also a conflict between the party and the intellectuals – writers, film-makers, etc. This did not begin in 1967, but long before. You can see this by looking at Czechoslovak literature and cinema, which had been among the most progressive in eastern Europe since 1964–5 – the so-called Czechoslovakian New Wave. Then there was the conflict between the Czechs and Slovaks – the unsolved national problem. There were the economic difficulties, which led Novotny to accept Šik's proposals for partial economic reform. All these contradictions were already present from 1963 on, and were steadily growing. From time to time Novotny tried to halt the process by administrative measures, but he no longer had the power to do so.

All these contradictions came to a head in autumn 1967 and January 1968, and culminated in this so-called Prague Spring. But this had been prepared for a long time previously. For example, in the ideological sphere, progressive intellectuals had organized themselves into discussion groups which had been working together for several years before 1967. One was the group around Radovan Richta, which was concerned with the scientific-technical revolution. Another group round Zdeněk

Mlynář was preparing reforms of the political system. There were several other groups too, working inside the party for specific reforms.

I think the Novotny regime falls into two distinct phases. In the first, prior to 1965, Novotny directed the repressive role of the party. But after the Twenty-Second Congress of the CPSU, when Stalin was once again condemned by Khrushchev, Novotny realized that it was impossible to stop the movement towards liberalization. Because there was a continuing trend towards de-Stalinization in the Soviet Union, he could not rely on Soviet support for a continuation of the old policies. He therefore, instead, decided to take the opportunity to get rid of the people most directly responsible for the trials – like Siroký, Kohler, Bacílek, Urválek, etc. They were all eliminated from the party leadership, new people were brought in, and Novotny tried to present himself as the leader of the liberal tendency. But, of course, he could not succeed, since he could not wipe out his own responsibility for the political trials.

What role did the crisis in the Czechoslovak economy play in this whole development?

Certainly it played a role but I do not think it was a decisive one. Economic difficulties always have political repercussions, particularly in socialist countries. They expose the inability of the bureaucratic-centralist system to develop production and increase the standard of living of the masses, thus creating dissatisfaction both in the leading circles and among the population in general. Since the party leadership wants to score economic successes to maintain its political monopoly, it accepts some proposals for economic reform which it hopes will boost production and improve its competitive position *vis-à-vis* the capitalist economies. In this way Novotny endorsed the proposals for economic reform, but it was to the credit of Ota Šik and other Czechoslovak economists that they clearly linked political with economic reform.

It is interesting to note that popular dissatisfaction with the economic situation in Czechoslovakia was greater in the recent period when living standards were much higher, than in the period immediately after the war when the masses believed that austerity was in the service of revolutionary ideas and socialist construction. Dissatisfaction among the people always starts in the period when the original socialist ideas have been discredited by Stalinist deformations and when the leadership has sought to replace political motivation by the slogan of competing with and overtaking the capitalist countries – which, of course, they are unable to do. By replacing revolutionary ideals with the promises of a consumer society, the bureaucrats only create trouble for themselves. On the other hand, it should be stated that an economic crisis itself is not sufficient to bring about a change in the situation since bureaucratic regimes have reserves with which to prevent an explosion caused by purely economic factors.

Perhaps we could turn now to the Prague Spring itself. What do you think of the criticism that has sometimes been made by Marxist analysts, that the Prague Spring involved liberalization – economic reforms, certain individual rights – rather than democratization, in the sense of real control by the workers over the decisive institutions of the state, genuine workers' power in the factory and in political life as a whole?

Yes, I am aware of this line of criticism, but I do not think that it corresponds exactly to the reality of what took place. I would say that the Czechoslovak 'new course' in the spring of 1968 was, in fact, directed more to democratization than to liberalization. The opposition was united in the fight against Novotny, because all agreed that there should be a division of functions between the First Secretary of the party and the president, that Novotny was unable to solve the real problems of the country and should be replaced. But part of this anti-Novotny opposition, of course, merely wanted changes in personnel and improvements in the party's methods of work. This group would include people like Indra, Piller, Bilak and so on, and it had a majority in the Central Committee. But there was a minority, which would include Smrkovsky, Kriegel, Šik, Špacek, etc, who soon became aware that merely to replace Novotny by somebody else was not enough, and that real structural changes were necessary in order to come back to the sources, to renew socialism as a power of the people, to renew the dialogue between the party and the masses, to change the role of the party from administrative to inspirational hegemony. This group did not have a clear programme, because it was effectively impossible under Novotny for those in opposition to meet or discuss. Thus the whole development of the Prague Spring began almost spontaneously, after the palace revolution which overthrew Novotny, and it soon led to a permanent conflict between these two groups. The working class, initially, was rather passive as a consequence of the de-politicization which it had undergone since 1948. The same was true of the peasants, who had never had any political representation in the system. The groups which reacted most quickly were the intellectuals, who had been prepared by their conflicts with Novotny in the previous years; the youth, in particular, the students, and to some extent the Slovaks. The working class on the whole adopted a wait-and-see attitude. They were not sure whether what had happened might not be some new trick. Moreover, they were also influenced by some of the older workers who said that the economy would collapse. They would have to work longer hours for the same pay, prices would rise and there might even be some unemployment. However, this initial passivity, or suspicion, on the part of the working class subsequently changed, when the workers had more information. I must stress that the demand for freedom of expression, particularly in eastern Europe, is not at all just an intellectual's demand as some people, even some people on the left, suppose – it is the basic condition for the workers and peasants to take part in politics. For example, the Czech workers were told that the Factory Legislation was for them, but they did not even know the financial balance sheet of their factories. They did not know if their factories were working with a surplus or a deficit, or what was planned for them. They had no information at all, even less than in a capitalist country. The explosion of information which followed the abolition of censorship set the working class in motion. This process accelerated after the adoption of the Action Programme of the party. This laid the basis for the workers' councils, though not very clearly, by initiating discussion on the forms in which the working class can really exercise power. This of course was a new problem for Czechoslovakia. There were only a few people who had studied the Yugoslav, Polish or Hungarian experience (nothing was published about them in Czechoslovakia) or who had read left literature from the West.

At all events, the discussion began and developed during May, June and July, with the creation of 'committees of initiative' which were to establish the workers' councils. The workers, for the first time for many years, found that their own speakers were able to appear on radio and television and write articles for the press. They saw that they were able to ask questions and obtain basic information. It was then possible for them to discuss the forms of the participation both through the workers' councils and through independent trade unions, through representation in the national committees, etc. In short, I think that there was a clear tendency towards democratization. I say 'tendency' because the Prague Spring was only the beginning. We can only see a tendency, we cannot say that it was definitely this or that. Do not forget the external pressure which started immediately after February. This was mainly directed not against intellectuals talking here and there, but against all measures which weakened the bureaucracy of the party and the state. The Russians were most upset by any talk about workers' self-management or workers' councils, of replacing state ownership by collective ownership, etc. On the latter question they said there was no difference; once the working class held state power, state ownership was the most socialist form of ownership in the means of production.

If there had been no Soviet intervention, I am convinced that it would sooner or later have come to a conflict within the Czechoslovakian 'new course'. For there were those who were for real, all-out democratization, and there were also those who were for certain concessions, certain measures of liberalization, but who wanted to maintain the existing structure. The latter were, of course, very much encouraged by the Soviet pressure. They said: 'we cannot do much more, because otherwise the Soviet Union will occupy us'. That was always the argument of those who were against full democratization. But I think the masses had been mobilized to such an extent, had become so active, that the tendency for a thorough-going reorganization would have won.

But what about the possibility that the economic policies would have led to the appearance of unemployment, as in Yugoslavia? Do you think then that a working-class opposition would have emerged within the party and ensured that this unemployment was abolished?

In that case, yes, but this argument about unemployment was, in fact, used a lot by the opponents of decentralization, that is to say by those in the economic apparatus of the party and the state. Of course, it may well be that certain factories or even certain branches of industry would have been closed because they were not economically viable. But I think that it would have been possible, in the framework of the socialist economy, to find alternative jobs for the workers. Of course, it is true that local sentiment is always strong. We had one case, for example, where they were proposing to shut down a small factory and said that the workers would all be given jobs in another one. But the latter was five kilometres away and the workers resisted, saying that they wanted to go on working in their own factory, even though it was a hundred years old and the machines were obsolete. Such minor social conflicts were inevitable. But I think that if the party had been able to draw up a real comprehensive plan for the country's future economic development, a plan altering the whole structure of the economy, which had simply been following the Soviet model, concentrating on heavy industry and neglecting branches such as chemicals, for which there were excellent conditions in Czechoslovakia, then it would have been possible to win over the mass of the workers to the new course. If the party had been able to transform the economy, something which clearly could not be done overnight but would take time, I think the people would have accepted certain temporary sacrifices; that is, if they had been convinced that this would be to their advantage in the long term. I think this was possible.

Perhaps there is a difference here between the Czechoslovakian and Yugoslav working classes. For if you look at the statistics published in 1968 about what the workers expected from the councils, there was no immediate demand for them to concentrate on raising wages. The workers said the councils should act to improve the management of the economy and make it more efficient; they should improve conditions of work, they should select really competent people to direct the factories, and they should also give more thought to planning. Nobody said 'now we can take all the money we have produced, and distribute it among ourselves'. One cannot eliminate that danger completely, but I think that in Czechoslovakia the people would have been able to solve this problem.

How about the tendency of a decentralized system to increase economic inequality? Do you think that would have happened in Czechoslovakia?

Yes, I think it would have happened and it was already happening even before 1968, as a reaction against the egalitarian system introduced in 1955. Under the latter, everybody in Czechoslovakia was within a narrow range of salaries. This means that there were no material rewards for responsible jobs, whether for intellectual work or for important posts in the factories. From the ideological point of view, you may say that this was progress. But in the transitional period of development of a socialist society, I think it is necessary to use both moral and material incentives. Precisely because a socialist society should favour technical and scientific development more than capitalist society does, its technical and scientific personnel should be paid accordingly. Of course even in this period, inequalities did exist, in the sense that even if people had identical salaries, some of them, party leaders for instance, had many other facilities.

Certainly Czechoslovakia in 1962 did not give an impression of great equality – quite the opposite. High party officials had cars, large flats, a very comfortable existence in general at a time when this was not true of the mass of Czech workers. There were even special shops where party officials could buy foreign produce and other goods not generally available. This was not equality, was it?

I was coming to that. I was speaking before about the great majority of the population, and I think there was equality among them. For example, if you walked through Prague on Sunday, it was difficult to perceive who was a university professor, who was an engineer and who was a worker. All were roughly on the same level. But, of course, the exception were the party leaders. The party bureaucracy had a lot of special privileges. They had been far more numerous in the fifties; by 1962 they were already diminishing, but they still certainly existed. For example there was a famous story about what happened in 1968, when the Party Treasurer was dismissed from the Central Committee and as a sort of defence he sent a letter to the Central Committee meeting (the letter has never been published, I might add) in which he enumerated how much money the various members of the leadership had received over and above their official salaries. The leaders named were obliged to pay into the party coffers all the party contributions which they had neglected to pay over the years on their earnings. In some cases this came to enormous sums of money. Even so, these privileges were far smaller in Czechoslovakia than in the Soviet Union or some other communist countries.

But I was mainly speaking before about the majority of the population, and I think it is true perhaps that we were tending in 1968 towards a greater differentiation of salaries among workers, and also among the intellectuals and the peasants. This differentiation was tied to the real contribution they made to the national economy, or to the productivity of their work. In general, it meant greater rewards for the intelligentsia who had been under-valued and underpaid. I do not think this would lead to any very great contradictions, and I do not think that we could apply the same system in Czechoslovakia as in China, with everybody having basically the same salary. I do not think this could be viable in a modern European socialist society. What do you think?

The equality of 'to each according to his needs' is surely the goal of socialism, isn't it?

Yes, it is the goal.

We could come very close to that goal in advanced industrial economies today.

What do you mean by advanced? In Czechoslovakia, which was the most advanced industrial country in the socialist bloc, in fact there was, and is, a terrible shortage of the most basic goods. It is necessary to queue for hours in the shops to get veal or whatever else happens to be in short supply. There is no poverty, of course, but you still cannot apply the formula 'to each according to his needs' until there is an abundance of goods.

Surely it is not just a question of shortages, it is also a question of a bureaucratic system of administration, which is not responsible to the workers and which must repress their initiative if it is to defend its monopoly of decision-making. Very often, large quantities of things are produced that nobody wants to consume. There is a sort of bureaucratic over-production of goods that can't be sold.

That is not by chance. This is a necessary result of a centralized planning system which imposes the plan of production from a

single centre without taking into consideration the real needs
of the country. There I would like to take up another left criticism
of the Prague Spring. I am referring to the view that Šik's economic reforms were designed to introduce a market economy in
Czechoslovakia. This is a misunderstanding of the real aim of the
reform. It was to combine the system of centralized state planning
with responsiveness to certain pressures of the market; but
market in the sense of socialist market, i.e. what the people
really need. The aim is precisely to prevent the production of
goods which are not needed and cannot be sold, and to ensure
that goods which are needed are on the market.

*The goal of revolutionary Marxists in a transitional society must
be to rediscover the appropriate contemporary form of workers'
power, corresponding to the Soviets in Russia during and after 1917.
Do you think that this could have been one possible line of development of the Prague Spring, or was the latter merely an attempt to
put a human face on bureaucratic socialism?*

I think we have already discussed the question of whether the
Prague Spring involved liberalization or democratization, and I
said that its momentum was towards democratization. The
expression 'socialism with a human face' was coined to make
clear that the aim was to build a socialist society different from
that which had been constructed in the Soviet Union and the
other socialist countries. But it is true that there was a real
difficulty in using basic Marxist concepts which had lost their
original meaning entirely for most people. For example, 'Soviet
Power' had no meaning beyond that of the Soviet Union; a
great power, symbol of 'order', with a specific economic, social
and political system which was considered by some communists as a model.

*Obviously, in the Soviet Union itself, Soviet power has not existed
for a very long time, has it? Since before Stalin even.*

Yes, it only lasted for a short period after the revolution. The
usual explanation is that this was due to foreign intervention and
civil war. It is true, of course, that these played their roles. But
the real tragedy in the Soviet Union was that certain measures
which were probably necessary as provisional measures for a
certain period were then taken as real socialist ones. I am referring

above all to the limitation of opposition inside the party – the ban on factions and discussion, which put the party on a semi-military footing appropriate only to a war situation.

Perhaps we could turn now to the question of foreign policy during the Prague Spring. Many people on the left were concerned about this and felt that Czech foreign policy was tending towards increased rapprochement with the West and decreased emphasis on the anti-imperialist struggle. But was there at the same time any fundamental discussion on what a socialist foreign policy should be? After all, one of the things that clearly began to happen during the Prague Spring was that a whole range of problems connected with the nature of Stalinism began to be examined. Many things were published which had previously been banned. Did this discussion of Stalinism go back to the theory of 'socialism in one country' and was there any discussion of foreign policy in terms of a return to proletarian internationalism?

There are two problems here. First on the ideological level, that of discovering the deep roots of Stalinism. There was a lot of discussion about this and many articles were written on the subject. Moreover, we were able to read certain texts which had previously been prohibited; for example, *Literary Listy* translated Isaac Deutscher and even some texts by Trotsky and Bukharin were published and some articles about the Moscow trials. But such things were discouraged by the party leadership, on the grounds that they would create problems with the Soviet Union whereas we should try for the time being to avoid anything which might worsen relations. It should never be forgotten, as left critics sometimes do forget, that the whole development of the Prague Spring took place in the shadow of Russian pressure. Furthermore, Moscow did not merely have the ability to exert economic, military and political pressure, it also had a fifth column inside Czechoslovakia, within the Security forces, army and state apparatus. This constant Russian pressure certainly explains why some things happened more slowly than many people would have liked – but it would hardly have been able to prevent them permanently.

The second problem concerns foreign policy. This was, in fact, the field least affected by the new course of 1968. This may seem paradoxical, since the Russians justified the invasion at the time principally by the approaches which Czechoslovakia was supposedly making to West Germany, the United States, etc. But, in fact, Czechoslovakia in 1968 was in total contrast, for example, to Rumania, where internal policy remains basically Stalinist while there is a certain freedom and initiative in international politics. In Czechoslovakia in 1968 it was the contrary. There was innovation in internal politics, but on the international level there were no particularly new developments and Czechoslovakia declared quite sincerely that it basically supported the policies of the Soviet Union.

Of course, what was new was that international policy was no longer a monopoly of the party and the Ministry of Foreign Affairs. It began to be possible for people to express their own views about it, which they had not previously been allowed to do, and it began to be influenced by public opinion. For example, take the question of relations between Czechoslovakia and Israel. In the Arab countries it was sometimes alleged that Czechoslovakia was moving closer to Israel. This was not true. Czechoslovakia continued its support for the Arab countries and it continued to supply them with armaments. What was new was that certain people, particularly among the intelligentsia, asked why we had this one-sided policy in the Middle East. They said that we should re-examine whether this policy was really progressive; whether these Arab countries were really socialist as we were told, or whether they were not, in fact, nationalist countries; whether it was correct to have broken off diplomatic relations with Israel when we had diplomatic relations with the United States who were waging the war in Vietnam. At that time I was the chairman of the Foreign Affairs Commission of Parliament, and I defended party policy at many meetings on this topic. At the same time I realized that these critics were quite logical in asking why we had not broken off diplomatic relations when the United States had started to bomb North Vietnam. For this was a far more blatant case of imperialist aggression than the situation in the Middle East. Moreover, communists were in prison in several of the Arab countries. As for West Germany, we only asked them to annul the Munich Agreement. Scheel was invited to Prague and I received him in my capacity of Chairman of the Foreign Affairs Commission. The Soviet Union attacked his visit, calling him a 'war-monger', but only one year later the 'war-monger' went on a friendly visit to Moscow.

Czechoslovakia continued its foreign policy on issues like Vietnam. True, not much popular enthusiasm was shown in support of Vietnam or Cuba, but this was because any popular initiative was quickly absorbed or neutralized by the state. Furthermore, if you are allowed to protest against the political repression in Greece or Spain, but not against student arrests in Poland or Czechoslovakia, you become easily demoralized. For example, the students once decided to collect money for Vietnam following a suggestion from the IUS, but the party came out against it. It was said that as the government had already given money to Vietnam, the best way the people could help Vietnam was to increase production. Again, during the Bay of Pigs invasion, the foreign students in Prague took the initiative and called for a demonstration at the American embassy. Many Czech students joined in, but it was stopped by the police in case it created problems with the Americans. In the course of time such expressions of international solidarity lost their attraction. The foreign policy at the popular level was characterized by confusion. For example, during the May Day Parade in 1968, some students were carrying placards saying 'long live Al Fatah' while others shouted 'long live Israel'. For some people, supporting Israel meant opposing the official party policy and that of the Soviet Union. This confusion had its roots in the fact that real problems were never discussed publicly or with the masses. I believe an absence of socialist internationalism is at present a weakness of the revolutionary movement in both western Europe and eastern Europe – there are socialists in the West who have closed their eyes to what is happening in our countries.

To conclude the question of foreign policy, there was no shift in the basic alignment. Some people did feel, however, that it should become more independent, that Czechoslovakia should not only repeat what the Soviet Union said.

Could we move on now to the Soviet military intervention? What, in your view, was the decisive reason for the Russian decision?

I think it was the fear of the Soviet bureaucracy that the Czecho-slovakian experiment would overcome its difficulties and succeed in creating a different kind of socialist society. For this would have exerted a powerful force of attraction on the neighbouring countries of east Europe and threatened Soviet hegemony over them.

I don't think the Russians really believed for a moment that Czechoslovakia was threatened by invasion from West Germany.

Nor do I think that they really believed there was any danger of counter-revolution. They knew the situation, and they knew that right-wing forces were much too weak to take to the streets in Czechoslovakia. Moreover, there was no intervention when the Czech party was genuinely under pressure in March and April. At this time, the party had lost the initiative. There was great pressure from below, but the party had no programme, until the Action Programme was published at the end of April. The 'Progressive Group' had not yet been formed. There was an explosion of information and almost complete freedom of expression; the Communist party was under fire and on the defensive. In this situation, the Russians did not intervene to prevent counter-revolution. With the publication of the Action Programme and the adoption of measures showing that it really meant to carry this programme out – I am thinking of the law on rehabilitation, the plan for the establishment of factory councils, the new party statutes, etc. – the party won back the initiative. Thanks to the external pressure, it even became a real national force supported by the majority of the people. When the decision was taken in June to call a Party Congress, it was already clear that the Congress would consolidate the position of the Dubček leadership. There was no danger of any split in the party itself, because the conservative group was quite small and isolated. It was clear that the Congress would give the party even more strength to carry out its policy. I think it was precisely this that the Russians feared. They saw that the new Central Committee, with its new statutes, would be much more difficult to control than the old one – which was after all still unchanged from Novotny's time. I think a definite date for the invasion was decided when the Russians realized that the date of the Congress could not be changed. At the Cierna meeting between the two Politburos at the beginning of August, the main pressure from Brezhnev was to postpone the Congress, which was already convened for 9 September 1968, and to put through certain changes of personnel before the Congress took place. It should be stressed that the Czechoslovak party did not seek to present its new course as a model for other countries. On the contrary. Some intellectuals went on about the eyes of the world being on Czechoslovakia, but the party was concerned to dispel any idea that it was setting itself up as a model. But the Soviet Union was well aware that if the Czech experiment was allowed to succeed, it would inevitably have repercussions in the other socialist countries. It was not accidental that Gomulka, Ulbricht and Shelest, the First Secretary of the Ukranian Communist Party, i.e. the leaders of three countries bordering on Czechoslovakia, should have been the most enthusiastic proponents of intervention.

Who else was pressing for it in the Soviet Union? Do you think the army command was enthusiastic about it?

That is difficult to say, I think it was seen more as a political than as a military necessity. But the army was certainly in favour of the invasion. Soviet officers with whom we talked after the intervention claimed that Stalin's greatest mistake, after his failure to prevent the German attack in 1941, was his failure to incorporate the east European countries as constituent republics of the Soviet Union in 1945.

But quite apart from whatever the Russian military may think, the Soviet leadership certainly sees the presence of the Red army as the only real guarantee of their political control over the other socialist countries. Czechoslovakia was one of the few countries with no Soviet troops on its territory. Novotny himself has said that he was asked several times to accept Soviet military bases, but that he had always refused. The Prague Spring provided a pretext to put Soviet troops into Czechoslovakia and I am convinced they will try to do the same in Yugoslavia and Rumania, if they have the chance. The party bureaucracy really does consider the army as the best means of controlling the eastern European countries; and as long as there were no Soviet troops in Czechoslovakia they were uneasy.

Incidentally, it is interesting to learn from the Piller Report that this issue had arisen as early as 1949, when Rákósi and Bierut wrote to Stalin and to Gottwald expressing their concern about developments in Czechoslovakia. They pointed out that the Czechs had so far failed to discover any agents of imperialism in the party and they claimed that Czechoslovakia was the weakest link since there were no units of the Soviet army on Czech soil.

Could you tell us something about the discussions which were taking place inside the Czech party before the invasion? About the possibility of invasion, about the appropriate response to the invasion threat, and about what could be done to make it less likely?

In fact I think there were very few people in responsible positions in the party who really considered the possibility of Soviet military intervention. First of all I think it was probably a mistake for Dubček to hide the true extent of Soviet pressure from the masses. It meant that nobody was aware of how great the pressure was. Of course, there were rumours, there were reports of articles hostile to the Czech development, but the daily pressure which was exerted by the Soviet leadership on Dubček and the other leaders was not known even to the party activists.

What was your own estimate of Soviet reaction to the developments in Czechoslovakia?

I knew something of the way they were thinking, but only through my personal contacts in the Soviet Union. My case was not typical and the position of the Soviet Union was not discussed within the Central Committee in a realistic way. At the Dresden meeting in March 1968 the first strongly critical reaction to the Czechoslovakian development was expressed by the other members of the Warsaw Pact. The Western press published some articles about this. Those responsible for radio, television and the press were convened to meet Dubček on his return from this meeting. He told us that economic relations and plans for development and co-operation were discussed, but he did not mention Soviet pressure. I asked Dubček whether the Western newspaper reports were correct in saying that Czechoslovakia had been criticized at Dresden. He replied that they were not. Later, after the invasion, Dubček was criticized by other members of the Czech delegation at Dresden who said that he had hidden from us the criticism by Ulbricht, Gomulka and the others. Dubček then replied that it was true that he had concealed this from us, but that to do so had been the unanimous agreement of the Czech delegation. Novotny was still in the Praesidium and they did not want to encourage the forces he represented; furthermore it was Dubček's sincere opinion during this whole period that to reveal the extent of Soviet pressure would create anti-Soviet feeling, and this he wished to avoid. He did his best to stop rumours about the Soviet position circulating, for this reason. Even in those party circles which were somewhat more aware of the real situation, there was no thought of a military intervention, but rather of some economic pressure or blockade. Dubček himself, and many other people including myself, were convinced that since Stalin had not dared to occupy Yugoslavia, then Brezhnev would not imagine he could do this to Czechoslovakia. After all Stalin at that time was militarily very strong and enjoyed much greater prestige in the international communist movement than the present Soviet leaders. We thought that after the Twentieth Party Congress and after what happened in Hungary, a crudely military intervention was no longer possible. Dubček personally was convinced that the Soviet Union would exert all kinds of pressure, but would not go this far. However, there were people like General Prchlik, who was head of the Department for Defence and Security, who wished to submit to the leadership a paper outlining the alternatives in case of a Soviet invasion. The army and the security forces had discovered that the objective of the Soviet army manoeuvres in Czechoslovakia in June and July had been to put itself in a position where it could control our communications systems. They had made maps of how this system worked, they had laid cables underground and they had established the location of all telephone and postal facilities, including those only used by state organizations. This was known to the security forces, though since some of the security officers were Soviet agents there were conflicting reports. Moreover, the existence of General Prchlik's suggestion for a contingency plan was passed on to the Soviet embassy through these people. This led to an immediate Soviet reaction. They asked how it was possible for a man capable of such a provocation to be head of the armed forces and a member of the Central Committee. There was an official diplomatic note from the Soviet Union directed against Prchlik, taking as a pretext the fact that he had called at a press conference for some reforms in the Warsaw Pact – very minor reforms which were later, in 1970, to be adopted. Dubček decided to sacrifice Prchlik and dismissed him from his post. I think this was a decisive moment. From this point on the Soviet Union knew that Czechoslovakia would not attempt to defend itself in the case of a military intervention. Prchlik was sacrificed as a symbol of our full confidence in the Soviet Union.

The question will be debated for many years whether any course of action could have been taken to avert the Soviet intervention. Some people in the party argued that it could have been avoided if Czechoslovakia had behaved in a more compliant manner. I do not believe this. The experience of Yugoslavia and Rumania shows that the only possibility of deterring the Soviet Union would have been to tell the Soviet leaders clearly that although we were willing to continue any discussions and wished to remain a loyal member of the Warsaw Pact, yet in the case of any attempt at a military solution, Czechoslovakia would defend herself and would mobilize the people and army. The failure to do this was to some extent an expression of the absence of a clear attitude towards democratization which we have already discussed. Our leaders hesitated to mobilize the masses and to give a clear lead to the country, to distribute arms to the people and declare that we would not be moved by threats. I personally am convinced that if such a line of action had been taken by Dubček, the Soviet Union would not have dared to launch the invasion. They would, of course, have continued to exert other types of pressure, but they would not have gone further than that. Some people said that any talk of resistance would simply goad the Soviet Union to extreme action and that Moscow was ready to destroy Prague. But if the Soviet representatives made threats of this sort, then it was just the application of psychological pressure. After all they did not want to create a Vietnam for themselves – it is not so easy for them to envisage massacring thousands of people in central Europe. The course of action adopted by the Czechoslovak leaders was incapable of opposing the invasion. It showed a serious lack of revolutionary spirit.

What was the situation when the invasion took place? Presumably as soon as it happened it was necessary to decide how to react? At what level was that decision taken and what forms of resistance were discussed inside the party?

We learnt of the invasion only after it had happened, at 11.20 p.m. on 21 August, while a meeting of the Praesidium was still in progress. We know today that certain members of the Praesidium were aware of what was about to happen – Bilak, Indra and some others. It seems that there may have been some misunderstanding between them and the Soviet Union. The pro-Soviet elements in the leadership had hoped to impose a resolution on the Praesidium declaring that there was a danger of counter-revolution and that the Party Congress, which was imminent and would have consolidated the Dubček leadership, would have to be postponed. However, this resolution had not been voted on at the time of the invasion. Some people say that the plan was not properly co-ordinated because while it was one o'clock in Moscow it was eleven o'clock in Prague. However, whether or not this played a part, the Praesidium, on learning of the invasion, adopted a resolution condemning it and making it clear that no intervention had been invited. The Praesidium asked the army not to resist and made arrangements for convening a meeting of the Central Committee next day.

Was the possibility of armed resistance discussed in the Praesidium?

No, not at all. The discussion turned on whether the invasion should be condemned. In fact the biggest discussion was about an amendment to the effect that the invasion was a violation of international law and of the norms governing the relations between socialist states. I think it is an illustration of the weakness of this leadership that they condemned the invasion, but without making any appeal to the people or letting them know what they should do. I was in the Central Committee building that night. They were saying that all was lost, the airport had been taken, tanks were moving forward everywhere and units from the airport were already beginning to surround the Central Committee building. The possibility of armed resistance had already been lost, though there were some in the army who were thinking that they should fight and some generals were removed from their posts because of this. But nothing could be done. When the president, who was chief of the armed forces, had given the order to put up no resistance, then the officers had to accept it. The time for contemplating armed resistance was earlier. What was now possible was to confront the occupiers with a political resistance which they could not ignore and to deny them any political solution on their terms. This was the time for the party leadership to mobilize the masses, to convene the Party Congress and to study other forms of action such as a general strike. Instead the leaders merely declared that they were against the occupation and did nothing but wait in the Central Committee building to be captured by the Soviet army. Until six or seven o'clock in the morning they had the opportunity to leave the building by a secret exit of which the Soviet units were unaware. We wanted Dubček to leave, to go to the CKD factory in Prague 9 and to organize political action from there. But Dubček thought that as they were the leaders of the party and the country they should stay at their posts and do their duty like the captain staying on the bridge of a sinking ship. Dubček is a very honest man and he thought he should sacrifice himself for others. But he was thinking legalistically; a revolutionary leader would have acted in a quite different way, he would have gone to the factories and mobilized the workers. This was proved by what happened. On the initiative of the City Committee of the party in Prague the scheduled Congress of the party was convened for an extraordinary meeting. All the delegates for this Congress had, of course, been elected prior to the invasion. The Congress was held on the 23rd in a proletarian district of Prague and there was nothing the occupying forces could do about it. The Russians did not want to send armoured cars into that district to shoot the workers. But although the convening of the Congress was to be a great success, there was still no clear decision on the resistance. Over one thousand two hundred delegates attended the Congress, which the occupation forces did not at all expect. At the Congress there was a long discussion as to whether to declare a general strike or only a one-hour strike. It is very interesting that many were afraid of declaring a general strike on the grounds that it was the workers' ultimate weapon and should not be lightly used. In the event the Congress decided to call for a one-hour general strike. It was observed throughout the country and was a full success, but of course it could not have the same effect as a proper general strike. On the other hand, the Soviet army did find itself in a political vacuum.

Their attempt to create a so-called workers' and peasants' government with a collaborator at its head did not succeed because of the universal opposition of the masses and because the Congress had made clear that the party was overwhelmingly against the invasion. At this point no potential collaborator had the courage to take on his shoulders the odious task of abetting the occupation. When the Soviet authorities realized that they had failed to secure the basis for a collaboration regime, they invited President Svoboda to go to Moscow. When news of this plan came through we were at the Congress in Prague 9. We tried to convince Svoboda from the Congress not to go to Moscow. He was still in his official residence in Prague Castle, and we spoke to him by phone. It was clear to us that the Soviet plan was in difficulties since they had no one through whom they could control the country politically. By this time Dubček and other top party leaders had been kidnapped and taken by plane to the Ukraine, where they were held at a military airport. If the occupying powers had succeeded in establishing the so-called 'revolutionary' government, then Dubček and the others would have all been shot as counter-revolutionaries. But since they failed, the Soviet leaders were forced to bring them to Moscow after about five days. They needed to negotiate with someone and they needed to find some leadership which would accept the occupation. The solidity of the resistance in Czechoslovakia itself meant that they were forced to bargain with these people whom they had intended to destroy. We tried unsuccessfully to persuade Svoboda not to go to Moscow, pointing out to him that it was not us who were in difficulties but rather the occupying forces. The Soviet Union was being condemned by the whole world, especially by various sections of the Communist and workers' movement itself. Although they had invaded Czechoslovakia, they had no control over it. The occupying armies were in a mess; they had shortages of essential supplies, including food. The ordinary Soviet soldier was very confused and demoralized. Everywhere our people were asking them why they were invading a brother socialist country and the Russian soldiers did not know what to answer. There were a number of suicides of Soviet soldiers at this time. A very impressive mass response to the occupation had developed. But although party militants were very active in this, it was difficult for us to draw the full political advantage from it. The leaders in whom the masses had confidence were cut off from them and could not be fully aware of what was happening in Czechoslovakia. If Dubček had been with us in the CKD factory at the Congress and if there had been a full general strike, then the situation would have been very different. I don't say that the Soviet forces would have immediately withdrawn, but the relationship of forces would have been very different. Of course all these problems belong to the past, but they are also problems of general revolutionary strategy. Similar situations will arise in the future. The lesson of Czechoslovakia is that nothing can really be achieved without the action of the masses.

There was, of course, an explosion of popular resistance in the days following the invasion. To what extent did the party organize this?

Those who were most active in organizing the resistance were party members but, in fact, we had no instructions to do what we did. For example, we very quickly developed a series of underground radio stations and newspapers. These were able to report the real progress of the occupation and the difficulties the occupying authorities were running into, to report the world-wide reaction to what happened and to give orientation to our people. But this was all organized on their own account by those who worked in radio, television and the other media. For they found they could enlist the support of citizens in every quarter, in the army and in the state organizations. Of course there were some agents of the occupying power, mainly members of the old security forces, but we were quickly able to neutralize their activities. The numbers of the cars they were using were broadcast over the radio and they found it very difficult to operate. Editors were arranging things for themselves and making sure that they could continue to produce their papers. The fact that the Party Congress came out so clearly against the invasion and accepted responsibility for opposing it gave it great moral strength and popular support. The occupying forces had an enormous concentration of military firepower, but so long as we maintained a solid front against them they had no political presence in the situation. It is true that they could kill a lot of people, but this did not give them the control of the situation they wanted. At the same time I believe that the resistance could have become much better co-ordinated and the force that existed could have been organized. But instead this phase of popular resistance was brought to an end by the Protocol signed in Moscow between our leaders and the Soviet leaders. For the Czechoslovak Communist party this was the beginning of the end. The people had been ready for resistance, they were ready to oppose the occupation by all forms.

The leaders of the party in Moscow were cut off from this development. But even if they thought we were defeated, it would have been better not to sign this Protocol. It would have been better to remain as symbols of a new *cause*, which could arise again when circumstances permitted, than to sign this political death-warrant. From this point Dubček and the others who signed were being used by the Soviet Union to keep people quiet and to help them get control of the situation again. Of course they were under intolerable pressure, but the course they adopted was to lead to their own destruction just as surely. At that time the Russians needed them because the people still had confidence in them. All those who were suspected of having collaborated with the invasion were completely discredited. The Moscow Protocol gave time for a thoroughly collaborationist element to establish itself under the protection of Dubček and soon to displace him. Initially, Dubček's prestige was so great that nearly everyone was prepared to go along with what had been done. On 31 August, the day after his return from Moscow, a meeting of the Central Committee was called. This was the old Central Committee but enlarged by the presence of eighty of the delegates to the Party Congress. Under the terms of the Moscow agreement the Party Congress was held to have been illegal. By enlarging the old Central Committee, Dubček tried to get round this by some compromise. At this meeting only one representative spoke out against the Moscow agreement, Sabata. Others may have doubted the wisdom of signing the Protocol, but they still had confidence in Dubček. After all, he wanted the best for our people and they felt they should not complicate his task. So when this young man from Moravia said we must destroy the Moscow agreement, they did not allow discussion of this. We may conclude that there were three mistakes made in the course of this whole development. The first mistake was that the leadership did not mobilize against the possibility of an invasion before it took place, and make it clear to the Soviet Union that it would not just be a walkover. The second was that they waited in the Central Committee instead of going to the factories and organizing resistance. The third was that they signed the Moscow agreement.

What has happened to the Communist party now, more than three years later, and what role will it play in the future?

Well, I would say that the whole process of normalization has made it into a quite different party now. Half a million of the most active members have been expelled or have left. There has been a return of the old Stalinist structure and methods of administration. It is not by chance that they are again glorifying Gottwald, who let his own friends be arrested and executed by Stalin. The Czechoslovak party is now really a branch of the Soviet party. Of course there were always remnants of Stalinism in our party. It cannot be said that this current development has just dropped from the heavens. In 1968 there were the elements for a split in the party. But at that time the new majority wanted to introduce a new statute whereby the minority could maintain its position and fight for it. The Stalinists were in a minority, but we didn't want to expel them; we wanted them to fight for their ideas, but with arguments.

What implications do you think this transformation of the party has for the future?

It means, and I think this applies elsewhere as well as in Czechoslovakia, that basic changes will not come from inside the party. Since the defeat of the Prague Spring the development of the party is such that a socialist renewal could not come from inside this new Stalinist party. This does not mean that all who are in it are completely lost, but those who would like things to change are in a minority and they are passive. In my opinion the renewal of socialism must come from groups who are outside the Communist party. Throughout eastern Europe the Communist parties are too closely tied to the established order, they have too rigid a structure, the power of the bureaucracy within them is too great to allow a real renewal from the inside. The Soviet Union has learnt the lesson of Czechoslovakia and will be more vigilant than before. I think the tactics of the struggle against the bureaucracy must be as follows. There must be pressure from the masses, expressed by groups outside the party, even from revolutionary groups which are in a small minority, young people, students and so forth. The party bureaucracy must be obliged to make certain concessions. But it must be made clear that these concessions are not the ultimate aim of the struggle. These concessions must be ones which assist further struggle. No time must be given to the bureaucracy to consolidate itself. The bureaucracy must be forced to further concessions by mobilizing the people for certain generally accepted goals, which then oblige the bureaucracy to retreat further. Of course, at the same time we should try to find allies within the party, within the trade unions and other official organizations. An opposition always develops inside the bureaucracy since it is not capable of solving the problems that confront it. Even when it knows how such a problem can be solved, it cannot implement its solution because it does not have the support of the masses on whom all solutions depend. Generally these parties are very isolated from the masses. This means we should try to combine pressure from the masses outside the party with encouragement of the opposition within it. The most important task we face is of bringing about in this process an alliance between the working class and the intelligentsia. In Czechoslovakia we discovered the importance of developing a programme which corresponds to the interests of the working class. In Poland, on the other hand, recent events have shown the power the workers have to shake the bureaucracy – but in the absence of any programme formulated by the intelligentsia, there were no political demands. The immediate demands, concerning prices and so on, were met, but no basic change occured in the political system. Whenever the working class and the intelligentsia are isolated from one another it is always a bad thing.

What then is your estimate of the significance of liberalizing trends within the governing bureaucracy?

The goal of revolutionary socialists and the goal of the liberalizers are quite different. But that does not mean that the path to an anti-bureaucratic revolution may not lie through some sort of period of liberalization in these countries. Such a liberalization at least allows the workers, the young people and the intellectuals the chance to organize themselves. In such a period they can find themselves; they can work out and express their aims before the confrontation. Otherwise there is a danger that a spontaneous explosion – for example between workers and police – will lead to bloodshed, but not to any political change. In fact such an explosion could even be used by reactionary and counter-revolutionary forces. This is a complicated problem because the political consciousness of the masses has been very much weakened and confused by the bureaucratic regimes. I think the people have first of all to clarify their ideas in a freer climate if they are to carry through a real revolution inside the revolution.

So you do not believe in the notion that the collapse of the bureaucratic regimes will be brought about by their economic difficulties?

First of all, I do not belong to the school of those who think the worse things get, the better is the chance for change. The economic difficulties will last for a long time, since the present bureaucratic-centralist system is not able to go to the root of these problems. This will produce a sort of permanent tension, which will sometimes explode in open clashes, as it did in Poland in December 1970. But without a political programme and political struggle, this cannot lead to a real ending of the present bureaucratic regimes. It will oblige them to make certain concessions, which is positive, but we should have no illusions about the partial and transient character of these.

How do you conceive the revolution needed in Czechoslovakia and similar countries?

I think the countries that call themselves socialist are, in fact, some transitional form of society – it is a sort of state socialism dominated by a bureaucracy which is not controlled by the workers. The path of revolution in these countries will be different from its course in a capitalist country. In some ways the position of the ruling stratum is weaker since it is not built into the structure of production; the bourgeoisie has been eliminated and basic industry has already been nationalized. The problem is to defeat the bureaucracy and to destroy the bureaucratic structures. I would call this a revolution inside the revolution. The bureaucracy is not a real social class and is not built into social relations like a bourgeoisie in a capitalist society. It constitutes a privileged elite which makes up for its social weakness by a concentration of political strength. It has international links with its counterparts elsewhere. It cannot be defeated except by a real revolutionary movement – this means by the masses and is quite different from any attempt to make the bureaucratic system itself more acceptable and human. Since the events of December 1970 such a process has been under way in Poland and we can see that it does not constitute a real movement towards socialism. I do not know exactly whether the Cultural revolution in China was a genuine mass movement, but I do not expect a development like that in eastern Europe. I do not think any top leader will appeal to the masses here to challenge the bureaucracy. The movement for renewal must come from below. Moreover I do not believe that it would be successful if it was confined to just one country in eastern Europe. Both Czechoslovakia in 1968 and Hungary in 1956 show that wherever any movement starts in an isolated way, on only a national scale, it can be suppressed by the Soviet army. I think this is an urgent reason for a practical form of internationalism between the peoples of eastern Europe, since a movement in two or three countries at the same time would be in a much stronger position *vis-à-vis* the Soviet Union. Tension between the Soviet Union and China could also help to weaken the Soviet leadership in the face of movements in eastern Europe.

As to how we will organize for this new revolution, we have been asking ourselves recently whether the future belongs to the system of political parties or not. The result of the analysis made by my friends in Czechoslovakia is that the old conception of the revolutionary party is not appropriate any longer to our situation. Lenin's theory of the party played a certain historical role, but we think that for us a much more suitable form of organization would be the movement. This would have a common ideological platform but not the rigid structure of the party. I am sure that the moving force in the renewal of socialism in our countries will be really democratic mass organizations; trade unions, workers' councils, local soviets and other forms of direct democracy.

Surely there is no contradiction between, on the one hand, workers' councils and soviets, as the form of organization of the revolutionary state, and, on the other, revolutionary parties which act as a force within these institutions? In the West we have had experience of amorphous, de-centralized movements and they usually turn out to be both undemocratic and ineffective. In the context of a soviet or workers' council, political parties could ensure the clarification of different policies and platforms: they would mean that such bodies could follow policies rather than personalities. In this sense political parties are surely complementary to institutions of popular power?

Well, I think a movement could develop political platforms in the same way. You know it is only a question of what we understand by the traditional political party. I agree with you that there is no contradiction between democratically organized parties and soviets or workers' councils. But I had in mind first of all the existing socialist countries and the existing Communist parties which monopolize all politics in a Stalinist fashion. I know that in Czechoslovakia the people will never willingly accept this system. All these parties are organized in more or less the same way and all of them impose themselves as the leading force in all state institutions and mass organizations. A democratically organized party would operate in a quite different way and could not assume that it would automatically be the leading force in society; if it wanted this position it would have to win it by gaining the confidence of the people. You have got to remember that revolutionaries in our countries are not confronted with a capitalist social structure. In our society there are no basic contradictions between social classes. This means that if we have several parties and movements they would not correspond to different class viewpoints; they would all operate within the framework of socialism, but they would have different conceptions of how socialism should be built. At the same time they should not be so rigidly organized as the traditional Communist parties. Of course these are just my own ideas and I believe we need much more discussion of such questions. At the present moment the opposition is not organized in the form of a political party, and it might prove artificial to develop one if the form of a movement arouses more confidence in the people.

It is a remarkable fact that oppositions do now exist in eastern Europe in nearly every country. Even in the Soviet Union there are underground journals and a core of open oppositionists for the first time since the twenties. Do you think there are any parallels between the new opposition which is emerging today and the main oppositional currents in the twenties and thirties?

Well, the situation has completely changed so naturally there are many differences. The Soviet Union's position in the world has altered greatly and the whole society is now much more developed. But there are perhaps some underlying similarities all the same. Firstly they were attacking the same system that we are attacking, the Stalinist system – but whereas they opposed it in its infancy we are now opposing it in its old age. This difference is already clear. The bureaucracy is no longer so effective as it was in the old days. It does not have such a clear conception of where it is going, it cannot accomplish the tasks it sets itself, and it has not been able simply to eliminate all its opponents. The second similarity is that our generation has again recovered the feeling that the situation can be changed. The old revolutionaries, the old Bolsheviks had this feeling because they had made a revolution. This gave them the courage to struggle for what they believed in despite the ruthlessness of the bureaucracy. Today we again feel that there can and must be a change and that we can help to bring it about. But for us the revolution does not lie in the past – it lies in the future.

September 1972
Interviewers:
Quintin Hoare
Robin Blackburn

Peaceful Coexistence and World Revolution

ERNEST MANDEL

(Reprinted from *Peaceful Coexistence and World Revolution*, New York 1970)

With the revolution of October 1917, the problems of socialism were added to the problems of relations between states. The class struggle on a world scale took a dual form: the struggle between social classes in each country, with its inevitable international repercussions, became intertwined with the relations between the USSR (and after 1945, other countries which had overthrown capitalism) and the bourgeois states.

Marxist theory, which had traditionally started from the general assumption that socialist revolution would triumph first in the most advanced countries of the world, had not prepared a set of guiding rules for revolutionists in these new conditions. It had paid little attention to the implications of the conquest of state power on the international conduct of revolutionary policies. Soviet and non-Soviet communist leaders had to work out *ad hoc* theories in this respect in the period immediately following the October revolution. Great controversies surrounded these problems, from the early days of Soviet power to the current period. The debates about the relation between the Brest-Litovsk peace negotiations and the revolution in central Europe; the controversies in the 1920s about the theory of permanent revolution and the possibility of building socialism in one country; the discussions at the international conferences of Communist parties in 1957 and 1960, and their explosion into the public Sino-Soviet rift around the problems of 'peaceful coexistence' and the subsequent polemics on the real nature of 'detente' – these can all be traced in the last analysis to the same context.

World revolution and the defence of Soviet Russia in Lenin's time

The Bolshevik leaders had to tackle these problems amidst chaos and civil war, beset by foreign intervention by a dozen capitalist powers, and under the heavy pressure of immediate burning needs. Nevertheless, it can be said that they tried to remain as faithful as possible to their revolutionary convictions, and that in the process they evolved a certain number of rules to prevent power politics and 'raison d'état' from getting the better of their principles.

Conceptually, they affirmed the unity of the interests of the Soviet state and world revolution in such a way as to subordinate, ultimately, the first to the second; the very conquest of power in Russia was seen and justified primarily as a contribution to the development of socialist revolution in other, more advanced countries. Institutionally, the newly founded Communist International was completely independent from the Soviet state and its diplomatic network or manoeuvres. If there was a personal union between the leaders of the state and the Russian representatives in the International, it only underlined that, in the last analysis, the Soviet section of the Communist International considered itself as part of the movement for world revolution.

These elementary principles did not solve the whole complex problem. Very early, even before the foundation of the Communist International, the problem of concluding a separate peace at Brest-Litovsk projected into the debate questions of the dialectics of self-defence and the self-perpetuation of the young workers' republic in relation to the prospects of world revolution. The opponents of the Brest-Litovsk peace in the revolutionary movement outside the Bolshevik party (the left SRs) as well as inside the Bolshevik party, accused Lenin of betraying world revolution by strengthening the Central powers through the conclusion of a separate peace. In part nationalist rather than internationalist motives explained this opposition to the Brest-Litovsk treaty. In part mistaken estimates of the *immediate* maturity of revolutionary conditions in Germany, Austria and Hungary, and erroneous evaluations as to the consequences of the Brest-Litovsk treaty upon the subsequent maturing of these conditions were at the bottom of the arguments of Lenin's opponents.

But what emerges from this whole debate is Lenin's principled conduct and his staunch adherence to the tenet of subordinating the interests of the Soviet state to those of world revolution. Not for one moment does he conceive of putting a brake upon revolutionary propaganda among German soldiers in order to receive less harsh peace conditions from the Central powers. At no time did he propose to the German revolutionists to 'help' save the Soviet state by moderating their opposition to the imperialist war machinery and state of their own rulers. On the contrary, he strongly approved of Trotsky's revolutionary agitation at Brest-Litovsk, whose effects in undermining war morale in central Europe should not be underestimated. The debate over the Brest-Litovsk separate peace treaty did not revolve around the question of whether world revolution should be sacrificed to the self-defence of the Soviet state. It revolved around the problem of whether world revolution would best be served by a desperate 'revolutionary war' by the young Soviet republic against the Central powers, which would lead rapidly to the occupation of revolutionary Petrograd and Moscow, or whether by deliberately trading space for time the Bolsheviks would thereby both save Soviet Russia and hasten the outbreak of a revolution in central Europe.

History proved Lenin to be right. One of his chief imperialist opponents at that time, German Imperial Chief of Staff Ludendorff, sadly stated in his memoirs that the balance sheet of Brest-Litovsk had accelerated the disintegration of the Reich.[1] By saving their young republic, Lenin and Trotsky had not made the outbreak of the German, Austrian and Hungarian revolutions more difficult; on the contrary, they had accelerated the revolutionary process in central Europe that came to a head less than nine months after the conclusion of the separate peace. And there are many indications that this assistance was not only moral and political, but that it also took very concrete material forms.[2]

The question of the defence of the Soviet state against foreign intervention loomed large among the innumerable political obligations which the Communist International took upon itself during the first years of its existence. This defence was conceived, in the first place, as a specific task for revolutionary action, for example, at the time of the threat of French intervention against Soviet Russia during the Polish campaign in 1920. But the means suggested for that defence were solely the means of revolutionary class struggle: demonstrations, strikes by specific groups of the working class (dockers, railway workers, workers in munition factories), or general strikes. In this way, the problems of the revolutionary defence of Soviet Russia, although implying certain specific tasks, blended harmoniously with those of preparing favourable conditions for an expansion of international revolution.

Three special aspects of Soviet foreign policy in Lenin's time exemplify this general approach to the problem of interrelating the defence of the Soviet state with the tasks of the developing world revolution. It is well known that Lenin rigidly applied his thesis of the right of all nationalities to self-determination immediately after the October revolution and accepted the independence of Finland headed by the counter-revolutionary Svinhufud government. He justified this action – which was evidently detrimental to the interests of Soviet Russia as a state, for example from the point of view of military self-defence – by the internal needs of the Finnish revolution and the communist movement in that country.

It is also known that Trotsky was opposed to Tukhachevsky's quick offensive towards Warsaw in 1920, because the Polish revolution was not yet ripe and such a military move would strengthen chauvinism among the Polish workers, and thereby slow down and not hasten the revolutionary process in that country; Lenin recognized that Trotsky was right in that respect.[3] Finally, when preparing the Rapallo and Genoa conferences, and trying to create a rift in the front of imperialist states against Soviet Russia, the Bolshevik government did not let this manoeuvre influence the strategic or tactical tasks of the German Communist party. The Communist International maintained its course towards a proletarian revolution in Germany; Lenin insisted on the necessity of winning a majority influence among the German workers in order to attain that goal.

Of late, an attempt has been made to present Lenin as the father of the 'theory of peaceful coexistence', and a parallel legend has been developed about Trotsky advocating 'instantaneous revolution' in all countries through military interventions of the Soviet state. Neither myth has any foundation, either in the theories or in the practices of the founders of the Soviet system and the Communist International.

Genuine misunderstandings (we don't concern ourselves with deliberate falsifications) arise from the dialectical nature of the interrelationship between the Soviet state and the world revolution. Defending the first and furthering the second cannot be conceived simply as a single process with a single logic. Both have a specific logic of their own.

The needs of defending the Soviet state by diplomatic and military means must be recognized as genuine and as a specific part of the general task of world revolution. In the same sense, the needs of furthering revolution imply specific tasks in each specific country, which must be recognized as genuine, and which cannot be confused with any of the needs of defending the USSR. Only if the special requirements of the two tasks are recognized can the unity of the movement be achieved on a higher level.

It is as wrong to advocate subordination of the strategy and tactic of the revolutionary movement in any country to the needs of defending the Soviet state as it is wrong to call upon that state to 'hasten' revolution in other countries by untimely military or diplomatic moves which would threaten its own security. World revolution must be seen as a process conditioned in the first place by a maturing of favourable objective and subjective conditions for the conquest of power by the proletariat in a successive series of countries, a maturing which can be strongly influenced but not artificially decided by what happens on the international scale. Both the internal policies of the revolutionary party and the international policies of the Soviet state should be conducted in such a way as to hasten and not to slow down these maturing processes.

It is only in this framework that the so-called theory of peaceful coexistence between states of different social natures, attributed to Lenin,[4] can be correctly understood. What it means is simply that the autonomy of tasks for the proletarian *state*, as long as world revolution has not triumphed in most countries, implies the necessity of accepting prolonged periods of armistice with the bourgeois states, during which all the prerequisites of inter-state relations (diplomacy, trade, etc.) should be used for strengthening its own positions. In that most general and abstract sense, the theory is of course correct. Its negation would imply the duty of a proletarian state to maintain permanent conditions of military warfare with its hostile environment, without taking into consideration any question of resources, relationship of forces, capacity of resistance, etc.

But such a trivial 'theory', expressing the simple need of physical survival and economic growth, cannot be construed to imply any 'general line' of the foreign policy of the workers' states, or even worse, of the world revolutionary movement.[5] 'Peaceful coexistence' between states of different social natures must be seen as what it is in fact: an armistice – and a temporary one – on *one* of the fronts of the international class war. This war goes on uninterruptedly on the other front, of internal class struggle in each country (which does not, of course, mean that it always takes the violent form of armed uprisings and clashes). It will periodically involve the workers' state in military conflicts.

Both fronts constantly interact upon each other until they blend into an immediate unity (at moments) of exacerbated social and military tension on a world scale. Any other position reflects either the abandonment of the goal of world revolution, or the reformist illusion that this goal can be achieved through the peaceful and gradual elimination of capitalism, nationally and internationally – an illusion which has been cruelly contradicted by reality for more than half a century.

'Socialism in one country' and the 'Soviet bulwark' in Stalin's time

After Lenin's death, a subtle transformation took place in this dialectical interrelationship between the defence of the interests of the Soviet state power and the furthering of world revolution. This transformation was so subtle that it was not recognized by most of the participants in the process, including its main author. As late as 1925, Stalin wrote in a pamphlet entitled 'Questions and Answers':

Let us come to the second danger. It is characterized by scepticism towards the proletarian world revolution and the national liberation movement of the colonies and vassal countries; by lack of understanding of the fact that, without the support of the international revolutionary movement, our country could not have resisted world imperialism; by lack of understanding of that other fact that the triumph of socialism in one country cannot be final (this country having no guarantee against an intervention) as long as the revolution has not won in the least several other countries; by a lack of that elementary internationalism which implies that the triumph of socialism in one country should not be considered an end in itself, but a means of developing and supporting the revolution in other countries.

This is the road leading to nationalism, to degeneration, to complete liquidation of the foreign policy of the proletariat, because those who are infected with this disease consider our country not as a part of the world revolutionary movement, but as the beginning and the end of that movement, as they believe that the interests of all other (revolutionary movements) must be sacrificed to those of our country.[6]

It would be an oversimplification to state that this process of transformation was actually initiated by Lenin's death. Already before 1924, indications of such a change had appeared.[7] Confusedly mingled with the debate about the possibility of achieving the construction of 'socialism in one country', the change found its first theoretical expression in the 'Draft Programme of the Communist International' written by the unfortunate Bukharin. From unconscious and piecemeal changes, the transformation became more and more open and deliberate in the early 1930s expressing itself in the decline and fall of the Comintern, and finally its dissolution by Stalin in 1943.

The coincidence between the beginning of this process and the end of the first post-war revolutionary wave in Europe could create the impression of a causal link between these two sets of phenomena: the Bolsheviks subordinated the interests of the Soviet state to those of world revolution as long as world revolution remained a practical proposition; they moved towards a subordination of the interests of the world communist movement to the task of consolidating the Soviet state, economically, diplomatically and militarily, as soon as it appeared to them that an international expansion of the revolution had ceased to be a likely short-term perspective. Or to put it in other terms: the survival of the Soviet state could be based either on revolutionary expansion, or on a division between its enemies. If expansion of the revolution became unlikely, it would be necessary to concentrate on divisions between imperialist enemies, even to the point of sacrificing some revolutionary interests.[8]

We shall not deny that many communist leaders and militants, both inside and outside the Soviet Union, *rationalized* the fundamental turn in the Comintern's policies in the 1920s in this way. There seems to be no point in questioning the sincerity of at least part of those who continue to cling to this kind of argument till this very day.[9] But Marxists cannot limit themselves to examining the motivations which parties and social layers invoke for explaining their own actions. They must check these motivations against the background of objective reality and of social interests; that is, they must try to explain the objective reasons which led social forces to behave in a certain way. From this point of view, it is easy to recognize that the reasons invoked for the new policies followed by the Soviet leaders beginning in the mid-1920s, and their supporters at home and abroad, do not hold water and do not offer a really satisfactory explanation for a change in behaviour which ended in a complete somersault.

First of all it must be recognized that if a temporary stabilization of capitalism indeed followed the first post-war revolutionary wave in Europe, this stabilization was only *temporary*, and the 1920s and 1930s were interlaced with grave social and political crises in several key countries. These bore testimony to the maturing of pre-revolutionary conditions – to say the least: the German crisis in 1923; the general strike in Britain in 1926; the Chinese revolution of 1925–7; the German crisis of 1930–3; the Spanish revolution of 1931; the Asturias uprising in Spain in 1934; the Spanish civil war particularly in the period 1936–7; the general strike with factory occupations in France in 1936 – just to name the most important crises, which put socialist revolution again and again upon the agenda of half a dozen major countries in Europe and Asia.

Secondly, the outcome of these crises, which ended in working-class defeats and strengthened the downward trend of world revolution, cannot be separated from the actual policies of the working-class parties participating in them, in the first place of the Communist parties, which were the only ones during that period with avowedly revolutionary objectives. The main contradiction in the apologetic positions adopted by those who justify Stalin's policy of subordinating the interests of the international socialist movement to the so-called interests of consolidating the Soviet state's power position in the world lies in the fact that the 'impossibility of world revolution', far from being an objective fact, resulted to a large extent first from the political mistakes and afterwards from the deliberate political options taken by the leaders of the Soviet Union themselves.[10]

Thirdly, by counterposing in a mechanistic way the interests of furthering world revolution to those of consolidating the Soviet state, the Soviet leadership under Stalin objectively demonstrated that it was moved by social motives quite distinct from those of furthering the *genuine* interests of the Soviet Union. In the light of subsequent history it would be hard to prove, for example, that the conquest of power by Hitler was in the interests of the Soviet Union.[11] In fact, a correct policy by revolutionary parties, which would lead to the maturing of favourable internal conditions in various countries, enabling them to conquer power, could be construed in no way whatsoever to lead to a weakening of the position of the USSR on a world scale. Post-Second World War history has proved this proposition to the hilt.

But, it may be asked, wouldn't the international extension of the revolution have sharpened the international-class struggle and increased international tensions, including tensions on an inter-state level? Indeed it would have – but it would have sharpened these tensions, *precisely as a result of a change in the international relationship of forces favourable to the Soviet Union.* That under these conditions, such a 'sharpening of tension' was not something detrimental to the interests of the Soviet Union seems rather obvious. Wouldn't the imperialists react under these conditions by unleashing war against the Soviet Union? This question cannot be answered in the abstract; it needs concrete examination, as will follow both in respect to the Spanish and Yugoslav civil wars. But what should be stressed at this point is the extreme oversimplification which is at the bottom of this kind of reasoning. In this kind of argument, the world bourgeoisie is represented as a group of conspirators who anxiously scan the skies for any 'pretext' offered them to start intervention against the Soviet Union. The *ne plus ultra* of revolutionary wisdom consists in not 'offering the pretext' for such intervention. History and social conflict are degraded to a vulgar spy game, each side busily engaged in 'outwitting' the other.

Is it necessary to stress that this representation of contemporary social conflict and international relations bears only the vaguest resemblance to reality? The historical reality is based upon contending forces, inside each country and internationally. What is decisive is the dynamics of the relationship between forces. In order to start an intervention against the Soviet Union, it is not enough for the bourgeoisie of one of the larger countries to be 'provoked' by the extension of the revolution; it is necessary, at the very least, to have reduced its own working class to a position of political and social weakness and/or ideological disarmament, where it has become unable to react in the manner in which the European working class did react, for example, in 1920–1. It is also necessary to have at its disposal the necessary point of intervention from a purely military and geographical point of view. Internal divisions in the imperialist camp are important indeed. But they cannot take precedence over the two factors which have just been stressed. Therefore, any change in the social relationship of forces which increases the militancy and revolutionary spirit of the working class of key imperialist countries makes it more difficult and not easier for imperialism to start a war against the Soviet Union. And any victory of socialist revolution in a new country often has precisely that effect upon the workers inside the key imperialist states.

It is therefore essential to view the change in the official USSR attitude towards world revolution expressed in Stalin's famous interview with the US journalist Roy Howard[12] as reflecting not the genuine global interests of the Soviet state or Soviet society, but those of a particular social layer inside that society, characterized by a basically conservative attitude to the world situation, *by a desire to maintain the international status quo*. Whatever may be the rationalization of this attitude by the Soviet leaders or their apologists, the social roots for this conservatism can only be discovered inside Soviet society itself, in the specific role of that leading stratum and its specific relationship to the basic classes of contemporary Soviet society, the working class and the peasantry.

It is not the purpose of this study to analyse in a detailed way the social nature and function of that upper stratum, the Soviet bureaucracy. This analysis was made before the war by Leon Trotsky, and further developed after the Second World War by his followers.[13] In our opinion, it remains fundamentally valid today. From the specific place of that bureaucracy in Soviet society flows its specific role in world politics. It is not a new class, but a privileged stratum of the proletariat which has usurped exclusive exercise of political power and total control over the social surplus product within the framework of a planned socialized economy. It can appropriate its essential privileges in the means of consumption only on the dual basis of the collective property of the means of production on one hand and political passivity of the Soviet masses on the other.

This role reflects the fundamentally contradictory and dual nature of the Soviet bureaucracy. On the one hand, it is genuinely attached to the new social order which has emerged in the Soviet Union from the October revolution and the violent destruction of private agriculture by Stalin's forced collectivization. It tries to defend this order – the basis for its power and privileges – by means which correspond to its own narrow special interests. By defending Soviet society, it objectively serves the international extension of the revolution, independently of its own desires and motives.[14]

On the other hand it is instinctively afraid of any upsetting of the international *status quo*, not only for psychological reasons which reflect its fundamentally conservative nature in Soviet society, but also because it fears the profound transformations which an extension of the international revolution would provoke, both in the political apathy of the Soviet working class and in the internal relationship of forces inside the world communist movement.[15] The transformation of the Communist International into a 'frontier guard' of the Soviet Union, elevated to the position of the 'main bulwark' of the world proletariat, to whose diplomatic and military defence every single workers' movement in every single country had to be subordinated, faithfully reflects the specific interests of that bureaucratic caste.[16]

At the end of this process of transformation, the initial relationship of the Soviet state to world revolution, as seen by Lenin, is completely overthrown. The Soviet Union is no longer seen as an instrument of furthering world revolution; on the contrary, the international communist movement is viewed as an instrument to further the immediate twists and turns of Soviet diplomacy.[17] The 'unity' of the Soviet Union and international revolution is degraded from the principled height where Lenin and Trotsky had placed it to the lowest level of pragmatic expediency: Communist parties have to ruthlessly sacrifice the militancy, consciousness and self-confidence of the working classes of their respective countries on the altar of the 'state power interests' embodied by the Soviet government. The outcome of this process historically was a tremendous weakening of the proletarian forces, which enabled Hitler to concentrate all the resources of the European continent against the Soviet Union with very little initial resistance by the defeated and disorientated masses of Europe, and which brought the Soviet Union within an inch of military collapse.

The Spanish and Yugoslav examples

The real interrelationship between the potential extension of Soviet power and the threat of imperialist intervention against the USSR can be most vividly understood if one analyses the concrete circumstances under which the problem was posed historically. The two outstanding cases are those of the Spanish revolution in the inter-war period and the Yugoslav revolution during and immediately after the Second World War.

The Spanish revolution of 1936 presented the world with one of the maturest examples of revolutionary conditions since those of Russia in 1917.[18] In answer to a fascist military putsch led by generals Sanjurjo, Mola and Franco, and notwithstanding the notorious lack of preparation, understanding and initiative of their official leaderships, the Spanish workers and poor peasants rose with an admirable revolutionary ardour, stormed military barracks and in a few days had crushed the uprising in all the large cities with the exception of Seville, had seized the factories and landed estates and started to build their own armed militia, which drove the fascist armies away from one province after another. With a minimum of revolutionary audacity and organization, the revolution could have crushed the uprising in a few months' time, among other things by promising the independence of Spanish Morocco to Franco's Moorish troops, by starting to divide up the land, by calling upon Franco's Spanish troops to desert in order to receive their property in the villages, and generally by consolidating the new socialist order born from the heroism of the July-August-September 1936 days.

The Communist International, assisted by the social-democracy and by the significant reformist illusions of the main Spanish anarchist leaders, crushed these prospects within a few months' time. Under the pretext of not 'alienating' the sympathy of the British and French bourgeoisie, they prevented the revolution from reaching its climax in the clear establishment of a socialist federation. They used the Soviet arms deliveries to Spain in order to impose their ruthless leadership first on the International Brigades, then on the Spanish government itself. One after another, the revolutionary conquests of the summer of 1936 were torn away from the workers and poor peasants in the name of re-establishing 'republican', (that is, bourgeois) 'law and order'. A regular bourgeois army with a 'regular' officer corps, took the place of the militias. Factories and landed estates were restored to their former owners. When the Barcelona workers rose in defence of their conquests, in answer to an open provocation,[19] they were first severely repressed and then abandoned by their own leaders. The Soviet leadership went so far as to attempt to export the infamous technique of the Moscow trials to Spain, with results which would appear grotesque were it not that hundreds of honest revolutionaries were killed in the process.[20]

The outcome was easily foreseen. The comedy of 'nonintervention' was not observed by the fascist governments, which generally respect only strength, not diplomatic agreements. But it was scrupulously respected by the social-democrat French prime minister, Léon Blum, supported by the CP, and eventually even the International Brigades were dissolved. Having been deprived of an early victory and pushed on to the defensive (which is always fatal in a revolution), the Spanish masses became more and more disoriented and dispirited when they saw that they were called upon to defend, not revolutionary conquests, but the same old 'law and order' that they had been rising against since 1934. Final defeat was only a question of time. The admirable spirit of resistance that the workers of the great cities showed for nearly three years under these extremely adverse conditions only underlines the favourable conditions for a rapid victory in 1936. Having completed the revolution they would have won the war. Instead, the CP called upon them to win the war first, and then to complete the revolution. This led to the crushing of the revolution, which could only produce defeat in the war.

The justification offered again and again by the apologists of Moscow's Spanish policies is that any alternative policy would have led to an 'imperialist united front' and an immediate threat of victorious intervention against the Soviet Union. But a responsible analysis of the concrete conditions prevailing at that time does not in the least warrant such a conclusion.

In the first place, we know today that Nazi rearmament in 1936 was only in its first infant stage; in the spring of 1936 the Nazis had only one armoured division; in fact, they trembled lest the French general staff answer the remilitarization of the Rhine valley with an immediate invasion of Germany, against which they had no force to mobilize.[21] Britain's situation was no different; it had no striking force to intervene in Europe.[22] The United States had not even started the preliminary stages of re-armament.

The only strong army on the European continent which could be considered a threat to the Red army – at that time probably the main military power in Europe – was the French army. But France was in the throes of a tremendous rise of workers' militancy. One million workers had just risen to occupy the factories and had voted Blum into power, with the support of a greatly strengthened Communist party. So scared were the upper classes that they were ready to adopt any measure of social reform in order at least to recover their main property.[23] It is completely ludicrous to think that, under such conditions, these workers would have permitted themselves to be mobilized to fall on the backs of their victorious Spanish brothers, not to speak of an attempt to have them travel over thousands of miles in order to attack the Soviet Union – in alliance with Hitler and Mussolini! It is absolutely certain that the attempt by any French government to push through such a policy would have proved suicidal, and would have been answered by an immediate uprising of the French working class.

On the other hand, it is also unrealistic, to say the least, to compare the internal situation in Nazi Germany or fascist Italy in 1936 with that prevailing in these countries in 1940 or 1941. Internal resistance was still fairly strong. Any foreign defeat would have meant immediate trouble for these governments.[24] Already the small military reverses suffered by the fascist Italian legion at Guadalajara led to increased anti-fascist activities inside Italy. A victorious Spanish and French revolution would have completely changed the relationship of forces inside Germany and Italy, and decisively weakened, if not overthrown, the dictatorship in at least one of these two countries.

It is probable that such a development would have strengthened the sympathies with Hitler and fascism inside the British and American bourgeoisie. But one should not forget that the year 1936 was the year of the great sit-down strikes in the United States and of a strong leftward trend inside Great Britain. The outcome of these tendencies would have been deeply modified in the event of socialist victories in Spain and France, not to speak of a collapse of fascism in Italy. Even if one supposes that eventually the right-wing bourgeois forces would have had the upper hand in these countries, it would have required many years and many changes in the world situation before Washington and London could threaten a war in alliance with Hitler, against the Soviet Union. It is much more probable that such a threat of war, even if it materialized, would not have been directed against the Soviet Union alone, but against a socialist Europe. We would have had a situation similar to the one emerging from the Second World War, but with the proletarian forces geographically, socially, politically and morally much stronger than they are today.

As pointed out above, the Spanish revolution was sacrificed to the idea that the attitude of world capitalism towards the Soviet state and world revolution depends in the last analysis upon the ability of the Soviet leadership to avoid 'provoking' its united hostility, and to 'placate' and 'divide' it instead. This conception radically discounts the real class struggle going on in the capitalist countries themselves.

Still clearer was the case of Yugoslavia, although the outcome there was, happily, more favourable than in the case of Spain.

From its inception, the Yugoslav revolution encountered distrust and attempts at strangulation by Stalin and his collaborators. Its attempts to organize proletarian brigades were severely reprimanded by Moscow; it was starved of military aid; and behind its back Stalin divided up the Balkans with Churchill in October 1944, imposing a 'fifty-fifty' solution on Yugoslavia.[25] In this way, a coalition government was formed in which bourgeois politicians acquired a certain weight.

The leadership of the Yugoslav Communist party, however, did not follow the injunctions of the Moscow leadership. It pushed the revolution through to victory. In a referendum, the decision in favour of the republic and against the monarchy was imposed through huge mass mobilizations and tremendous propaganda.[26] The socialist transformation of the economy was quickly achieved. The remnants of the old bourgeois state apparatus and army, already reduced to a shadow of their former strength during the civil war that was superimposed upon the resistance struggle against Nazi occupation, were completely eliminated. Nothing was left of the coalition government decided at Teheran and Yalta. Socialist revolution triumphed.

During this whole process, Stalin did not cease to express his misgivings and criticisms of the YCP's revolutionary orientation. He feared lest the 'great coalition' of the Second World War would be broken through this 'Yugoslav adventurism'. He saw a military showdown looming ahead.

In fact, the development of the Yugoslav revolution was accompanied by strong international tension, especially in the Trieste area, in the same way as the victory of every single revolution since 1945, or even the victory of the October revolution, increased international tension. It is one of the facts of political life, that civil war has the tendency to spill over national frontiers. But in no case did an actual world war arise out of the international tensions provoked by internal revolutionary victories. Tito's achievement of a socialist revolution no more 'provoked world war' than the victory of Mao Tse-tung in 1949, Ho Chi Minh in 1954, or Castro in 1959.[27]

In order to understand the reasons for this astonishingly constant factor, it is sufficient to state that world capitalism – and especially the leading layers of the American ruling class – react to the world situation as a whole, and not to each separate country or event, isolating it from the overall context. If it is true that each victorious revolution modifies the world relationship of forces at the expense of capitalism, it is also true that the reactions of world capitalism against such a revolution must then follow in a general context unfavourable for capitalism and for imperialist intervention. The capitalist leadership is therefore torn between conflicting needs – the need to stop currents going against its interests, and the need to take into consideration the deteriorated overall situation which is highly unfavourable for a general counter-offensive.

For this reason, the relationship between victorious revolution and war after 1917, and again after 1945, has been one of limited counter-revolutionary military interventions following upon each new victory of the revolution, rather than general world war. By trying to achieve a few limited victories which neutralize the effects of the previous defeat, imperialism reacts to new extensions of the revolution first by attempting to restore a favourable balance of power, before it considers launching a general counter-offensive, including a possible war of intervention against the USSR.

We shall come back to this point in trying to draw up a general balance sheet of the international developments of the last twenty years. But we can already arrive at a seemingly paradoxical conclusion: it is not revolutionary victories but, up to a certain point, defeats of the revolutionary forces, which hasten the movement towards world war. This certainly was so in the period 1936–9.

It was not because the Spanish revolution was victorious, but because it was lost, and because the tide therefore turned sharply towards the right and towards the disenchantment and passivity of the masses in France, Britain, Czechoslovakia, etc., that Munich became possible, and as a result of Munich, the occupation of the Sudetenland, the preparation of the liquidation of Poland and the beginning of the world war by Hitler. During the eighteen months between the revolutionary upsurge of the French and Spanish workers in June-July 1936, and the rape of Austria in the beginning of 1938, the relationship of forces in Europe was decisively changed in favour of German imperialism.

282 *Ernest Mandel*

Surely, the defeat of the Spanish revolution had something to do with this change! Surely, at the end of this phase there occurred precisely what the Stalin leadership had so desperately tried to avoid: the 'ganging up' of all great European powers against the USSR (between Munich and the occupation of Prague). If this front of imperialists was broken, it was not because Stalin had made enough sacrifices in order to gain the good graces of the stock exchanges of Paris and London, but because Hitler proved too greedy, and the Western imperialists convinced themselves that he wanted to crush them completely in his proposed embrace.

In the same way, one has to view the immediate post-war developments in Europe in 1944–5. The Atlantic Pact was not concluded to 'punish' the Soviet Union for having let Tito make a revolution in Yugoslavia. On the contrary, imperialism was fully aware of the use it had made of the moderating influence which Stalin, through the local Communist party leaderships, had exercised upon the situations in Greece, Italy and France when they came dangerously near to revolution.[28] The North Atlantic Pact was concluded, and imperialism could establish its first worldwide military alliance against the USSR (NATO), after the revolutionary situations in Greece, France and Italy ended in a restoration and consolidation of capitalism, with the help of local CP leaderships and with the full consent of Stalin. In this sense it is correct to say that not the victory of the revolution in Yugoslavia, but its defeats in Greece, Italy and France, brought about a worldwide alliance against the USSR.

There is an apparent element of paradox in this reasoning. After all, one could argue, the western powers had divided Europe with Stalin at Yalta, and to a large extent, both sides had respected the actual line of division, which reflected a given balance of power. The conclusion of the North Atlantic Treaty could be viewed as an imperialist measure to consolidate 'its own' sphere of influence, in the same way as the elimination of bourgeois politicians, bourgeois democracy and private property in eastern Europe could be viewed as a similar move by Stalin to consolidate the Soviet sphere of influence.

The flaw in this kind of argument is its completely static conception, which forgets that every defensive move always contains the germs of a future offensive. Behind NATO was not only 'containment' but also the hope of a future 'roll back'. 'Containment' was facilitated by the fact that in Italy and France the potential socialist revolution was nipped in the bud by the CP leaderships. This again facilitated the possibility of a 'roll back'. The hope that 'containment' would not occur because Stalin deliberately intervened to block the spread of revolution to the West proved to be an illusion. In fact, if one examined the concrete motivation which led to the establishment of NATO, one would have to conclude that the victory of the Yugoslav revolution, or the fear of a victorious revolution in France or Italy, played a much lesser role than the actual military conquests of the Red army, the events in countries where there was no revolution, like Poland and eastern Germany, and the strengthening of the strategic positions of the USSR.[29] What 'provokes' imperialism is not only the extension of the revolution; it is its very existence, or rather the consolidation of its power base in the USSR itself.[30] In the long run, the only way not to 'provoke' the capitalists is to consolidate and restore capitalism everywhere, including the Soviet Union. If one is not ready to pay *that* price, any other move then becomes simply a matter of calculation as to its effects, not upon the imperialists being 'provoked' – which they always are – but upon the overall balance of forces.

We see here the basic reformist fallacy[31] in the strategies of 'peaceful coexistence' and 'socialism in one country'. Underlying both is the hope that somehow, in some way, world imperialism will reconcile itself to the existence of the USSR, and 'let it alone', if only the USSR lets world imperialism alone also. Ironically, the same people who base themselves upon this illusion also state that 'in the long run' the world relationship of forces will be decisively changed by the economic and military strengthening of the USSR.[32] But surely, imperialists recognize this also, and must therefore strive, in the long run, not only to 'contain' revolution but also to destroy the USSR. Therefore, the main question is whether this test of strength is unavoidable in the long run. Once one agrees on this unavoidability, one will then concentrate on achieving the best possible relationship of forces for that moment. Military and economic strengthening of the USSR, attempts to divide the imperialist camp and victorious extensions of the revolution (especially in the main fortresses of imperialism) are then seen not as conflicting, but parallel, developments, tending to create a more favourable relationship of forces for that test of strength. The history of Europe from 1933 to 1941 bears this analysis out to the hilt. And there is every indication that since 1945, imperialism, above all US imperialism, has not ceased for one minute to prepare for the Third World War.[33]

The Chinese revolution and the nuclear threat to mankind's existence

Two developments of world-shaking importance after the Second World War might be thought to modify the general framework of the relationship between the international expansion of revolution and the continuing 'armistice' between the great state powers sketched above: the victory of the Chinese revolution in 1949, and the beginning of the nuclear arms race in the early fifties.[34] The establishment of the People's Republic of China broke the capitalist encirclement around the Soviet Union and thereby created an entirely new strategic world situation, in which the workers' states enjoyed a tremendous superiority in 'conventional' armies and weapons on the continents of Europe and Asia. The rapid progress of the USSR's nuclear industry destroyed the American monopoly of nuclear weapons, and Washington's illusion of being able to depend on 'nuclear diplomacy', to offset the advantages of the 'socialist camp' by threatening nuclear destruction of the Soviet Union. The nuclear stalemate achieved in the late 1950s and maintained ever since implies a potential nuclear destruction of the United States as well as of the USSR in the event of a nuclear war.[35]

The victory of the Chinese revolution gave a tremendous impetus to the colonial revolution, which had started with the July 1942 uprising in India and the substantial weakening of the old imperialist powers – Britain, France, the Netherlands, Belgium, Japan, Portugal – in Asia and Africa, during and after the Second World War. In order to save its essential economic positions, imperialism tried to switch progressively from direct to indirect rule, from outright colonialism to 'neo-colonialism'.

But the colonial revolution was difficult to canalize in channels controlled by imperialism; it had the tendency to grow over into anti-imperialist and anti-capitalist revolutionary mass uprisings: Indonesia, Kenya, Vietnam, Algeria, Cuba, Congo, Bolivia, Santo Domingo, etc. In some cases, like South Korea, Malaya and Santo Domingo, strong imperialist intervention in the form of full-scale colonial war succeeded in momentarily defeating the revolution. In other cases, the colonial wars ended with im-

perialism handing over political power to the bourgeois-nation-
alist or petty-bourgeois leaderships of the liberation movements,
in the hope of saving at least some of its property (Indonesia,
Morocco, Kenya, Algeria). In other cases the revolution has
gone through a series of vicissitudes but is still in progress, after
having suffered partial but not final defeats. In North Vietnam
and Cuba, the liberation movement triumphed and the anti-
imperialist revolution transformed itself into a socialist revolution and established new workers' states. The Arab countries
present a complex picture, but the tendency towards permanent
revolution became clear at least in Egypt and Syria and manifested itself embryonically in Iraq, Yemen and South Arabia.

In the mid-1950s, the illusion was created that a politically
powerful 'third world' had emerged. Although it was generally
recognized that the countries newly liberated from direct colonial
rule were economically weak and faced grave inner social
contradictions, many people thought that the sheer weight of
their hundreds of millions of inhabitants, united around the idea
of 'nonalignment' and of 'positive neutrality', would serve as a
buffer between the imperialist and 'socialist' camps, and thereby
gradually reduce world tensions. The Bandung conference of
1955 epitomized these hopes, embodied in the personalities of
Nehru and Sukarno.[36]

But these illusions were quickly destroyed. The economic
weakness of the colonial bourgeoisie appeared more and more
pronounced, and led it to become more and more dependent upon
foreign (i.e. essentially imperialist) 'aid'.[37] The inner social
contradictions slowly eroded whatever prestige the Nehrus,
Sukarnos and Kenyattas had acquired during the national
liberation struggle. Mass agitation and mass uprisings also led
them to lean more and more upon imperialist aid and support.
Instead of a 'buffer zone' between the 'two camps', the 'third
world' became a gigantic arena of social and political polarization,
in which violent clashes and civil wars progressively multiplied.
On the agenda was not the stabilization of any 'state of national
democracy' as Moscow indicated,[38] but a struggle between
bourgeois states and pauperized masses striving to establish
proletarian states.

This was the general framework in which the Sino-Soviet
dispute (preceded by the compromises arrived at during the
1957 and 1960 international conferences of Communist parties)
exploded. Some of the questions raised by that dispute appear

to be of a conjunctural nature. The People's Republic of China's *de facto* relations with imperialism were of a different nature than those of the Soviet Union. US imperialism had no diplomatic relations with China. It kept that great country outside the United Nations and deprived it of its rightful seat in the Security Council. It maintained an economic blockade of China. It financed and sustained the Chiang Kai-shek puppet regime in Taiwan, symbol of the fact that the Chinese civil war was not yet completely finished and that imperialism continued to intervene in this civil war against the mass of Chinese workers and peasants. It has encircled China with missile, air and naval bases with the acknowledged purpose of military (including nuclear) aggression against China. This situation was obviously different from the relations between Washington and Moscow, which were not only based upon normal diplomatic recognition and exchange, but even upon repeated, and partially successful, attempts at periodic collaboration in many fields.

In that delicate situation the Soviet bureaucracy, guided by its basically conservative motives in international affairs, committed the unforgivable mistake (nay, crime, from the point of view of the interests of world socialism) of joining the blockade and attempted *quarantine* of the Chinese revolution. After 1960, Moscow cut off all its economic aid to the Chinese, at a moment when the Chinese economy was going through the severe strains of the failure of the second phase of the 'great leap forward'. It thereby brutally arrested industrial development in China in several key fields. It refused China assistance in the development of nuclear weapons, thereby objectively contributing towards the imperialist nuclear blackmail of China. It went so far as to give military aid to the Indian bourgeoisie, at a moment when it was undeniable that these weapons could be used against the People's Republic of China and even against the Indian masses.

Whatever may be our criticism of the sectarian attitude and polemics which the Maoist leadership has developed in recent years against the USSR and the pro-Moscow Communist parties; and whatever may be our refusal to accept as valid and in conformity with socialist principles a whole series of measures and trends (along with more healthy ones) appearing inside China in the course of the 'great proletarian cultural revolution', it seems to us undeniable that at the bottom of the Sino-Soviet rift lay the detrimental attitude of the Soviet bureaucracy to the Chinese revolution, which we have sketched in the preceding paragraphs.[39] We therefore say that Moscow bore the main responsibility for the negative results of the Sino-Soviet rift, that is the rift on a *state* level which weakens the whole of the anti-capitalist forces on a world scale. (This should not be confused with the public *ideological debate*, in itself a welcome departure from the monolithism of Stalin's time.)

We define, nevertheless, as conjunctural all those aspects of the debate on revolutionary global strategy which flow from specific attitudes and actions of the Soviet bureaucracy and its Chinese counterpart. For even if these actions had not occurred, and if the Soviet and Chinese leaders had been glowing representatives of soviet democracy and proletarian internationalism,[40] the new world situation which emerged from the victory of the Chinese revolution and from the nuclear arms race would have posed new problems of revolutionary strategy.

The attempt to deny that the nuclear arms race has introduced a new factor into the discussions on the relationship of war, peace and revolution has been undertaken by Maoist and pro-Maoist forces.[41] It is not very serious and rather irresponsible. We are, of course, no experts on nuclear physics and biophysics. But if scientists warn us that a global nuclear war, with a general utilization of the nuclear weapons which are today stockpiled, could lead to a complete destruction of human civilization or even to a planet on which all life would be destroyed, we have to take these warnings very seriously and examine them on their scientific merit – and not from the viewpoint of whether they tend to 'stimulate' or to 'dampen' revolutionary enthusiasm in certain circles. Scientific socialism cannot base itself upon myths, illusions and blind faith in man's destiny. It has to start from an objective and critical appraisal of reality and its evolution. And there seems to be no doubt that the nuclear stockpiles have reached such a terrifying degree of destructive capacity that even if humanity were to survive a nuclear world war, the problem of physical survival would be posed under entirely different circumstances than under present conditions, not to speak of the prospects of socialism.

A classical revolutionary 'guide to action' was the rule: go into the army, learn the use of weapons and turn them against your own ruling class. But nuclear weapons obviously cannot be turned into weapons for civil war, because they destroy workers and capitalists indiscriminately and alike. This example alone is sufficient to prove that the nuclear arms race has indeed changed something in the world. Indeed, if one takes the scientists' warnings seriously, one should conclude that to prevent nuclear world war must become one of the major strategic goals of the world revolutionary movement.

But by posing the problem in this way, one has not at all concluded in favour of the travesty of 'peaceful coexistence' which has been the guiding line of the Communist party of the Soviet Union and most of the parties which follow its orientation during the last period. The question remains one *of the most effective ways* to avoid nuclear world war. The question basically boils down to this: whether or not imperialism will reconcile itself to the existence and economic-military strengthening of the 'socialist camp' (including China), provided these countries in no way whatsoever 'assist' the international extension of revolution. We have already recalled the answers given by the Eisenhower and Kennedy administrations in the Sputnik period, which clearly recognized in the growing economic and military strength of the 'socialist' camp alone, a mortal threat to the survival of world capitalism. This is the basic reason why disarmament, including nuclear disarmament, under conditions of surviving capitalism, surviving class struggle on a world scale, is and remains an illusion.[42] Even if international expansion of the revolution were to completely fade away, there would be no 'peaceful coexistence' in any meaningful sense, but just an uneasy armistice combined with a constant jockeying for better positions in the inevitable future showdown.

But international revolution cannot 'fade away', because it is by no means 'provoked', 'initiated' or 'triggered off' by 'foreign aggression', but springs from the deep inner social conflicts and contradictions in capitalist society, in the colonial and semi-colonial countries and in the 'advanced' countries themselves.[43] To hope for a disappearance of 'violent revolution' from this world is to hope for a reconciliation of the vast majority of mankind with unbearable and inhuman social, economic, political and cultural conditions. Such a hope is illusory, irrational, and not very ethical at that.

Once this is recognized as one of the basic truths of our time, the next question which arises is this: will imperialism 'reconcile' itself to a gradual spread of world revolution, a gradual shrinking of its own socio-economic domain, or will it try to oppose this process by force, armed interventions and counter-revolutionary aggressions? One should, of course, greatly prefer that imperialism stay passive in the face of world revolution. One could even hope that certain weaker and demoralized sectors of the world bourgeoisie would eventually swing over to such a passive attitude. But to expect such a gradual surrender from the strongest, most aggressive and most vital sectors of world capitalism, the leading circles of US imperialism, at the pinnacle of their economic and military power, is again an utter illusion. Experience has borne out during the last seven years that imperialism has decided to oppose by every means at its disposal, above all armed intervention, any threat of a new victorious revolution.

There remains but one question to be answered: which attitude on the part of the Soviet Union would in the long run best contribute to avoiding nuclear world war: a gradual retreat before imperialist aggression and blackmail, or a resolute intervention on the side of the various revolutionary peoples and movements attacked by imperialism? If past experience can offer any guidance, the answer would be obvious. Retreat or hesitation in the face of aggression does not 'appease' the aggressor. It only makes him bolder and leads him to escalate his aggression, which will eventually provoke a test of strength at a point so near to the vital interests of both contending powers, that world war will be much more unavoidable than if the test of strength had taken place at the periphery, during the first stage of the aggression.

But it is precisely the 'nuclear stalemate' which gives this argument much greater force than it had in the past. Nuclear world war is nuclear suicide, for the American bourgeois class as well as for the whole of mankind. Under present conditions, when this class is at the pinnacle of its power, it would be ludicrous to assume that it is ready to commit suicide for the sake of 'saving Vietnam from Communism'. It will continue its aggression only so long as the risks incurred are relatively small compared with the potential loss. The higher the risks become, the smaller will be the danger of escalation. It therefore follows that the stronger the 'socialist' camps' 'counter-escalation' in face of any imperialist aggression, at any point of the globe, the smaller will be the risk of new aggressions and of new 'escalations'.

We do not advocate any irresponsible actions on the part of the Soviet Union. *If* there existed a democratically united command of all anti-capitalist forces on a world scale; and *if* it moved to co-ordinate its actions in an efficient way, surely such a 'counter-escalation' could take a dozen different forms, from those proposed by Ernesto 'Che' Guevara of creating 'two, three, many Vietnams', to those of prudent military moves forcing the imperialists to send their reserves to various points of the globe. Surely, the logic of such a 'counter-escalation' is obvious: instead of allowing the enemy to concentrate his tremendous forces upon each small country and each revolution separately, thereby enabling him to crush these revolutions successively, to force him, rather, to disperse and spread his forces over a wider and wider range of countries and continents, and to tackle half a dozen uprisings, revolutions and military manoeuvres simultaneously.

So obvious is this logic and so elementary the political and military truth which it reflects, that one cannot believe the Soviet leaders to be so naïve as to be blind to these rules, in their 'total devotion to the cause of peace'. Peace, after all, is more and more threatened by their constant withdrawal in face of aggression. The only possible conclusion, again, is that their pathetic adherence to the myth of 'peaceful coexistence', in the face of blatant imperialist aggression, can only be explained by their specific *social interest*, by their fundamental conservatism, which clashes not only with the interests of world revolution but also with those of the Soviet peoples and the Soviet Union itself.

The examples of Cuba and Vietnam

The examples of Cuba and Vietnam underline the importance of this analysis. In the western press, the 1962 Caribbean crisis is often interpreted as a Kennedy 'masterstroke'. Kennedy 'called Khrushchev's bluff'.[44] We are far from approving all the tactical moves of the Soviet government on that occasion, especially the somewhat high-handed manner in which the sovereignty of revolutionary Cuba was treated. But one should not forget that after the failure of the 'Bay of Pigs' invasion, the pressure on the Kennedy administration to start a new aggression against Cuba was constantly growing. In fact, prior to the shipping of Soviet missiles to Cuba, rumours of a new incipient invasion of Cuba were numerous.[45] The balance sheet of Khrushchev's somewhat erratic dispatching and withdrawing of nuclear weapons to Cuba is, after all, that no such invasion took place. Soviet protection insulated the Cuban revolution from the kind of counter-revolutionary aggression which struck down the revolution in the Dominican republic three years later.

Ever since the victory and the consolidation of the Cuban revolution, Washington has made clear its resolution to oppose by every means at its disposal any new extension of the revolution. It did so by numerous military coups, in the Congo, Brazil and Indonesia, just to name the most important ones. It did so by open military intervention in the Dominican republic, Vietnam and Thailand. But it did not act in a reckless way. It prudently probed each step. First came the increase of military advisers in South Vietnam, then a large-scale invasion of South Vietnam with the building of huge military bases. Then came a swift but limited air attack against the Democratic Republic of Vietnam, allegedly in retaliation for an attack against an American vessel in the Bay of Tonkin. Only when each of these successive steps was not followed, on behalf of the Soviet Union, by anything else but verbal protests and a certain limited increase of material help to Hanoi, did Washington decide to generalize uninterrupted bombing of North Vietnamese territory, first making exceptions of 'sanctuaries' in and around Hanoi and Haiphong, and later not even sparing these any more.

Can there be any doubt that, should these aggressions be marked with success and be answered with further retreats by the Soviet leadership, a mortal danger would loom ahead for all workers' states which lie in the immediate shooting distance of imperialist power, that is, China, North Korea, Cuba, and in a certain sense, also the German Democratic Republic? And can there be any doubt that, at some point in this chain of aggression, the Soviet leadership will have to intervene, for reasons of military self-defence, and that the danger of a nuclear world war will be much greater then than today, given the fact that both aggression and Soviet retaliation would be located around 'targets' much nearer to the nerve centres of the USSR?

One could argue that the strategy of 'counter-escalation' to neutralize imperialist aggression involves a certain element of risk, and hinges dangerously on the assumption of rational behaviour by the leaders of American imperialism. We do not deny the validity of this objection. The only point we stress is the fact that the myth of 'peaceful coexistence' in the face of growing imperialist aggression involves a much greater risk and hinges upon the assumption that the aggressor will become 'appeased' by a few peripheral victories – an assumption that flies in the face of all historical experience.

Precisely because nuclear world war is nuclear suicide, it is logical to assume that imperialism will answer the spread of world revolution not by such a war, but by limited local wars. The more it gets away with them, the more it will multiply them. The more it is defeated in them the more it will be deterred from renewing the experience. Only when the international situation has changed so much that the leading circles of American imperialism have become desperate and certain of defeat, like Hitler in 1944, can there be a real threat that they would risk collective suicide by nuclear war rather than accept defeat.

We do not underestimate this threat – as it is underestimated by many of those who justify the hoax of 'peaceful coexistence' with the argument of avoiding nuclear war. We believe that as long as capitalism survives, this threat will be there, and will even grow stronger, because it is a function not of the strength but of the weakness of the surviving imperialist fortress. But such an analysis leads to a reappraisal of the decisive historic importance of the revolution inside the imperialist countries – not only for solving the economic problems which victorious revolutions in relatively backward countries have such difficulties in solving, but also for ensuring mankind's survival. For this survival depends in the last analysis upon the possibility of a nuclear *disarming* of the US monopolists, and this disarming cannot be achieved from without, that is, by any force outside the United States. It is the task of the progressive and socialist forces *inside* the United States itself.

We seem far from our starting point: the connections between world revolution and inter-state relations. And yet, in a certain sense, we have arrived back at our point of departure. The alternative to the illusions of 'socialism in one country' and 'peaceful coexistence' is not 'revolutionary war' launched by Moscow, 'preventive nuclear war', or 'simultaneous revolution' everywhere which is irresponsible adventurism. It is a comprehensive and co-ordinated strategy of world revolution, which is based upon support for revolutionary uprisings in a successive and growing number of countries, as a function of the maturing of favourable conditions for these uprisings inside the respective countries. It is, in a word, class struggle united in a dialectical way, on a world scale. And in the long run, the class struggle and the socialist revolution in the imperialist countries themselves will play the key role in the final test of strength globally.

For a whole historical period, the centre of world revolution has passed to the underdeveloped countries. But it is in Japan, in western Europe and in the United States, that the fate of mankind will be decided in the last analysis. And the struggle between the opposing class forces inside the United States itself will decide whether there will or won't be nuclear world war, i.e. will decide the life-and-death question facing mankind in our epoch.

Brussels 1970

Notes

1. Erich Ludendorff, *Meine Kriegserinnerungen 1914-18*. Berlin 1919, pp. 519, 517, 407, etc.

2. On the eve of the German November 1918 revolution, the Imperial Government broke off diplomatic relations with Soviet Russia, using as a pretext the fact that an accident at a Berlin railway station had revealed that diplomatic boxes sent to the Soviet embassy contained large quantities of communist propaganda in the German language.

3. For a detailed analysis of these discussions, see Isaac Deutscher, *The Prophet Armed*, London 1954, pp. 459–73.

4. We say the 'so-called theory' because Lenin nowhere formulated it in these words. The only statements which the defenders of that theory today use to support themselves (for example, E. Kardelj, *Le Communisme et la Guerre*, pp. 66–71), are statements concerning the need of normal diplomatic or commercial relations between Soviet Russia and the capitalist countries. That the Soviet state and the Communist International were right to struggle to break the imperialist blockade against the workers' state seems rather a truism. To transform that concrete struggle, at a concrete historical juncture, into a 'strategic line of the world communist movement' seems ludicrous.

5. In the 'Open Letter of CPSU Central Committee to All Party Organizations and All Communists of the Soviet Union,' of 14 July, 1963, the 'Leninist principle of peaceful coexistence' is said to have been 'proclaimed the general line of the Soviet foreign policy' by that party.

6. J. Staline, *Questions et Réponses*, Paris 1925, pp. 17–18.

7. Radek's policy of 'national communism', his opportunist manoeuvring with the followers of extreme chauvinists like Schlageter, was a significant departure from genuine internationalism. See Ruth Fischer, *Stalin and German Communism: A Study in the Origins of the State Party*, Cambridge, USA 1948; and Ypsilon (pseudonym for Johann Rindl and Julian Gumperz), *Pattern for World Revolution*, New York 1947.

8. What is involved here is not the question of the legitimacy of manoeuvres between enemies, of exploiting inter-imperialist conflicts, etc. What is involved is the question of whether manoeuvres, compromises, etc., have no limits, and whether the crossing of these limits does not endanger the objective fruits of these compromises. In this sense, a comparison between the Brest-Litovsk treaty and the Hitler-Stalin pact is very instructive. In the first case, a maximum propaganda use was made of the negotiations, in order to further international revolution. In the second case,

the world Communist movement was degraded to the point of 'defending' the Hitler-Stalin pact, and German Communists wrote that 'German imperialism' (presumably Hitler) was no longer to be considered the main enemy. *Die Welt*, 18 October, 1939.

9. Some people explain the USSR's survival in the Second World War as a result of these manoeuvres. This is an obvious mistake in reasoning. If the imperialists didn't unite against the Soviet Union, but continued to fight against each other, one camp allying itself with the USSR, it is because intra-imperialist contradictions were stronger, under the immmediate circumstances, than the common hostility against the USSR. This was largely independent of the USSR's propaganda or foreign policy. Lenin made a similar point after 1918 when he said that notwithstanding all their hatred for Bolshevism, the imperialists didn't succeed in uniting against it. And this at a time when the Bolsheviks continued the circulation of revolutionary propaganda!

10. The wrong policies of the Comintern certainly played a key role in the defeat of the Chinese revolution in 1927, in Hitler's coming to power in 1933 and in the defeat of the Spanish revolution of 1936–7.

11. Some people who are obsessed by the idea of 'all capitalists ganging up against the USSR' go so far as to say that Stalin was right to enable Hitler to come to power, because as a result of this, the Anglo-Saxon imperialists allied themselves to the USSR in the Second World War! The absurdity of such reasoning does not need to be elaborated, especially if one knows that Hitler's aggression against the USSR brought the Soviet Union within an inch of military defeat in 1941.

12. On 1 March, 1935, Stalin told the president of the Scripps-Howard newspapers that it was a 'tragi-comic misunderstanding' to attribute to the Soviet Union 'plans and intentions of world revolution'. *The Stalin-Howard Interview*, New York 1936.

13. See Leon Trotsky, *The Revolution Betrayed*, New York 1965; and *In Defence of Marxism*, New York 1965. See also the theses of the fifth world congress of the Fourth International: 'Montée et déclin du stalinisme', 'Déclin et chute du stalinism', *Quatrieme International*. December 1957, pp. 59 and 82.

14. The existence of the Soviet Union has objectively facilitated the victory of the Yugoslav, Chinese, Vietnamese and Cuban revolutions, even if the subjective policies of Stalin, Khrushchev and their followers tried to prevent the victories of these revolutions.

15. Experience has fully borne out the rationality of these fears: The victory of the Yugoslav as well as the victory of the Chinese and of the Cuban revolutions has created deep rifts, if not de facto splits, in the world Communist movement, on which the Soviet bureaucracy has now a much more limited hold than before or during the Second World War.

16. Extreme examples of such ruthless submission are: the opposition of the Indian Communist Party to the great uprising of the Indian people of July 1942; the opposition of the French Communist Party to the Algerian national movement in the spring and summer of 1945 (going as far as to approve the imperialist repression of the rising people who were condemned as 'fascist'); the attempts of French CP cabinet ministers to force their comrade, Ho Chi Minh, to stay within the French colonial empire, re-baptized the 'French Union', and the fact that these ministers remained in the imperialist government even after the colonial war of reconquest had been started against the Vietnamese revolution in early 1946!

Peaceful Coexistence and World Revolution 295

17. Walter Duranty cabled from Moscow that the first reaction to the outbreak of revolution in Spain in 1931 was 'a melancholic editorial in *Pravda* . . . in the first place because the USSR is excessively and perhaps unjustly nervous in relation to the war danger, and views with alarm any attempt to upset, anywhere, the European status quo . . . In addition, the policy of the Kremlin is based today more on the success of socialist construction in Russia than on world revolution' (*New York Times*, 18 April, 1931). Already in 1931!

18. The best analyses of the Spanish revolution are those of Felix Morrow, *Revolution and Counterrevolution in Spain*, London, and Pierre Broué et Tamine, *Revolution and Civil War in Spain*, London 1972.

19. The regular army attempted to take away from the workers' militias the Central Telephone Office, which the militias had occupied in July 1936 when they won it from the fascists after great sacrifices.

20. The sentence pronounced by the 'Central Espionage Tribunal' of the Spanish Republic against the executive committee of the POUM, dated 29 October, 1938, a verdict which, far from condemning the members of that committee, called for the suspension, 'temporarily', of the struggle for their specific goals, that is, the socialization of the economy and the establishment of the dictatorship of the proletariat, while participating in the general people's struggle against the fascist military uprising (a participation which the Tribunal does nowhere deny or denigrate!).

21. William L. Shirer, *Aufstieg und Fall des Dritten Reiches*, Munich 1963, Band I, p. 324. The German generals confirmed this during the Nuremberg Trials. Many other sources can be quoted to the same effect, among them Walter Goerlitz, *Der deutsche Generalstab*, (Frankfurt), p. 440.

22. See Winston Churchill, *The Gathering Storm*, Harmondsworth 1966, pp. 601–6.

23. During his testimony before the Riom trial, conducted against him by the Pétain regime, Blum proudly recalled that the employers' organizations came to beg him to become prime minister 'because the workers had confidence in him', and he could become the intermediary between the workers and the employers 'to stop this terrible movement [the occupation of the factories – E. M.].' Here are some characteristic expressions of Blum's: 'As early as Friday morning, M. Lambert-Ribot, who had been my colleague for long years in the Council of Ministers, before he, like a great many representatives of high public bodies and the universities, entered the service of the employers' organizations, M. Lambert-Ribot, with whom I had always maintained friendly relations, pressed me through two friends, through two different intermediaries, appealing to me to endeavour to establish a contract between the top employers' organizations such as the Comité des Forges and the Confédération Générale du Travail on the other.' Léon Blum, *L'Histoire Jugera*, Paris 1945, pp. 277–8. 'The employers not only did not ask him to use force but beseeched him not to use it. They told him, "in the present state of things, that could only lead to a bloody conflict." ' ibid., p. 279. 'But I must tell you that at that moment in the bourgeoisie, and in particular in the management world, I was considered a saviour, I was awaited and expected as a saviour.' ibid., p. 28.

24. Walter Goerlitz relates that even pilots of the 'Condor Legion', which Hitler sent to Spain, deserted to the side of the Spanish workers. *Der Deutsche Generalstab*, p. 442. H. B. Gisevius notes that popular opposition remained strong in the years 1936–7, although these were the 'calmest' years of the Nazi regime. *Bis zum bittern Ende*, Darmstadt 1947, p. 266.

A strong underground Communist Party organization in Berlin, counting several thousand active members, had been rebuilt in 1934–6 and was dismantled by the Gestapo only in the beginning of 1937, using the 'spy scare' spread by the Moscow trials and Stalin purges in the USSR.

25. Vladimir Dedijer, *Tito Parle*, Paris 1953, p. 231. The decisive historic steps on the road to the Yugoslav revolution, which were the decisions of the second session of the Antifascist People's Liberation Council of Jajce in the autumn of 1943, were considered 'a stab in the back of the Soviet Union' by the Moscow leadership, which continued its efforts to arrive at a compromise between the Communist-led resistance movement and the Royal Yugoslav Government in emigration. Mosa Pijade, *La Fable de l'aide soviétique à l'insurrection nationale yougoslave*, Paris 1950, p. 69 etc.

26. Even today, one can see on the walls of small towns and villages many remnants of the intense propaganda campaign which was conducted in Yugoslavia at that time.

27. Stalin was convinced that his alliance with Britain and the United States would be put to a terrible test by the victorious socialist revolution in Yugoslavia. Only when he saw, to his surprise, that the Western imperialists weren't gravely shocked by Tito's successes, did he partially change his attitude. Mosa Pijade, op. cit., p. 69.

28. See Charles de Gaulle, *Mémoires de Guerre, vol. 3, Le Salut*, Paris 1959: 'Their [the masses'] aversion to the former structures was exasperated by poverty, concentrated by the Résistance, and exalted by the liberation. Here, then, was an extraordinary occasion for the "party". By deliberately mixing up the insurrection against the enemy with the class struggle and posing as the champion of both kinds of revolt, the "party" had every opportunity of taking the leadership of the country by social fraud, even if it could not do it through the Conseil de la Résistance, the committees, and the militias.' pp. 112–13. 'Taking into account the events which have occurred since, and today's needs, I judge that the return of Maurice Thorez to the leadership of the Communist Party at present offers more advantages than disadvantages. This will be the case as long as I am at the head of the state and nation. To be sure, day after day the Communists will shower us with frauds and invectives. However, they will not attempt any insurrectional movement. Still better, as long as I govern, there will not be a single strike . . . As for Thorez, while trying to advance the interests of Communism, he was, on several occasions, to render service to the public interest. Immediately following his return to France, he helped eliminate the last vestiges of the "patriotic militias" that some of his people were trying to maintain in a new clandestinity. To the extent that the grim and harsh rigidity of his party permitted, he opposed the encroachments of the Comités de Libération and the acts of violence which some overexcited teams sought to undertake. To many workers, in particular miners, who listened to his harangues he continually gave the order to work to their utmost and to produce no matter what the cost. Was this out of a political tactic? There is no reason for me to try to unravel it. It is enough for me that France was served.' pp. 118–19.

29. Harry S. Truman, *Years of Trial and Hope*, New York 1956, vol. II, pp. 240–3. In fact, in the whole chapter concerning the creation of the Atlantic Pact, Yugoslavia isn't even mentioned; nor is the fear of 'subversion' in France and Italy.

30. This was quite apparent throughout the Kennedy era, when the apprehension of bourgeois public opinion in the United States was centred

less around the 'world spread of Communism', than around the 'sputnik', the 'missile gap', the USSR's advances in space technology, scientific education, etc.

31. There is an obvious parallel between social democratic reformism inside a capitalist country and Stalinist or Khrushchevist reformism in the world capitalist framework. In both cases we are confronted with the reified dialectic of *partial conquests*, the defence of which becomes a goal in itself, which takes precedence over the overall goal. This expresses the particular interests of a bureaucratic stratum which parasitically lives upon these conquests, but can only live on them insofar as they remain partial.

32. This is the line taken by the programme of the Communist Party of the Soviet Union adopted at the twenty-second congress.

33. The question could be posed, why didn't US imperialism immediately launch an attack against the Soviet Union in the summer and autumn of 1946, when it enjoyed an overwhelming military and economic superiority and a monopoly of nuclear arms? Three subjective, sociopolitical obstacles prevented such a course from being realistic. In the first place, the peoples of Western Europe were not ready to accept this turn, which consequently would have most probably led to victorious anti-capitalist revolutions in these countries. Secondly, public opinion was not ready for it in the United States, and it would have created a grave internal crisis, much graver even than the crisis created by the present Vietnam war. See *The Forrestal Diaries*, New York 1951, pp. 100–29. Thirdly, and this was paramount in the minds of the military leaders, the American soldiers were not ready to continue the war, and certainly not against a former ally. They wanted to go home immediately, and even revolted against postwar occupation of Europe and the Far East. See Harry S. Truman, op. cit., pp. 506–10; Mary-Alice Waters, *GIs and the Fight Against War*, New York 1967.

34. A UPI dispatch from Washington, dated 23 October, 1951, for the first time mentions the fact that 'American specialists on nuclear matters' consider that Soviet nuclear tests could profoundly modify the relationship of forces. Malenkov announced on 8 August, 1953, that the Soviet Union had manufactured an H-bomb.

35. An Agence-France Press release of 9 October, 1953, carried a statement by President Eisenhower of the same date that the USSR was able to conduct a nuclear attack against the United States.

36. Malek Bennabi, an Egyptian ideologue, published a book which summarizes all these hopes and illusions. *L'Afro-Asiantisme*, Cairo 1956. Many echoes of them can be found in official Soviet and Communist literature of the period.

37. For the period 1960–6, the average annual 'aid' of imperialist countries to underdeveloped countries amounted to $9 billion; during the same period, the average annual aid of 'socialist' countries to underdeveloped countries was less than $500 million. These figures are net, that is, after deduction of repayments of underdeveloped nations.

38. This formulation was used in the programme of the Communist Party of the Soviet Union adopted at the twenty-second congress to describe those states of the underdeveloped world which are supposed to be 'neither capitalist nor socialist'.

39. In *The Unfinished Revolution*, Isaac Deutscher recalls how Lenin, in one of his final writings, denouncing the brutal repression which Stalin and his cronies had unleashed in Georgia, expressed his fear that the 'great-Russian, chauvinistic scoundrel and oppressor' would cause infinite

damage to the communist cause by his arrogant behaviour towards Asian peoples. Lenin, in notes written on 31 December, 1922, expressed the historic warning that such behaviour could cause suspicions as to the sincerity of the Russian Communists' adherence to internationalist principles among the awakening peoples of the East.

40. One should stress the fact that the Chinese leaders are also responsible for peddling the myth of 'peaceful coexistence' for many years; that they opportunistically supported the disastrous right-wing line of the leadership of the Indonesian Communist Party, leading to the catastrophic defeat of October 1965 (Mao Tse-tung sent a public letter to Aidit on the fortieth anniversary of the Communist Party of Indonesia, approving the 'correct' line of the party!); that they instructed the Bengali Communists to soft-pedal revolutionary struggles in East Pakistan, because the reactionary Pakistan military dictatorship was the only bourgeois government in Asia which keeps very friendly relations with Peking. See Livio Maltan, *Party, Army and Masses in China*.

41. *Débat sur la ligne générale du movement communiste international*, Peking 1965, pp. 247–61.

42. In addition, one has to consider the tremendous importance of armament production in the 'countercyclical' economic strategy of 'mature' monopoly capitalism and the impossibility of that capitalism finding 'peaceful' outlets of a similar magnitude without endangering the whole logic of production for private profit.

43. In the case of Vietnam, it can easily be documented that civil war broke out in the South as a result of Diem's terrorism against left-wing and progressive circles of the population, after the Geneva agreements, *years* before the North decided to intervene in order to support the Southern guerrillas. See Nguyen Kien, *Le Sud-Vietnam depuis Dien-Bien-Phu*, Paris 1963; Hans Henle, *Chinas Schatten ueber Suedost-Asien*, Hamburg 1964; a summary of many sources can be found in Juergen Harlemann and Peter Gaeng, *Vietnam Genesis eines Konflikts*, Frankfurt 1966.

44. For example, *The Economist*, 10 June, 1967.

45. A few weeks before the October 1962 Caribbean crisis, *The Economist* published an editorial in its 6 October issue entitled, 'Obsessed by Cuba', which started with the following paragraph: 'There are plenty of good reasons for being worried about Cuba, and it may seem odd to put the correspondence columns of *Time* magazine and the *New York Herald Tribune* at the top of the list. But in fact the most disturbing thing about recent developments in Cuba is the effect they have had on the American state of mind; these two papers in particular (though not only they) convey the furious impatience – and the reluctance to see Cuba in context – that seem to mark the current mood in the United States. The widespread demand for President Kennedy to "do something" and damn the consequences, has reached a point where an outsider can fairly say what he thinks.' The Russians always insisted on the fact that, before sending missiles to Cuba, they had reliable information that Washington had prepared a new invasion of that island. See 'Open Letter of CPSU Central Committee to All Party Organizations and All Communists of the Soviet Union', 14 July, 1963.

PART THREE
Class Struggle and Bourgeois Power

In a discussion of the political ideas of Rosa Luxemburg and Leon Trotsky, Norman Geras points out that bourgeois democracy has been the normal political regime of the advanced capitalist countries since the Second World War. In this political system government is based on the consent of the governed, secured through electoral competition between parties which solicit a popular mandate to representative assemblies every few years. In practice the executive apparatus has a large measure of autonomy from the elected bodies and officials; the state apparatus itself is built on a hierarchical, bureaucratic basis, and its higher levels are directly integrated into the ruling class by many personal and social ties. The interests of big business, and the dictates of the national and international capitalist market, cannot be ignored by either legislative or executive. The electoral process itself is bound to reflect the extra-parliamentary concentrations of economic and social power. But these concentrations can include the power of an organized labour movement; indeed, in one way or another, they are bound to. Norman Geras discusses both the advantages and the risks that such a system entails for the bourgeoisie. In this excerpt from his book *The Legacy of Rosa Luxemburg* Geras takes as his point of departure the sharp contrast between Luxemburg's conception of bourgeois power and class struggle and the conceptions to be found in the writings of Eduard Bernstein and the Russian Mensheviks.

Based on antagonistic class relations, capitalist society spontaneously generates class conflicts. This is the primary source of all the social energy required to overthrow the political and economic structures of capitalism. When a proletarian upsurge achieves national scope, then the nature of the bourgeois political order and the depth of the capitalist crisis will determine the tactics and strategy required to lead the workers' movement to victory. Revolutionary tactics and strategy will be those that accumulate and concentrate the force of the proletarian class struggle in an escalating challenge to the prevailing order. Antonio Gramsci's writings on the workers' councils that erupted in Turin in 1919 and 1920 furnish a vivid picture of the creativeness of a proletarian upsurge. He contrasts the new forms of organization thrown up in the struggle with the circumscribed routines of the traditional workers' organizations. These articles by Gramsci were widely read in Turin at the time and helped to give shape to the movement of factory occupations and workers' control of production. With solidarity actions in every other part of Italy, the revolutionary democracy of the workers' councils was a formidable threat to the enfeebled and disorganized Italian bourgeois state. However, the Socialist party failed to consolidate and direct that explosion of proletarian class struggle. Neither the Socialist party nor the trade-union federation put forward a transitional programme for socialist revolution based on building and extending organs of workers' power throughout Italy. Gramsci insisted that the elements of such a proletarian solution to the crisis were already present in the actions of the workers of northern Italy. Ignoring this the Socialist party and trade unions led the movement to defeat. Before long the Italian bourgeoisie was looking to the fascists to ensure that they would never again have to face such a mortal peril.

Tom Nairn traces the history of the Labour party, indicating the structural reasons why its variety of socialism could be so easily absorbed by the bourgeois order. The Labour party was founded by, and subsequently has derived its substantive support from, the trade unions. This fact has ensured the Labour party a solid proletarian base and permitted it to become more simply an electoral and parliamentary machine than was the case for the Continental social-democratic parties which pre-dated the trade unions. The militants at the base of the trade unions in Britain were not required to play any direct role in the Labour party, while the constituency parties were rarely to play any role in the industrial struggle. The isolation of Labour politics from the source of proletarian class militancy was bound to enfeeble it, and to leave it without any social basis for withstanding the pressure of bourgeois institutions. The negative effects of the Labour party's undemocratic structure, and the separation of the economic and political spheres of action, was aggravated by a circumstance that Tom Nairn does not explore. Since its

inception the Labour party has excluded from direct participation the majority of organized Marxist militants within the
workers' movement. It has long operated a system of bans and
proscriptions against such militants; and it has refused to accept
affiliation from Marxist political organizations, beginning with
its refusal to accept the application for affiliation made by the
Communist party in the early 1920s. These exclusions certainly
help to explain the frustrated dialectic which has afflicted the
Labour party's internal political life and the hopelessness of the
Labour left vividly evoked by Tom Nairn.

The election of the Popular Unity government of Salvador
Allende in 1970 greatly stimulated the extra-parliamentary
movement of workers and peasants in Chile. The government
promised land reforms and nationalizations. The Chilean landowners and capitalists sought to sabotage this programme and
thus provoked a wave of land seizures and factory occupations.
In the working-class districts Supply Committees were established
to guarantee the distribution of food and other goods which the
capitalist interests were seeking to disrupt. The Allende government refused to abandon its programme of nationalizations and
social transformation but it failed to give organization and
coherence to the popular movement surging beneath it. The
Chilean armed forces overthrew the government and began the
bloody suppression of the workers' movement. Ralph Miliband
here examines the significance of these tragic events for socialists
everywhere.

Luxemburg and Trotsky on the Contradictions of Bourgeois Democracy

NORMAN GERAS

(Extract from *The Legacy of Rosa Luxemburg*, London 1976)

Well before 1905 some general indications can be found in Rosa Luxemburg's writings of the directions her thought would take when brought to bear on the problems of the Russian revolution. These are no more than indications. It was the momentous events of 1905 itself which enabled her to concretize them into a rounded-out strategic perspective for Russia. However, they already provide a clear anticipation of what her response would be to the Menshevik 'orthodoxy' on the Russian revolution: a blunt rejection of what she was to refer to on one occasion as 'gigantic stupidities'.[1] Two such anticipatory indications stand out in particular: Luxemburg's assertion of the inherent prematurity of the proletarian conquest of power; and the theme, pervading all her writings, of the historical bankruptcy of bourgeois democracy and liberalism.

Inherent immaturity

The first was elaborated, at the turn of the century, against Bernstein, whose argument in favour of gradualism included the notions that the proletariat was neither mature enough to take power nor fit yet to wield it, and that the exercise of proletarian power would in these circumstances be an impracticable, costly and disastrous experiment. The dictatorship of the proletariat, according to Bernstein, was, in a word, premature: a most happy conclusion on his part seeing that he deemed it to be ethically inadmissible in any case, since it violated the norms of 'democracy' and, as such, belonged 'to a lower civilization ... an age which did not know ... the present methods of the initiating and carrying of laws'.[2] Luxemburg's retort was not limited to the observation that beneath Bernstein's fears of a premature conquest of power there lay in reality 'nothing more than a *general opposition to the aspiration of the proletariat to possess itself of state power*'. Examining the argument concerning prematurity on its own terms, she also pointed out that it betrayed a mechanistic conception of the struggle for socialism to imagine that the necessary degree of proletarian political maturity could be produced or measured by factors extraneous to the class struggle itself, to the proletariat's struggle for, and exercise of, power and to the successes, failures and lessons of that whole process. Outside of the experience it provided there was no school of political maturity for the proletariat. For that reason, initiatives and even conquests of power which were, in an historical sense, premature would be unavoidable: 'These "premature" attacks of the proletariat constitute a factor, and indeed a very important factor, creating the political conditions of the final victory . . . in the course of the long and stubborn struggles, the proletariat will acquire the degree of political maturity permitting it to obtain in time a definitive victory of the revolution.' It should be borne in mind, however, that Luxemburg's argument here was developed in the context of a controversy about the general strategic orientation of the German SPD and justifies neither the inference that she believed socialist revolution to be on the agenda *everywhere and immediately*, nor the imputation to her of *tactical* recklessness. Her contention was simply that the proletariat's struggle for power could not be postponed until it was completely assured, in advance, of a definitive victory in ideal conditions, since that would be a postponement *sine die*. No revolution could even begin if its precondition was the complete political maturity of the proletariat, and no conquest of power be undertaken if it had to be legitimated by guarantees of perfect success. Where the conditions for the revolutionary seizure of power emerged, the proletariat could and must, nevertheless, attempt, within the limits of its strength, to implement its historical objectives. 'There can be no time', Luxemburg wrote, 'when the proletariat, placed in power by the force of events, is not in the condition . . . to take certain measures for the realization of its programme.'[3]

Prospects of bourgeois democracy

The significance of this argument in the present context and its distance from simple 'rebel's impatience'[4] are revealed by a consideration of the second theme, Luxemburg's diagnosis of the contemporary condition and prospects of bourgeois democracy. The programme of German Social Democracy, adopted at Erfurt in 1891, contained not only those demands, the so-called maximum programme, in which the party expressed its ultimate, socialist objective, but also a set of immediate demands – the minimum programme, to be fought for and won on the terrain of capitalist society itself – concerning the acquisition and extension of bourgeois rights and liberties and the improvement of the material conditions of the working class. Luxemburg's attitude to the minimum programme was far from being cavalier, despite her sustained fight against the way in which it was understood and projected, first by the revisionists, then by the party leadership and the political 'centre' from which the leadership drew its support. She vigorously opposed the revisionist attempt to excise the maximum programme from the perspectives of the SPD. From 1905 onwards she opposed, equally vigorously, the party's actual practice of delaying the struggle for socialism to some unspecified future even while continuing to affirm and reaffirm its currency. She tirelessly exposed as illusory and false the conceptions on which this contradictory practice was based: that the trade-unionist and parliamentary struggle for the minimal demands could be a substitute for a strategy of mass struggle leading towards the conquest of power; that secreted within that day-to-day, bread-and-butter struggle was some automatic trajectory towards socialism; that the trade-union and electoral strength of the working class could 'become', through organic growth and a Social-Democratic majority in the Reichstag, the dictatorship of the proletariat; that bourgeois parliamentarism itself might be the organ of proletarian dictatorship and democracy. Yet, at no time and in no way did Luxemburg belittle the importance to be attached to the struggle of the working class for elementary bourgeois-democratic rights. She believed, on the contrary, that that struggle was now the '*only* support' capable of sustaining bourgeois democracy, and that one of Social-Democracy's most urgent contemporary tasks was 'to save bourgeois parliamentarism from the bourgeoisie'.[5]

Underlying this belief were two arguments, both of them expressed during the course of the revisionist controversy, though Luxemburg continued to adhere to them thereafter. The first was that the institutions of bourgeois democracy, albeit no substitute for the dictatorship of the proletariat which they could not render superfluous, were needed by the working class nevertheless, since the rights of organization and expression which they allowed, and the very struggle for the defence and enlargement of those rights, constituted at least part of the indispensable preparation for its conquest, and exercise, of power. The second was that these same institutions of bourgeois democracy had, from the point of view of the bourgeoisie, exhausted their historical function and would be, indeed were being, progressively abandoned by it. Luxemburg challenged Bernstein's naïve and unilinear view according to which some law of progress guaranteed that democracy was the exclusive or even natural political form for capitalist relations of production, all other reactionary political phenomena being no more than accidental aberrations from the general law. Not only was this false historically, since capitalism had already coexisted with numerous political forms, from absolute monarchy through constitutional monarchy and democratic republic to Bonapartism. It also provided a dangerously mystifying perspective for the future. Bourgeois democracy, according to Luxemburg, had played a necessary though limited historical role in the bourgeoisie's struggle against feudalism and in its mobilization of the masses in that cause. But so soon as this struggle was completed or compromised, so soon as its 'stimulating fire' went out, as she contended it had already done on a more or less international scale, then bourgeois democracy lost its historical purpose, became useless and dispensable to the bourgeoisie itself. Threatened by a rising working class and racked by the convulsions of imperialist rivalry and militarism, the bourgeoisie would not hesitate to jettison its own democratic institutions. Since these had now lost the kind of support provided by this class in its 'heroic' period, Luxemburg's prognosis for them, should the workers' movement fail in their defence, was uniformly bleak. Hence the assertions that 'democratic institutions . . . have completely exhausted their function as aids in the development of bourgeois society', that 'liberalism . . . is now absolutely useless to bourgeois society', that 'bourgeois democracy must logically move in a descending line', that 'bourgeois parliamentarism has . . . completed the cycle of its historical development and has arrived at the point of self-negation', that 'parliamentarism has lost all significance for capitalist society'.[6] Hence the references, in a later period, to 'the inner wretchedness of bourgeois liberalism', to the 'merciless trampling down of the last remnants of . . . bourgeois liberalism and bourgeois progress', to 'the miserable breakdown of the last remnants of . . . bourgeois democracy'.[7]

The limitations of Luxemburg's foresight

There is in all this an evident underestimation on Luxemburg's part of bourgeois democracy's potential use, to the capitalist class, and potential life span, as one form of capitalist rule, within the metropolitan centres of imperialism. It should first be said, however, that her whole conception was in no respect inferior, neither analytically nor predictively, to the rosy Bernsteinian vision, an essentially liberal one, against which it was directed. She understood that the bourgeoisie would nowhere again be prepared to wage, let alone lead, an energetic revolutionary fight for the democratic objectives of the bourgeois revolution. She recognized that there were no lengths, however undemocratic, to which it would not go in defence of its rule and in pursuit of imperialist ambitions. She grasped earlier and better than anyone else that the European working class had reached an historical turning-point, that the epoch of peaceful growth and struggle in the context of capitalist stability lay behind it, while ahead there stretched a period of economic crisis and violent political conflict. Her writings can be seen as one long effort to erect a signpost at that turning-point in order to save the working class from misdirection on a new terrain. When the policy of the SPD which she had criticized for a decade came to fruition, during the First World War, in the *Burgfrieden* and the party's support for the 'Fatherland', she anticipated the general essence, if not the precise and convulsive forms, of the unparalleled calamity which this capitulation foreshadowed and which, twenty years later, would overtake the German and European working class and European Jewry in the shape of triumphant Nazism.

In 1915 Luxemburg wrote the following prescient lines: 'German freedom . . . has been endangered by this attitude of the social democracy far beyond the period of the present war. The leaders of the social democracy are convinced that democratic liberties for the working class will come as a reward for its allegiance to the fatherland. But never in the history of the world has an oppressed class received political rights as a reward for service rendered to the ruling classes . . . The indifference with which the German people have allowed themselves to be deprived of the freedom of the press, of the right of assembly and of public life, the fact that they not only calmly bore, but even applauded the state of siege is unexampled in the history of modern society . . . That such a thing is possible in Germany today, that not only the bourgeois press, but the highly developed and influential socialist press as well, permits these things without even the pretence of opposition bears a fatal significance for the future of German liberty. It proves that society in Germany today has within itself no foundation for political freedom, since it allows itself to be thus lightly deprived of its most sacred rights. Let us not forget that the political rights that existed in Germany before the war were not won, as were those of France and England, in great and repeated revolutionary struggles, are not firmly anchored in the lives of the people by the power of revolutionary tradition. They are the gift of a Bismarckian policy granted after a period of victorious counter-revolution that lasted over twenty years. German liberties did not ripen on the field of revolution, they are the product of diplomatic gambling by Prussian military monarchy, they are the cement with which this military monarchy has united the present German empire. Danger threatens the free development of German freedom not . . . from Russia, but in Germany itself. It lies in the peculiar counter-revolutionary origin of the German constitution, and looms dark in the reactionary powers that have controlled the German state since the empire was founded . . . The passive submission of the social democracy to the present state of siege . . . has demoralized the masses, the only existing pillar of German constitutional government.'[8]

Judged against a period which was bracketed by two bloody and destructive world wars, a period in which bourgeois democracy, where it survived, was subject to severe strain and pressure and, where it did not, made way for the most murderous variant of capitalist rule, Luxemburg's forecasts concerning the destiny of bourgeois democracy in the advanced countries are actually remarkable in one sense for their perspicacity. Nor is it entirely surprising if she did not see beyond this grim and extended reality to the era of renewed capitalist stabilization and expansion which followed it and in which bourgeois democracy was better able to prove its capacity for survival and revival. Theoretically, of course, her conception of capitalist accumulation precluded the possibility of such economic recovery, predicating an increasing aggravation of the problem of realizing surplus-value on the shrinkage of the non-capitalist environment. But there is a more important point here. Historically, capitalist recovery, after 1945, was in part the product of the preceding series of massive and repeated defeats for the European working class. No Marxist of Luxemburg's generation could fully foresee or measure them, much less all their effects, before the First World War, even though in her own case the onset of the war provided her with an inkling of their possibility. It may be added that that recovery could, in any case, be no more lasting or permanent than the period which produced a Bernstein, for all that it too, at its peak, spawned its own soothing myths. The stability enjoyed by advanced capitalism after the Second World War has already, and quite visibly, begun to fracture.

Bourgeois rule and popular consent

Even now, however, bourgeois democracy is far from being useless to the bourgeoisie. Luxemburg's early admonition of its demise in favour of more reactionary variants of capitalist rule, her failure to appreciate its potential resilience in the major countries of developed capitalism, must also partly be put down to a somewhat unilateral definition of its historical role: her belief that it was a political form specific to the bourgeoisie's struggle against feudalism. In fact, it is a form which has shown itself to be sturdiest where, and in the measure that, that struggle has been consummated,[9] a form of the bourgeoisie's consolidated ascendancy and not merely of its fight for it. From the point of view of the bourgeoisie there are excellent reasons for giving this political form its support. Bourgeois democracy performs the function, a not so heroic one this, of securing and maintaining the consent of the masses to their own exploitation and subordination. This point should not be oversimplified but nor can it be evaded. In a polemical observation, which may appear to contradict the bald manner in which it is here expressed, Trotsky once wrote for example: 'Anyone who would say that in England, France, the United States, and other democratic countries, private property is supported by the will of the people would be a liar. No one ever asked the consent of the people.'[10] The truth of this observation is that bourgeois democracy obtains the consent of the masses not by revealing their subordination to them, but by concealing it from them, much as the wage form conceals the existence of their exploitation. It throws up a screen (which is not just a fiction, however, but a real structure with real effects) of elections, parliamentary legislation and debate, equal democratic rights, etc., behind which the central, executive apparatuses of the state and their points of contact/access to the capitalist class are obscured. It thus creates the illusion in the masses that they control this democratic state at least as much as anybody else. What they consent to is not something which they know to be their own subordination in the light of the clearly presented historical alternative of its abolition but a structure which they understand quite otherwise. A kind of consent is secured from them nevertheless, even if it is misguided and misinformed, even if it is never entirely perfect from the point of view of the capitalist class, because pierced by the experience of a rather less benign reality, contradictory, and therefore in need of reinforcement by the constant threat, and periodic use, of violence.

Trotsky himself understood this. He explained it clearly in a series of writings on Germany embodying not only brilliant, and still unsurpassed, conjunctural analyses of the rise of Nazism, but also the elements of a theory of the capitalist state not to be found in the previous Marxist canon, not in Marx, nor in Lenin, nor in Luxemburg, and one which, to this day, has not been properly assimilated in Marxist research – still less by the most influential currents within the workers' movement. One of Trotsky's main concerns in these writings was precisely to elucidate the different forms and methods of bourgeois rule and the different social blocs they attempt to construct, and lean on, for their support. On the subject of bourgeois democracy he wrote: 'In a developed capitalist society, during a "democratic" regime, the bourgeoisie leans for support primarily upon the working classes, which are held in check by the reformists. In its most finished form, this system finds its expression in Britain during the administration of the Labour government as well as during that of the Conservatives.'[11]

Bourgeois democracy's strength in eliciting such support derives from mechanisms of ideological legitimation and political integration incomparably more powerful than those available to the alternative, overtly repressive forms of bourgeois rule and for want of which the latter employ systematic terror. All bourgeois democracies, to be sure, also possess an armed, repressive apparatus which they use not only as a last resort, when these other mechanisms begin to fail decisively, but also on a more regular basis: piecemeal or in generous doses depending on the nature of the case. They rely upon 'a combination of repressions and concessions'.[12] But the basic pillar of their strength is a dense and complex structure of institutions and practices, many of them external to the state apparatus itself – of elections, legislative, executive and advisory bodies, political parties, pressure groups and trade unions, newspapers and other mass media, etc. – through which the needs and demands of the masses are processed. This structure has a dual character. On the one hand, it does provide the workers' movement with the organizational and political means for opposing the more blatant forms of exploitation and oppression, for defending the workers' most immediate interests, and for winning material gains on their behalf. This provision is the source of bourgeois democracy's self-legitimating power, and explains why it is no *mere* fraud and why an attitude of sectarian, ultra-left abstentionism towards it will not win the confidence of politically conscious workers. On the other hand, this structure largely succeeds in sublimating and neutralizing, or sabotaging, such genuinely anti-capitalist demands and initiatives as do emerge, by taking them through its many 'competent' and 'specialized' channels, i.e. away from the masses, out of their direct control and sight – generally with the assistance of reformist workers' parties and trade-union leaders. This is why bourgeois democracy is *in large measure* a fraud, not class-neutral, not democratic *tout court*, and why the purely parliamentary road to socialism is a vain hope. The costs of this type of policy to the bourgeoisie, costs attendant on not having a prostrate workers' movement at its command, are not to be denied. But it has often been prepared to bear them, especially in the advanced countries where it could most afford to. Their levels of wealth and position within the imperialist nexus made possible, over long periods, fundamental concessions to the working class in terms of rising standards of living.

Risks

From the point of view of the bourgeoisie there are also certain risks. The organizational strength which the working class is able to build up can become a serious threat to bourgeois rule once it begins to be released in the direction of forms of proletarian self-activity and self-organization which overflow bourgeois democracy's constricting framework and paralyse its function as the political expropriator of the initiatives of the masses. Bourgeois democracy *itself* furnishes points of support from which such initiatives towards proletarian democracy and power can be launched. This is why abstentionism is also a miserable substitute for a socialist strategy which can learn how to use these points of support in a revolutionary way, opening up the contradiction within bourgeois democracy in order to dispatch it once and for all. The bourgeoisie has, in any case, been prepared to live with these risks up to a point. But only up to a point. Wherever and whenever the dam has begun to burst, it has moved, in the most resolute and bloodiest possible fashion, to liquidate all the paraphernalia of democratic government; and no one has yet produced a convincing reason for thinking that things are now different in this respect, though before 11 September 1973 Chile was offered in place of a reason. Luxemburg was therefore entirely correct to insist that the capitalist class is *everywhere* less sentimental about democracy than about its own continued rule. Nor was she alone in doing so. It has been a central principle of revolutionary Marxism, supported by good evidence, that the road to socialism cannot bypass the preparation of the working class and its allies for armed self-defence and armed struggle. Accordingly, the denial of this principle by individuals and organizations within the labour movement, whether Social-Democratic or Communist, has always marked their passage towards, or destination at, a meliorative, reformist perspective unable to get beyond or, sometimes, even see beyond the end of capitalist society.

None of this, however, adds up to bourgeois democracy's uselessness to the bourgeoisie in an epochal sense. It is not just that it has proved its worth, in certain conditions and over a considerable period of time, as a means of containing and integrating the masses. The course of liquidating it into naked repression, particularly where it has achieved any real hold, also entails both risks and costs for the bourgeoisie. For this course amounts to an open declaration of war on the workers' movement, a war whose outcome is never entirely certain. Even if the bourgeoisie triumphs, this is likely to be at the expense of a profound economic dislocation, and of a generalized ideological and social crisis which it will not quickly be able to repair. Furthermore, the hands into which it thereby entrusts its rule, whether those of military chieftains or those of fascist demagogues, have not always proved as pliable to its will or as sensitive to the long-term dictates of capitalist accumulation as have its democratic representatives and functionaries. It is out of fears and considerations of this kind that the bourgeoisie, though often forced to resort to them, is less than enthusiastic about what Trotsky, in a reference to fascism, termed 'the "plebeian" means of solving its problems'.[13] While, therefore, there is every reason, both defensive and offensive, for the workers' movement to be alert and vigorous in its attention to bourgeois democracy, a point on which Luxemburg was, once again, perfectly correct to insist, it is not true to suggest, as she did, that the bourgeoisie for its part will carelessly or light-mindedly abandon it. By the same token, it is not universally true to say that the workers' movement is its *only* contemporary support. On the contrary, where the workers' movement is the only such support, there bourgeois democracy is doomed in a much shorter-term sense than Luxemburg intended, frequently a conjunctural one. Withdrawing its support from democratic institutions which are beginning to jeopardize its rule, the bourgeoisie will either succeed in finding the means to overturn them or it will fail, and if it fails in *that* then the ultimate sanctions of its hegemony will have crumbled. The working class will understand this.

The capitalist class, to conclude here, has continued to give support to bourgeois democracy in certain conditions not because this class is, in the twentieth century, a revolutionary or progressive force, but because it is not. It has used bourgeois democracy, where it could, to arrest that one form of revolutionary progress which has been haunting it for over a century and which is now more urgent than ever, the emancipation of the working masses from exploitation. Bourgeois democracy still performs this function for it in the countries of advanced capitalism today. How long it can continue to do so is a problem that has yet to be resolved.

Notes

1. Letter to Emmanuel and Mathilde Wurm, 18 July 1906, cited in P. Frölich *Rosa Luxemburg*, London 1972, p. 124.

2. E. Bernstein *Evolutionary Socialism*, New York 1961, pp. 146–7; and see pp. 101–9, 155, 161–3, 196–7, 218–19.

3. 'Social Reform or Revolution' in M.-A. Waters (ed.) *Rosa Luxemburg Speaks*, New York 1970, pp. 81–3.

4. Kautsky's later characterization of Luxemburg's position. See C. E. Schorske *German Social Democracy 1905–17*, New York 1970, p. 185.

5. 'Social Reform or Revolution', Waters, op. cit., p. 76; 'Social Democracy and Parliamentarianism' in R. Looker (ed.) *Rosa Luxemburg:*

Selected Political Writings, London 1972, p. 110.

6. 'Social Reform or Revolution', Waters, op. cit., pp. 56, 73–6, 80–1; 'Social Democracy and Parliamentarianism', Looker, op. cit., pp. 106–10.

7. 'What Now?', Looker op. cit., p. 172; 'The Idea of May Day on the March', in Howard *Selected Political Writings of Rosa Luxemburg*, New York and London 1971, p. 318.

8. 'The Junius Pamphlet', Waters, op. cit., pp. 297–9.

9. As the last quoted passage indicates, Luxemburg herself was aware of this. It did not, however, restrain her from statements, of the kind noted above, which across all national histories declared bourgeois democracy to be generally moribund.

10. *Leon Trotsky on Britain*, New York 1973, p. 72.

11. Leon Trotsky, *The Struggle Against Fascism in Germany*, New York 1971, p. 158.

12. ibid., p. 281.

13. ibid., p. 282.

Anatomy of the Labour Party

TOM NAIRN

(Reprinted from *New Left Review*, 27 and 28, 1964)

The British Labour party is obviously one of the greatest political forces of the capitalist world. With its six million and more members, it is by far the largest of social-democratic parties. The twelve million votes cast in its favour at the last General Election were the votes of the majority of the working class – of a working class undivided on religious or ideological grounds, and sociologically the dominant class in an overwhelmingly proletarian nation. The Labour party is no mere opposition party. It is used to power, although the modalities of that power may seem limited.

Such are the evident indices of the Labour party's strength and importance. But inseparably associated with this strength there are less evident weaknesses, and both strength and weakness are aspects of a unique historical and political evolution full of its own characteristic contradictions, too little analysed until now. As a part of its well-known general antipathy to theory, the British Left has been notably averse to thinking critically about itself. The Labour party did not come into being in response to any theory about what a socialist party should be; it arose empirically, in a quite piecemeal fashion, like so much in British bourgeois society before it. And it rapidly became accepted as a permanent, inevitable feature of that society – a kind of monument about which it was pointless, if not impious, to ask too searching questions. Something of the mindless complacency of British bourgeois society was in this way transmitted to British socialism. And besides this, the Labour party dominates the scene so totally in Britain, it embraces so much and has sunk such deep roots that any radical change in it seems unthinkable, out of the question – what criticism could affect a leviathan like this? The very proportions of Labourism defy analysis.

Any adequate account of the Labour phenomenon must, naturally, be historical in its orientation. And a historical analysis must bear in mind Gramsci's stricture to the effect that: 'the history of a party . . . cannot fail to be the history of a given social class . . . writing the history of a party really means nothing but writing the history of a country from a particular, monographic point of view, throwing one aspect of it into relief.'[1] This is perhaps especially true of a party like the Labour party. Its empirical, undoctrinaire origins, the thoroughly indigenous nature of all its roots, signify a particularly intimate bond with the society that gave birth to it. Like other mass socialist parties, it is essentially a novelty – nothing else than the embryo of a new society altogether – but this element is concealed and qualified in its case by a singularly dense integument tying it to the past. This integument is at once party psychology, and mass psychology, the ideology and customs of Labourism and beyond them the reflexes of the Labour movement and of the working class as a whole. It is linked to, and in part dependent upon, a specific kind of organization and bureaucratic control. It was the natural, effective instrument of adaptation of a working-class movement to a society which itself – during the whole existence of Labourism – leaned instinctively and whole-heartedly towards the past.

Only from an examination of this matrix as a whole is it possible to define the basic problems of Labourist socialism. This study, naturally, cannot hope to treat such a complex of themes other than summarily – to look for a correct approach to it, by asking questions, rather than by formulating answers. But we must also try to see to what extent the situation of the Labour party under Harold Wilson is a new one. British society as a whole has begun to change more rapidly and consciously, after a long era of stagnation, generating a multitude of tensions and new contradictions. What new possibilities and dangers confront the Labour party under these conditions? What new problems are being added to the old ones?

British trade unionism

After the defeat of Chartism began the greatest era of prosperity for British capitalism, the twenty-five years from 1850 until about 1875. Cyclical crises practically disappeared. 'Shortly before the middle of the century there began everywhere a substantial advance in the standard of living. At first this was due not to rising wages but to falling prices; but later, when prices again rose, wages . . . rose more than enough to meet them . . . Revolts and mass movements gave place to the well-organized but moderate trade unions and co-operative societies of the new order.'[2] The epoch of integration had begun. This moderate trade unionism, whose basic structures and outlook endure to this day, was to become the nucleus of Labourism. Not until 1918 did it turn aside, even nominally, from a general acceptance of the conditions of capitalist society.

While early trade unionism of the Owenite period had been all-embracing in its organization and idealistic in its philosophy, trade unions after 1850 were fragmentary in structure and set themselves no general ideal greater than that of acceptance by the great Victorian bourgeoisie as 'respectable' institutions. Early trade unionism had tried to organize all grades of workers. After the defeats, in changed economic and psychological conditions – the development of industry, and especially metallurgical industry, was producing wider differences between skilled and unskilled operatives – the trade unions became organizations of the 'labour aristocracy'. A fundamental aspect of the new unionism was, in the words of the major historians of British trade unionism, 'the principle of the protection of the vested interests of the craftsman in his occupation'.[3] The Preface to the rules of the most important of the new unions, the Amalgamated Society of Engineers, actually compared the position of the skilled worker to that of the professional man: a qualified doctor, it points out, is entitled to certain privileges, and to protection by the law against charlatans – why should this not be true of the skilled worker who has gone through his apprenticeship? But since the law does not protect *his* 'privileges', the trade union must do so.

On this narrowly corporative basis – directed against the employers, in the first place, but also against the mass of unskilled workers – were built up organizations of great strength and resilience. Indeed, this strength of the new 'craft unions' lay in their very limitations, as compared to the older and more ambitious bodies. Their corporativism echoed that of the working class as a whole, showing the same positive and negative aspects. On the one hand, it was a model form of working-class resistance, appreciated as such in many other countries – for instance, by the large delegation of Parisian workers which visited London for the Universal Exhibition of 1862.[4] On the other hand, it was a form of integration into the characteristic hierarchies of Victorian society, an assimilative process affecting a vital sector of the proletariat. Politically, the new trade union leaders were committed to Liberalism – that is, to the classical British party of the industrial bourgeoisie, reposing on the twin pillars of Protestantism and Free Trade. Through them, the workers in effect allied themselves with the bourgeoisie against the power of the landlords, expressed in the Conservative party.

But not, as in under-developed countries, with a *weak* bourgeoisie struggling to assert itself against an all-powerful, regressive feudalism! In Britain, the agrarian question had in reality become completely secondary and the aristocracy could only govern in the general interests of the bourgeoisie even when in power – hence, the subordination of the working class to the Liberals was no more than a characteristic piece of mystification. Yet, until 1914 this tactic of diverting the political passions of the masses towards a fight against 'landed privilege' was to remain efficacious. David Lloyd George was its last great practitioner.

It was this period that occasioned Engels's famous outburst: 'The English proletariat is actually becoming more and more bourgeois, so that this most bourgeois of all nations is apparently aiming at the possession of a bourgeois aristocracy and a bourgeois proletariat *as well as* a bourgeoisie.'[5] Marx too thundered constantly in his letters, denouncing the 'sheepish attitude of the workers' and their 'Christian, slavish nature.'[6] He did not make the mistake committed by so many later observers and critics of the British working-class movement – that of blaming exclusively the 'treachery' of leaders for what was wrong. It is doubtful, indeed, if any other working-class movement has produced as many 'traitors' – or at least as many *unashamed*, magnificently naked traitors – as has Labourism. But the angry denunciation of leaders in which sectarians and the Labour Left wing have always indulged has served only to conceal the underlying conditions of betrayal, the circumstances in the party, the movement, the class itself which have generated corrupt and half-hearted leadership. Labourism is a system which *cannot* be led by revolutionaries. To retrace the origins of Labourism in Victorian trade unionism is to see the inevitability of the moderation afflicting this, the nucleus of all later developments. If, in general, it is true to say that trade unions are 'a type of proletarian organization specific to the period when capital dominates history . . . an integral part of capitalist society, whose function is inherent in the regime of private property',[7] the problem is to understand why classical British trade unionism shows such an especially profound and permanent subordination to the categories of its own capitalist society. The answer does not lie in the stupidity of leaders, or – as Marx cried in another moment of exasperation – in the biological traits of the British workers, those 'thick-headed John Bulls, whose brain-pans seem to have been specially manufactured for the constables' bludgeons'.[8] With great energy and courage, the British workers had already proved this was not so.

Although always an organ of adaptation to capitalist society, trade unions have occupied a great variety of roles in the evolution of the working-class movement in different countries, and stood in different relationships to political and revolutionary organizations. But in Britain, from 1850 until around 1890, they were the working-class movement. There was nothing else. There were no socialist ideas or movements with any influence, until the 1880s there was not even a significant radical movement to which the workers could look for support. The voices of intellectual protest were few, and remote from politics and the working class: distorted by the immense pressures of Victorian conformity, they tended towards an impossible and Utopian rejection of capitalism and industrialism as such (as with Ruskin and William Morris) or retreated into obscurity and eccentricity (like the novelists Meredith and Samuel Butler). In such a void – following earlier defeat – profound subordination was unavoidable. With the passage of time, the bourgeoisie disposed of more and more ample means of corruption, both material and spiritual. Its world economic dominance enabled it to concede something to the superior strata of skilled workers, those involved in the first trade unions, while to all the inherent mystifications of British bourgeois society was added the sense of belonging to a superior race, that which owned a large part of the world and supplied the wants of the rest. Belonging to it was a kind of privilege, even in misery. From the 1880s onwards, when British capitalism was for the first time challenged on world markets, this feeling of superiority was enormously increased by the new climate and mystique of imperialism.

The workers could not by themselves throw off the crushing weight of this complex of historical conditions. Resistance was only possible in the terms imposed by the system. For forty decisive years, class conflict – whose concrete form is always determined by the entire field of social forces at any given time – was reduced to relatively mild and tolerable proportions. Bourgeois society had succeeded, at least temporarily, in assimilating the working-class movement. By the end of the period, habits and traditions had been formed, founded on the strength and prestige of the trade unions, enduring reflexes which impressed themselves on all that happened later.

The entire political existence of the British working class was conditioned by the prior existence of this trade unionism. Trade unionism was to dominate politics absolutely – the contrary of what happened in, for example the evolution of the German working class. When the workers began to think politically for themselves, slowly and still hesitantly, in the last decade of the century, they could only start from the accomplished fact of trade unionism. How could any working-class political movement have any success, if it did not somehow lean upon the trade unions and make use of their strength, their funds, their prestige? All the more so, because of the great expansion of the unions in the last ten years of Victoria's reign, after the London dock strike of 1889. This strike and the events following it constituted the entry into trade unionism of masses of unskilled workers. In part, the trade union movement was reconstructed on a less exclusive basis, with large 'general' unions of unskilled workers supplementing the old 'craft' unions. Total trade union membership rose in a few years from around 750,000 to one-and-a-half million, and by 1900 there were two million trade unionists.

This growth and partial change in the character of trade unionism had been produced by the more severe cyclical crises and generally more difficult conditions imposed on British capitalism since the ending of its world monopoly. It coincided with the beginning of serious socialist agitation in Britain, conducted by the first Marxist group, the Social-Democratic Federation (founded in 1883), the Fabian Society (founded in 1884), and the most important socialist party – and forerunner of the Labour party – the Independent Labour party (founded in 1893). And it gave rise to something of a counter-offensive by the employers, culminating in the Taff Vale court case (1901) when a legal decision in effect abolished the right to strike. The last two factors together moved the trade unions towards political action. But of the two, the second was alone really decisive – the trade union leaders were only convinced of the necessity for working-class politics when such action became necessary to safeguard trade unionism itself.

The historical function of trade unionism – the function 'inherent in' capitalist society, in Gramsci's words – was the protection of the workers' material standards of life and work, through a constant struggle against the mechanisms of the capitalist system. In itself, this did not require a consciousness of the working class as being more than one section of society, with particular problems arising out of its particular situation. Its ideal does not have to be any more than that of obtaining a 'square deal' for the workers, in the general terms permitted by that situation. Such 'economism' – as Lenin called it – can embrace political action or not, in differing circumstances. Indeed, it can involve the consciousness and action of the working class as a whole, or not, according to the needs and degree of evolution of the working class. The last decades of the century saw the British working class, through its trade unions, first of all acquire a more comprehensive consciousness of its essential unity (in contrast to the fragmentation of the craft unions), and then attempt to pursue its collective interests through forms of political action. But without stepping beyond the limits of 'economism'.

A non-Marxist universe

Who were the socialists that tried, without success, to convert the trade unions to more ambitious ideas at this time? Plainly – in view of what was said above about the nature of British bourgeois society, and about the specific deprivations and mystifications inflicted on the British proletariat – the arrival of Marxist ideas in Britain should have been of the greatest importance. Was not Marxism the evident, only answer to the intellectual and political voids of British historical development? At once the natural doctrine of the working class, and the summing-up of the Enlightenment and all the highest stages of bourgeois thought into a new synthesis? Its superiority to British bourgeois conservatism was such, surely, that by appropriating it the working class could compensate for the burdens oppressing its evolution and attain its own *hegemonic* ideology?

A few years after the foundation of the Social-Democratic Federation, however, Engels frankly admitted the problems it was confronting: 'One can see that it is by no means easy to drill ideas into a big nation in a doctrinaire and dogmatic way, even if one has the best of theories, developed out of its own conditions of life . . .'[9] In fact, the task was to prove impossible. The reason is, in part, that Marxism – in the elementary form embraced and propagated by the Federation – was *not* really developed out of the 'conditions of life' of Britain and the British proletariat. It was based upon an extensive analysis of the *economic foundations* of that life, certainly – but the dominating characteristic of social life in general was, precisely, the variety of ways in which those foundations were masked for the average consciousness, the web of false relations and ideas woven around them. Marx and Engels had devoted little time to examination of these superstructures. This cannot be considered a reproach to them, but it plainly imposed special problems to their disciples in Britain. A theory can only become practically effective and a cultural and political force when it is felt to echo experience; but experience, actual consciousness, is mediated through the complex of superstructures and apprehends what underlies them only partially and indirectly. Hence, in Britain it was vitally necessary to decipher social reality as a whole, in order that Marxism could penetrate the working-class movement. This required a creative development of Marxist ideas – Marxism can never be 'applied', every genuine use of it implies a development of the theory itself – on a very considerable scale. At this time, unfortunately, the British intelligentsia had other preoccupations. It was engaged on discovering Hegelian idealism and re-expressing it in the appropriate imperialistic terms (as in Bosanquet's *Philosophical Theory of the State*, for instance, published in 1901); one sector had undertaken a timorous revolt against Victorian puritanism, inspired by G. E. Moore's *Principia Ethica*, but this was confined strictly to personal and aesthetic terms.

As was indicated above, therefore, the nullity of native intellectual traditions proved to be the most serious of obstacles to socialism. The Marxists of the Social-Democratic Federation – and their later successors – were destined to remain a small and sectarian group. The leaders of Labourism thought that, however appropriate Marxism might be in foreign countries, it just had no reference to Britain. Nevertheless, some kind of theory was objectively necessary to the working-class movement. The trade unionists had adhered originally to *laissez-faire* liberalism; when this was no longer possible and they had committed themselves to autonomous political action, they tried for as long as possible to avoid any doctrine justifying such action. Pure empiricism reigned during the first decades of labourist politics. When the movement had become a great mass force, however, threatening to depose liberalism politically (after the World War), empiricism had to be at least adulterated with something else capable of furnishing a minimum of cohesion. The void left by the failure of the Marxists had to be filled by the other socialist currents active from the 1880s onwards.

'British socialism'

These indigenous theories were uninteresting and, in any wider perspective, quite unimportant. Essentially, they reflected nothing but the intellectual parochialism of the bourgeoisie, its complacent self-absorption and optimism. They adapted and transformed third-rate bourgeois traditions into fourth-rate socialist traditions, imposing upon the working class all the righteous mediocrity and worthless philistinism of the pious Victorian petty bourgeois. Fabian socialism was derived Utilitarianism, the timid and dreary species of bourgeois rationalism embraced by the British industrial middle class during the Industrial Revolution. In it, bourgeois rationalism became socialist rationalism chiefly through the substitution of the State for the magic forces of the *laissez-faire* capitalist market: the former was seen as bringing about the 'greatest happiness of the greatest number' almost as automatically as the latter had been. According to this ideology of minor functionaries, although the working class made socialism *possible* (with their votes), the new society would actually be created by an eternal 'elite of unassuming experts . . . exercising the power inherent in superior knowledge and longer administrative experience'.[10]

The Independent Labour party's socialism, on the other hand, was derived from the religion of the Protestant sects. This was possible because since the seventeenth century sectarian Protestantism had always been to a certain extent a movement of popular protest against the official or 'established' religion, Anglicanism, which was (unlike Catholicism) clearly seen *as* the religion of the ruling classes. Militant Protestantism died hard, in a nation whose great revolution had after all been carried out under the aegis of Puritanism. But long before the foundation of the Labour party, this tradition had decayed into a relatively subordinate, impotent – and therefore acceptable – force, a kind of domesticated national voice of conscience, forever indignant at the 'excesses' of capitalism and at the iniquitous conduct of the very rich and the very poor alike (the vices of the latter being essentially identified with alcohol). Such was the cadaver passed on to the Labour movement. If the ideas of Fabianism were few and tedious, this post-Christian socialism had no ideas at all. The dissenting sects had viewed intellect with the gravest suspicion, as being probably associated with the Devil; the forms and attitudes of protest bequeathed by them to Labourism, therefore, could produce only a sort of ethical, sentimental socialism founded not upon any idea of what the world is objectively like but upon the conviction of its wrongness and injustice. Socialism, hence, was apprehended primarily as a moral crusade propelled by emotions of outrage at injustice and suffering. Speaking of the greatest propagandist of Independent Labour party socialism, G. D. H. Cole points out how in spite of Robert Blatchford's immense influence as a journalist, 'his contribution to socialist *thought* . . . was next to nothing. He was neither a theorist nor a planner, and to socialist doctrine he neither contributed nor sought to contribute any original idea'.[11]

It is of the utmost importance to grasp the relationship between these two currents of socialist ideology, for this relation has been the key structure of Labourist ideology. Although it came into being bit by bit with the gradual formation of the Labour party from 1900 onwards, one can perceive what constitutes the link from a consideration of their respective characters.

In the first place, what they had in common was sufficient to permit them to come together in one body and act in alliance. They both accepted – the Fabians by clear conviction, the ILP socialists for want of an alternative – the *evolutionary* character of socialism. Socialism had to be constructed piece by piece, in discrete instalments, over a long period of time. This evolutionism, in effect, denied entirely that a decisive struggle for *power* played any necessary role in the process – the conditions of British bourgeois society had clothed the fact of power so well, and reduced the conflict of classes so much, that this mystification was entirely natural. The Fabians actually thought of the whole capitalist epoch in history as being, not the domination of one class over others, but a mere 'period of anarchy' in social affairs, a period of 'administrative nihilism' in between feudal administration on the one hand and the new collective, socialist administration on the other.[12] Society was recovering spontaneously from this deplorable anarchy, as State intervention and control were extended, and socialists had simply to assist this natural, healthy tendency by the appropriate propaganda and action in support of nationalization and municipalization. Since present society was not in essence a power-structure but a sort of historical mistake, socialism could not be a struggle to replace one hegemony with another.

The logical consequence of evolutionism was, in concrete terms, *parliamentarism*. That is, there could not be any good reason why parliamentary action should not suffice, to build socialism up piece by piece. Again, although the ILP was much less enthusiastic about parliament than the Fabians, it nevertheless accepted it in practice. Instinctively, the workers and advanced trade union militants in the ILP distrusted these things – but they saw no alternative, no other theory justifying their diffidence. So, how could they fail to be persuaded by such an orator as James Ramsay MacDonald, leader of the Labour party for most of the first thirty years of its existence, and (as he liked to conceive himself) the 'poet of socialism'? 'The spirit of constructive socialism', intoned the hero, 'arises from political democracy. With the approach of the sun to the earth in spring, the breeze warms and the wayside bursts out into colour. Life is the companion of the hours of spring. So is socialism the companion of democracy . . .'[13] If the British Parliament was 'democracy', in this ineffable conception, it was also a great deal more. Accepting it as one's life companion signified more for the nascent socialist movement than an easy march towards socialism.

The British parliamentary system was no recently constructed, banal affair, a mere instrument of government; with its feudal origins and almost uninterrupted history, its antique rites and (even up to 1914) remarkably aristocratic composition, it was by far the most prestigious of assemblies. This immemorial institution could not be ignored, or merely *utilized* by socialists; the 'Mother of Parliaments' imposed her own conditions on whoever entered her. In other words, in Britain the parliament was an integral, central aspect of the entire complex of mystifications constituting bourgeois hegemony, a sort of living myth rather than a bourgeois machine. For centuries, the different sections of the British ruling class had been used to arrange their differences in it; its traditional two-party order expressed internal divisions inside a fundamentally united class, not a total class conflict – hence the mild and amicable custom it showed, its *camaraderie*, its well-known reputation as 'the best social club in the world'. The menace of such an atmosphere for

Labourism, as the representative of a new class and a *real* class conflict, is obvious. And the problem was magnified by the great progress already realized by the old parties in adapting to the new age of mass democracy. There had been very extensive adult male suffrage since 1867, and the Conservative and Liberal parties had evolved from being groups of 'notables' into mass organizations seeking to exploit the new electorate – even on this plane, therefore, the new working-class political movement could not hope to change the political system, by asserting itself as a new type of party representing hitherto excluded masses. Everything combined to make it appear as simply a new competitor for votes on the political market, of essentially the same type as the other two; the system was prepared to absorb it, in every respect.

The common subjection to these ideas, and to this fatal context of political action, gave rise to the inevitable preponderance of one of the two socialist tendencies mentioned over the other. They signified the permanent hegemony of Fabianism, ideologically. The Fabians were in essence technicians of reform – perhaps the most able reformers of this kind produced by socialism in any country. Their whole interest and effort was always concentrated upon what was immediately possible for specific ends and in the actual condition of society; their acute sense of the possible, their great respect for the facts that concerned them, their armoury of information and argument, all these things made them *effective* reformers. And these perspectives were, naturally, the perspectives proper to so-called 'evolutionary' socialism and parliamentarism.

The socialists of the Independent Labour party, by contrast, were predominantly working-class in origin (the party was strong above all in the great northern industrial towns, while the Fabians were Londoners) and lacked the formation and outlook of the technocrats. Their revolt against society was, in a sense, far more *real* than that of the Fabians: they reacted against capitalism with passion, they took the ultimate aim of the socialism movement seriously and wanted to see the beginnings of a real change in their own lifetime – not in some indefinite future state, at the end of an interminable series of partial reforms. *Instinctively*, they, in fact, rejected the perspectives of evolutionism and parliamentarism; but because they accepted the latter *intellectually*, they were constrained to accept the leadership of Fabians within the wider ambit of the working-class movement.

Lacking ideas (that is, lacking intellectual cadres) capable of formulating what they felt, tied in the archaic web of neo-Protestant moralism, they never had a clear conception of what should be *done* practically in order to realize their socialist dream.

The Fabians, on the other hand, invariably knew what to do. Some idea of their competence and prescience can be gathered from the contents of the *Minority Report of the Poor Law Commission*, published in 1909. This report on the reform of the state assistance laws concerning the poor and unemployed, written mostly by the leading Fabians Sidney and Beatrice Webb, anticipates with great accuracy the entire development of social legislation since that date. It is, as G. D. H. Cole points out 'the first full working out of the conception and policy of the Welfare State – more comprehensive . . . than the Beveridge Report of 1942, which in many respects reproduced its ideas'.[14]

This meant, in effect, that within the limits of Labourism the actual modalities of action were dominated by the Fabians. The ILP tradition was destined to become – so to speak – the *subjectivity* of the political wing of Labourism, the emotions of the movement in contrast to its Fabian 'mind' or 'intellect'. When the two traditions were united inside the Labour party, other factors also contributed to the hegemony of Fabianism. But one can see how the Fabians were bound to be naturally in command – how ILP socialism, in spite of its working-class base, in spite of a certain authenticity of reflex and feeling rendering it infinitely more humanly admirable than Fabianism, could only become a 'left' opposition fixed in more or less impotent attitudes of protest. It was destined to become a left wing permanently, necessarily in rebellion against Fabian mediocrity – but unable to formulate and develop coherently this revolt, intellectually empty, paralysed inside the larger body of Labourism, a permanent minority opposition lacking the resources to assume hegemony of the movement in its turn.

Second-best socialism

These considerations may help us to identify the second fundamental problem of Labourism. Because of the size and power of trade unionism, it was – we saw above – bound to dominate the nascent political movement. The dilemma confronting all the socialist pioneers is described by Cole in these words (speak-

ing of the Independent Labour party): 'They speedily realized
that . . . they must either induce the trade unions to throw in
their lot with them or be content to build up very slowly a party
based on individual membership on the Continental socialist
model. As they were not prepared to wait, most of them preferred the shorter cut of a Labour party based mainly on trade
union affiliations, even though they realized that they could get
such a party only by a considerable dilution of their socialist
objectives . . .'[15] The Labour party was, indeed, a kind of historical
'short-cut' to socialism (but a short-cut that has proved very much
more long and difficult than the early socialists believed, perhaps
longer than the alternative would have been). It did not emerge,
however, only because the socialists 'were not prepared to wait'.

A complex combination of factors really determined the
decision and made it certain that the growth of socialism could
only proceed 'very slowly'; we have tried to identify them above.
The overpowering conservatism of British society, deeply
embedded in the working class itself and now aggravated by
imperialism; the failure of the intellectuals to attack this conservatism and provide the basis of a genuine 'British socialism';
the slow evolution of all socialist ideas and the corresponding
movement, in isolation from the movements in other European
countries, leading to the dominance of the unions and their
prudent, economist philosophy – all these things brought about
the 'second best' solution of Labourism. When the unions finally
agreed to co-operate in setting up a working-class political
movement at the time of the Taff Vale decision, the socialists
were in fact only too happy to accept the union's conditions.
The proposed political party would be not socialist, but devoted
to 'the direct interest of Labour' – that is, trade unionism
translated on to the political plane, a political party like a kind
of super trade union representing the interests of the class as a
whole in the way that an individual union treats the interests of
its members. Although the trade unions were furnishing the
finances and laying down the general orientation of the new
party, the greater part of its active organizers and leaders were,
naturally, socialists. The Fabian Society and the Independent
Labour party were affiliated to the new organization, in the same
way as the trade unions, and furnished the cadres. Here was the
matrix within which the character of British socialism was
formed, the character which the Labour party as a whole would
assume when it became a socialist party, at last, in 1918.

It is the internal dynamic of this socialism which constitutes the second basic problem of the Labourist movement. We have already seen the elements found within it, and their relationship. In the Labour party, Fabianism became the dominant, right-wing leadership tradition, the source of the ideas governing most of the action of the party. Its leaders were all to be either avowed Fabians (Attlee, Gaitskell) or implicit Fabians, whatever their apparent background and orientation (MacDonald, Henderson, Lansbury). The Independent Labour Party became the Labour left wing, in chronic instinctive protest against the leadership but intellectually subordinate to it and incapable of effectively replacing it. Labourism, therefore, acquired from the beginning *a peculiarly weak left*. This is, in a sense, the intimate tragedy of Labourism – for the left has always expressed the most vital working-class elements, the most active and genuine socialist forces *potentially* able to develop their own hegemony over party and state. But expressing them in the fashion and under the conditions indicated, the Labour left has really completely frustrated these forces, putting them at the disposition of the right-wing reformists. It has been unable even to seriously influence the leadership, except under rare circumstances and momentarily.

Hence, the Fabian-inspired leadership tradition, permanently supported by the trade unions, could acquire a great stability and continuity – a kind of dynasty, in fact, with its own characteristic internal procedures of recruitment and co-ordination, almost independent of the party in general. And this permanent, organic power in its turn of course *obstructed* any further real evolution of the left wing – it is as if the Independent Labour Party tradition, which was apparently the beginning of a real British mass socialist party, was *paralysed* by entry into the matrix of Labourism and the conditions it found therein. Hardie and the other ILP leaders anticipated that they would be able to rapidly convert the Labour party to socialism, their socialism. Instead, the conditions of Labourism, and their own weakness, transformed them into a mere permanent opposition, always urging the Labour party to move left and always unable to make it move, only half conscious of their own position and its true meaning, unable to act within Labourism but unable to see any alternative to Labourism, oppressed by Fabian triviality and timidity but with no workable alternative to offer – such was the result of the 'short cut' to socialism which Labourism had seemed to represent. Such was the paradox of Labourism – the distinctive form of socialism which arose out of British conditions, and in effect prevented any *further* socialist evolution from taking place.

It can be seen, then, that the 'left' of Labourism is different in nature, and occupies quite a different function, from those of socialist parties elsewhere. Its non-Marxist aspect is only one part of a much deeper peculiarity. Obviously, too, this peculiarity and all its consequences for the Labour party, the second fundamental problem of Labourism, are closely connected to the first problem previously distinguished. In part, the Independent Labour Party's socialist tradition and then the Labour party left wing have been what they have been because of a historical factor already discussed in this review: the integration of the intelligentsia into the general fabric of British conservatism, that secular, insular stultification which effectively prevented the intellectuals from contributing what was necessary to the emergent working-class movement, isolating the latter and throwing it back into second-hand, second-rate substitutes, a narrow and debased socialist culture inherently incapable of meeting the tremendous challenge of the struggles awaiting it. And both 'problems' of Labourism are, of course, from another point of view *defining characteristics* of Labourism. In the case of the left, for instance, it is clear that the Labour party has only been able to become the one great political expression of the British working class and survive in the same form for so long, *because* it has had a left wing of the general type analysed. Other socialist traditions and ideas would not have been able to tolerate the Labour party, and it would not have been able to tolerate them – schisms of the kind familiar in other movements would inevitably have occurred, decisively altering the political evolution of the working class and the whole nation.

Hypocrites and traitors

From 1906 onwards, the Labour party functioned essentially as a kind of trade union 'pressure group' (or, more widely, as a 'pressure group' for the working class as a whole). It was not a very effective pressure group. Its supine acceptance of parliamentarism made of it for most of the time a subordinate attachment of the Liberal party. Something of the evolution of the early Labour party can be seen in the contrast between two statements by the same man, Ben Tillett, one of the trade union militants who had played a prominent role in founding both the Independent Labour Party and the Labour party. Speaking in 1893, he asserted that socialists should aim first of all 'to capture the trades unionists of this country, a body of men well organized, who paid their money, and were socialists at their work every day, and not merely on the platform, who did not shout for blood-red revolution, and when it came to revolution sneaked under the nearest bed . . . With his experience of unions, he was glad to say that if there were fifty such red revolutionary parties as there were in Germany, he would sooner have the solid, progressive, matter-of-fact, fighting trades unionism of England than all the hare-brained chatterers and magpies of continental revolutionists'.[16] Here was the authentic spirit of Labourism: proudly anti-theoretical, vulgarly chauvinist, totally deluded by the false social-democratic contrast between 'revolution' (conceived as twenty-four hours of 'blood-red' violence) and 'evolution' (conceived as a sort or arithmetic adding-up of social-ism by little, regular instalments). Yet the same Ben Tillett, fifteen years later, published a well-known pamphlet with the title *Is the Parliamentary Party a Failure?* in which he denounced the Labour deputies as 'sheer hypocrites' who 'repaid with gross betrayal the class that willingly supported them'.[17] But the Labour 'Parliamentary Party' was only the logical consequence of the outlook and policy Tillett himself had preached in 1893. 'Hypocrisy' and 'betrayal' were the natural result of the 'solid, progressive, matter-of-fact' economism and philistinism he had defended; ordinary trade unionists were *not* 'socialists at their work every day', and the Labourist assumption that they were and that a great political movement could be founded on them just as they were led to the creation of politicians who were not 'socialists at *their* work every day', either. The missing dimension characteristic of Labourism emerges clearly from Tillett's remark: socialist education, the complex, difficult task of changing consciousness to express (and, by expressing, develop) the instincts of the masses at their work every day. Labourism's relation to the class it represents is in essence a *passive* one. Historically, it accepts the working class and the organizations the latter evolved in its long development, the trade unions, as given, decisive facts – arriving late upon the scene, the organ of a class already profoundly adapted to the conditions of bourgeois society and imbued with its conservatism, it sees its function as no more than a continuation, a further step in this evolution.

But the evolutionary models at the root of Labourist thought and action are false. Their falseness is the crucial falseness of Labourism as a whole. The advance on to the political plane embodied in the Labour party is not really another step on the same evolutionary road, a 'natural' process of growth on the same basis. There is a factor of novelty involved in it, requiring a more radical and complete change than the analogy allows – a qualitative change, as it were. The political place is the plane of power: a political party lays claim to a specific form of hegemony over society as a whole, and a socialist party intends using such hegemony to remodel society. The problems of hegemony are of an order different from those confronting trade unions – at least, trade unions as they existed in Britain up to 1906. They impose upon a hitherto subordinate social class and its organizations a vast, energetic development, a new tension and perspective, violent and positive adjustments in the field of culture – if the hegemony is to be really new, in fact, a sort of metamorphosis. The drive towards this change does not arise mechanically from the working class – least of all from the British working class as it was in the imperialist era – and is not transmitted to political leaders by a passive link between the latter and the former.

An apparent paradox is the key to this typical central defect of Labourist socialism. The political potential of the working class is not realized when the political movement founded on it accepts as determinant the structures and outlook already created by the workers in their struggle as a subordinate class. These structures cannot *really* determine the form and content of a political movement – hence, as the entire story of Labourism so clearly demonstrates, when political parties embrace this basis they finish by being determined by quite different factors. That is, by the pressures of bourgeois society outside the proletariat, by paralysing conventions and myths. The miserable 'respectability' of the new-born Labour party, its abject political manoeuvring, its lead-heavy 'moderation' – its whole apparatus of 'betrayal' – arose paradoxically from its purely proletarian basis. The latter apparently determined the nature of the political, socialist movement; but because in reality – for the reasons indicated – it could not do so, the effective political culture of the socialist movement was bound to be not proletarian but bourgeois. The way was left open for what may be more accurately defined as a sub-bourgeois political culture, for the sweepings of the great Anglo-Saxon ethos, a servile imitation of the ruling class's corpus of ideas and customs quite dissociated from the latter's historical *raison d'être*. The paradox functions even on the plane of personalities: to the solidly working-class character of the Labour party's militants – immediately visible at any Labour Party Conference – there corresponded *necessarily* ruling cadres derived directly from the ruling class, imbued with its outlook and traditions, such as Attlee, Gaitskell, Dalton and many others.

Does this mean that the working class can only evolve a socialist movement truly expressing its political potential under the tutelage of revolutionary intellectuals, of an intelligentsia whose own sociological origins are not proletarian? This, in turn, is surely only one aspect of the truth. The conception of the intellectuals mechanically 'manipulating' the working class ('fomenting' trouble, in the classical reactionary image) is a mere antithesis to the conception of the political movement arising spontaneously out of the working class. In reality, only a dialectical relationship between leaders and masses, 'intellectuals' and 'executants', can create a genuinely proletarian and socialist political movement. And it was the absence of this dialectic which crippled and hypostatized Labourism in a mould that was to become chronic, resisting all later pressures for change. The historical failure of the intellectuals – the particular '*trahison des clercs*' incarnated in Labourism – signifies therefore not the lack of an elite mandarin class benevolently bestowing its wisdom upon the workers from above, but the lack of a kind of catalyst element a socialist movement requires in order to be itself.

Socialism, declared the poet of socialism in 1912, 'must begin with the facts of social unity, not with those of class conflict, because the former is the predominant fact in society'.[18] So it was not surprising if, two years later, after its ignominious and subordinate parliamentary career, the new Labour party plunged into active participation in the Great War. With even less difficulty than in other European countries, the official Labour movement was transformed into an instrument of government policy. 'By 1914,' it has been pointed out, 'the more enlightened members of Britain's ruling orders had come to see the leaders of Labour *both* as opponents and as allies.'[19] After 1914, they ceased for years to be opponents. The Labour party took part in government for the first time when it entered the war-time coalition of 1915, and later played a more important role (with three Ministerial posts) in the new Lloyd George coalition of 1916. The war also led to a general weakening of socialist influence within the Labour movement, and to hostility between the trade unionists and the socialists of the ILP – chiefly because of the pacifist protest against the war among certain ILP leaders.

But if the Great War brought about a further assimilation of the Labour movement, and a further weakening of the already feeble socialist influence upon it, in other respects its effects were quite different. As so often in the Labour party's history, one is in the presence of paradox. The Great War also *made* the Labour party, in the form we know today, and constituted therefore an essential milestone in socialist development. War conditions forced the government to evolve a very extensive system of state control of the economy – including prices and rents – in a country previously devoted to '*laissez-faire*'. This was seen by the Labour movement as a proof of the inadequacy of capitalism, and as a sort of 'war-time socialism' that could be preserved and extended after the war. A part of the Fabian vision was being realized in practice, before the eyes of the Labour movement, and this was far more persuasive than any rhetoric to the 'empirical', 'practical' trade union leaders. More generally, the shock of the war created a sense of new possibilities, and a vague demand for a new world, propitious to the advance of socialist ideas. Even the Liberal Prime Minister Lloyd George felt in 1917 that he had to advise a Labour delegation that 'The whole state of society is more or less molten . . . you can stamp upon that molten mass almost anything, so long as you do so with firmness and determination . . . Think out new ways; think out new methods . . . Don't always be thinking of getting back to where you were before the war; get a really new world.'[20]

In the same year, the Russian revolutions added another stimulus. How strong this stimulus was, was demonstrated in one of the most extraordinary episodes of Labour party history, the famous Leeds Convention of 1917. At this meeting, organized for the purpose of welcoming the Russian revolution, British workers were astonished by the spectacle of the poet of socialism and other equally improbable personages supporting a resolution that demanded 'the establishment in every town, urban and rural district, of Councils of Workmen and Soldiers' Delegates

(Soviets) for initiating and co-ordinating working-class activity
. . . and for the complete political and economic emancipation
of international labour.'[21] This euphoric cry for a repetition of
the Russian revolution in Britain soon vanished without trace,
but the fact that it happened at all showed how the Labour
movement had become temporarily open to change and new
ideas.

The modern Labour party

Hence, the Great War accomplished what the small British
socialist groups had not been able to accomplish. Under the
influence of these great external pressures, the Labour movement as a whole moved towards the acceptance of a form of
socialism: at last, the Labour party could become a socialist
party and not a mere trade union party. But, because this happened at a time when the socialists themselves were particularly
weak, it took the shape of an absolutely *minimal* conversion
to the new idea. The socialists were in a poor position to foster
and push further the process of conversion. If the majority of
trade union leaders liked the abstract notion of socialism more
than previously, they disliked and distrusted most actual socialists
more than previously and were not prepared to envisage a
radical transformation of the Labour party. The key figure in
the transition was Arthur Henderson. He saw that the possibility
existed for the Labour party to become a real, national political
party, and that a real political party must have an ideology –
in the case of the Labour party the new ideological appeal *could*
only be socialist in orientation. One more prudent, empirical
step forward, one more cautious phase of British 'evolution',
one more insanely complex compromise, and the instrument of
British socialism was there at last, occupying its proper place
in the British firmament mid-way between the House of Lords
and the Boy Scouts. The product of endless, grudging, political
manoeuvrings and an infinity of sorry compromises, a half-
hearted mixture of socialism, trade unionism, Protestant moralism and all-engulfing respectability, the Labour party arrived
haltingly and late upon the historical scene; yet its arrival also
coincided with, and partly expressed, new and wider stirrings in
the consciousness of the masses and in spite of its shortcomings
it powerfully developed this consciousness. The new horizons
it offered were part mirage, part real. Time would disentangle the

two – as we shall see. But to present new, partly autonomous perspectives to the working class, even with so many qualifications and defects, and so late, was a great, permanent achievement in this country of the past.

A new constitution was drafted for the party (principally by Henderson and Sidney Webb), and approved at a special Conference in February 1918. It remains in force today, with only minor changes. The new constitution was designed to give the party a new organization corresponding to its new ideology and ambitions. Hitherto, it had been simply a collection of 'affiliated' organizations, mostly trade unions and socialist groups, and had had no individual members of its own; now it was to recruit members like other social-democratic parties. Hitherto, it had led an uncertain, mediate existence in an undefined limbo somewhere between politics and trade unionism; now the political embryo was to develop into a full political being, with real political aims, drawing its force from a nation-wide network of political militants instead of from other organizations, at second hand.

The speeches and discussions about the new constitution show a consciousness of how important the change was. This was something like a re-birth of the Labour party. Consciousness, however, again fell far short of the objective implications of the development, as had happened at the birth of the party. We saw already how new and great the problems of a socialist political movement are, in comparison with those of trade unionism, how exacting are the new dimensions of power; in 1917 and 1918, Henderson and the other leaders still only partially recognized these dimensions. To the original 'short-cut' of Labourism they could only add another empirical, improvised 'short-cut' in the general direction of socialism.

The social changes envisaged by socialism are vast. They can only be realized by generations of men, through difficult struggles we are only beginning to understand. And if any one thing is certain about socialism, it is that such changes – if they are to be conscious and controlled – require the dedication and active participation of vast numbers of people. They cannot be brought about by a few dozen party leaders, or a few hundred men in a parliament, whatever the laws they make. But what is a party's way to such mass energy, to a harnessing of the popular will which alone can really bring a new social order into being? Its way is the people in it, its socialist militants, those now commonly referred to even on the left by the odious label of 'the rank and file'. From a socialist point of view, they *are* the party and the movement, it is they who can turn ideas into a material force and become the guiding nucleus of otherwise indeterminate energies. Because of what socialism will be, and because a socialist party must as far as it can prefigure this feature in its own existence, it follows that socialists must be conscious of being the movement, must feel that it is theirs and entirely governed by them – because an all-embracing democracy will be part of socialism, it cannot fail to be a constitutive element of any real socialist movement. Hence, one may say that certain principles of organization follow from the very meaning of socialism, and impose themselves upon any socialist party. Whatever problems lie in the way of such democracy – problems indicated by many critics in the past – the effort to realize and maintain it is nevertheless a fundamental obligation of any socialist party, and one of the vital indices of its real nature.

We have already seen something of the ideological deficiencies of the British socialist tradition. In the events of 1918 and the new Labour party constitution we see crystallizing *organizational* deficiencies that precisely parallel such cultural weakness, and render it permanent by embodying it in a great new national structure. This aspect of Labourism is little understood or re-marked upon – yet it is clearly of fundamental importance, and any discussion or criticism of Labourism not taking it into account can only be superficial. Within the Labour party itself, one finds the greatest confusion about simple organizational questions, and the most total ignorance about how the party works and ought to work. The Labour Right has customarily ignored these problems for the good and sufficient reason that the present organization of the party keeps them permanently in power; they study the niceties of its manipulation, not the principles of its structure. The Left has ignored them, because it has always felt – with characteristic moralism – that men's souls can be converted to the cause by preaching, however they happen to be organized. And if socialists themselves are not concerned to understand their organization – that is, their own society, their way of life – why should those outside the Labour party understand it better?

In fact, the Labour party's organizational structure is a perfect embodiment of the whole historical experience of the Labour movement in Britain, and incarnates both its achievements and its failings. Arrived at 'empirically', that is by a blind series of piecemeal compromises among various historical forces, it naturally expresses on the practical plane the dominant balance of such forces. But we saw how in Britain the dominant pattern of working-class life and institutions had, inevitably, become a conservative one capable of generating at most a kind of class-sectional or corporative outlook. The trade unions were the guardians of this outlook, as well as of the standard of living of the workers. Hence, the continuation of their hegemony over the Labour party after 1918 meant the continued hegemony of this outlook within Labourism – whereas the objective task posed to socialism in Britain was the reform of this world-view, this fruit of subordination and defeat, it remained fixed in the heart of socialism itself, the rock-like basis upon which the Labour party was built. The re-birth of 1918, the step into the future of socialism, was also a step back into the past, a decision to remain anchored in the history whose outlines we considered previously.

There is no better illustration of the true meaning of British 'empiricism' or 'evolutionism' than the story of the Labour party's formation. This philosophy of cautious, practical realism and profound respect for the past, a perfect ruling-class intellectual organ tried and tested through centuries of experience, was inherited by the working class – as we saw – for lack of anything better or more fitting; deprived of its original purpose and *raison d'être*, it immediately turns into something else altogether, and all its principal characteristics assume a different sense. Realism turns, in Labour leaders, into mere cowardice, a kind of timid hypnosis in the face of events; practicality turns into wilful short-sightedness, a ritual pragmatism wielded to exorcise the sort of theoretical thinking socialism requires; dignified reverence for the past becomes a depraved fetish-worship of idols which seem to change into dust at the very touch of such falsity – the symbols of a nationalism whose significance should, after all, be transformed utterly by the social revolution Labourism nominally stands for. Born out of an iron ring of conceptions like these, the modern Labour party could only be a compromise. Not a crafty, innocent compromise of the kind the British are forever boasting about, but one in which all the forces pressing towards the future are mortgaged absolutely to the past and have the life drained from them in useless, secondary struggles.

The dead souls of Labourism

Transforming itself into a socialist party, the Labour party remained an organ of trade unionism, a trade union 'pressure-group'. The one was simply grafted on to the other. In theory, as with other political parties, the controlling body of the party is the Annual Conference. Over eighty per cent of the votes which can be cast at this Conference come from the trade unions: in recent years they have represented about five million members, as against the one million members from the individual members and militants of the party. This vast mass of inactive members are counted, like Gogol's dead souls, as so many votes at the Labour Party Conference, far outweighing those of the active members.

It may be objected that, surely, a high proportion of active trade unionists must be Labour party activists as well. Does not this redress the balance to some extent? In reality, it serves only to accentuate the paradox of the dead souls of Labourism, for in most cases, of course, the trade unionist actively supporting the party is *also* an 'individual' member enrolled in one of the Constituency parties. A high proportion of the individual militants are, naturally, trade unionists. The great double political effort of the latter, in the trade unions and the Labour party directly, cannot however come near equalling the crushing weight of the dead souls, the purely nominal voices which theoretically govern the destiny of the Labour party, and sometimes of Britain as a whole.

Because they are dead souls, and not an active political force, these voices cannot, of course, really have this power. They are wielded by the men who do have the power, that is, the delegates to the Labour Party Conference. These delegates are, in fact, representatives of the *leaderships* of the different trade unions, of the great variety of bureaucratic organs which control British trade unionism. A few large unions, in turn, have a preponderant share of the trade unions majority.

In what sense, then, is this great power employed by the trade union leaders? British trade unionism is not a centralized or coherent force – like everything else, it grew up on an empirical, piecemeal basis and no later attempts at rationalization have succeeded. Hence, no one line is represented by the trade union delegations at the Labour Party Conference. However, although

a small minority of unions are traditionally left-wing in orientation, the substantial majority has consistently, throughout the
party's history, supported characteristic Fabian policies of
extreme caution. We discussed above some of the reasons for
the corporative and conservative attitudes of the working class.
They are commonly found in their most aggressive form among
trade union bureaucrats, who rise to power entirely within the
ambit of this narrow, tradition-bound type of trade unionism
and identify its categories with their own success and position.

Earlier, we examined the nature and relationships of the
socialist currents present in Labourism, and saw how the dynamic
inherent in them led to a kind of Fabian hegemony over a
chronically weak left wing. Now, it is possible to see how this
dynamic takes its place within the larger dynamic of the Labour
party. Fabianism was intrinsically superior to Labour Leftism,
and in the British context was bound to dominate it unless it
could evolve greatly and find a superior intellectual expression.
But the Labour party's distinctive organization also gives a
permanent bureaucratic form to such dominance, and imposes
a permanent bureaucratic barrier to the further evolution of the
Left. Although there are a few exceptions – the most notable case
has been Ernest Bevin – the trade unions have not used their
power in the Labour party to elect trade unionists into the leadership of the party in parliament. Their hegemony has not brought
about the active hegemony of trade unionism over all the other
elements in the movement – for the simple reason that, as was
pointed out already, British trade unionism did not contain
within itself the capacity needed for political and cultural hegemony, even the minimal hegemony of a right-wing social-
democratic party. It could only result in the active hegemony
of the intellectual group most congenial to the majority of trade
union leaders, the moderate Labour Right. The permanent
alliance between these forces – sometimes called simply the
'labour alliance' – has been the heart of Labourism, the central
nerve slowly evolved through the dark empirical processes we
have observed.

The British trade union leaders have always made clear their
distrust of 'intellectuals', their innate reverence for the 'practical'
and for moderate, unintellectual 'reasonableness'. Nevertheless, in
the Labour party they have always, in fact, maintained in power
a clique of intellectuals, and through their agency one particular
stratum of the intelligentsia has been able to achieve an extra-

ordinary unity and continuity of domination over the British working-class movement. The clue to this paradox lies, naturally, in the characteristics of the stratum in question. It is composed of a type of 'intellectual' who does not, in a sense, appear *as* an intellectual because of his profound acceptance of the prevailing categories of social existence. Contemptuous of rebels, the British trade union bureaucrats could only bestow power upon the unrebellious, traditional intelligentsia – upon 'intellectuals' reared within the old conformity of British intellectual life, educated in the customary fashion at the ancient universities, and wishing to change society not against but in accordance with its essential taboos. If, therefore, the corporative tendencies of trade unionism represented a sort of instinctive, primitive conservatism, by means of the 'labour alliance' this is joined to a much more refined and intellectually-elaborated conservatism, to the deeply-rooted, solid, but very un-radical traditions of the British liberal intelligentsia. In this coalition of forces, the ideological dead weight of the past upon the working class assumes a precise organizational form. The British form of socialism, the force of the future, remains deeply and paradoxically tied to the past, not only in its ideas and sentiments but in its practical structures.

Parliamentary socialism

One might say that the design of Labourism systematically *alienates* the socialist militant, the individual member who is in the movement primarily out of his political conviction and who naturally feels that socialism is something to be realized within the horizons of the living. Labourism inevitably canalizes such revolutionary energy, since it is the unique representative of the working class and of indigenous socialist traditions; it exploits its socialists, who have always played the most important of roles in the everyday functioning of the party; and ultimately it frustrates them in virtue of its very character, alienating all the forces which will not yield to built-in mediocrity. Yet so far we have only seen one dimension of this alienation. In the party as a whole, as a social organism of national scale, the dead souls of political trade unionism are the determining factor. Through the block-vote majority a right-wing majority on the National Executive Committee is almost automatically secured. The most important recent analyst of British political parties points out that the trade unions 'can determine, if they wish, who shall occupy eighteen of the twenty-eight places on the National Executive Committee.'[22] The same author shows how this majority has invariably conformed to the political line proposed by the right-wing parliamentary leaders, and how – since the more important trade-union leaders prefer to devote their time to trade-union affairs, within their own unions or on the General Council of the Trade Union Congress – it has consisted 'at almost every stage in the modern history of the party . . . of second and sometimes third rank union leaders . . . prepared to play a modest role and support the initiative of the Leader of the party'.[23]

Yet such omnipresent modest mediocrity is only one type of obstacle interposed between the Labour party's genuine socialists and power. For the National Executive Committee is not, in reality, the ruling body of the party. In theory, the Annual Conference is the mainspring of the party, the source of its power; and the National Executive Committee is the organ of the Conference, existing to realize Conference decisions. In theory, the socialists of Great Britain meet once a year to decide the destinies of Labourism, to orient the party anew and lay down new policies democratically. In theory, therefore, the members of the NEC and the Labour Members of Parliament are simply their agents. And indeed how could it be otherwise? As we observed, how can a real socialist movement be anything but radically democratic, how can socialists be themselves except in a party they feel to be entirely theirs – a party whose essence defies the alienation of the society outside it?

In practice, the NEC is a subordinate body in the Labour party. So is the Annual Conference, and indeed most of what one understands by 'the party', the whole national and local organization, the mass of ordinary members. The 'party', in this sense, exists to serve another organ, another 'party' which appears almost as separate and autonomous, the head in relation to which the rest functions as a supporting body. This organ is, of course, the Parliamentary Labour party. While the constitution, the formal organization, of the Labour party accords supremacy to the Annual Conference and the NEC, the *real* dynamic of its organization places ultimate power with the group of Labour Members, in the Mother of Parliaments.

The ideological subservience of Labourism to parliamentary necromancy was mentioned above, and its relation to British evolutionism. This too has its practical, organizational expression in the party's physiology. We saw how the lateness of the Labour party's coming prevented it from being an innovator on the general scene of British political life. The age of mass politics arrived before it, the great bourgeois parties had already adapted themselves considerably to the exigencies of a huge new electorate by the end of the nineteenth century. But they did so, naturally, in accordance with bourgeois traditions – that is, empirically and untheoretically, altering the substance and leaving the external forms intact as far as possible. Once, parliaments were the direct, organic expression of the ruling class and of the (relatively) secondary divisions found within that class. In Britain as elsewhere the 'notables' assembled in an institution whose symbolic supremacy reflected the true pattern of social power. The enfranchisement of the masses changed the whole character of political life: it either introduced, or threatened to introduce, the class conflict into political life. The only way this new, menacing force could be either expressed or – on the other hand – controlled and checked was by the formation of the essential organs of modern politics, the mass political parties of the late nineteenth and twentieth centuries.

In the case of Britain, their emergence was brilliantly chronicled by the French theorist Ostrogorski. As he pointed out, the formation of these great political machines meant that in reality parliament could no longer be itself the supreme power in the state, in the old fashion. Instead, it was bound to be transformed progressively into a mere terrain of conflict among the parties, the means of access to power – an instrument in a conflict, as it were, no longer the unique, unequivocal voice of permanent social hegemony. The mystique of the elective parliament was disappearing in – as he thought – the chaos and corruption of party-political life. In Britain, however, this process was by no means carried through to its logical conclusion. While the traditional ruling-class parties, the Conservatives and Liberals, did become great machines of this type they were also successful in *concealing* the transformation and in preserving the essential mystique of Westminster and the façade of the Old British Constitution. The machines, the 'parties' in the distinctive contemporary sense, remained subordinate to the groups of Liberals and Conservatives elected to parliament – the 'parties' in the old sense of notable factions. Until recently the names of the parties did not appear beside the names of the candidates on election ballot papers in Britain. The parties outside parliament remained, from a constitutional point of view, bodies with no *right* to control parliament and parliamentarians, and lay down the policies of the 'parties' inside parliament.

Obviously, this was a fundamentally conservative tactic aimed at avoiding the possibly dangerous consequences of the new regime of parties. It was a constitutional equivalent of the conservatism we have already observed in other fields. For the hitherto subordinate masses, for the new working-class and socialist movements seeking to fight on their behalf, the democracy of the parties was of course the only *possible* kind of democracy – the great party machine which represented a hideous threat to Ostrogorski and other nostalgic apologists for the *status quo*, represented emancipation to them, the only kind of collective self-expression permitted by the conditions of bourgeois society. But it could only fulfil their need by being a genuine innovation – in other words, by definitely establishing the ascendancy of the new mass organization over its delegates in parliament, by providing a basically democratic link between the masses and the representatives claiming to be carrying on their struggle at that level. Only in this way could the class struggle in social reality hope to find any voice in politics. This is precisely what the 'British Constitution' tries to avoid. This is the true meaning of the clearly anachronistic interpretations of it prevalent since the end of last century. And this was the trap laid for the Labour movement by British parliamentarism – the trap into which it fell completely and blindly, and from which it has never emerged. Recent developments in the Labour party, which we will examine later on, have indeed powerfully confirmed its parliamentary servitude.

Summing up the evolution of Labourism in this respect, McKenzie observes that the origin and essential significance of the two principal modern parties were quite different: 'While the Conservative party in Parliament created a mass organization to serve *its* purposes, Labour began as a movement in the country which created a parliamentary party to give the working-class a voice in the House of Commons . . .'[24] Nevertheless, he continues, this apparently vital difference was soon forgotten, for the Labour party '. . . began increasingly to resemble the other great parliamentary parties as it came to rival them in size and strength. By the time the Parliamentary Labour party had taken office in 1924 its transformation was almost complete. By accepting all the conventions with respect to the office of Prime Minister and of Cabinet government it ensured that effective power within the party would be concentrated in the lands of the leadership of the PLP.' The new democracy of the Labour movement had been obliterated by the old democracy of the British Constitution. The Labour party, too, was to become merely an electoral machine in the service of parliamentarians. The British ruling class had acquired, so to speak, a double defence against socialism: in practice, the modern party system itself – even where the domination of parliament by the parties is assumed – has usually been a heavy brake on the class struggle, but at the same time the system necessarily contains a dangerous *potential* for change or even revolution that can never be quite forgotten, and British constitutional custom is in essence a barrier against the party system in its characteristic modern form, a unique first line of defence insuring old England against *all* the risks and perils of the modern political world. The ancient 'supremacy' of parliament in political life was conserved, as a corrupting fetish that separated the political leaders of the working-class movement from their mass following and utterly broke the democracy that is a pre-condition of socialism.

How has this almost inconceivable imbroglio been tolerable to Labour party militants? In part, because of the chronic theoretical inertia of even the left wing; in part, because of the extraordinary ignorance of the party already referred to among the party members themselves, which allowed myths to flourish wholesale. The most important of such myths was the idea that the Annual Conference and the NEC decided the 'general lines' or the 'objectives' of party policy, while the Parliamentary Labour group had the function of realizing these principles in parliamentary terms. It was Aneurin Bevan himself who stated that the PLP was to 'interpret policies in the light of the parliamentary system. Any other procedure would merely confuse the whole situation'.[25] It does not seem to have struck him how totally, permanently, inextricably 'confused' the situation was already, since by a permanent and fortunate coincidence the PLP was always able to control what happened at Annual Conferences and so exactly *which* policies it was going to 'interpret'. He emphasized the point further in the same speech: 'It is quite impossible for a conference of 1100 people, *even if it were constitutionally proper*, to determine the order in which the Parliamentary Labour Party and a Labour government introduces legislation into the House of Commons . . .'

Much of the misery of Labourism is concentrated in these words. The quasi-divine secrets of parliamentary ritual, incomprehensible to the dull minds of simple socialists. The rules of the 'British Constitution', absolute limits to all human thought and action. And all in the mouth of the greatest of Labourism's rebels, addressing dismayed militants who, in attempting to do the simplest thing in the world – assert their collective democratic right of control – were merely 'confusing the whole situation'! Superficially, in so much of its thought and action, British labourism appears as woodenly practical and dull, sunk in hopelessly dusty routines and indescribably boring rhetoric. Yet a disabused analysis of its true character brings constantly to light a crazy logic reminiscent of the wanderings of Alice in her child's Wonderland, an upside-down impossible world where incredible contradictions are so natural that they no longer cause an eyebrow to be raised.

The dynamic of Labourism appears to conservatives as a kind of reassuring stability, a permanent insurance policy against 'extremists' and 'socialist cranks'; to socialists, it appears rather as an ingenious vicious circle designed to perpetually promise advance towards socialism and perpetually move away from it in reality. Tracing out the main lines of the Labour party's anatomy, we have seen how the circle works. Its mainspring is the solid, conservative pillar of the trade-union majority, the flock of ghost-members whose votes are manipulated by the trade-union leaders. This is – suitably enough – the main body of the army supporting the Fabian right-wingers. They count on it to secure them a reliable majority at the Annual Conference and on the National Executive Committee, but even if – as has happened just *once* on an important question in the party's history – the dead souls refused to be regimented into line, this would not be fatal to the Right. Controlling the Parliamentary party, it can and has maintained that, in any case, what happens at Annual Conferences is without importance. The Labour MPs are elected by their constituents, according to the principles of the Constitution, which states that their first responsibility is to those electing them and their second responsibility is – to their own consciences! The Labour party outside parliament has no right to come between an MP and his conscience! This would be rank totalitarianism, as Gaitskell chose to put it.

Of course, the system would be breached were it possible for

the Left to gain a majority of MPs within the Parliamentary
party. But, although it is possible for a fairly constant minority
of left-wingers to find their way into the PLP, the party leadership
and the trade unions together exert sufficient control over the
processes of candidature to guarantee their authority in this
respect as well. At the same time, the pretence or myth of the
Labour party's democratic character is invariably maintained
on the level of rhetoric. The painful and shameful impotence of
the socialist militants at the base of the party has never been
more neatly and cruelly depicted than by Richard Crossman, in a
moment of lucidity: '. . . the Labour party required militants,'
he has pointed out, 'politically conscious socialists to do the
work of organizing the constituencies. But since these militants
tended to be "extremists", a constitution was needed which
maintained their enthusiasm by apparently creating a full party
democracy while excluding them from effective power. Hence
the concession in principle of sovereign powers to the delegates
at the Annual Conferences, and the removal in practice of most
of this sovereignty through the trade union block vote on the
one hand, and the complete independence of the Parliamentary
Labour party on the other.'[26]

Nonentities, fanatics, cranks and extremists

Such was the improbable political machine built up from 1918
onwards. It was built up around a word: 'socialism'. Looked
at critically, in relation to the actual functioning of the Labour
party, this word seems in turn dream and utter delusion, justification and mask, essence and mere appearance. The essential
meanings attached to it were as clearly expressed at the 1918
Annual Conference as at any later occasion; they are little changed
today. The new constitution of the party contained 'Clause 4',
committing the movement 'To secure for the producers by hand
or brain the full fruits of their industry, and the most equitable
distribution thereof that may be possible, upon the basis of the
common ownership of the means of production and the best
obtainable system of popular administration and control of
each industry and service'.[27] Even then, at its moment of most
daring advance, the language of Labourism was tired and bureaucratic: the future of mankind was dressed in words raked out of
the bottom of a minor functionary's filing-cabinet.

The spirit behind the words inspired even less faith in their supposed meaning. In the very first debate on the very first resolution proposed by the NEC to the first Conference after the adoption of the new constitution, the issues were made sufficiently clear. This resolution was about 'Social Reconstruction' after the Great War, and envisaged '. . . the gradual building up of a new social order based . . . on the deliberately planned co-operation in production and distribution, the sympathetic approach to a healthy equality, the widest possible participation in power, both economic and political, and the general conscious-ness of consent which characterizes a true democracy'.[28] It was not easy to pierce this astounding miasma of well-turned clichés. But the more clairvoyant of the left-wingers noticed the absence of any definite reference to the *ownership* of the means of pro-duction and distribution, and a Mr Fairchild of the British Socialist party[29] rose to protest. This resolution was hardly in accordance with the fine new constitution, he pointed out, and might even be interpreted as advocating 'co-operation' between workers and employers. 'The resolution entails the creation of an army of bureaucrats and experts', he insisted, 'and there is no recognition of the claims of *Labour* to direct the means of production in the interests of the class represented at this Conference . . .'[30]

No less a person than the father of Fabianism, Sidney Webb, came to reply to Fairchild – a typical example of the left-wing group Webb collectively characterized elsewhere as 'nonentities . . . fanatics, cranks, and extremists . . .'[31] It was true, he admitted it, that the constitution said what Mr Fairchild claimed. But really, they all had a great deal of work to do, including no fewer than twenty-six more resolutions and '. . . they did not want repeatedly, over and over again, to ring the changes on the old shibboleths . . .'[32] It is a little hard to see how the *first* discussion of the party's new objective could be a monotonous repetition of anything . . . but, of course, this is precisely the point. Once was, indeed, far too often for Webb and the leadership majority – for them, the great new principle and hope, the new socialist image assumed by the party was already a 'shibboleth' to be evaded in all the concrete work of the party.

Socialism, in short, belonged in its proper place, the constitu-tion, where it could be admired occasionally and referred to in moments of emotion. The nonentities, fanatics, cranks and extremists who wished to relate it in a significant fashion to the actual *work* of the Labour party had to be suppressed. Another lesson was administered to them in the discussion of resolution number VII. This dealt with unemployment, and accomplished the not inconsiderable feat of omitting all reference to the cause of unemployment, the capitalist system. Would it not be better to attack the capitalist system openly, someone objected, and so demonstrate to the ruling class their outlook and intentions? Again Webb rose to answer the objection. It was quite unnecessary to '. . . bring in once again an old shibboleth. They had heard the same speech over and over again . . . and it got a bit monotonous'. Capitalism, as the cause of social evil, and socialism, as its cure; both were 'shibboleths' to the Labour Right, at the very foundation of the modern Labour party. It is quite wrong to think that the leadership has 'betrayed' socialist principles, at any of the later dramatic turnings in the party's history. 'Betrayal' was always an integral part of it, inseparable from it. Nor was this betrayal the result of individual hypocrisy or moral degeneration, as the Left has too often said; it followed logically from the whole orientation of Fabianism. Evolutionism, or 'gradualism', divorce the end-state of socialism from the actual steps taken to achieve it: the former exists at an intangible distance from the latter, hence they cannot be judged solely by their efficacy in promoting it – they are seen as good 'in themselves', justifiable by more immediate criteria deriving from society as it is here and now. The Left, on the other hand, wants each step to be meaningfully *related* to the end – an insistence which *is* fanatical and extremist, in evolutionary perspectives.

This tension – or something close to it – has existed in all socialist and communist parties. The peculiarity of the Labourist version lies in the relative strength and character of the two poles creating the tension. As we saw, for many different reasons the right-wing, moderate tendency was exceptionally powerful in Britain – it was, and still is, rooted in the profound and diffused conservatism of British society, of a social regime that had succeeded better than most others in suffocating the class struggle. And the left-wing pole of force provided by Nonconformity, traditional radicalism, and the ILP and Labour-Left tendencies was exceptionally weak – and even subordinate to the other in vital respects. Objectively, the task set to the left is the overcoming of this tension *dialectically*, through an ideological and practical synthesis uniting the immediacy of reforms with the remoter ideal of a socialist society. Incapable of rising to these difficult heights, the Labour Left is forced into crude and repetitious formulations of its position, into a mindless passion which is only the obverse of its ideological subjection. We saw how the Labour Left wing was, as it were, the 'subjectivity' of the movement, and how the distinction of right from left in Labourism is like a distinction between a barren – and therefore petty and cramped – intellect, and an impotent source of feeling, a passion with no voice.

The analogy can be carried further. The profundity and apparent permanence of the determining conditions have made of the Labour Left a *neurotic* subjectivity – that is, a contradictory complex of ideas and attitudes unable to comprehend its own nature but also *unwilling* to do so, detesting the terrible weight lying upon it and yet completely loyal to Labourism, gripped in an oppressive dream which it *chooses* and clings to rather than face a reality still more painful. The 'short-cut' to socialism embraced so eagerly at the beginning of the century has turned into a permanent, intolerable labour of Sisyphus – but would not the Labour party's socialists be even more impotent if they renounced the labour, and abandoned the party as hopeless? The failure of the Communist party, and a desert of futile left-wing sects, stand as a warning against this.

Hence, the extreme and constant inner tension generated by Labourism has never exploded. Its own inherited inadequacies, and the evident lack of any practical alternative to the Labour party, have tied the socialists of the left wing remorselessly into the pathological internal dialectic of Labourism. We saw how two basic conditions of Labourism as a system were, firstly, the very defective ideological matrix behind British socialism, and secondly – and intimately related – the weakness of the entire left-wing political tradition incorporated into Labourism. Now, considering the organizational dimension of Labourism, we have seen another of its fundamental characteristics: Labourism is in part an organized *contradiction* between the two really vital sectors of the working-class movement, a system according to which they mutually inhibit one another instead of engaging in a genuine dialectic of growth towards socialism.

What is the main justification of Labourism, put forward by socialists at its birth and still advanced by its apologists? What is the cry that rings out at every Labour Party Conference, to repress all serious dissent and maintain the incredible system intact? That Labourism attains the *unity* of the working-class movement, in a definitive and final form from which any departure would be treason and defeat. This call touches the deepest chord in the entire historical experience of the working class – the dispossessed, fragmented into atoms by the alienating pressures of capitalist society, who found and asserted themselves wholly through uniting in collective action. It echoes everything most sacred in the secular struggle of trade unionism, everything that renders it more than merely another facet of the bourgeois order, everything which connects it potentially to socialism and to the future beyond the bourgeois order. It suggests that an organization embracing trade unionism and socialism together, and summing up all the latent might of the working class, *must* be right in principle.

The truth inherent in this call cannot be denied. It deserves to be called the truth of Labourism, its characteristically positive element. Yet we have seen in how many ways, and how profoundly, the Labour party betrays its own truth – the historical falsehood with which it is organically linked, the antagonistic and regressive form which it gives to 'unity' in the concrete. At a moment when the question of uniting working-class forces has appeared again as a living possibility in more than one country, it is important to grasp fully the lesson of Labourism. In any given period, the working-class movement as a whole – like the working class itself – contains many contradictory tendencies: in part it is tied to the past, in part it looks hesitatingly towards the future, it is both the product of capitalism and the social force which can overthrow capitalism, struggle and subordination vie with one another in every interstice of its thought and action. Any unified movement must reflect these contradictions to some extent. Hence, its ultimate significance depends entirely upon which elements hold the initiative within it, upon how it actually expresses the contradictions in reality and in turn modifies their conflict. We have seen why, in Britain, the conservative burden borne by the workers was so heavy, so embedded in organization and popular psychology, why their type of class-consciousness contained subordination in its own texture.[33] This meant that it was absolutely necessary for a revolutionary left to dominate any unitary organization such as Labourism, assuming as its first task the reform of this massive nexus of traditional consciousness – that is, the nexus which in fact constituted the heart of Labourism. The conflicts inside Labourism could not have been avoided, by any different interplay of forces. But they might have been rendered conflicts of growth – instead of what we have seen, sterile and misdirected battles within a senseless dynamic, an economy founded upon the preservation of the dead weight of the past and insertion into the empirical evolutionism of the ruling class. Labourism's unity has paralysed the vital contradiction of tendencies inside it, imprisoning British socialism instead of liberating it, and deforming its whole development.

The instrument of Labourist involution has been the trade-union majority, the permanent hegemony of trade unionism over socialism. This fact, however, constitutes a criticism of the trade unions only in a very limited sense. By and large, they could not help being what they were; nor could they act other than they did inside the framework provided by the Labour party. This is the whole tragedy of Labourism. British trade unionism could not avoid stifling British socialism within one unified body, given the immense strength of the former and the weakness and incoherence of the latter. The price paid by the British Left for 'unity', therefore, was high – half a century of frustration for the most vital and militant forces in the working class, the formation of the permanent Fabian dynasty as their leadership.[34]

The Labour party encountered many vicissitudes in the twenty years after 1918, most of them unfavourable to it. It gradually increased its parliamentary representation, displacing the Liberal party as His Majesty's official Opposition, and formed the first Labour Government in 1924. This short-lived, minority government accomplished nothing, but was less of a disaster than the second Labour Government of 1929–31. The latter suffered the full impact of the Great Depression, totally unprepared, and had the task of trying to restore British capitalism to health 'without the shadow of a constructive, or even a defensive, policy'.[35] Inevitably, MacDonald and the other Labour leaders were forced to attack working-class interests in order to 'save the pound', by reducing wages and payments to the unemployed, and this was too much. The trade unions rebelled, as well as the left wing. Disappointed by the reluctance of the working class to follow the logic of Labourist inter-classism to its rational conclusion, MacDonald abandoned class and party to form the infamous 'National' government in coalition with Liberals and Conservatives. The 'National' government easily won the elections of 1931 and 1935, and by the beginning of the war in

1939 the Labour party had scarcely recovered its position and strength of ten years previously. In between the two periods of government, the Labour party had stood apart from the crucial test of the working class, the General Strike in defence of the miners in 1926, as if it did not exist.

Significant as they were in many ways, from our point of view these traumatic experiences are not of first importance. The Labour party survived MacDonald and humiliating defeat by the 'National' regime without a major scission – it threw off individual leaders, but not the basic ideological traditions of leadership they represented. There were small left-wing rebellions, but the greater part of the left remained loyal. We have already explored some of the reasons for this extraordinary cohesion, in the face of events that would surely have shattered most socialist parties. Another can be seen in the excuse so constantly offered by the Labour Right for the miserable showing of both Labour governments: that is, that since both were minority governments dependent upon Liberal support the principles of Fabianism had not really been tried, Labourism had not had a genuine chance to prove itself. In spite of their acute discontent, this argument appealed to the pragmatic instincts of the left and to the universal sense of 'fair-play'. It held the left wing in its accustomed role of trying to push the leadership 'further to the left', and left untouched the assumption underlying this role: that socialists and the Labour leadership were in fact travelling along the same road, towards the same destination. Fundamentally, in spite of many superficial symptoms of torture and crisis, Labourism drifted along intact through the inter-war years. It was waiting for power, for the chance to prove itself.

The chance was given it in 1945. The third Labour Government of 1945–50 is the decisive happening in the history of Labourism, after 1918. In retrospect, the Labour party seems always to have been tensed for this moment. A great electoral triumph, massive popular support, an overwhelming majority in parliament – Labourism's moment of self-realization had arrived at last, it entered upon its inheritance. But, as we have seen, the contradictions and confusions it was made of were such that its period of affirmation was bound also to be a period of crisis and disintegration; being a bundle of disparate forces united in a delusion, Labourism could not rise to express its true character without at once threatening this unity, without disentangling dream from reality in a way fatal to its own continued existence.

Its political victory necessarily presaged its own division and defeat. This fact is the key to most of what has happened to the Labour party, between 1945 and the present day.

The zenith of Labourism

The First World War had made the Labour party. The Second World War provided it with its great historical opportunity – by far the most favourable opportunity that ever confronted any socialist party.

Up until 1939, the Labour party had existed in the midst of an inert, backward-looking society full of taboos and rigidities, a society whose metabolism was essentially the using-up of old accumulated stocks of economic and political capital. It had experienced a relative decline in wealth and power for over fifty years, faced with competition from the younger, more modernized and energetic capitalist systems of other countries, especially Germany and the United States. Yet this decline and stagnation had not produced any dramatic repercussions within society, no violent mass movements had arisen on either right or left to demand radical changes. The conservative torpor following the Industrial Revolution was stiffened further by imperialism, into an impenetrable blanket of complacency – while change accelerated everywhere else, it was as if time stood still for the British, fixed in a pattern that could never need more than minor modifications. Economically, the empire was an indispensable cushion against the effects of the Great Depression. Germany, Britain's main competitor, was twice ruined by war and suffered more from the Depression. Thus, external circumstances protected this fossilized regime and permitted British capitalism to adapt to modern times '. . . slowly and in the most inefficient manner, with the maximum wastage of unemployed human potential and amidst the desolation of whole regions of the land.'[36]

Then, from 1939 until 1945, circumstances altered completely and administered a violent shock to British society. The war shook the crumbling edifice of British conservatism to its foundations. Violent collective effort replaced the old myopic sloth of the 'National' regime as the keynote of the national ethos. Abruptly, the ruling class discovered that it needed the working class in order to escape annihilation; the masses of unemployed vanished, there was soon an acute labour shortage, and the status

M

of the workers rose miraculously. The pseudo-feudal class structure and all the social impedimenta associated with it were thrust into abeyance, and 'war-time socialism' introduced an egalitarianism – even a sort of semi-heroic proletarian ideology – in complete contrast to anything known before 1939. An extensive system of state economic planning and control replaced *laissez-faire*. After 1941, with the Soviet alliance, communism became fashionable.

It is true that this awakening was neutralized to some extent by the extreme nationalist colour it assumed, as in Churchill's famous war-time speeches. Yet even this was not entirely negative, seen from a socialist point of view. Britain was an extraordinarily fragmented nation culturally, the collective consciousness reflecting those stratifications discussed above – in fact, such divisions were an essential feature of British-style conservatism. The British 'nation' had never been integrally re-made in a bourgeois revolution, as had France in the years after 1789. Instead, as we saw, the bourgeoisie had clung to and utilized anachronistic forms in its own affirmation – retaining, on the collective cultural level, a semi-aristocratic idiom quite unrelated to its own experience. The world-renowned 'frigidity' and lack of ready communication of the British is certainly in part a product of this cultural history – in effect, of the absence of a valid, universal vehicle of expression within the hegemonic class. The universal cultural 'language' was the dialect of a ruling elite assimilated to the aristocracy, and bred chronic inarticulacy everywhere else in society because of its inherent limitations. At the same time, success in inhibiting the class-struggle had permitted the formation of a powerful sentiment of national unity – a unity which, because of such extreme cultural fragmentation and mass inarticulacy, could only exist *on the lowest possible level*, with the minimum of ideal content. The war re-created this unity on a higher level, in spite of the imperialist and racialist rhetoric that was so common, giving it a new democratic content, a meaningful popular voice. It brought about '. . . the emergence in Britain of a new popular radicalism, more widespread than at any time in the previous hundred years'.[37]

This was the situation inherited by Labourism in 1945. Half a revolution had already been accomplished by the war. Capitalism was a discredited memory, associated with unemployment and the slump. Public opinion was malleable and open. The vague image of a new world of social relationships, half dream, half reality in the peculiar context of the war, hung over society, a more significant vision of the future than socialist propaganda had ever fashioned. Britain was not ruined by the war; economically, she remained a major nation, politically she was free from any threat of intervention. Not one of the obstacles that have blocked or distorted the rise of socialism everywhere else was present. The chance was unique.

The Labour party did not exploit this chance. The reasons for this failure must be obvious, after what has been said of the party's character. The parliamentarism and moderatism of the Labour leaders had been greatly reinforced by service under Churchill in the war-time coalition government. A conscious, political revolution was needed to realize the potentialities of the situation; but the ideas implicit in any revolutionary action, the idea of hegemony and the struggle for hegemony, the idea of the class-struggle as the basis of the political or party battle – all were further away than ever. The Labour party advanced a few cautious steps on the evolutionary road long marked out. However, it did accomplish these steps fully, under the new favourable circumstances, as the previous Labour governments had not been able to. Fabianism was put into practice. This was sufficient to open the critical drama of Labourism: since then, it has been beset by an inevitable, chronic malady, at times debated openly, at times wilfully ignored, almost always misrepresented and misunderstood. The English Ideology makes practice the touchstone of all reality and value, and no one had held to this faith more keenly than the Fabians. Now Fabianism was to be tested and found wanting, disconcertingly, in its own sacred terms. Practicality had been its essence, its virtue (as against the 'fanaticism' and 'idealism' of the left); now practice itself was to demonstrate the delusion in this 'practicality', the ideological sleight-of-hand behind it.

The success and failure of Fabianism

The Labour programme of 1945, 'Let us face the Future', was directly descended from the original statement of 1918, Sidney Webb's *Labour and the New Social Order*. It proposed the nationalization of the coal mines, the gas and electricity industries, all principal transport services, the Bank of England, and the iron and steel industry. These were the industries and services 'ripe for public ownership'. The economy as a whole was to be 'planned', in the public interest, but in reality the government's powers over the private sector were very limited and were decreased with the passage of time: this was a form of planning without objectives or powers, affecting the economy only marginally. The Labour Government did not even have the information and statistics required for the most minimal planning.[38] A new range of social services was also in the programme, many of them agreed on by all parties; the most important was the National Health Service, making all forms of medical care free. In foreign policy, the Labour party's main aspiration was to function as a mediating and uniting influence between the USA and the USSR; but doubt of its capacity to do this arose at the first international conference attended by Attlee and the new Foreign Minister, Ernest Bevin, formerly secretary of the Transport and General Workers' Union, and the leading force in British trade unionism. Both Roosevelt and the American Secretary of State, Byrnes, were disconcerted by Bevin's aggressiveness towards the Russians.[39] Shortly afterwards, Bevin disclosed his views on colonialism: 'I am not prepared to sacrifice the British Empire,' he told a critic, 'because I know that if the British Empire fell . . . it would mean the standard of life of our constituents would fall considerably.'[40]

By 1948, most of this programme had been achieved. The details of its execution, the particular effects it had on society, do not concern us here. In general, Labour's reforms ended by being accepted as necessary even by conservatives. The major exception was the plan to nationalize the steel industry: while nationalization was a convenient fate for bankrupt and deficitary industries like coal-mining and the railways, capitalists were determined to retain a profitable key industry like steel in private control. The Labour Government left this part of the programme until the last moment, and carried out the nationalization in a weak manner which made it simple for the Conservative Government of Churchill to restore the industry to private ownership after 1951. It is more important for us to grasp the general sense of the evolution of British society from 1948 onwards, and the relationship between this evolution and the traditional 'evolutionary' perspectives at the centre of Fabianism.

Fabian gradualism had seen the goal, socialist society, as produced by successive instalments of reform which would one day 'add up' to socialism. As we noticed, they did not think there was any real barrier of force capable of reacting against this long-term trend: Sidney Webb described it as the 'inevitable outcome' of the universal franchise, a 'stream of tendencies' against which all opponents were 'ultimately powerless'.[41] In Britain at least – where everyone was reasonable – socialism would be a march of events, guaranteed by the ordinary machinery of democracy: once started, nothing would halt it. The Labour Government of 1945–50 was the start.

And yet, from 1948 onwards, its progress resembled anything except an irresistible march of events. Apparently its first programme should have launched it forward in a momentum carrying it across all obstacles. But in reality the Labour party's loss of confidence was the dominating fact, after these first achievements. Instead of finding itself, Labourism had obviously lost its way; success engendered inertia, not automatic advance. Then the inertia turned into retreat. The Labour party lost the elections of 1951, then (by a much larger majority) those of 1955 and those of 1959. During most of this period, there seemed no good reason why Conservatism should not retain power for ever. Labourism's loss of heart became bitter internal conflict and paralysis, year after year; the mass hope of 1945 became indifference, apathy, even hostility – all remote from the mild, reasonable optimism the Fabians had counted on. British socialism had encountered a barrier invisible to its eyes, its old world-view. Like the barrier of sound an aircraft meets at a certain speed, this force had flung it back into confusion and impotence.

What had happened? The electorate had not behaved as expected; the first experience of socialism ought to have impressed all rational beings and made certain further progress. Why not? Clearly, because the Labour reforms had not been in reality exactly what Labour leaders had believed they would be – self-explanatory 'instalments' of the socialist future, 'islands of socialist virtue in a sea of capitalist greed'.[42] And what had prevented them from being this? Partly, no doubt, the limited and bureaucratic form given to nationalization – from the origins of the movement, Labour leaders had been inflexibly opposed to the conception of workers' control. Partly the fact that the purpose of the deficiary public sector was to 'serve the public', and the 'public' consisted mostly of the industries in the capitalist sector; caught between a weak government policy and the pressures of the private sector, the state industries could not help becoming subordinate to the latter – and so, an instrument assisting the re-birth of capitalism, of the new wave of capitalist prosperity and ideology destined to drown Labourism in the fifties. The complex of forces which had turned their work into something other than what was intended was the critical factor ignored or minimized by Fabianism: the general dynamic of the system as a whole, the hegemonic pattern rooted in a certain organization of the economy and certain institutions, and incarnated in a ruling class. Here was the vast power which had turned against Labour's arithmetical dose of 'socialism' and transformed its meaning so utterly – making of it, finally, an integral structure reinforcing the conservative renaissance.

Perhaps – a defender of Labourism might object – there is too much retrospective wisdom in this analysis. Could the party itself possibly have understood what was happening, fifteen years ago? Given its indifference to theoretical questions, was not Labourism bound to grope blindly forward at that point, slowly absorbing the hard lesson of practical experience? But it is difficult to see any real excuse for what followed in such reflections. Whether the party's theorists were able to analyse the situation or not, it was at least evident from 1951 onwards that British socialism had met a major obstacle and was in a crisis *needing* the most intensive debate. The acid test of practice had exposed essential defects in the movement's whole historical programme and outlook; the very meaning of its existence was no longer clear. A searching revision of its theoretical basis was the prelude to any future.

The incredible slowness of response to this crisis, the protracted confusion and uncertainty which actually followed, are the final condemnation of Labour's so-called 'empiricism'. In the awful decade following the Attlee government, Labourism demonstrated its inability to learn from the hard experience it had always cherished ideologically. In a sense, of course, it is true that practice is the real test of theory, both the matrix and the eventual meaning of ideas. But, paradoxically, practice only bears such truth in it when it exists in the light of ideas – when, in spite of its primacy, it remains part of a dialectic relationship to theory, a relationship in which the theoretical element has real autonomy and worth. In other words, acute ideal consciousness is a necessary condition of *real* 'empiricism', of the vital capacity to respond directly to and learn swiftly from practical experiences.

The British ruling class had avoided this necessity: para-doxically, it had been able to adopt a kind of fetishistic pseudo-empiricism as its ideological banner *because* it had never been forced to undertake any great, conscious practical reformation of society. What is British 'empiricism' and British faith in practical 'instinct' except systematized indifference to ideas? And how did this anti-ideology come to exist? Because hard facts, the demands of practical experience, had never coerced the bourgeoisie into looking for something better – its good fortune had preserved that basic stupor of outlook which a popular expression calls 'muddling through'. Piously accepting this stupor as the last word in realism, British socialists had shrunk socialism to fit it – pretending, so to speak, that socialism was not a colossal, intractable, practical problem but a mere question of 'evolution', not a revolution but a piece of Sunday-afternoon tinkering. From 1951 onwards, this superstitious trance stood exposed in the cold wind of disproof. Yet for years the only result was a further numbing of sensibility, a sterile involution only half-related to circumstances.

Nobody would deny that in certain respects the 1945–51 Labour Government was successful. In others, nobody can deny the failure of its work. This paradox contains, precisely, the lesson of the experience, the lesson for which Labourism was unprepared and which – if assimilated – would be fatal to Labourism. In themselves, and for their immediate, short-term effects, the Labour reforms were necessary – from any point of view – and some of them were popular. But in society nothing exists and has meaning 'in itself'. Its true meaning emerges from its relationship to the whole social complex at a given moment – that is, to a complex organism having a definite character and central dynamic, *the* general meaning of society. Hence a phenomenon can have one face at the particular, isolated level, and another face when seen in relationship to its context. The nationalization of the mines vastly improved the standard of living and conditions of work of the miners, and abolished one of the most ugly phases of the class-struggle in Britain; but the rationalization of the mining industry and its whole structure of costs, effected after nationalization, has made of it the prey of the private sector monopolies and reinforced their position in a way the old coal industry could never have done. And so with the other reforms, in their different ways.

In other words, from a socialist point of view reforms have a socialist sense only when carried out as parts of a strategy aiming at the heart of society, at the pattern of social hegemony which bends everything into its own design – they are socialist reforms only when really placed within a revolutionary perspective, seen and executed as such. Society, its pre-existing 'natural' tendency, its 'evolutionary' force – these are enemies, on the whole, not allies. Unless socialism is tensed against them in every fibre, in every moment, in an arc of action as wide and varied as the forces of hegemony themselves, it will be imprisoned and petrified by these forces, the liberating potential of its work annulled for ever. This recognition was fatal to Fabianism and the assorted ideological baggage associated with it. It struck the foundations away from Labourism, as it had existed up to 1950.

The Labour party had failed to grasp the revolutionary opportunity furnished by the conditions of 1945. It had failed, in the sense indicated, even according to the much more modest traditional criteria it had always respected. The shadow of this failure is the dominating fact in the evolution of the party since 1950, and an essential part of the explanation of Wilson and Wilsonism. For about ten years after the defeat of 1951, Labourism seemed to drift at the mercy of events, feebly trying to discover a new formula. Then, at the same time as external conditions had changed radically – and in a way favourable to the Labour party – the rise of Wilson appeared magically to fill the void, heal the chronic dissensions of the party and re-knit a unity and purpose comparable to those known previously. A large part of his power derives from his role as restorer – whether real or illusory – of the innocence existing before the Fall.

Labour in limbo

During the 1950s the Labour party was haunted by its failure. But, characteristically, the compulsions agitating it were expressed only partially and fitfully in the actual debates of the era. The traditional left-right battle became more acrimonious and bitter – but it remained in substantially the same terms as before, in an objective situation which had changed profoundly. The society which emerged out of the first Labour regime was significantly different from the old one, and presented different problems. At the same time as left-wing parties in other European countries, and in addition to the basic dilemma mentioned, Labourism had to confront the new difficulties of a more and more prosperous capitalist society relatively free from recessions. The growing revolt against colonialism, the great new interrogatives in ideology and international relations created by the disintegration of Stalinism after 1955 – these familiar questions too were bound to exercise its mind. If it did not deal with them very effectively, perhaps this was due in part to the fundamental doubt in its heart.

Naturally, since nothing can really stand still in an explosive era, the stagnation and vacillation of the movement was also retreat, and brought about what Williams calls '. . . the visible moral decline of the labour movement'.[43] In the fifties, he claims, 'both politically and industrially, some sections of the movement have gone over, almost completely, to ways of thinking which they still formally oppose. The main challenge to capitalism was socialism, but this has almost wholly lost any contemporary meaning . . .' Under the pressures of renascent capitalism, equipped with new methods and new appeals, more confident than ever and reinforced by Labour's own legislation, the Labour party seemed to be sliding backwards into more and more hopeless positions.

The decisive experience of 1945–50 had in reality placed Labourism squarely at a parting of the ways. A tormenting crossroads lay in the facts themselves, and compelled some response. The old straight way to socialism – to which all the party's essential mechanisms were geared – was lost in the sands.

No route now connected the day-to-day life of the party to its goal, the rainbow-light it had called 'socialism'. Therefore, the party had either to abandon the goal – or re-invent and rediscover everything, from the beginning, find a new way to a new, better-understood goal. These alternatives were inevitable, whatever was to be the fate of the *word* 'socialism'. Obviously, social-democratic revisionists can cling to the word and re-define it to mean a particular species of capitalist society; a novel revolutionary conception, too, can be attached to the same word. But it did not seem that the magic of even this word could go on confusing the issue for Labourism, after 1951.

What were the full implications of this choice? We saw how tenuous and imaginary the links between concrete action and the ultimate ideal were, in Fabianism – how, instead of a significant unity, the entire bias of thought and activity were thrown into the former. Obviously, in it the goal and conception of 'socialism' – as a global state-of-affairs somehow qualitatively different from bourgeois society – were inherently liable to atrophy. The adverse shock of the 1945–50 government and its

results were bound to produce just this disintegration, and make
the Fabian tradition tend to identify its being and purpose more
openly with the particular reforms, the concrete 'practical',
'empirical' projects which had always been in the centre of its
attention. The logic of the Labour Right response to fundamental
set-back was abandonment of the ideal, an overt embracing of
technicism as the party's universe. The British ruling class, too,
was essentially pragmatic; but its disposition to empirical change
was wrapped up in a hard cortex of sentimental conservatism and
ritual, so that its reform always appeared as reluctant. The way
forward for Fabianism was simply to strip pragmatism of this
pious traditionalism, and replace it with a more aggressive,
pseudo-scientific rationale: their new man was to be the zealous,
hard-headed social engineer, even more deeply immersed in a
practical present, equally indifferent to romances of the past and
the future. Hence, the logical reaction of Fabian socialism to its
defeat was to cease being 'socialist' in the old sense, and to
define a new role of opposition in the characteristically British
political world – a kind of pure, non-ideological reformism.

The strengths of this approach are evident: its basic continuity
with the past, with British socialist 'empiricism' (now in fact
given a more intense and mystifying form than ever) – and at
the same time a break with the past, with piety and 'evolutionism'
and the inconvenient old dogma of 'socialism', sufficient to give
an appearance of hardy novelty and boldness. Associated with
this – perhaps necessarily – was a more unashamed *populism* than
the party had been able to allow itself in the past. Socialism had
been linked – however minimally and ineffectively – with the
notion of *forming* public opinion in a new, better mould, with an
educative function deriving from the socialist ideal itself. Post-
socialist technicism could only think in terms of giving people
what they want, here and now – that is, in terms of a mere
consumers' ideology. Technicism entails the dominance of
'experts'; but it exonerates itself from the accusation of being a
technocrats' dictatorship by claiming to do only what people
want.

The other direction at Labour's crossroads led not to abandonment but into the heart of socialism's problems. What went
wrong after 1945 was, in essence, what has always been wrong
with Labourist socialism itself. Hence, any authentic socialist
response to it entailed a critical task of great dimensions. It
was necessary to try and understand what had been wrong with

the notion of socialism employed by the party, and with the party's relationship to that notion in its ordinary activity; this implied a drastic revision of Fabian orthodoxy, ideologically, and beyond ideology the criticism was bound to invest the whole movement, its structure and functioning – all connected to and expressive of the party's philosophy, as we saw. Logic is fatal to Labourism, in its traditional forms. No adequate reaction could possibly have stopped at the programmatic level – it could not have stopped anywhere short of the attempt to re-define British socialism integrally, as ideology, as organization, as immediate policy.

But this was just the difficulty. The first line of response to Labourism's crisis mentioned was, by and large, that of the Labour leadership in the decade after 1950 – though it adopted it only slowly and in hesitant stages, holding on to old myths and confusing the issues at the same time. The second, surely, should have been that of the Labour party's left wing? Was not the crisis of Fabianism its long-awaited opportunity to come forward as the valid alternative it had always claimed to be? Was not the end of 'British Socialism' the possible beginning of socialism in Britain? But such a decisive break with Labourist tradition – and with *itself*, its own past function in the movement – was altogether beyond the powers of the left. The right took its logical course away from the checkmate of 1951, but the left could not. We saw how the weakness of the left wing had always been one of the fundamental traits of Labourism, how it had fallen into the role of a permanent, 'neurotic' opposition. This formation was to prevent it from grasping the opportunity – and so condemn it, as has become more and more clear in the last few years, to final sterility and exhaustion.

Consequently, if the Labour party's great experience of 'British Socialism' in practice had withered away the latter, this development in its turn exposed and destroyed the pretensions of Labour Leftism no less completely. In the last decade, the left-wing scene in Britain has changed greatly. The Labour leadership tradition has been transforming itself; new movements, new ideas and new modes of action – some with world-wide influence – have arisen outside Labourism, and have also – as we shall see below – reacted upon Labourism. But in this era of change, the left wing of Labourism has remained on the whole stationary, as if cut off from all the vital currents and tensions. Some of the sources of this weakness were discussed above.

In the long travail of the fifties they appeared as a kind of umbilical cord which tied the left to everything dead, and compelled it to look permanently backwards into a mythical past. As a left-wing speaker put it, succinctly, at the 1955 Annual Conference of the party – 'To a Socialist there is no necessity in 1955 to re-state a Socialist policy.'[44] In other words – the old, traditional vision of the party had been all right, in substance, so that further progress signified loyalty to that vision. According to this conception, the right had *betrayed* Socialism after 1948 – here was the cause of the movement's malady! It was necessary only to return to 1945, and another victory like that of 1945, another period of advance like that of 1945–48, would cure the movement. A second left-winger rose to support the one quoted, at the same Conference – 'If we are to impress the workers of this country . . . we must quite definitely get back to the old-fashioned socialism we knew . . . Our party must get back to Socialist principles, the principles on which the party was founded, as quickly as possible.'

How can one deny the hopelessness of such typical left-wing attitudes? How can one fail to observe that Labourism's mortal crisis stemmed, precisely, from the sacred 'Socialist principles . . . on which the party was founded', that the condition and outlook of 1945 were the very things which had led to the failure oppressing the party, and that in 1955 there was an urgent necessity not simply to re-state a 'Socialist policy' – for to think primarily in terms of 'policy' was already a concession to the right – but to elaborate a policy, an ideology, a critical account of the period of government, in short a coherent global position worthy of the adjective 'socialist'?

The result, the general situation out of which Wilsonism and the present inner state of the party have emerged, has been described as one where '. . . Old Left and New Right in the Labour party are unconscious allies in delaying any relevant analysis and challenge. The invocation of old habits . . . combines with the rejection of socialism as a radically different human order, to leave the ruling interpretations and directions essentially unchallenged.'[45] The particular episodes and personalities of the period are of less importance to us here. Aneurin Bevan was the leader of the left for the greater part of it; after his reconciliation with the leadership, in 1957, and his death in 1960, no comparable figure appeared to dominate the left-wing scene – a fact testifying, in its own way, to the decline of the 'Old Left'. Hugh Gaitskell, who succeeded Attlee as Leader in December 1955, was to become the guide of the right-wing trend outlined above, through the systematic 're-thinking' of Labour programmes which he initiated between 1957 and 1959. The climax of the conflict, and its most revealing moment, came only after the third electoral defeat in 1959.

The defeat was used by Gaitskell and the right as the excuse for a major offensive to finally convert the movement to the new post-socialist ideas. They maintained that the election had been lost because the party was still seen as attached to 'out-moded' and 'irrelevant' notions such as nationalization of the means of production; hence, it was essential to change the Constitution so as to make clear the party's devotion to a permanent 'mixed economy' (Labour's euphemism for an advanced-capitalist economy with a strong public sector). Here was to be the consummation of the right's logical reaction from 1945–50. What was wrong with the party, Gaitskell said, was its association with ideals rendered *dépassé* by the work of the Labour Government, and the subsequent better conduct of the capitalists. In substance, the socialist Kingdom of Heaven was here already. But the party contained elements that still pined for unreasonable further instalments, and the Constitution appeared to support these ignorant malcontents with its notorious 'Clause 4'.[46]

In spite of the great power of the right, and the immediate cogency its arguments derived from the fact that many of the left-wing positions really were *dépassé*, it could not win the battle. This was due – paradoxically – to the very same conservatism in the party which had so reliably and for so long kept the right in power. In discussing class consciousness, we saw how the inward-turned, densely corporative character dominant in Britain could function paradoxically as guardian of the positive class values, instead of only as a form of class subordination – resisting invasion and assimilation as well as tying the working class down to a static conservatism. It was against a barrier of this sort that Gaitskell and the revisionists struck. They were moving too far, too fast, to carry their traditional allies with them. Exasperated by the defeat of 1959, they wanted to carry the party's revisionism to its logical, honest conclusion, breaking with the old totem of 'socialism' and diminishing as far as possible the class appearance and outlook of the movement – its 'Victorian image', as they said.

But the majority of the movement – including the elements which had supported the political *substance* of their revisionism

– were more attached to the past, more sentimentally 'Victorian'
than they were. The trade union leaders were not impressed by
logic. It seemed to them that the old confusion had worked well
enough; while of course, after forty years, 'Clause 4' and the
other venerable furnishings of Labourism had almost taken a
place alongside the monarchy and Yorkshire pudding. The
repercussions of Gaitskellite revisionism might end by totally
changing the nature of the movement – for would it be possible,
or useful, in the long run for the trade unions to continue their
intimate association with a political party which had renounced
so formally and completely its 'class' character? In addition, a
practical consideration was important: Gaitskellism would
decisively alienate the socialist left – who would then replace the
left-wing militants so active at the base of the party, the loyal
exploited few so important in keeping the machine running?
Gaitskell had originally been *the* man of the great trade union
leaders.[47] Now he had become too dogmatic, there was a threat
to the vital functioning of the movement in his desire to push
matters to the logical, doctrinaire conclusion – hence, surpris-
ingly, many trade union leaders joined hands with the left in
opposing the constitutional changes.

By itself, the left wing would not have been able to defeat
Gaitskell. The 'Clause 4' episode does not therefore count as a
left-wing victory. Nevertheless, it was clearly an episode the left
could exploit – a victory at one remove, as it were, a gift of fate
arriving unexpectedly, and undeservedly, in spite of the long
impotence of the left. And it was quickly followed by another
dramatic event, still more surprising, still more propitious to
the left.

The Old Left's last chance

At the same time as Gaitskell's revisionist campaign was developing in the Labour party, another movement was gathering
strength outside it. The Campaign for Nuclear Disarmament
(CND) had rapidly become a nation-wide popular protest,
with its chief force among young people but affecting also many
sectors of the labour movement. Naturally, the left had embraced
this cause wholeheartedly and attempted to convert the whole
party to it. For the first time in the party's history, it succeeded.
An effective CND campaign at the trade union conferences
preceding the Labour party Annual Conference of 1960 ensured

that a majority of the trade union delegations would support a policy of unilateral abandonment of nuclear weapons – in direct conflict with the leadership's traditional defence policy (scarcely distinguishable from that of the Conservatives). By a kind of miracle, the dead souls and stolid bureaucrats were moved away from their generations of allegiance to rightist moderation. The fear of nuclear extinction had penetrated even into the stony recesses of British trade union conservatism, and the earth moved under the time-honoured structures of Labourism. The left won its first direct victory on a major policy question, in spite of Gaitskell's frantic pleading with the Conference. A year before the party's official socialist façade had been preserved; now, reinforced by the dynamic influence of the CND, the left had gone on to a genuine triumph. Nothing in the desert of the previous decade had presaged such a dramatic twist in events – could the left wing consolidate its advance, and permanently shatter the neo-Fabian dynasty?

The actual history of the year following the 1960 Conference is perhaps the bitterest in the Labour party's history. What happened is well known. Gaitskell simply defied the Annual Conference's decision, and said that the official policy of the party in parliament (and so of any Labour government) would not be changed. The mechanisms making this evasion possible were analysed above.[48] The leadership, in effect, took shelter behind the pre-historic code of the 'British Constitution' – with its rule that no 'extra-parliamentary' body may interfere with what goes on in that transcendental sanctum, the Holy of Holies, the House of Commons – to protect itself from its own party and its own party's democracy. As long as their position had been secure, the leaders had aquiesced in the myth that the Annual Conference decided party policy – after all, the Conference is the party's great holiday, a mixture of Congress and fete whose magic derived from the conviction that the ordinary people attending it could actively help to change the world. When their rule was threatened, the myth was demolished in an hour. The anonymous socialists constituting the Labour party were put firmly in their proper place – as servants, who were permitted to discuss important questions now and then and make their opinions known to the masters. Gaitskell – who the previous day had pleaded with the delegates to give the party a 'sensible' defence policy – made a speech pointing out that the delegates had no right to give the party any policy at all, since this might interfere with the 'consciences' of Labour MPs and with their sacrosanct 'promises' to the constituents that had elected them.

At the same time, obviously the leadership could not content itself with treading on the pretentions of the Annual Conference. Unfortunately, it would continue to need the party outside the walls of Westminster, and it would be inconvenient if the electoral machine were to have a mind different from that of the parliamentary party for any length of time. Gaitskell declared that he would 'fight, fight, and fight again' to restore the movement to sanity and the H-bomb. The bourgeois press and all official opinion realized that a hero had been born – by far the most promising chief of the Labour party since Ramsay MacDonald, a man capable of forming a 'National' government any day. His hardness more than made up for his lack of poetry.

The left, for its part, was presented with an equally clear picture – in order to gain any advantage from its victory, it too would have to 'fight, fight, and fight again' to have the will of the majority executed. If it did not, then it could scarcely hope to go on to other victories – worse than that, the very *sense* of its mode of activity was being destroyed by Gaitskell in his attack on the constitutional question, the hope (or illusion) of power the left had cherished for forty years was being menaced. Nor was the question in itself difficult, or dubious. On simple democratic grounds alone – not to mention the word 'socialism' – the left's case was quite unanswerable. In a world where the French revolution had actually happened, not a shred of logic could decently protect the phantasmagoric mish-mash of inanities emitted by the right and the hordes of *bien-pensant* political commentators on the subjects of democracy and political rectitude.

E. P. Thompson has commented perceptively on '. . . the lack, in the British twentieth-century labour movement, of Jacobin virtues'.[49] The minuscule dose of Jacobinism required to reduce Gaitskell and the 'British Constitution' to their appropriate size on the historical scene proved outside the powers of the Labour party's left wing. The right did fight back, in the year following the 1960 Conference, with a massive campaign entitled 'The Campaign for Democratic Socialism' and in 1961 sanity was restored – against very little opposition. Most of the unions were docilely reconverted to support of the official line by propaganda axed on the leading question – 'Are you in favour of making Great Britain defenceless?' A bureaucratically organized victory like this signifies little in itself. It was the inadequate opposition to it which signified much, brutally accentuating again the terrible weaknesses of the left, and their familiar source – the absence of a coherent intellectual position transcending the particular enthusiasms and policy crusades of left-wing socialism. The nuclear question had become inseparable from a whole complex of questions: not only in defence and foreign policy, but now in the sacred field of constitutionalism as well – while underlying everything were pressing interrogations about Labourism itself, its organization and meaning. The problem always confronting the Labour Left was re-presented, swollen to new and critical dimensions, by Gaitskell's drive towards a more dogmatic right-wing hegemony. Successful counter-attack had to be comprehensive or else futile, all or nothing. Incapable of all, the left was reduced to nothing.

The period since this demolition of the left has been one of quiescence, internally. Only two years after his Conference set-back of 1960, Gaitskell had apparently established a more total domination over the party than ever. He led Labourism into opposition to the Conservative Government's attempt to join the Common Market, basing his position on the alleged 'betrayal of the Commonwealth' by the Conservatives. The movement was united behind him as it had not been for many years – the same left that had cursed him as a traitor in 1960 now saw him as an increasingly progressive and left-inclined leader, clever enough to find a new moral crusade the entire party could agree upon. Such disconcerting vacillations of attitude result inevitably from the left's lack of an ideology. The only alternatives it has ever had have been either to leave the party, to resign, to threaten a split – or to submit, collaborate, make the best of a bad job within the rigid structures of Labourism, and tell itself that it may make things a little less bad than they would otherwise be and that in any case there is no 'practical' alternative. This chronic and impossible choice – illustrated to perfection in the career of Aneurin Bevan – is imposed by the left's lack of any *real* alternative, of a permanent point of view superior to the shabby middle-class limbo of Fabianism and containing in itself the source of a socialist hegemony over the movement, and ultimately over society.

A permanent question-mark

Such was the party inherited by Harold Wilson in 1963. We have
seen how it was modelled out of the distinctive historical experience of the British working class, how it bears the stamp of
the relation evolved between that class and British bourgeois
society. British society, with its permanent, massive congealment
of classes along clearly visible lines, had petrified the class conflict
in a form tolerable to itself. Labourism was the issue of this
petrification, the half-socialism which the working class could not
transcend in its chronically inhibited cold war against society.
Enmeshed in the dense web of archaic superstructures drafted
on to British capitalism, in spite of – and even *because* of – its
solidly corporative class-consciousness, the working class could
not distance itself aggressively from society and constitute its
own autonomous movement towards social hegemony.

The cutting instrument needed for this task was lacking. That
is, an intellectual stratum torn adrift from the social consensus
with sufficient force and capable of functioning as catalyst to
the new force striving for expression against the consensus.
Hence the working class could only find its affirmation on the
basis of its traditional corporate institutions, the trade unions,
in a political movement emanating from and tied to them – 'The
Labour party reflects trade unionism and cannot surpass it,'
G. D. H. Cole observed in 1913.[50] But, as we saw, it was forced
to surpass it by the inherent necessities of political action; and
could only acquire as its new politico-intellectual dimension an
organizing group derived from the old conformist intelligentsia.
This stratum, functioning as connective tissue between the working
class and tradition, established an easy ascendancy over Labourism and permanently repressed all more revolutionary developments within it – the very organization of the movement systematized and made definitive the modalities of the 'short-cut to
socialism', the compromise supposed to last a few years. Having
found expression in Labourism, the working class was also
imprisoned in it: the socialist left that ought to have in turn
transformed Labourism into Socialism, in fact, sank into hopeless
subordination to the system. 'British Socialism' did not break the
ossification of British society but became another layer of it.

Obviously, all these basic characteristics are still present in
Harold Wilson's Labour party. The experience which ought to

have demonstrated to socialists that Labourism was no more than an unacceptable half-way-house – the government of 1945–50 – did not, in fact, disrupt the Labourist compromise. Objectively, it confronted the movement with the bankruptcy of Fabian 'socialism'; but subjectively, only the Fabian Right was capable of responding to the challenge in its own fashion, while the left lost the chance to take up again the drive of the pioneer socialists and push Labourism further towards socialism. The questions all remained in suspense. The vast interrogation mark surrounding the continued existence of Labourism is still there. If the Labour party carries on upon the lines whose significance finally emerged from 1945–50, then how can it still be a socialist movement? If it ceases to be one, then how can socialists still participate in it – and, in the absence of the minimal goal holding the movement together, what will keep the trade unions participating in it in the long run? Is not the Labour party bound to become either more, or less, than it has been in the past: either a genuine socialist movement, or a mere reformist party continuing the old liberal tradition?

However, the Wilson era is by no means simply a continuation of the past whose outline we have traced. Although the Labour party cannot escape permanently the critical dilemma forced on it, all its problems at present appear in a vastly different light from a few years ago. The reason is, not that Labourism has changed internally, but that the external conditions it faces are in rapid flux. Born in an epoch of glacial immobility, built in time with the sluggish pulse of declining imperialism, the Labour party is now living through the disappearance of the bone-deep conservatism which formerly shrouded it. Suddenly, British society has slid into an era of change. More or less violent adaptations are imposed on every aspect of it. This is, at once, the new opportunity offered to Labourism, and the emergence of new problems for it in addition to the chronic ones described above – the profile of a new Labour government's dilemmas.

The future

Labourism was the product, the incarnation, of class stasis and intellectual stasis; it was the negation of any moving dynamic between theory and practice, the heavy domination of practice – in certain precise historically established forms – over theory and consciousness. It goes without saying that Labourism would be different in a historical situation where such stasis no longer endured. This is why one must approach with caution the familiar dilemma of whether any new left-wing movement must be 'inside' or 'outside' the Labour party, whether it should try to take over Labourism or replace it with something else. The fact is, that the existence of any forceful left-wing tendency, with a mind of its own and some basis in the trade unions – a left capable of hegemony and not only protest – would transform Labourism. Nobody can say how Labourism would react under a new strain of this sort. Would it be possible to preserve the positive side of Labourism – the unity it asserts among working-class organizations – on a higher, socialist level? Would a disintegration of the system be inevitable, as part of the ensuing battle?

Only one thing is certain: Labourism, which has survived every internal and external vicissitude since its foundation, which has drifted on immutably through defeat and the disintegration of its ideals, would no longer be able to function in the same way. Hegel first stated the paradox that a party only becomes real when it is divided against itself, when contradictions battle within it. Labourism was what it was because *not* divided against itself in this vital sense – as we saw, it centred upon a phoney dialectic, a pathological battle of appearances with no possibility of resolution. What it would become when lifted out of such unreality by an authentic challenge, when lacerated by contradictions which it could not stifle or ignore – nobody can say.

October 1964

Notes

1. Gramsci, *Note sur Machiavelli*, p. 22.
2. G. D. H. Cole, *A Short History of the British Working Class Movement*, p. 126.
3. S. and B. Webb, *History of Trade Unionism*, p. 199.
4. Bruhat, Dautry and Tersen, *La Commune de Paris*, p. 39.
5. Engels, letter to Marx, October 7th, 1858, in *Marx and Engels on Britain* (Moscow 1953), pp. 491–2 [cf. p. 383 of this reader].
6. Marx, letter to Engels, 17 November, 1862, in op. cit., p. 492.
7. Gramsci, *L'Ordine Nuovo*, p. 36.
8. Marx, letter to Engels, 27 July, 1866, in op. cit., p. 495.
9. Engels, letter to Sorge, 7 December, 1889, in op. cit., p. 522.
10. Beatrice Webb, *Our Partnership*, p. 97.
11. G. D. H. Cole, *A History of Socialist Thought*, vol. III, Part I, p. 167.
12. See Sidney Webb, 'The Basis of Socialism: Historic' in *Fabian Essays* (1889).
13. James Ramsay MacDonald, *The Socialist Movement*, p. 107.

14. G. D. H. Cole, op. cit., p. 207.

15. G. D. H. Cole, *A History of the Labour Party from 1914*, p 152.

16. G. D. H. Cole, *British Working Class Politics, 1832–1914*, p. 141.

17. See R. Miliband, *Parliamentary Socialism*, p. 28.

18. James Ramsay MacDonald, *Syndicalism: a Critical Examination*, p. 50.

19. R. Milliband, *Parliamentary Socialism*, p. 38.

20. Labour Party Annual Conference Report, 1917, p. 163.

21. S. Graubard, *British Labour and the Russian Revolution*, p. 38.

22. Robert McKenzie, *British Political Parties* (2nd edition), p. 517.

23. Robert McKenzie, op. cit., p. 519.

24. Robert McKenzie, op. cit., p. 639.

25. Labour Party Annual Conference Report, 1947, pp. 212–14.

26. R. H. S. Crossman, introduction to *The English Constitution* (new edition) by Walter Bagehot, 1963.

27. G. D. H. Cole, *History of the Labour Party from 1914*, p. 72.

28. Labour Party Annual Conference Report, 1918, p. 43.

29. op. cit., p. 44.

30. op. cit., p. 44.

31. Beatrice Webb, *Diaries*, 19 May, 1930.

32. Labour Party Annual Conference Report, 1918, pp. 44 and following section.

33. P. Anderson, article 'Origins of the Present Crisis', in *New Left Review* No. 23, January–February 1964, pp. 41–2.

34. See M. Duverger, *Political Parties*, p. 166.

35. G. D. H. Cole, *Short History of the British Working Class Movement*, p. 432.

36. M. Barratt Brown, *After Imperialism*, p. 144.

37. R. Miliband, op. cit., p. 272.

38. A. A. Rogow and P. Shore, *The Labour Government and British Industry*, 1945–51, pp. 45–6.

39. J. Byrnes, *Speaking Frankly*, p. 79.

40. Speech in House of Commons, 21 February 1946.

41. Sidney Webb, *Fabian Essays* (1889), pp. 65–7.

42. R. Miliband, op. cit., p. 288. Perhaps the best analysis of the question is in John Hughes, *Nationalized Industries in the Mixed Economy* (Fabian Society Pamphlet, 1962).

43. Raymond Williams, *The Long Revolution*, p. 301.

44. Labour Party Annual Conference Report, 1955, p. 114.

45. Raymond Williams, op. cit., p. 333.

46. Raymond Williams, op. cit., p. 47.

47. For an ingenuous but revealing journalistic account of the period, see L. Hunter, *The Road to Brighton Pier* (1958).

48. L. Hunter, op. cit., pp. 42–7.

49. Edward Thompson, *The Making of the English Working Class*, p. 183.

50. G. D. H. Cole, *The World of Labour*, p. 15.

The Turin Workers' Councils

ANTONIO GRAMSCI

(Reprinted from *New Left Review*, 51, 1968; translated from *Ordine Nuovo* 1919-20)

Workers' democracy

An urgent problem today faces every socialist with a lively sense of the historical responsibility that rests on the working class and on the party which represents the critical and active consciousness of the mission of this class.

How are the immense social forces unleashed by the war to be harnessed? How are they to be disciplined and given a political form which has the potential to develop and grow continuously into the basis of the socialist state in which the dictatorship of the proletariat is embodied? How is the present to be welded to the future, satisfying the urgent necessities of the one and working effectively to create and 'anticipate' the other?

The aim of this article is to stimulate thought and action. It is an invitation to the best and most conscious workers to reflect on the problem and collaborate – each in the sphere of his own competence and activity – towards its solution, by focusing the attention of their comrades and associations on it. Only common solidarity in a work of clarification, persuasion and mutual education will produce concrete, constructive action.

The socialist state already exists potentially in the institutions of social life characteristic of the exploited working class. To link these institutions together, co-ordinating and ordering them in a highly centralized hierarchy of instances and powers, while respecting the indispensable autonomy and articulation of each, means creating a true and representative workers' democracy here and now. Such a democracy should be effectively and actively opposed to the bourgeois state, and already prepared to replace it in all its essential functions of administration and control of the national heritage.

Today, the workers' movement is led by the Socialist party and the Confederation of Labour.[1] But for the great mass of workers, the exercise of the social power of the party and the Confederation is only achieved indirectly, by prestige and enthusiasm, authoritarian pressure and even inertia. The scope of the party's prestige widens daily, spreading to previously unexplored popular strata; it wins consent and a desire to work effectively for the advent of Communism among groups and individuals which have never previously participated in political struggle. These disorderly and chaotic energies must be given permanent form and discipline. They must be organized and strengthened, making the proletarian and semi-proletarian class an organized society that can educate itself, gain experience and acquire a responsible consciousness of the duties that fall to a class that achieves state power.

Only many years or decades of work will enable the Socialist party and the trade unions to absorb the whole of the working class. These two institutions cannot be identified immediately with the proletarian state. In fact, in the Communist republics, they have continued to survive independently of the state, as institutions of propulsion (the party) or of control and partial implementation (the unions). The party must continue as the organ of Communist education, the dynamo of faith, the depository of doctrine, the supreme power harmonizing and leading towards their goal the organized and disciplined forces of the working class and the peasantry. Precisely because it must strictly carry out this task, the party cannot throw open its doors to an invasion of new members, unused to the exercise of responsibility and discipline.

But the social life of the working class is rich in institutions, is articulated by a multiplicity of activities. These precisely demand development, co-ordination, and interconnection in a broad and flexible system that will include and order the entire working class.

The workshop with its internal commissions,[2] the socialist circles and the peasant communities are the centres of proletarian life in which we must work directly.

The internal commissions are organs of workers' democracy which must be freed from the limitations imposed on them by the management, and infused with new life and energy. Today, the internal commissions limit the power of the capitalist in the factory and perform functions of arbitration and discipline. Tomorrow, developed and enriched, they must be the organs of proletarian power, replacing the capitalist in all his useful functions of management and administration.

The workers should proceed forthwith to the election of vast delegate assemblies, chosen from their best and most conscious comrades, under the slogan: 'All Power in the Workshop to the

Workshop Committee', co-ordinating this slogan with another:
'All State Power to the Workers' and Peasants' Councils'.

A vast field of concrete revolutionary propaganda would open
up before the Communists organized in the party and in the ward
circles. In accord with the urban sections, the ward circles should
make a survey of the workers' forces in their zone, and become
the seat of the ward council of workshop delegates, the ganglion
that knits together and centralizes all the proletarian energies
of the ward. The system of elections could be varied according
to the size of the ward, but the aim should be to get one delegate
elected for every fifteen workers, divided into categories (as in
English factories), arriving by electoral stages at a committee
of factory delegates which included representatives of the whole
work process (manual workers, clerical workers, technicians).
The ward committee should also try to include delegates from the
other categories of workers living in the ward: servants, coach-
men, tram-drivers, railway workers, road-sweepers, private
employees, clerks, and others.

The ward committee should be an expression of *the whole
working class* living in the ward, a legitimate and authoritative
expression that commands respect for a discipline invested with
spontaneously delegated power, and that can order the immediate,
integral cessation of all work throughout the ward.

The ward committees should be enlarged into urban commissions, controlled and disciplined by the Socialist party and the
craft federations.

Such a system of workers' democracy (integrated with the
corresponding peasant organizations) would give a permanent
form and discipline to the masses. It would be a magnificent
school of political and administrative experience, and it would
incorporate the masses into its framework down to the last man,
so that tenacity and perseverance become habitual for them, and
they get used to regarding themselves as an army in the field
which needs a strict cohesion if it is not to be destroyed and
reduced to slavery.

Each factory would constitute one or more regiments of this
army, with its commanders, its interconnecting services, its
general staff, whose power will be delegated by free election, not
imposed in an authoritarian fashion. Assemblies, held within the
workshop, and ceaseless propaganda and persuasion by the most
highly conscious elements, should radically transform the workers'
psychology. It should increase the readiness and capacity of the

masses for the exercise of power, and diffuse a consciousness of the rights and duties of comrade and worker that is concrete and effective, since it has been spontaneously generated from living historical experience.

As we have said, these brief proposals have been put forward only to stimulate thought and action. Every aspect of the problem deserves coherent subsidiary treatment, elucidation and integration, in breadth and depth. But the concrete, integral solution of the problems of socialist life can only arise from Communist practice: collective discussion, sympathetically modifying consciousness, unifying it and inspiring it with active enthusiasm. It is a Communist and revolutionary act to tell the truth, to arrive together at the truth. The 'dictatorship of the proletariat' must cease to be a mere formula, an occasion for showy revolutionary phraseology. He who wants the end must also want the means. The dictatorship of the proletariat is the installation of a new, typically proletarian state, which will bring together the institutional experiences of the oppressed class and make the social life of the working class and the peasantry a highly organized and extensive system. This state cannot be improvised; the Russian Bolshevik government laboured eight months to diffuse and concretize the slogan 'All Power to the Soviets', and the Russian workers had known Soviets since 1905. Italian Communists must treasure the Russian experience and save time and labour: the work of reconstruction itself will demand so much time and so much labour that every day, every act must be devoted to it.

21 June 1919

The factory council

The proletarian revolution is not the arbitrary act of an organization that asserts itself to be revolutionary, or a system of organizations that assert themselves to be revolutionary. The proletarian revolution is a very long historical process that manifests itself in the rise and growth of determinate forces of production (which we summarize by the expression: 'proletariat') in a determinate historical context (which we summarize by the expressions: 'private property, capitalist mode of production, factory system, organization of society in a democratic-parliamentary state'). In a given phase of this process, the new productive forces are unable to develop or to organize themselves autonomously within the official order of the human community. Then the revolutionary act occurs: it is a direct bid to overthrow this order of things violently, to destroy the whole apparatus of economic and political power in which revolutionary productive forces are oppressively constricted. The revolutionary act is also a direct bid to overthrow the machinery of the bourgeois state and to construct a type of state in which liberated productive forces find both the adequate form for their further development and expansion, and the necessary fortress and weaponry to suppress their adversaries.

The true process of the proletarian revolution cannot be identified with the development and action of revolutionary organizations of a voluntary and contractual type, such as the political party or the trade unions. These are organizations born on the terrain of bourgeois democracy and political liberty, as an affirmation and development of political freedom. These organizations, in so far as they both embody a doctrine which interprets the revolutionary process and predicts its development (within certain limits of historical probability), and are acknowledged by the broad masses as their expression and embryonic apparatus of government, are – increasingly so – the direct and responsible agents of the successive acts of liberation which the whole working class will launch in the course of the revolutionary process. But all the same they do not incarnate this process. They do not supersede the bourgeois state: they do not and cannot embrace the multiple epicentres of revolution which capitalism throws up in its implacable path as a machine of exploitation and oppression.

During the economic and political predominance of the bourgeois class, the actual unfolding of the revolutionary process takes place subterraneously, in the darkness of the factory and in the obscurity of the consciousness of the countless multitudes that capitalism subjects to its laws. It is not controllable and documentable: it will be so in the future when the elements that constitute it (the feelings, the desires, the mores, the germs of initiative and of habit) are developed and purified by the evolution of society and the new place that the working class comes to occupy in the field of production. The revolutionary organizations of the political party and the trade union are born on the terrain of political liberty and bourgeois democracy, as an affirmation and development of liberty and of democracy in general, where the relationships of citizen to citizen subsist.

The revolutionary process takes place on the terrain of production, in the factory, where the relations are those of oppressor to oppressed, of exploiter to exploited, where freedom for the worker does not exist, where democracy does not exist. The revolutionary process occurs where the worker is nothing and wants to become everything, where the power of the proprietor is unlimited, is the power of life and death over the worker, over the worker's wife and over the worker's children.

When we say that the historical process of the workers' revolution which is immanent in the human community under capitalism, whose intrinsic laws are those of an objective concatenation of a multiplicity of actions that are uncontrollable, because they are created by a situation that has not been willed by the worker and is not foreseeable by the worker – when we say that this historical process has exploded into the light of day, has it become a controllable and documentable force?

We say this when the whole working class has become revolutionary: no longer in the sense that it refuses in a general way to collaborate with the ruling institutions of the bourgeois class and represents an opposition within the framework of democracy, but in the sense that the working class, as it is to be found in a factory, launches a movement that must necessarily result in the founding of a workers' state – that is, shape a human society altogether different from anything that has previously existed, in a universal form that embraces the whole workers' International and hence the whole of humanity. We say the present period is revolutionary precisely because we can see that the working class, in all countries, is tending to generate from within itself, with the utmost vital energy (if with the mistakes, gropings and encumbrances natural to an oppressed class which has no historical precedent, and must do everything for the first time), proletarian institutions of a new type: representative in basis and industrial in arena. We say the present period is revolutionary because the working class tends with all its energy and all its will-power to found its own state. That is why we claim that the birth of the workers' Factory Councils represents a major historical event – the beginning of a new era in the history of humanity. The revolutionary process has exploded into the light of day. It has become controllable and documentable.

In the liberal phase of the historical evolution of the bourgeois class and the society dominated by the bourgeoisie, the elementary cell of the state was the proprietor who subjugated the working class to his profit in the factory. The proprietor was also the entrepreneur and the industrialist. Industrial power and its source was in the factory, and the worker never succeeded in freeing himself from the conviction that the proprietor was necessary: his person was identified with that of the industrialist, with that of the manager responsible for production and hence also for the worker's wages, his bread, his clothing, his roof.

In the imperialist phase of the historical evolution of the bourgeois class, industrial power has become separated from the factory and is concentrated in a trust, in a monopoly, in a bank, in the state bureaucracy. Industrial power does not have to answer for what it does and hence becomes more autocratic, ruthless and arbitrary. But the worker, freed from obedience to the 'boss' in a servile atmosphere of hierarchy, and stimulated by new social and historical conditions, achieves priceless gains in independence and initiative.

In the factory the working class becomes a determinate 'instrument of production' in a determinate organic system. Every worker enters 'at the dictate of chance' to play a part in this system: at the dictate of chance so far as his own will is concerned, but not at the dictate of chance as regards the assignation of his work, since he represents a specific necessity in the process of labour and production. It is only for this that he is taken on: it is only for this that he is able to earn his bread. He is a cog in the machine of the division of labour, in a working class constituted into an instrument of production. If the worker acquires a clear consciousness of the 'determinate necessity' of his situation and makes it the basis of a representative apparatus of a state type (that is, not voluntary or contractual, through the membership card, but absolute and organic, part of a reality that is a precondition of bread, clothes, housing, industrial production) – if the working class does this, it achieves something of deep significance. It initiates a new history, the era of workers' states that must coalesce to form a Communist society: a world organized on the model of a large engineering works, an International in which every people, every part of humanity acquires a characteristic personality by its performance of a particular form of production and not by its organization as a state with particular frontiers.

In so far as it builds this representative apparatus, the working class effectively completes the expropriation of the primary machine, of the most important instrument of production:

the working class itself. It thereby rediscovers itself, acquiring consciousness of its organic unity and counterposing itself as a whole to capitalism. The working class thus asserts that industrial power and its source ought to return to the factory. It presents the factory in a new light, from the workers' point of view, as a form in which the working class constitutes itself into a specific organic body, as the cell of a new state, the workers' state – and as the basis of a new representative system, a system of councils. The workers' state, which is born within a specific matrix of production, creates the conditions for its own development and for its ultimate disappearance as a state, with its organic incorporation into the world system of the Communist International.

In the council of a large engineering works today, every work team (by craft) is united, from the proletarian point of view, with the other teams in the section, and every branch of industrial production merges with all the other branches, throwing into relief the productive process: so throughout the world, English *coal* will mix with Russian *petrol*, Siberian *grain* with Sicilian *sulphur*, *rice* from Vercelli with *wood* from Styria . . . in a single organism, subject to an international administration which governs the richness of the world in the name of all humanity. In this sense the workers' Factory Council is the first cell of a historical process which should end in the Communist International, no longer as a political organization of the revolutionary proletariat, but as a reorganization of the world economy and of the whole human community, on a national and international scale. Every revolutionary action has value and is historically real, in so far as it participates in this process and is conceived as an initiative to free it from the bourgeois superstructures that restrict and obstruct it.

The relations that should link the political party and the Factory Council, the trade union and the Factory Council, are already implicit in the argument that has been presented. The party and the trade union should not impose themselves as tutors or ready-made superstructures for the new institution, in which the historical process of the revolution takes a controllable historical form. They should become the conscious agents of its liberation from the restrictive forces concentrated in the bourgeois state. They ought to set themselves the task of organizing the general external (political) conditions in which the process of the revolution can achieve its maximum speed, and liberated productive forces find their greatest expansion.

5 June 1920

Unions and councils – I

The proletarian organization that, as a total expression of the worker and peasant masses, is centred on the Confederation of Labour is undergoing a constitutional crisis similar in nature to the crisis in which the democratic parliamentary state is vainly struggling. This crisis is a crisis of power and sovereignty. The solution of the one is the solution of the other. By solving the problem of the will for power in the sphere of their class organization, the workers will succeed in creating the organic foundations of their state and will victoriously counterpose it to the parliamentary state.

The workers feel that the complex of 'their' organization, the trade union, has become such an enormous apparatus that it now obeys laws internal to its structure and its complicated functions, but foreign to the masses who have acquired a consciousness of their historical mission as a revolutionary class. They feel that their will for power is not adequately expressed, in a clear and precise sense, in the present institutional hierarchy. They feel that even in their own home, in the house they have built tenaciously, with patient effort, cementing it with their blood and tears, the machine crushes man and bureaucracy sterilizes the creative spirit. Banal and verbalistic dilettantism cannot hide the absence of precise ideas for the necessities of industrial production, or a lack of understanding for the psychology of the proletarian masses. These *de facto* conditions irritate the workers, but as individuals they are powerless to change them: the worlds and desires of each single man are too small in comparison to the iron laws inherent in the bureaucratic structure of the trade-union apparatus.

The leaders of the organization are oblivious to this deep and widespread crisis. The clearer it becomes that the working class is organized in forms that do not accord with its real historical structure: the more certain it is that the working class is not organized into an institution that perpetually adapts itself to the laws that govern the intimate process of the real historical development of the class itself: the more these leaders persist in blindness, and work to resolve dissensions and conflicts within the organization 'legalistically'. Eminently bureaucratic in spirit, they believe that an objective condition, rooted in the psychology that develops in the living experience of the workshop, can be overborne by speeches that move the emotions and with an agenda voted unanimously in an assembly stupefied by oratorical din and verbosity. Today, they are stirring themselves to 'keep up with the times' and, to show that they are still capable of 'trenchant thought', they are reviving the old and threadbare syndicalist ideology, insisting painfully on establishing an identity between the Soviet and the trade union, insisting painfully on the claim that the present system of union organization already constitutes the foundation for a Communist society, the system of forces which should embody the dictatorship of the proletariat.

In the form in which it exists at present in Western Europe, the trade union is a kind of organization which not only differs essentially from the Soviet, but also differs considerably from the trade union as it is steadily developing in the Russian Communist republic.

The craft unions, the Chambers of Labour,[3] the industrial federations and the General Confederation of Labour are the types of proletarian organization specific to the historical period dominated by capital. It can be maintained that they are in a certain sense an integral part of capitalist society, and have a function which is inherent in the regime of private property. In this period, when individuals are only valued as owners of commodities, which they trade as property, the workers too are forced to obey the iron laws of general necessity; they become traders in their sole property – their labour power and professional skills. More exposed to the risks of competition, the workers have accumulated their property in ever broader and more comprehensive 'firms', they have created these enormous apparatuses for the concentration of work energy, they have imposed prices and hours and have disciplined the market. They have hired from outside or produced from inside a trusted administrative staff, expert in this kind of speculation, able to dominate market conditions, to lay down contracts, to evaluate commercial risks and to initiate profitable economic operations. The union's essential nature is competitive, not Communist. The union cannot be the instrument for a radical renovation of society, it can provide the proletariat with proficient bureaucrats, technical experts on industrial questions of a general kind, but it cannot be the basis for proletarian power. It offers no possibility of fostering the individual abilities of proletarians which make them capable and worthy of running society; it cannot produce the leadership which will embody the vital forces and rhythm of the progress of Communist society.

The proletarian dictatorship can only be embodied in a type of organization that is specific to the activity of producers, not wage-earners, the slaves of capital. The Factory Council is the nuclear cell of this organization. For all branches of labour are represented in the council, in proportion to the contribution each craft and each branch of labour makes to the manufacture of the object the factory produces for the collectivity; it is a class institution and a social institution. Its *raison d'être* is in labour, in industrial production, i.e. in a permanent fact, and no longer in wages, in class divisions, i.e. in a transitory fact – precisely the one that we wish to supersede.

Hence the council realizes the unity of the working class, gives the masses a cohesion and form of the same nature as the cohesion and form the masses assume in the general organization of society.

The Factory Council is the model for the proletarian state. All the problems inherent in the organization of the proletarian state are inherent in the organization of the council. In the one and in the other the concept of the citizen gives way to the concept of the comrade: collaboration to produce well and usefully increases solidarity and multiplies ties of affection and fraternity. Everyone is indispensable, everyone is in his place, everyone has his function and his position. Even the most ignorant and backward of workers, even the most vain and 'civil' of engineers will eventually convince himself of this truth in the experience of factory organization; all eventually acquire a Communist consciousness, so that they can understand the great step forward that the Communist economy represents as against the capitalist economy. The council is the best adapted organ for the mutual education which develops the new social spirit that the proletariat has successfully expressed out of the rich and living experience of the community of labour. In the trade union, workers' solidarity was fostered by the struggle against capitalism, in suffering and sacrifice. In the council, it is positive and permanent, it is embodied in even the least moments of industrial production. It is a joyous consciousness of being an organic whole, a homogeneous and compact system that by useful work and the disinterested production of social wealth, affirms its sovereignty, realizes its power and freedom to create history.

The existence of an organization in which the proletariat is structured homogeneously as a productive class, making possible a free, spontaneous flowering of respected and capable leaders and individuals, will have fundamental effects on the constitution and spirit that informs the activity of the trade unions.

The Factory Council, too, is based on the crafts. In every department, the workers are differentiated into teams and each team is a labour unit (a craft unit); the council is made up precisely of commissars whom the workers elect by departmental crafts (teams). But the union is based on the individual, while the council is based on the organic and concrete unity of the craft as it is realized in the discipline of the industrial process. The team (craft) feels its distinctness from the homogeneous body of the class, but at the same time, it also feels its enmeshment in the system of discipline and order that makes possible the development of production and its exact and definite functioning. As an economic and political interest the craft is an indistinct and perfectly solidary part of the class body; it is distinct from it as a technical interest and as a development of the particular tool it utilizes in the work-process. In the same way, all industries are homogeneous and solidary in their aim to perfect the production, distribution and social accumulation of wealth, but each industry has distinct interests where the technical organization of its specific activity is concerned.

The existence of the councils gives the workers direct responsibility for production, leads them to improve their work, institutes a conscious and voluntary discipline, and creates the psychology of the producer, the creator of history. The workers will carry this new consciousness into the union, and the latter, instead of pursuing the simple activity of the class struggle, will devote itself to the fundamental work of imprinting a new configuration on economic life and labour technique; it will devote itself to the elaboration of the forms of economic life and professional technique proper to Communist civilization. In this sense, the trade unions, made up of the best and most conscious workers, will realize the highest moment of the class struggle and the dictatorship of the proletariat: they will create the objective conditions in which classes will no longer be able to exist or re-emerge.

The industrial unions in Russia are doing this. They have become the organs in which all the individual undertakings of a certain industry are amalgamated, interconnected and articulated, forming one great industrial unit. Wasteful competition is being eliminated, the main services of administration, supply, distribution and storage are being unified in great centres. Work systems, manufacturing secrets and new applications are immediately made available to the whole of the industry. The multiplication of bureaucratic and disciplinary functions inherent in relations of private property and individual enterprise is being reduced to minimal industrial necessities. The application of union principles to the Russian textile industry has made possible a reduction in the bureaucracy from 100,000 employees to 3500.

Factory organization will bind the class (the whole class) into a homogeneous and cohesive unit that can adapt flexibly to the industrial process of production and dominate it, bringing it under final control. So factory organization will embody the proletarian dictatorship, the Communist state that destroys class dominion in the political superstructures and in their general interconnections.

Craft and industrial unions will be the rigid backbone of the great proletarian body. They will elaborate individual and local experience and store it up, realizing that national equalization of the conditions of labour and production on which Communist equality is concretely based.

But if it is to be possible to impress on the unions this positive class and Communist direction, it is essential that the workers turn their whole will and credence to the consolidation and diffusion of the councils, to the organic unification of the working class. On this homogeneous and solid basis all the higher structures of the Communist dictatorship and economy will flourish and develop.

11 October 1919

Unions and councils – II

The trade union is not a predetermined phenomenon: it *becomes* a determinate institution, that is, it assumes a definite historical form to the extent that the strength and will of the workers who are its members impress a policy and propose an aim that define it.

Objectively, the trade union is the form that labour as a commodity necessarily assumes in a capitalist regime when it organizes to dominate the market. This form is an office of functionaries, technicians (when they are technicians) of organization, specialists (when they are specialists) in the art of centralizing and leading the workers' forces in order to establish an advantageous balance between the working class and the power of capital.

The development of trade-union organization is characterized by two facts: 1. the union embraces an ever-larger number of workers; 2. the union concentrates and generalizes its scope so that the power and discipline of the movement are focused in a central office. This office detaches itself from the masses it regiments, removing itself from the fickle eddy of moods and currents that are typical of the great tumultuous masses. The union thus acquires the ability to sign agreements and take on responsibilities, obliging the entrepreneur to accept a certain legality in his relations with the workers. This legality is conditional on the trust the entrepreneur has in the *solvency* of the union, and in its ability to ensure that the working masses respect their contractual obligations.

The emergence of an industrial legality is a great victory for the working class, but it is not the ultimate and definitive victory. Industrial legality has improved the working class's material living conditions, but it is no more than a compromise – a compromise which had to be made and which must be supported until the balance of forces favours the working class. If the officials of the trade union organization regard industrial legality as a necessary, but not permanently necessary compromise; if they devote all the means at the disposal of the union to improving the balance of forces for the working class; and if they make all the indispensable moral and material preparations for the working class at a given moment to be able to launch a successful offensive against capital and subject it to its law, then the trade union is a revolutionary instrument and union discipline, even when it is used to make the workers respect industrial legality, is revolutionary discipline.

The relations which should prevail between union and Factory Council must be considered from this viewpoint: from our judgement of the nature and value of industrial legality.

The Factory Council is the negation of industrial legality. It tends at every moment to destroy it, for it necessarily leads the working class towards the conquest of industrial power, and indeed makes the working class the source of industrial power. The union represents legality, and must aim to make it respected by its members. The trade union is responsible to the industrialists, but it is responsible to them in so far as it is responsible to its own members: it guarantees continuity of labour and income to the workers and their families, that is, bread and a roof over their heads. By its revolutionary spontaneity, the Factory Council tends to unleash the class war at any moment; by its bureaucratic form, the trade union tends to prevent the class war ever being unleashed. The relations between the two institutions should be such that a capricious impulse on the part of the councils could not cause a step backward by the working class, a working class defeat, in other words; the council should accept and assimilate the discipline of the union, while the revolutionary character of the council exercises influence on the union, as a reagent dissolving its bureaucratism.

The council tends to move beyond industrial legality at any moment. The council is the exploited, tyrannized mass, forced to perform servile labour; hence it tends to universalize every rebellion, to give a revolutionary scope and value to each of its acts of power. The union, as an organization totally committed to legality, tends to universalize and perpetuate this legality. The relations between trade union and council should create the conditions in which the movement away from legality – the proletarian offensive – occurs at the most opportune moment for the working class, when it has that minimum of preparation that is indispensable to a durable victory.

The liaison between unions and councils can only be established by one link: the majority or a substantial part of the electors to the councils should be organized in the union. Every bid to link the two institutions in a relation of hierarchical dependence can only lead to the destruction of both.

If the conception that makes the council a mere instrument in the trade union struggle is materialized in a bureaucratic discipline and rights of direct union control over the council, the council is sterilized as a force of revolutionary expansion – as a form of real development of the proletarian revolution that tends spontaneously to create new modes of production and labour, new modes of discipline, a Communist society. The emergence of the councils is a result of the position the working class has won on the terrain of industrial production; the council is a historical necessity of the working class. Thus any bid to subordinate it hierarchically to the trade union will sooner or later result in a clash between the two institutions. The power of the councils consists in the fact that they are close to and coincide with the consciousness of the working masses who are seeking their autonomous emancipation, who wish to affirm their freedom of initiative in the creation of history: the whole mass participates in the life of the council and feels itself to be something through this activity. Only very small numbers of members participate in the life of the union; its real strength lies in this fact, but this fact is also a weakness that cannot be put to the test without grave risks.

If, moreover, the union were to lean directly on the councils, not to dominate but to become a higher form of them, the typical tendency of the councils to move beyond industrial legality at any moment and unleash decisive actions in the class war would be reflected in the union. The latter would forfeit its ability to make commitments and would lose its character as a disciplinary and regulative force over the working class.

If its members establish a revolutionary discipline in the union, which appears to the masses as a necessity for the victory of the workers' revolution and not as slavery to capital, this discipline will undoubtedly be accepted and made its own by the councils. It will become the natural form of the councils' action. If the union office becomes an organ of revolutionary preparation, and appears as such to the masses in the practice it executes, in the men who compose it and the propaganda it develops, then its centralized and absolute character will be seen by the masses as a major revolutionary strength, as one more (and a very important) condition for the success of the struggle to which they are basically committed.

In Italian conditions, the union bureaucrat conceives industrial legality as a permanent state of affairs. He too often defends it from the same viewpoint as the proprietor. He sees only chaos and wilfulness in everything that emerges from the working masses. He does not understand the worker's act of rebellion against capitalist discipline as a rebellion; he perceives only the physical act, which may in itself and for itself be trivial. Thus the story about the 'porter's raincoat' has been as widely disseminated and interpreted by stupid journalists as the fable of the 'socialization of women in Russia'. In these conditions union discipline can only be a service to capital; in these conditions every bid to subordinate the councils to the unions can only be judged as reactionary.

Communists want the act of revolution to be as far as possible conscious and responsible. They therefore want the choice of the moment to unleash the workers' offensive (to the extent that there is a choice) to remain in the hands of the most conscious and responsible section of the working class: that which is organized in the Socialist party and participates most actively in the life of the organization. Therefore, the Communists cannot wish that the union lose any of its disciplinary control and its systematic centralization.

By constituting themselves into permanently organized groups in the unions and the factories, the Communists must introduce the conceptions, theses and tactics of the Third International; they must influence union discipline and determine its aims; they must influence the deliberations of the Factory Councils and transform the rebellious impulses produced by the situation capitalism has imposed on the working class into consciousness and revolutionary creativity. The Communists in the party have the greatest interest in this, for on their shoulders rests the heaviest historical responsibility: to promote by incessant activity relations of natural interpenetration and interdependence between the various institutions of the working class that will enliven its discipline and organization with a revolutionary spirit.

12 June 1920

The party and the revolution

The Socialist party, with its network of sections which in their turn are the fulcrum of a compact and powerful system of ward circles in the great industrial centres; with its provincial federations, tightly unified by the currents of ideas and activities that radiate from the urban centres; with its annual congresses for the discussion and resolution of immediate, concrete problems, which embody the highest sovereignty of the party, exercised by the mass of the members through precise delegations, with limited powers; with its leadership, which emanates directly from the congress and constitutes its permanent executive and organ of control – the Socialist party constitutes an apparatus of proletarian democracy which might easily in political fantasy be regarded as 'exemplary'.

The Socialist party is a model of a 'libertarian' society, voluntarily disciplined by an explicit act of consciousness. To imagine the whole of human society as a colossal Society party, with its requests for admission and its resignations, cannot but encourage the contractualist prejudices of the many subversive spirits who are influenced by J. J. Rousseau and anarchist pamphlets rather than by the historical and economic doctrines of Marxism. The Constitution of the Russian Soviet Republic is based on exactly the same principles as the Socialist party; the government of Russian popular sovereignty functions in forms suggestively similar to the forms of government in the Socialist party. Hence it is not surprising that these elements of analogy and instinctive aspirations should give rise to the revolutionary myth which conceives the installation of proletarian power as a dictatorship of the system of Socialist party sections.

This conception is at least as utopian as that which acknowledges the unions and the Chambers of Labour as the proper forms of the revolutionary process. Communist society can only be conceived as a 'natural' formation built on the means of production and exchange; and the revolution can only be conceived as the act of historical acknowledgement of the 'naturalness' of this formation. Hence the revolutionary process can only be identified with a spontaneous movement of the working masses caused by the clash of the contradictions inherent in common human life under a regime of capitalist property. Caught in the pincers of capitalist conflicts, and threatened by condemnation without appeal to the loss of civil and spiritual rights, the masses break with the forms of bourgeois democracy and leave behind the legality of the bourgeois constitution. Society could well collapse, all production of useful social wealth might slump, precipitating men into a bottomless abyss of poverty, barbarism and death, if there is no reaction by the historically conscious masses of the people to find a new framework, to build a new order in the process of the production and distribution of wealth. The proletariat's organs of struggle are the 'agents' of this colossal mass movement; the Socialist party is indubitably the most important 'agent' in this process of destruction and neo-formation, but it is not and cannot be conceived as the form of this process, a form malleable and plastic to the leaders' will. German Social Democracy (understood as an ensemble of political and trade union institutions) paradoxically forced the process of the German proletarian revolution violently into its own organizational forms, thinking it could dominate history.

It has created *its own* councils by *fiat*, with a secure majority of its own men on them; it has hobbled the revolution and domesticated it. Today it has lost all contact with historical reality, except for the contact of Noske's fist on the workers' backs, and the revolutionary process follows its own uncontrolled and as yet mysterious course, which will burst forth again in unknown founts of violence and agony.

The Socialist party achieves the same results with its intransigence in the political domain as the trade unions do in the economic field: it puts an end to free competition. With its revolutionary programme, the Socialist party pulls out from under the bourgeois state apparatus its democratic basis in the consensus of the governed. It influences ever wider popular masses and assures them that the state of distress in which they are caught is not a passing phase, nor an unavoidable evil, but corresponds to an objective necessity: it is the ineluctable moment of a dialectical process which must overflow in violent turbulence to regenerate society. Thus the party is identified with the historical consciousness of the popular masses and governs their irresistible spontaneous movement. It is an incorporeal government, which functions through a myriad spiritual links; it is a radiation of prestige, only becoming an effective government in culminating movements: by an appeal to the streets, by a physical array of militant forces, poised to ward off a danger or dissolve a cloud of reactionary violence.

Once the party has successfully paralysed the functioning of the legal government over the popular masses, the most difficult and delicate phase of its activity opens before it: the phase of positive activity. The conceptions the party disseminates operate autonomously in the individual consciousness, and they cause new social configurations to emerge in line with these conceptions. They produce institutions that function by internal laws, an embryonic apparatus of power in which the masses realize their government, and acquire a consciousness of their historical responsibility and peculiar mission: the creation of the conditions for a regenerative communism. As a compact and militant ideological formation, the party influences this intimate elaboration of new structures, this industry of millions and millions of social infusoria preparing the red reefs of coral whose growth will break the strength of the oceanic tempest in the not so distant future, and bring back peace to the waves, establishing a new balance of currents and climes. But this influx is organic, it grows from the circulation of ideas, the maintenance intact of the apparatus of spiritual government, from the fact that the myriads of workers who establish the new leaderships and institute the new order know that the historical consciousness that moves them has its living embodiment in the Socialist party: it is justified by the doctrine of the Socialist party, and has a powerful bulwark in the political strength of the Socialist party.

The party remains the superior hierarchy of this irresistible mass movement. It exercises the most effective of dictatorships, a dictatorship born of its prestige, of the conscious and spontaneous acceptance of an authority that is acknowledged as indispensable to the success of the work undertaken. It would be disastrous if a sectarian conception of the party role in the revolution claimed to materialize this hierarchy, and fix in mechanical forms of immediate power an apparatus governing the masses in movement, forcing the revolutionary process into the forms of the party. The result would be to divert a number of men and to 'dominate' history, but the real revolutionary process would escape the control and influence of the party which would unconsciously become an organ of conservatism.

The propaganda of the Socialist party insists on these irrefutable theses. The traditional relations of capitalist appropriation of the product of human labour have changed radically. Before the war, Italian labour agreed without serious or explosive resistance to the appropriation of sixty per cent of labour-produced wealth at the hands of the tiny capitalist minority and the state, while the tens of millions of the working population had to be content with a scarce forty per cent for the satisfaction of elementary needs and higher cultural life. Today, after the war, a new situation has emerged. Italian society only produces one half of the wealth it consumes; the state is colossally in debt to future labour, that is, it is progressively enslaving Italian labour to the international plutocracy. To the two groups who take a slice out of production (the capitalists and the state) it has added a third, purely parasitic one: the petty-bourgeoisie of the military-bureaucratic caste which formed during the war. It seized precisely that half of the wealth which is unproduced and becomes a debt to future labour: it seizes it directly as stipends and pensions, and indirectly because its parasitic function presupposes the existence of a whole parasitic apparatus. If Italian society only produces fifteen billion *lire* of wealth while it consumes thirty, and these fifteen are produced by a daily eight hours' labour on the part of the tens of millions of the working population who receive six to seven billions as their wages, a capitalist balance-sheet can only be re-established normally in one way: by forcing the tens of millions of the working population to give for the same mass of wages, one, two, three, four or five hours more labour daily. This is unpaid labour, labour which goes to increase capital, so it can return to its accumulatory function; which goes to the state so that it can pay its debts; or which consolidates the economic situation of the salaried petty-bourgeoisie and rewards it for its armed services to the state and capital in forcing the working population to exhaust itself at machines and on patches of earth.

In this general situation of capitalist relations, the class struggle cannot be aimed at any goal other than the conquest of state power by the working class so they can turn this ruthless power against the parasites and force them to return to the ranks of labour, and abolish at one stroke the monstrous slice they grab today. To this end the whole labouring masses must co-operate, they must become a conscious formation according to the place they occupy in the process of production and exchange. Thus every worker and every peasant is summoned by the councils to collaborate in the effort of regeneration, and to constitute the apparatus of industrial government and dictatorship: the present form of the class struggle for power is embodied in the councils. This, then, is the network of institutions in which the revolutionary process is developing: the council, the trade union, the socialist party. The council is an historical product of Italian society, defined by the necessity to dominate the productive apparatus, born of the conquest of self-consciousness by the producers. The union and the party are voluntary associations, stimulants of the revolutionary process, 'agents' and 'administrators' of the revolution; the union co-ordinates the productive forces and imprints on the industrial apparatus a communistic form; the Socialist party, the living and dynamic model of a social life in common that unites discipline with freedom, gives the human spirit all the energy and enthusiasm of which it is capable.

27 December 1919

Two revolutions

Any form of political power can only be historically conceived and justified as the juridical apparatus of a real economic power. It can only be conceived and justified as the defensive organization and developmental condition of a determinate order in the relations of production and distribution of wealth. This basic (and elementary) canon of historical materialism sums up the whole complex of theses we have been trying to develop organically with respect to the problem of the Factory Councils. It sums up the reasons why, in dealing with the real problems of the proletarian class, we have given a central and pre-eminent place to the positive experience determined by the profound movement of the working masses in the creation, development and co-ordination of the councils. We have therefore maintained: 1. that the revolution is not necessarily proletarian and Communist if it proposes and obtains the overthrow of the political government of the bourgeois state; 2. nor is it proletarian and Communist if it proposes and obtains the destruction of the representative institutions and administrative machine through which the central government exercises the political power of the bourgeoisie; 3. it is not proletarian and Communist even if the wave of popular insurrection places power in the hands of men who call themselves (and sincerely are) Communists. The revoltuion is proletarian and Communist only in so far as it liberates the proletarian and Communist forces of production, forces that have been developing within the society ruled by the capitalist class. It is proletarian and Communist in so far as it advances and promotes the growth and systematization of proletarian and Communist forces that can begin the patient, methodical work necessary for the construction of a new order in the relations of production and distribution: a new order in which a class-divided society will become an impossibility, and whose systematic development will therefore tend to coincide with the withering away of state power, with a systematic dissolution of the political organization that defends the proletarian class, while the latter itself will dissolve to become mankind.

The revolution that is achieved by the destruction of the bourgeois state apparatus, and the construction of a new state apparatus, concerns and involves all the classes oppressed by capitalism. Immediately, it is determined by the brute fact that,

in the conditions of famine left by the imperialist war, the great
majority of the population (made up of artisans, small landowners, petit-bourgeois intellectuals, extremely poor peasant
masses and backward proletarian masses) are no longer guaranteed even the elementary needs of daily life. This revolution
tends to have a predominately anarchistic and destructive
character and to manifest itself as a blind explosion of anger, a
tremendous release of fury, without any concrete object, which
only results in a new state power if fatigue, disillusionment and
hunger finally impose the necessity for a new constitutional
order and a power to enforce respect for that order.

This revolution may result merely in a constituent assembly
that tries to heal the wounds inflicted on the bourgeois state
apparatus by popular anger. It may go as far as Soviets, the
autonomous political organization of the proletariat and the
other oppressed classes, but which in this case do not dare go
beyond their organization to change economic relations, so that
they are cast aside by the reaction of the propertied classes.
It may go as far as the complete destruction of the bourgeois
state machine, and the establishment of a situation of permanent
disorder, in which the existing wealth and population dissolve
and disappear, shattered by the impossibility of any autonomous
organization. It may go as far as the establishment of a proletarian and Communist power which is exhausted by repeated
desperate attempts to create in an authoritarian manner the
economic conditions necessary for its survival and growth, and
is finally overturned by capitalist reaction.

In Germany, Austria, Bavaria, the Ukraine and Hungary,
we have seen these historical developments unfold; the revolution
as a destructive act has not been followed by the revolution as
a process of reconstruction towards communism. The existence
of external conditions – a Communist party, the destruction of
the bourgeois state, highly organized trade unions and an armed
proletariat – is not enough to compensate for the absence of
another condition: the existence of productive forces tending
towards development and growth, a conscious movement of
the proletarian masses in favour of substantiating its political
power by economic power, the will on the part of the proletarian
masses to introduce proletarian order into the factory, to make
the factory the nucleus of the new state, and to build the new
state as an expression of the industrial relations of the factory
system.

That is why we have always maintained that the duty of the existing Communist nuclei in the party was to avoid particularistic obsessions (the problem of electoral abstentionism, the problem of the constitution of a 'true' Communist party) and instead work for the creation of the mass conditions in which it would be possible to resolve all particular problems as problems in the organic development of the Communist revolution. In fact, can a Communist party really exist (one which is an active party, not an academy of doctrinaires and petty politicians who think and express themselves 'well' where communism is concerned) if the masses do not have the spirit of historical initiative and the aspiration towards industrial autonomy that should be reflected and synthesized in the Communist party? Since the formation of a party and the emergence of the real historical forces of which parties are the reflections do not occur all at once out of nothing, but according to a dialectical process, is not the major task of the Communist forces precisely that of giving consciousness and organization to the essentially Communist productive forces that must be developed, and which by their growth will create the secure and lasting economic base of the political power of the proletariat?

Similarly, can the party abstain from participation in electoral struggles for the representative institutions of bourgeois democracy, if one of its tasks is the political organization of all the oppressed classes about the Communist proletariat, and to obtain this it must become the governmental party for these classes in a democratic sense, given that it can only be the party of the Communist proletariat in a revolutionary sense?

In so far as it becomes the party of 'democratic' trust for all the oppressed classes, in so far as it keeps in permanent contact with every group of working people, the Communist party leads all sections of the people to acknowledge the Communist proletariat as the ruling class that must replace the capitalist class in state power. It creates the conditions in which it is possible to identify the revolution that destroys the bourgeois state with the proletarian revolution, with the revolution that expropriates the expropriators and inaugurates the development of a new order in the relations of production and distribution.

Hence, in so far as it claims to be the specific party of the industrial proletariat, and works to provide a precise consciousness and a policy for the productive forces produced by the development of capitalism, the Communist party creates the economic preconditions for the state power of the Communist proletariat. It creates the conditions in which the proletarian revolution can be identified with the popular revolt against the bourgeois state, the conditions in which this revolt becomes an act liberating the real productive forces that have accumulated within capitalist society.

These various series of historical events are not detached and independent; they are moments in a single dialectical process of development during which relations of cause and effect interlace, reverse, and interweave with one another. But the experience of revolutions has shown that, since Russia, all other two-stage revolutions have failed and the failure of the second revolution has prostrated the working classes in a state of demoralization which enabled the bourgeois classes to reorganize in strength and begin the systematic annihilation of every bid by the Communist vanguard to reconstitute itself.

For those Communists who are not content to chew monotonously the cud of the basic principles of communism and historical materialism, and are alive to the reality of the struggle, grasping reality as it is, from the viewpoint of historical materialism and communism, the revolution as the conquest of social power for the proletariat can only be conceived as a dialectical process in which political power makes possible industrial power and industrial power political power. The Soviet is the instrument of revolutionary political struggle which permits the autonomous development of that Communist economic organization whose Central Economic Council is established on the basis of Factory Councils, and settles the plans of production and distribution, thereby suppressing capitalist competition. The Factory Council, as a form of producers' autonomy in the industrial field and as the basis of Communist economic organization, is the instrument of a mortal struggle against the capitalist regime in so far as it creates the conditions in which class-divided society is suppressed and any new class division is rendered 'materially' impossible.

But for Communists alive to the struggle, this conception will not remain an abstract thought; it will become an incitement to struggle, a stimulus to greater efforts of organization and propaganda.

Industrial development has produced a certain degree of mental independence and a certain spirit of positive historical initiative in the masses. These elements of the proletarian revolution must be given form and organization; the psychological conditions for their development and generalization throughout the labouring masses must be created by the struggle for the control of production.

We must promote the organic constitution of a Communist party which is not a collection of doctrinaires or little Machiavellis, but a party of Communist revolutionary action, a party with a precise consciousness of the historical mission of the proletariat and the ability to guide the proletariat in the realization of that mission – hence, a party of the masses who want to free themselves from political and industrial slavery autonomously, by their own efforts, through the organization of the social economy, and not a party which uses the masses for its own heroic attempts to imitate the French Jacobins. To the extent that it can be achieved by party action, it is necessary to create the conditions in which there will not be two revolutions, but in which the popular revolt against the bourgeois state will be able to find the organizational forces capable of beginning the transformation of the national apparatus of production from an instrument of plutocratic oppression to an instrument of Communist liberation.

3 July 1920

The question of force

There are two powers in Italy, the power of the bourgeois state and the power of the working class: the second is progressively destroying the first. Only one function of the bourgeois state is alive today: its self-defence, the preparation of arms and armed men for its defence. It stands with its rifle permanently at the shoulder, ready to fire just as soon as the enemy takes on a concrete form and is embodied in the institution that will begin to exercise its new power. The power of the working class grows more and more massive every day; it is present in the strikes, the agitation, the fears of the governing class, the convulsions of the government officials, the trepidation of the capitalists and the continuous rabid snarling of all the watchdogs guarding the strong-room. The power of the working class could be embodied in a council system tomorrow, or even today, if all that was necessary was the revolutionary enthusiasm of the proletariat and a majority of the population on the proletarian side.

Today, the struggle between these two powers is on the brink of armed and organized violence. The bourgeois state only survives because it possesses a centre of co-ordination for its military might and because it still has the initiative: it is in a position to manoeuvre its troops and concentrate them on the revolutionary epicentres, drowning them in a torrent of blood.

This problem of force is finding its resolution in the process of revolutionary development. Every day new groups of the working population are welcomed into the general movement of the national and global proletarian revolution. Italian capitalism has its deepest roots and the seat of its hegemony in Northern Italy, in the industrial centres of Northern Italy. The Communist revolution, which in Italy presents itself as a revolution in industrial technique, as a problem of the equalization of the conditions of agricultural labour and the conditions of industrial labour, will have its major seat in the North. The class of factory workers will be confronted with the tremendous problem produced by the war: how can it succeed in building a state organization that has the means to industrialize agriculture and is able to provide the peasants with the same conditions of labour as the workers, so that it will be possible to exchange one hour of agricultural labour with one hour of industrial labour, so that the proletariat is not destroyed by the countryside in the exchange of commodities produced in absolutely non-comparable conditions of labour? This problem, which the capitalist industrialists are unable to solve, and which, if it is not resolved, will smash the bourgeois state, can be resolved by the workers, by a workers' state in Italy – as it has been resolved and is being resolved by the Russian workers' state. It will be resolved by the urban industrial workers who will become the principal agents of the Communist revolution.

If the workers, concentrated in the industrial cities, are to be the principal actors in the Communist revolution, the principal actors in the pre-revolutionary activity will rather be the peasant masses. Movements of the rural masses will definitively destroy the power of the bourgeois state, by destroying its military might. No army is large enough to subdue the countryside in revolt: regiments that seem invincible when they are amassed in the streets of a city, are a joke in the immensity of open fields: the cannons, machine-guns and flame-throwers that would scythe down a crowd of workers in closed streets and squares, are impotent in the immensity of the rural horizon.

The bourgeois state feels this danger is imminent: the countryside is going over to the revolution. From Apulia to Novara, from Novara to Brescia and Bergamo, the peasant masses are emerging from their torpor and engaging in grandiose actions. The Popular party[4] is deeply shaken by these gigantic clashes. Under the impulse of the poor peasants who militate under its banners, the left wing of the Popular party is adopting extremist and revolutionary attitudes. The bourgeois state detects this danger and would like to accelerate events in the industrial cities and solidly Communist centres. For these will become the fulcrum of the revolution; they will provide its soul and aims, and will construct the new society from the ruins of the old. Hence it is enough for an internal commission to move the hands of a factory clock to set hundreds of royal guards[5] and *carabinieri* in motion, to threaten an Armageddon. The working class must be on its guard, it must maintain discipline in its revolutionary trenches, a discipline whose substance is patience, proletarian critical sense, and trust in its own forces and future. The revolutionary situation is developing implacably, smashing the bourgeois state and destroying capitalist power. The working class will win; the proletariat, as it wills the revolution, must concern itself with a durable victory, a *permanent* victory. It is the depository of the future, the living energy of history; it must not expose itself to a repression that would put it out of action for too long a period. The bourgeois state would be glad to take its mercenary troops away from the cities and send them against the peasants if it could smash the workers and secure its rear. The working class is the most politically educated section of the whole working people; it must face the problem of force and realize that it can be largely resolved by the action of the peasant masses. The Russian working class was able to wait from July to November in 1917; in these months, the Russian peasants isolated Kerensky's state; then the workers launched their assault and resolutely seized power.

The normal development of the revolution will largely resolve the problem of armed force and the victory of the working class over bourgeois state power. But part of this problem must be solved by the general political action of the proletariat and its political party, the Socialist party. The bourgeois state is changing the national army into a mercenary army. Following a minutely prepared plan, soldiers have been transferred from their regiments to the legions of *carabinieri*, while retaining their special skills. *Carabinieri* corps of artillerymen, mortar-men, machine-gunners, flame-throwers, and others have been formed. Parliament is not concerned by this activity of the government, which exceeds its powers and its constitutional limits. Parliament should ask the government to explain this activity, to force it at least to unmask its intentions, to show in the clear light of day how the bourgeois dictatorship works. It ignores basic charters and devotes the whole administrative apparatus and all its financial resources to a single end: its defence against the majority of the population whose supreme representative and sovereignty it claims to be.

26 March 1920

Towards a renewal of the Socialist party

1. In Italy at the present time, the class struggle is defined by the fact that industrial and agricultural workers throughout the national territory are irrevocably determined to pose the question of the ownership of the means of production in explicit and violent terms. The intensification of the national and international crises which are steadily annihilating the value of money demonstrates that capital is *in extremis*. The present order of production and distribution can no longer satisfy even the elementary demands of human life, and it only survives because it is fiercely defended by the armed might of the bourgeois state. Every movement of the Italian working people tends irresistibly towards the realization of a gigantic economic revolution that will introduce new modes of production, a new order in the productive and distributive process, and give the initiative in production to the class of industrial and agricultural workers, by seizing it from the hands of the capitalists and landowners.

2. The industrialists and landowners have achieved a maximum concentration of class discipline and power: a line promulgated by the General Confederation of Italian Industry[6] is immediately carried out in every factory in the land. The bourgeois state has created a body of armed mercenaries[7], organized to function as an executive instrument carrying out the wishes of this new and powerful organization of the propertied classes; it tends to restore capitalist power over the means of production by a widespread application of the lock-out and terrorism, forcing the workers and peasants to let themselves be expropriated of an increased quantity of unpaid labour. The recent lock-out in the Turin engineering factories[8] was an episode in this plan of

the industrialists to bring the working class to heel: they profited by the lack of revolutionary co-ordination and concentration in the Italian workers' forces with a bid to smash the solidarity of the Turin proletariat and drive into oblivion the prestige and authority of the factory institutions (councils and shop commissions) that had initiated the struggle for workers' control. The length of the agricultural strikes in the Novara area and Lomellina show that the landowners are prepared to destroy production so as to reduce the agricultural proletariat to despair and starvation, implacably subjecting it to the hardest and most humiliating conditions of labour and existence.

3. The present phase of the class struggle in Italy is the phase that precedes: either the conquest of political power by the revolutionary proletariat and the transition to new modes of production and distribution that will make possible a rise in productivity – or a tremendous reaction by the propertied classes and the governmental caste. No violence will be spared in this subjection of the industrial and agricultural proletariat to servile labour: a bid will be made to smash inexorably the working class's institutions of political struggle (the Socialist party) and to incorporate its institutions of economic resistance (unions and co-operatives) into the machinery of the bourgeois state.

4. The workers' and peasants' forces lack revolutionary co-ordination and concentration because the leading institutions of the Socialist party have shown no understanding at all of the phase of development that national and international history is at present traversing, nor of the mission resting on revolutionary proletarian institutions of struggle. The Socialist party is a spectator of the course of events. It never has an opinion based on the revolutionary theses of Marxism and of the Communist International; it does not launch slogans which can be adopted by the masses; it does not lay down a general line, or unify and concentrate revolutionary action. As a political organization of the vanguard of the working class, the Socialist party should develop an overall action to raise the working class to the level from which it can win the revolution, and win it lastingly. Since it is composed of that part of the working class that has not let itself be demoralized and prostrated by the physical and spiritual oppression of the capitalist system, but has succeeded in maintaining its own autonomy and a spirit of conscious and disciplined initiative, the Socialist party should embody the vigilant revolutionary consciousness of the whole of the exploited class. Its

task is to focus in itself the attention of all the masses so that its directives become the directives of all the masses, so that it can win their permanent trust and become their guide and intellect. Hence it is essential that the party live permanently immersed in the reality of the class struggle fought by the industrial and agricultural proletariat, that it be able to understand its various phases and episodes, its manifold manifestations, drawing unity from this manifold diversity. It should be in a position to give a real leadership to the movement as a whole and impress on the masses the conviction that there is an order immanent in the present terrible disorder, an order that will systematically regenerate human society and make the means of labour suit elementary vital needs and civil progress. But even since the Bologna Congress[9], the Socialist party is still a merely parliamentary party, immobilized within the narrow limits of bourgeois democracy and preoccupied solely by the superficial political declarations of the governmental caste. It does not possess the features of party autonomy which should characterize the revolutionary proletariat, and the revolutionary proletariat alone.

5. After the Bologna Congress, the central institutions of the party should immediately have initiated and carried through an energetic drive to homogenize and unify the revolutionary membership of the party, in order to give it the specific and distinct features of a Communist party belonging to the Third International. But the polemic with the reformists and opportunists has not even been started; neither the party leadership, nor *Avanti!*[10] has counterposed a truly revolutionary conception to the ceaseless propaganda the reformists and opportunists have been disseminating in Parliament and in the trade union organizations. Nothing has been done by the central organs of the party to give the masses a Communist political education, to induce the masses to eliminate the reformists and opportunists from the leadership of the unions and co-operatives, or to give individual sections and the most active groups of comrades a unified line and tactics. The result is that while the revolutionary majority of the party has not found any expression of its thought or executor of its intentions in the leadership or the press, the opportunist elements, on the contrary, have been strongly organized and have exploited the prestige and authority of the party to consolidate their positions in Parliament and the unions. The leadership has allowed them to centralize and to vote for

resolutions that contradict the principles and tactics of the Third International, and are hostile to the party line. The leadership has granted absolute autonomy to subordinate institutions, allowing them to pursue actions and disseminate ideas that are opposed to the principles and tactics of the Third International. The party leadership has been systematically absent from the life and activity of the sections, of the institutions and of individual members. The confusion that existed in the party before the Bologna Congress and could be explained by a wartime regime has not disappeared; it has even increased terrifyingly. It is natural that in such conditions the confidence of the masses in the party should have declined and that in many places anarchist tendencies have tried to gain the upper hand. The political party of the working class only justifies itself when by a strong centralization and co-ordination of proletarian action, it counterposes a real revolutionary power to the legal power of the bourgeois state and limits its freedom of initiative and manoeuvre. If the party cannot unify and co-ordinate its efforts, if it reveals itself as a merely bureaucratic institution, with no spirit or will, the working class tends instinctively to build itself another party, and it moves over towards those anarchistic tendencies that bitterly and ceaselessly criticize the centralization and bureaucracy of political parties.

6. The party has been absent from the international movement. Throughout the world the class struggle is increasing in scale. Everywhere workers are forced to renew their methods of struggle, and often, as in Germany after the military coup,[11] to rise up with arms in their hands. The party has not bothered to explain these events to the Italian working people, or to justify them in the light of the ideas of the Communist International. It has not taken the trouble to carry out the vast educational activity needed to make the Italian working people conscious of the fact that the proletarian revolution is a world phenomenon and that each single individual event must be considered and judged in a world context. The Third International has already met twice in Western Europe: in December 1919, in a German city; in February 1920, in Amsterdam. The Italian party was represented at neither of those two meetings. The party's militants were not even informed by the central organs of the discussions and deliberations that took place at them. There is a ferment of polemic in the Third International about the doctrine and tactics of the Communist International; this has even led to internal

splits (for example, in Germany[12]). The Italian party has remained completely cut off from this vigorous debate of ideas which is steeling revolutionary consciousness and building the spiritual unity of action of the proletariat in every country. The central organ of the party does not have its own correspondents in France, England, Germany or even in Switzerland; a strange state of affairs for the paper of the Socialist party that represents the interests of the international proletariat in Italy, and a strange state of affairs for the Italian working class, which has to obtain its information from the warped and tendentious reports provided by bourgeois papers and news agencies. As the party organ, *Avanti!* should be the organ of the Third International. There should be a place in *Avanti!* for all the reports, polemics and discussions of proletarian problems that are relevant to the Third International. *Avanti!* should contain a ceaseless polemic, in a spirit of unity, against all opportunist deviations and compromises; instead, *Avanti!* stresses manifestations of opportunist thought, such as the recent speech in parliament by Claudio Treves in which was interwoven a petit-bourgeois conception of international relations and a defeatist counter-revolutionary theory designed to demobilize proletarian energies[13]. This absence from the central organs of any preoccupation with keeping the proletariat informed of the events and theoretical discussions that are unfolding within the Third International can also be observed in the activities of the publishing house. It is still publishing unimportant pamphlets or writings spreading the ideas and opinions of the Second International, while it neglects the publications of the Third International. Writings by Russian comrades that are indispensable to an understanding of the Bolshevik revolution have been translated in Switzerland, in England and in Germany, but they are unknown in Italy: Lenin's *State and Revolution* is just one example of many. When works are published, they are execrably translated, and errors of grammar and of simple common sense often make them incomprehensible.

7. The above analysis has already revealed the indispensable renovation and organization we feel must be carried out by the party's membership. The party must acquire its own precise and distinct features: from a petit-bourgeois parliamentary party it must become the party of the revolutionary proletariat in its struggle for the advent of Communist society by way of the workers' state: a homogeneous, cohesive party with its own

doctrine, tactics and rigid and implacable discipline. Non-Communist revolutionaries must be eliminated from the party, and its leadership, freed from preoccupation with the preservation of unity and balance among the various tendencies and leaders, should turn all its energies to the organization of the workers' forces on a war footing. Every event in national and international proletarian life should be analysed immediately in manifestos and circulars by the leadership, using them to promote the arguments of Communist propaganda and the education of revolutionary consciousness. The leadership should keep constantly in touch with the sections, and become the motor centre of proletarian action in all its manifestations. The sections should promote the constitution of Communist groups in all factories, unions, co-operatives and barracks, ceaselessly diffusing through the masses the ideas and tactics of the party, and organizing the creation of Factory Councils for the exercise of control over industrial and agricultural production. It should pursue the necessary propaganda for an organic conquest of the unions, the Chambers of Labour and the General Confederation of Labour, and should form the trusted elements that the mass will delegate for the formation of political Soviets and for the exercise of the proletarian dictatorship. The existence of a cohesive and highly disciplined Communist party with factory, trade union and co-operative cells, that can co-ordinate and centralize in its central executive committee the whole revolutionary action of the proletariat, is the fundamental and indispensable condition for any experiment in Soviets. In the absence of such a condition every proposed experiment should be rejected as absurd and useful only to the opponents of the idea of Soviets. Similarly, we should reject the proposal of a little socialist parliament,[14] for it would rapidly degenerate into a tool of the reformist and opportunist majority in the parliamentary group for the dissemination of democratic utopias and counter-revolutionary projects.

8. The leadership should immediately prepare, compose and distribute a programme of revolutionary government by the Socialist party, examining the concrete solutions that the proletariat, when it is the ruling class, will give to all the essential problems – economic, political, religious, and educational – that assail the various strata of the Italian working population. Basing itself on the idea that the party's power and activity is founded solely on the class of industrial and agricultural workers,

who are totally without private property, and that it regards the other strata of working people as auxiliaries of the strictly proletarian class, the party must issue a manifesto in which the revolutionary conquest of political power is explicitly proposed, in which the industrial and agricultural proletariat is invited to prepare itself and arm itself, and in which the principles of Communist solutions to present problems are indicated: proletarian control of production and distribution, disarmament of mercenary armed bodies, control of local government by workers' organizations.

9. On the basis of these considerations, the Turin Socialist Section proposes backing an agreement with those groups of comrades from all sections who would like to meet together to discuss these proposals and approve them; an organized agreement that will prepare for a congress in the near future, devoted to discussion of the problems of proletarian organization and tactics, and which will examine the activity of the executive organs of the party in the meantime.

8 May 1920

Notes

1. Founded at Genoa in 1892, The Italian Socialist party (PSI) represented the Second International in Italy. Unlike its French and German equivalents, it did not support the entry of Italy into the war in May 1915, but neither did it adopt a Zimmerwaldist attitude. The result was that it survived the war with the three wings characteristic of pre-war Socialist parties: a reformist wing on the right; a 'maximalist' (orthodox) centre; and a revolutionary wing on the left. The General Confederation of Labour (CGL) was the Socialist federation of trade unions. Founded in 1906, its pre-war membership rose to 384,000, about half the organized workers in Italy. After the war, the CGL membership rose rapidly to 2,000,000; its Catholic (CIL) and syndicalist (USI) counterparts claimed 1,160,000 and 800,000 members respectively. The CGL was dominated by reformists like its post-war secretary, D'Aragona.

2. '*Commissioni interni*': roughly equivalent to the shop steward committees set up in Britain during the First World War. The internal commissions had long been demanded by the engineering workers' union (FIOM) in Turin before they were acknowledged by the government (but not fully by the employers) in 1915. Most were dominated by revolutionary workers, though a few were tools of the management.

3. '*Camere del Lavoro*': The first chambers of labour were set up in Milan in 1889 on the model of the French '*bourses de travail*'. Like the British trades council, they provided a central organization for all the working-class institutions in a commune or province, developed a wide range of welfare activities and planned and directed the local class struggle. Whereas the later-founded trade unions were based on the aristocracy of

skilled workers, and tended towards conservatism, the Chamber of Labour united all workers, and represented the radical wing of the working-class forces.

4. *Il Partito Popolare:* The Popular party was founded in 1919 by a Sicilian priest, Don Luigi Sturzo, and in the same year it obtained 100 seats in the Chamber of Deputies out of a total of 508 (the PSI got 156). A non-confessional Catholic and rural petit-bourgeois party, it had a large peasant following. It was a forerunner of the modern Christian-Democrat Party (DC).

5. *Guardia Regia:* a force of 377 officers and 25,000 men founded by Prime Minister Nitti (in office June 1919 to June 1920) in the autumn of 1919 in a reorganization and reinforcement of police and security forces.

6. The General Confederation of Italian Industry (*Confindustria*): Militant organization of Italian capitalists; originally founded in 1910, on the basis of a Turin industrialists' league. Re-established in 1920 under the leadership of Gino Olivetti.

7. The Royal Guard; see note 5 above.

8. When daylight saving was introduced in the Fiat works in Turin without consulting the internal commission, a worker was dismissed for turning back the clock. Protest by the workers resulted in a lock-out on 28 March, 1920. This incident, the so-called 'clock-hands strike', led to the Turin general strike of April, 1920.

9. The Bologna Congress of the PSI was held from 5 October to 8 October 1919. The Congress adopted Serrati's maximalist motion, including adhesion to the Third International, and rejected a reformist motion and an extreme left abstentionist motion.

10. *Avanti!*: The official daily newspaper of the PSI, founded in 1896.

11. The Kapp putsch of March 1920 was defeated by a general strike in Berlin. The Weimar government had to use *Freikorps* divisions to suppress armed workers in Berlin and the Ruhr who hoped to extend the movement into a proletarian insurrection.

12. The 'Bremen Radicals', one of the left-wing Socialist groups that united in January 1919 to form the German Communist party (KPD), split away later the same year and formed the German Workers' Communist party (KAPD) on an abstentionist and ouvrierist platform.

13. Claudio Treves was one of the leaders of the reformist wing of the PSI. The speech in question, known as the 'expiation speech' was made on 30 March, 1920. Treves argued that while the bourgeoisie could no longer maintain its power in Italy, the proletariat was unable to seize power from it. Hence the tragedy and 'expiation' of the ruling classes.

14. This was a proposal to bring together in an assembly the socialist Deputies and spokesmen from the major political, trade union and co-operative organizations of the party, to work out proposals for an alternative government policy, and to put pressure on the existing government. The reformist bureaucracy would have controlled such an assembly and excluded much of the left from it.

The Coup in Chile

RALPH MILIBAND

(Reprinted from *Socialist Register 1973* edited by Ralph Miliband and John Saville)

1

What happened in Chile on 11 September 1973 did not suddenly reveal anything new about the ways in which men of power and privilege seek to protect *their* social order: the history of the last 150 years is spattered with such episodes. Even so, Chile has at least forced upon many people on the left some uncomfortable reflections and questions about the 'strategy' which is appropriate in Western-type regimes for what is loosely called the 'transition to socialism'.

Of course, the Wise Men of the left, and others too, have hastened to proclaim that Chile is not France, or Italy, or Britain. This is quite true. No country is like any other: circumstances are always different, not only between one country and another, but between one period and another in the same country. Such wisdom makes it possible and plausible to argue that the experience of a country or period cannot provide conclusive 'lessons'. This is also true; and as a matter of general principle, one should be suspicious of people who have instant 'lessons' for every occasion. The chances are that they had them well before the occasion arose, and that they are merely trying to fit the experience to their prior views. So let us indeed be cautious about taking or giving 'lessons'.

All the same, and however cautiously, there are things to be learnt from experience, or unlearnt, which comes to the same thing. Everybody said, quite rightly, that Chile, alone in Latin America, *was* a constitutional, parliamentary, liberal, pluralist society, a country which had politics: not exactly like the French, or the American, or the British, but well within the 'democratic', or, as Marxists would call it, the 'bourgeois-democratic' fold. This being the case, and however cautious one wishes to be, what happened in Chile does pose certain questions, requires certain answers, may even provide certain reminders and warnings. It may for instance suggest that stadiums which can be used for purposes other than sport – such as herding left-wing political prisoners – exist not only in Santiago, but in Rome and Paris or for that matter London; or that there *must* be something wrong with a situation in which *Marxism Today*, the monthly 'Theoretical and Discussion Journal of the (British) Communist party' has as its major article for its September 1973 issue a speech delivered in July by the General Secretary of the Chilean Communist party, Luis Corvalan (now in jail awaiting trial, and possible execution),[1] which is entitled '*We Say No to Civil War! But Stand Ready to Crush Sedition*'. In the light of what happened, this worthy slogan seems rather pathetic and suggests that there is something badly amiss here, that one must take stock, and try to see things more clearly. In so far as Chile was a bourgeois democracy, what happened there is about bourgeois democracy, and about what may also happen in other bourgeois democracies. After all, *The Times*, on the morrow of the coup, was writing (and the words ought to be carefully memorized by people on the left): '. . . whether or not the armed forces were right to do what they have done, the circumstances were such that a reasonable military man could in good faith have thought it his *constitutional* duty to intervene'.[2] Should a similar episode occur in Britain, it is a fair bet that, whoever else is inside Wembley Stadium, it won't be the Editor of *The Times*: he will be busy writing editorials regretting this and that, but agreeing, however reluctantly, that, taking all circumstances into account, and notwithstanding the agonizing character of the choice, there was no alternative but for reasonable military men . . . and so on and so forth.

When Salvador Allende was elected to the presidency of Chile in September 1970, the regime that was then inaugurated was said to constitute a test case for the peaceful or parliamentary transition to socialism. As it turned out over the following three years, this was something of an exaggeration. It achieved a great deal by way of economic and social reform, under incredibly difficult conditions – but it remained a deliberately 'moderate' regime: indeed, it does not seem far-fetched to say that the cause of its death, or at least one main cause of it, was its stubborn 'moderation'. But no, we are now told by such experts as Professor Hugh Thomas, from the Graduate School of Contemporary European Studies at Reading University: the trouble was that Allende was *much* too influenced by such people as Marx and Lenin, 'rather than Mill, or Tawney, or Aneurin Bevan, or any other European democratic socialist'. This being the case, Professor Thomas cheerfully goes on, 'the Chilean coup d'état cannot by any means be regarded as a defeat for democratic socialism but for Marxist socialism.' All's well then, at least for democratic socialism. Mind you, 'no doubt Dr Allende had his heart in the right place' (we must be *fair* about this), but then 'there are many reasons for thinking that his prescription was the wrong one for Chile's maladies, and of course the result of trying to apply it may have led an "iron surgeon" to get to the bedside. The right prescription, of course, was Keynesian socialism, not Marxist'.[3] *That's* it: the trouble with Allende is that he was not Harold Wilson, surrounded by advisers steeped in 'Keynesian socialism' as Professor Thomas obviously is.

We must not linger over the Thomases and their ready understanding of why Allende's policies brought an 'iron surgeon' to the bedside of an ailing Chile. But even though the Chilean experience may not have been a test case for the 'peaceful transition to socialism', it still offers a very suggestive example of what may happen when a government does give the impression, in a bourgeois democracy, that it genuinely intends to bring about really serious changes in the social order and to move in socialist directions, in however constitutional and gradual a manner; and whatever else may be said about Allende and his colleagues, and about their strategies and policies, there is no question that this is what they wanted to do. They were not, and their enemies knew them not to be, mere bourgeois politicians mouthing 'socialist' slogans. They were not 'Keynesian socialists'. They were serious and dedicated people, as many have shown by dying for what they believed in. It is this which makes the conservative response to them a matter of great interest and importance, and which makes it necessary for us to try to decode the message, the warning, the 'lessons'. For the experience may have crucial significance for other bourgeois democracies: indeed, there is surely no need to insist that *some* of it is bound to be directly relevant to any 'model' of radical social change in this kind of political system.

2

Perhaps the most important such message or warning or 'lesson' is also the most obvious, and therefore the most easily overlooked. It concerns the notion of class struggle. Assuming one may ignore

the view that class struggle is the result of 'extremist' propaganda and agitation, there remains the fact that the left is
rather prone to a perspective according to which the class struggle
is something waged by the workers and the subordinate classes
against the dominant ones. It is of course that. But class struggle
also means, and often means *first of all*, the struggle waged by
the dominant class, and the state acting on its behalf, against
the workers and the subordinate classes. By definition, struggle
is not a one-way process; but it is just as well to emphasize that
it is actively waged by the dominant class or classes, and in many
ways much more effectively waged by them than the struggle
waged by the subordinate classes.

Secondly, but in the same context, there is a vast difference
to be made – sufficiently vast as to require a difference of name –
between on the one hand 'ordinary' class struggle, of the kind
which goes on day in day out in capitalist societies, at economic,
political, ideological, micro- and macro-, levels, and which is
known to constitute no threat to the capitalist framework within
which it occurs; and, on the other hand, class struggle which
either does, or which is thought likely to, affect the social order
in really fundamental ways. The first form of class struggle
constitutes the stuff, or much of the stuff, of the politics of
capitalist society. It is not unimportant, or a mere sham; but
neither does it stretch the political system unduly. The latter
form of struggle requires to be described not simply as *class
struggle*, but as *class war*. Where men of power and privilege
(and it is not necessarily those with most power and privilege
who are the most uncompromising) do believe that they confront
a real threat from below, that the world they know and like
and want to preserve seems undermined or in the grip of evil
and subversive forces, *then* an altogether different form of struggle
comes into operation, whose acuity, dimensions and universality
warrants the label 'class war'.

Chile had known class struggle within a bourgeois democratic
framework for many decades: that was its tradition. With the
coming to the Presidency of Allende, the conservative forces
progressively turned class struggle into class war – and here too,
it is worth stressing that it was the *conservative forces* which
turned the one into the other.

Before looking at this a little more closely, I want to deal with
one issue that has often been raised in connection with the
Chilean experience, namely the matter of electoral percentages.

It has often been said that Allende, as the presidential candidate of a six-party coalition, only obtained thirty-six per cent of the votes in September 1970, the implication being that if only he had obtained, say, fifty-one per cent of the votes, the attitude of the conservative forces towards him and his administration would have been very different. There is one sense in which this may be true; and another sense in which it seems to me to be dangerous nonsense.

To take the latter point first: one of the most knowledgeable French writers on Latin America, Marcel Niedergang, has published one piece of documentation which is relevant to the issue. This is the testimony of Juan Garces, one of Allende's personal political advisers over three years who, on the direct orders of the President, escaped from the Moneda Palace after it had come under siege on 11 September. In Garces' view, it was precisely after the governmental coalition had increased its electoral percentage to forty-four per cent in the legislative elections of March 1973 that the conservative forces began to think seriously about a coup. 'After the elections of March,' Garces said, 'a legal coup d'état was no longer possible, since the two-thirds majority required to achieve the constitutional impeachment of the President could not be reached. The right then understood that the electoral way was exhausted and that the way which remained was that of force.'[4] This has been confirmed by one of the main promoters of the coup, the Air Force general Gustavo Leigh, who told the correspondent in Chile of the *Corriere della Sera* that 'we began preparations for the overthrow of Allende in March 1973, immediately after the legislative elections'.[5]

Such evidence is not finally conclusive. But it makes good sense. Writing before it was available, Maurice Duverger noted that while Allende was supported by a little more than a third of Chileans at the beginning of his presidency, he had almost half of them supporting him when the coup occurred; and that half was the one that was most hard hit by material difficulties. 'Here,' he writes, 'is probably the major reason for the military putsch. So long as the Chilean Right believed that the experience of Popular Unity would come to an end by the will of the electors, it maintained a democratic attitude. It was worth respecting the Constitution while waiting for the storm to pass. When the right came to fear that it would not pass and that the play of liberal institutions would result in the maintenance of Salvador

Allende in power and in the development of socialism, it preferred violence to the law.'[6] Duverger probably exaggerates the 'democratic attitude' of the right and its respect for the Constitution before the elections of March 1973, but his main point does, as I suggested earlier, seem very reasonable.

Its implications are very large: namely, that as far as the conservative forces are concerned, electoral percentages, however high they may be, do not confer legitimacy upon a government which appears to them to be bent on policies they deem to be actually or potentially disastrous. Nor is this in the least remarkable: for here, in the eyes of the right, are vicious demagogues, class traitors, fools, gangsters and crooks, supported by an ignorant rabble, engaged in bringing about ruin and chaos upon a hitherto peaceful and agreeable country, etc. The script is familiar. The idea that, from such a perspective, percentages of support are of any consequence is naive and absurd: what matters, for the right, is not the percentage of votes by which a left-wing government is supported, but the purposes by which it is moved. If the purposes are wrong, deeply and fundamentally wrong, electoral percentages are an irrelevance.

There is, however, a sense in which percentages *do* matter in the kind of political situation which confronts the right in Chilean-type conditions. This is that the higher the percentage of votes cast in any election for the left, the more likely it is that the conservative forces will be intimidated, demoralized, divided, and uncertain as to their course. These forces are not homogeneous; and it is obvious that electoral demonstrations of popular support are very useful to the left, in its confrontation with the right, so long as the left does not take them to be decisive. In other words, percentages may help to *intimidate* the right – but not to *disarm* it. It may well be that the right would not have dared strike *when it did* if Allende had obtained higher electoral percentages. But if, having obtained these percentages, Allende had continued to pursue the course on which he was bent, the right would have struck whenever opportunity had offered. The problem was to deny it the opportunity; or, failing this, to make sure that the confrontation would occur on the most favourable possible terms.

3

I now propose to return to the question of class struggle and
class war and to the conservative forces which wage it, with
particular reference to Chile, though the considerations I am
offering here do not only apply to Chile, least of all in terms of
the nature of the conservative forces which have to be taken into
account, and which I shall examine in turn, relating this to the
forms of struggle in which these different forces engage:

(a) *Society as Battlefield*. To speak of 'the conservative forces',
as I have done so far, is not to imply the existence of a homogeneous economic, social or political bloc, either in Chile or
anywhere else. In Chile, it was among other things the divisions
between different elements among these conservative forces
which made it possible for Allende to come to the presidency
in the first place. Even so, when these divisions have duly been
taken into account, it is worth stressing that a crucial aspect
of class struggle is waged by these forces as a whole, in the sense
that the struggle occurs all over 'civil society', has no front, no
specific focus, no particular strategy, no elaborate leadership
or organization: it is the daily battle fought by every member of
the disaffected upper and middle classes, each in his own way,
and by a large part of the lower middle class as well. It is fought
out of a sentiment which Evelyn Waugh, recalling the horrors
of the Attlee regime in Britain after 1945, expressed admirably
when he wrote in 1959 that, in those years of Labour government, 'the kingdom seemed to be under enemy occupation'.
Enemy occupation invites various forms of resistance, and everybody has to do his little bit. It includes middle-class 'housewives'
demonstrating by banging pots and pans in front of the Presidential Palace; factory owners sabotaging production; merchants
hoarding stocks; newspaper proprietors and their subordinates
engaging in ceaseless campaigns against the government; landlords impeding land reform; the spreading of what was, in
wartime Britain, called 'alarm and despondency' (and incidentally
punishable by law): in short, *anything* that influential, well-off,
educated (or not so well-educated) people can do to impede a
hated government. Taken as a 'detotalized totality', the harm
that can thus be done is very considerable – and I have not
mentioned the upper professionals, the doctors, the lawyers,
the state officials, whose capacity to slow down the running of
a society, of any society, must be reckoned as being high. Nothing

very dramatic is required: just an individual rejection in one's daily life and activity of the regime's legitimacy, which turns by itself into a vast collective enterprise in the production of disruption.

It may be assumed that the vast majority of members of the upper and middle classes (not all by any means) will remain irrevocably opposed to the new regime. The question of the lower middle class is rather more complex. The first requirement in this connection is to make a radical distinction between lower professional and white collar workers, technicians, lower managerial staffs, etc., on the one hand, and small capitalists and micro-traders on the other. The former are an integral part of that 'collective worker', of which Marx spoke more than a hundred years ago; and they are involved, like the industrial working class, in the production of surplus value. This is not to say that this class or stratum will necessarily see itself as part of the working class, or that it will 'automatically' support left-wing policies (nor will the working class proper); but it does mean that there is here at least a solid basis for alliance.

This is much more doubtful, in fact most probably untrue, for the other part of the lower middle class, the small entrepreneur and the micro-trader. In the article quoted earlier, Maurice Duverger suggests that 'the first condition for the democratic transition to socialism in a Western country of the French type is that a left-wing government should reassure the "classes moyennes" about their fate under the future regime, so as to dissociate them from the kernel of big capitalists who are for their part condemned to disappear or to submit to a strict control.'[7] The trouble with this is that, in so far as the 'classes moyennes' are taken to mean small capitalists and small traders (and Duverger makes it clear that he does mean them), the attempt is doomed from the start. In order to accommodate them, he wants 'the evolution towards socialism to be very gradual and very slow, so as to rally at each stage a substantial part of those who feared it at the start.' Moreover, small enterprises must be assured that their fate will be better than under monopoly or oligopolistic capitalism.[8] It is interesting, and would be amusing if the matter was not very serious, that the realism which Professor Duverger is able to display in regard to Chile deserts him as soon as he comes closer to home. His scenario is ridiculous; and even if it were not, there is no way in which small enterprises *can* be given the appropriate assurances. I should not like to give the impression that I am advocating the liquidation of middle and small urban French *kulaks*: what I *am* saying is that to adapt the pace of the transition to socialism to the hopes and fears of this class is to advocate paralysis or to prepare for defeat. Better not to start at all. *How* to deal with the problem is a different matter. But it is important to start with the fact that as a class or social stratum, this element must be reckoned as part of the conservative forces.

This certainly appears to have been the case in Chile, notably with regard to the now notorious 40,000 lorry owners, whose repeated strikes helped to increase the Government's difficulties. These strikes, excellently co-ordinated, and quite possibly subsidized from outside sources, highlight the problem which a left-wing government must expect to face, to a greater or lesser degree depending on the country, in a sector of considerable economic importance in terms of distribution. The problem is further and ironically highlighted by the fact that, according to United Nations statistical sources, it was this 'classe moyenne' which had done best under Allende's regime in regard to the distribution of the national income. Thus, it would appear that the poorest fifty per cent of the population saw its share of the total increase from 16.1 per cent to 17.6 per cent; that of the 'middle class' (45 per cent of the population) increased from 53.9 per cent to 57.7 per cent; while the richest 5 per cent dropped from 30 per cent to 24.7 per cent.[9] This is hardly the picture of a middle class squeezed to death – hence the significance of its hostility.

(b) *External conservative intervention.* It is not possible to discuss class war anywhere, least of all in Latin America, without bringing into account external intervention, more specifically and obviously the intervention of United States imperialism, as represented both by private concerns and by the American state itself. The activities of ITT have received considerable publicity, as well as its plans for plunging the country into chaos so as to get 'friendly military men' to make a coup. Nor of course was ITT the only major American firm working in Chile: there was in fact no important sector of the Chilean economy that was not penetrated and in some cases dominated by American enterprises: their hostility to the Allende regime must have greatly increased the latter's economic, social and political difficulties. Everybody knows that Chile's balance of payments very largely depends on its copper exports: but the world price of copper, which had almost been halved in 1970, remained at that low level until the end of 1972; and American pressure was exercised throughout the world to place an embargo on Chilean copper. In addition, there was strong and successful pressure by the United States on the World Bank to refuse loans and credits to Chile, not that much pressure was needed, either on the World Bank or on other banking institutions. A few days after the coup, the *Guardian* noted that 'the net new advances which were frozen as a result of the US pressure, included sums totalling £30 millions: all for projects which the World Bank had already cleared as worth backing.'[10] The president of the World Bank is of course Mr Robert McNamara. It was at one time being said that Mr McNamara had undergone some kind of spiritual conversion out of remorse for his part, when US Secretary of State for Defence, in inflicting so much suffering on the Vietnamese people: under his direction, the World Bank was actually going to *help* the poor countries. What those who were peddling this stuff omitted to add was that there was a condition – that the poor countries should show the utmost regard, as Chile did not, for the claims of private enterprise, notably American private enterprise.

Allende's regime was, from the start, faced with a relentless American attempt at economic strangulation. In comparison with this fact, which must be taken in conjunction with the economic sabotage in which the internal conservative economic interests engaged, the mistakes which were committed by the regime are of relatively minor importance – even though so much is made of them not only by critics but by friends of the Allende government. The really remarkable thing, against such odds, is not the mistakes, but that the regime held out economically as long as it did; the more so since it was systematically impeded from taking necessary action by the opposition parties in Parliament.

In this perspective, the question whether the United States government was or was not directly involved in the preparation of the military coup is not particularly important. It certainly had foreknowledge of the coup. The Chilean military had close associations with the United States military. And it would obviously be stupid to think that the kind of people who run the government of the United States would shrink from active involvement in a coup, or in its initiation. The important point here, however, is that the US government had done its considerable best over the previous three years to lay the ground for the overthrow of the Allende regime by waging economic warfare against it.

(c) *The conservative political parties.* The kind of class struggle conducted by conservative forces in civil society to which reference was made earlier does ultimately require direction and political articulation, both in Parliament and in the country at large, if it is to be turned into a really effective political force. This direction is provided by conservative parties, and was mainly provided in Chile by Christian Democracy. Like the Christian Democratic Union in Germany and the Christian Democratic party in Italy, Christian Democracy in Chile included many different tendencies, from various forms of radicalism (though most radicals went off to form their own groupings after Allende came to power) to extreme conservatism. But it represented in essence the conservative constitutional right, the party of government, one of whose main figures, Eduardo Frei, had been President before Allende.

With steadily growing determination, this conservative constitutional right sought by every means in its power this side of legality to block the government's actions and to prevent it from functioning properly. Supporters of parliamentarism always say that its operation depends upon the achievement of a certain degree of co-operation between government and opposition; and they are no doubt right. But Allende's government was denied this co-operation from the very people who never cease to proclaim their dedication to parliamentary democracy and constitutionalism. Here too, on the legislative front, class struggle easily turned into class war. Legislative assemblies are, with some qualifications that are not relevant here, part of the state system; and in Chile, the legislative assembly was solidly under opposition control. So were other important parts of the state system, to which I shall turn in a moment.

The Opposition's resistance to the government, in Parliament and out, did not assume its full dimensions until the victory which the Popular Unity coalition scored in the elections of March 1973. By the late spring, the erstwhile constitutionalists and parliamentarists were launched on the course towards military intervention. After the abortive putsch of 29 June, which marks the effective beginning of the final crisis, Allende tried to reach a compromise with the leaders of Christian Democracy, Alwyn and Frei. They refused, and increased their pressure on the government. On 22 August, the National Assembly which their party dominated actually passed a motion which effectively *called* on the Army 'to put an end to situations which constituted a violation of the Constitution'. In the Chilean case at least, there can be no question of the direct responsibility which these politicians bear for the overthrow of the Allende regime.

No doubt, the Christian Democratic leaders would have preferred it if they could have brought down Allende without resort to force, and within the framework of the Constitution. Bourgeois politicians do not like military coups, not least because such coups deprive them of their role. But like it or not, and however steeped in constitutionalism they may be, most such politicians will turn to the military where they feel circumstances demand it.

The calculations which go into the making of the decision that circumstances do demand resort to illegality are many and complex. These calculations include pressures and promptings of different kinds and weight. One such pressure is the general, diffuse pressure of the class or classes to which these politicians belong. 'Il faut en finir', they are told from all quarters, or rather from quarters to which they pay heed; and this matters in the drift towards putschism. But another pressure which becomes increasingly important as the crisis grows is that of groups on the right of the constitutional conservatives, who in such circumstances become an element to be reckoned with.

(d) *Fascist-type groupings.* The Allende regime had to contend with much organized violence from fascist-type groupings. This extreme right-wing guerrilla or commando activity grew to fever pitch in the last months before the coup, involved the blowing up of electric pylons, attacks on left-wing militants, and other such actions which contributed greatly to the general sense that the crisis must somehow be brought to an end. Here again, action of this type, in 'normal' circumstances of class conflict, are of no great political significance, certainly not of such significance as to threaten a regime or even to indent it very much. So long as the bulk of the conservative forces remain in the constitutional camp, fascist-type groupings remain isolated, even shunned by the traditional right. But in exceptional circumstances, one speaks to people one would not otherwise be seen dead with in the same room; one gives a nod and a wink where a frown and a rebuke would earlier have been an almost automatic response. 'Youngsters will be youngsters', now indulgently say their conservative elders. 'Of course, they are wild and do dreadful things. But then look whom they are doing it to, and what do you expect when you are ruled by demagogues, criminals and crooks.' So it came about that groups like *Fatherland and Freedom* operated more and more boldly in Chile, helped to increase the sense of crisis, and encouraged the politicians to think in terms of drastic solutions to it.

(e) *Administrative and judicial opposition.* Conservative forces anywhere can always count on the more or less explicit support or acquiescence or sympathy of the members of the upper echelons of the state system; and for that matter, of many if not most members of the lower echelons as well. By social origin, education, social status, kinship and friendship connections, the upper echelons, to focus on them, are an intrinsic part of the conservative camp; and if none of these factors were operative, ideological dispositions would certainly place them there. Top civil servants and members of the judiciary may, in ideological terms, range all the way from mild liberalism to extreme conservatism, but mild liberalism, at the progressive end, is where the spectrum has to stop. In 'normal' conditions of class conflict, this may not find much expression except in terms of the kind of implicit or explicit bias which such people must be expected to have. In crisis conditions, on the other hand, in times when class struggle assumes the character of class war, these members of the state personnel become active participants in the battle and are most likely to want to do their bit in the patriotic effort to save their beloved country, not to speak of their beloved positions, from the dangers that threaten.

The Allende regime inherited a state personnel which had long been involved in the rule of the conservative parties and which cannot have included many people who viewed the new regime with any kind of sympathy, to put it no higher. Much in this respect was changed with Allende's election, in so far as new personnel, which supported the Popular Unity coalition, came to occupy top positions in the state system. Even so, and in the prevailing circumstances perhaps inevitably, the middle and lower ranks of that system continued to be staffed by established and traditional bureaucrats. The power of such people can be very great. The writ may be issued from on high: but they are in a good position to see to it that it does not run, or that it does not run as it should. To vary the metaphor, the machine does not respond properly because the mechanics in actual charge of it have no particular desire that it should respond properly. The greater the sense of crisis, the less willing the mechanics are likely to be; and the less willing they are, the greater the crisis.

Yet, despite everything, the Allende regime did not 'collapse'. Despite the legislative obstruction, administrative sabotage. political warfare, foreign intervention, economic shortages, internal divisions, etc. – despite all this, the regime held. That, for the politicians and the classes they represented, was the trouble. In an article which I shall presently want to criticize, Eric Hobsbawm notes quite rightly that 'to those commentators on the right, who ask what other choice remained open to Allende's opponents but a coup, the simple answer is: not to make a coup.'[11] This, however, meant incurring the risk that Allende might yet pull out of the difficulties he faced. Indeed, it would appear that, on the day before the coup, he and his ministers had decided on a last constitutional throw, namely a plebiscite, which was to be announced on 11 September. He hoped that, if he won it, he might give pause to the putschist, and give himself new room for action. Had he lost, he would have resigned, in the hope that the forces of the left would one day be in a better position to exercise power.[12] Whatever may be thought of this strategy, of which the conservative politicians must have had knowledge, it risked prolonging the crisis which they were frantic to bring to an end; and this meant acceptance of, indeed active support for, the coup which the military men had been preparing. In the end, and in the face of the danger presented by popular support for Allende, there was nothing for it: the murderers had to be called in.

(f) *The military.* We had of course been told again and again that the military in Chile, unlike the military in every other Latin American country, was non-political, politically neutral, constitutionally-minded, etc.; and though the point was somewhat overdone, it was broadly speaking true that the military in Chile did not 'mix in politics'. Nor is there any reason to doubt that, at the time when Allende came to power and for some time after, the military did not wish to intervene and mount a coup. It was after 'chaos' had been created, and extreme political instability brought about, *and the weakness of the regime's response in the face of crisis had been revealed* (of which more later) that the *conservative dispositions* of the military came to the fore, and then decisively tilted the balance. For it would be nonsense to think that 'neutrality' and 'non-political attitudes' on the part of the armed forces meant that they did not have definite ideological dispositions, and that these dispositions were not definitely conservative. As Marcel Niedergang also notes, 'whatever may have been said, there never were high ranking officers who were socialists, let alone Communists. There were two camps: the partisans of legality and the enemies of the left-wing government. The second, *more and more*, numerous, finally won out.'[13]

The italics in this quotation are intended to convey the crucial dynamic which occurred in Chile and which affected the military as well as all other protagonists. This notion of dynamic process is essential to the analysis of any such kind of situation: people who are thus and thus at one time, and who are or are not willing to do this or that, *change* under the impact of rapidly moving events. Of course, they mostly change *within* a certain range of choices: but in such situations, the shift may nevertheless be very great. Thus conservative but constitutionally-minded army men, in certain situations, become just this much more conservative-minded; and this means that they cease to be constitutionally-minded. The obvious question is what it is that brings about the shift. In part, no doubt, it lies in the worsening 'objective' situation; in part also, in the pressure generated by conservative forces. But to a very large extent, it lies in the position adopted, and seen to be adopted, by the government of the day. As I understand it, the Allende administration's weak response to the attempted coup of 29 June, its steady retreat before the con-servative forces (and the military) in the ensuing weeks, and its loss by resignation of General Prats, the one general who had appeared firmly prepared to stand by the regime – all this must have had a lot to do with the fact that the enemies of the regime in the armed forces (meaning the military men who were pre-pared to make a coup) grew 'more and more numerous'. In these matters, there is one law which holds: the weaker the government, the bolder its enemies, *and* the more numerous they become day by day.

Thus it was that these 'constitutional' generals struck on 11 September, and put into effect what had – significantly in the light of the massacre of left-wingers in Indonesia – been labelled *Operation Djakarta*. Before we turn to the next part of this story, the part which concerns the actions of the Allende régime, its strategy and conduct, it is as well to stress the savagery of the

repression unleashed by the coup, and to underline the responsibility which the conservative politicians bear for it. Writing
in the immediate aftermath of the Paris Commune, and while
the Communards were still being killed, Marx bitterly noted that
'the civilization and justice of bourgeois order comes out in its
lurid light whenever the slaves and drudges of that order rise
against their masters. Then this civilization and order stand forth
as undisguised savagery and lawless revenge.'[14] The words apply
well to Chile after the coup. Thus, that not very left-wing magazine *Newsweek* had a report from its correspondent in Santiago
shortly after the coup, headed 'Slaughterhouse in Santiago',
which went as follows:

Last week, I slipped through a side door into the Santiago
city morgue, flashing my junta press pass with all the impatient
authority of a high official. One hundred and fifty dead bodies
were laid out on the ground floor, awaiting identification by
family members. Upstairs, I passed through a swing door and
there in a dimly lit corridor lay at least fifty more bodies,
squeezed one against another, their heads propped up against
the wall. They were all naked.

Most had been shot at close range under the chin. Some
had been machine-gunned in the body. Their chests had been
slit open and sewn together grotesquely in what presumably
had been a pro forma autopsy. They were all young and,
judging from the roughness of their hands, all from the
working class. A couple of them were girls, distinguishable
among the massed bodies only by the curves of their breasts.
Most of their heads had been crushed. I remained for perhaps
two minutes at most, then left.

Workers at the morgue have been warned that they will
be court-martialled and shot if they reveal what is going on
there. But the women who go in to look at the bodies say
there are between 100 and 150 on the ground floor every day.
And I was able to obtain an official morgue body-count from
the daughter of a member of its staff: by the fourteenth day
following the coup, she said, the morgue had received and
processed 2796 corpses.[15]

On the same day as it carried this report, the London *Times*
commented in an editorial that 'the existence of a war or something very like it clearly explains the drastic severity of the new

regime which has taken so many observers by surprise'. The 'war' was of course *The Times*'s own invention. Having invented it, it then went on to observe that 'a military government confronted by widespread armed opposition (?) is unlikely to be over-punctilious either about constitutional niceties or even about basic human rights'. Still, lest it be thought that it *approved* the 'drastic severity' of the new regime, the paper told its readers that 'it must remain the hope of Chile's friends abroad, as no doubt of the great majority of Chileans, that human rights will soon be fully respected and that constitutional government will before long be restored'.[16] Amen.

No one knows how many people have been killed in the terror that followed the coup, and how many people will yet die as a result of it. Had a left-wing government shown one tenth of the junta's ruthlessness, screaming headlines across the whole 'civilized' world would have denounced it day in day out. As it is, the matter was quickly passed over and hardly a pip squeaked when a British Government rushed in, eleven days after the coup, to recognize the junta. But then so did most other freedom-loving Western governments.

We may take it that the well-to-do in Chile shared and more than shared the sentiments of the Editor of the London *Times* that, given the circumstances, the military could not be expected to be 'over-punctilious'. Here too, Hobsbawm puts it very well when he says that 'the left has generally underestimated the fear and hatred of the right, the ease with which well-dressed men and women acquire a taste for blood'.[17] This is an old story. In his *Flaubert*, Sartre quotes Edmond de Goncourt's Diary entry for 31 May 1871, immediately after the Paris Commune had been crushed: 'It's good. There has been no conciliation or compromise. The solution has been brutal. It has been pure force ... a bloodletting such as this, by killing the militant part of the population ('la partie bataillante de la population') puts off by a generation the new revolution. It is twenty years of rest which the old society has in front of it if the rulers dare all that needs to be dared at this moment.'[18] Goncourt, as we know, had no need to worry. Nor has the Chilean middle class, if the military not only dare, but are able, i.e. are allowed, to give Chile 'twenty years of rest'. A woman journalist with a long experience of Chile reports, three weeks after the coup, the 'jubilation' of her upper-class friends who had long prayed for it.[19] These ladies would not be likely to be unduly disturbed by the massacre of left-wing militants. Nor would their husbands.

What did apparently disturb the conservative politicians was the thoroughness with which the military went about restoring 'law and order'. Hunting down and shooting militants is one thing, as is book-burning and the regimentation of the universities. But dissolving the National Assembly, denouncing 'politics' and toying with the idea of a Fascist-type 'corporatist' state, as some of the generals are doing, is something else, and rather more serious. Soon after the coup, the leaders of Christian Democracy, who had played such a major role in bringing it about, and who continued to express support for the junta, were nevertheless beginning to express their 'disquiet' about some of its inclinations. Indeed, ex-President Frei went so far, stout fellow, as to confide to a French journalist his belief that 'Christian Democracy will have to go into opposition two or three months from now'[20] – presumably after the military had butchered enough left-wing militants. In studying the conduct and declarations of men such as these, one understands better the savage contempt which Marx expressed for the bourgeois politicians he excoriated in his historical writings. The breed has not changed.

4

The configuration of conservative forces which has been presented in the previous section must be expected to exist in any bourgeois democracy, not of course in the same proportions or with exact parallels in any particular country – but the pattern of Chile is not unique. This being the case, it becomes the more important to get as close as one can to an accurate analysis of the response of the Allende regime to the challenge that was posed to it by these forces.

As it happens, and while there is and will continue to be endless controversy on the left as to who bears the responsibility for what went wrong (if anybody does), and whether there was anything else that could have been done, there can be very little controversy as to what the Allende regime's strategy actually was. Nor in fact is there, on the left. Both the Wise Men and the Wild Men of the left are at least agreed that Allende's strategy *was* to effect a constitutional and peaceful transition in the direction of socialism. The Wise Men of the left opine that this was the only possible and desirable path to take. The Wild Men of the left assert that it was the path to disaster. The latter turned out to be right: but whether for the right reasons remains to be seen. In any case, there are various questions which arise here, and which are much too important and much too complex to be resolved by slogans. It is with some of these questions that I should like to deal here.

To begin at the beginning: namely with the manner in which the left's coming to power – or to office – must be envisaged in bourgeois democracies. The overwhelming chances are that this will occur via the electoral success of a left coalition of Communists, Socialists and other groupings of more or less radical tendencies. The reason for saying this is not that a crisis might not occur, which would open possibilities of a different kind – it may be for instance that May 1968 in France was a crisis of such a kind. But whether for good reasons or bad, the parties which might be able to take power in this type of situation, namely the major formations of the left, including in particular the Communist parties of France and Italy, have absolutely no intention of embarking on any such course, and do in fact strongly believe that to do so would invite certain disaster and set back the working-class movement for generations to come. Their attitude *might* change if circumstances of a kind that cannot be anticipated arose – for instance the clear imminence or actual beginning of a right-wing coup. But this is speculation. What is not speculation is that these vast formations, which command the support of the bulk of the organized working class, and which will go on commanding it for a very long time to come, are utterly committed to the achievement of power – or of office – by electoral and constitutional means. This was also the position of the coalition led by Allende in Chile.

There was a time when many people on the left said that, if a left clearly committed to massive economic and social changes looked like winning an election, the right would not 'allow' it to do so – i.e. it would launch a pre-emptive strike by way of a coup. This has ceased to be a fashionable view: it is rightly or wrongly felt that, in 'normal' circumstances, the right would be in no position to decide whether it could or could not 'allow' elections to take place. Whatever else it and the government might do to influence the results, they could not actually take the risk of preventing the elections from being held.

The present view on the 'extreme' left tends to be that, even if this is so, and admitting that it is likely to be so, any such electoral victory is, *by definition*, bound to be barren. The argument, or one of the main arguments on which this is based, is that the achievement of an electoral victory can only be bought at the cost of so much manoeuvre and compromise, so much 'electioneering' as to mean very little. There seems to me to be rather more in this than the Wise Men of the left are willing to grant; but not *necessarily* quite as much as their opponents insist *must* be the case. Few things in these matters are capable of being settled by definition. Nor have opponents of the 'electoral road' much to offer by way of an alternative, *in relation to bourgeois democracies in advanced capitalist societies*; and such alternatives as they do offer have so far proved entirely unattractive to the bulk of the people on whose support the realization of these alternatives precisely depends; and there is no very good reason to believe that this will change dramatically in any future that must be taken into account.

In other words, it must be assumed that, in countries with this kind of political system, it is by way of electoral victory that the forces of the left will find themselves in office. *The really important question is what happens then.* For as Marx also noted at the time of the Paris Commune, electoral victory only gives one the *right* to rule, not the *power* to rule. Unless one takes it for granted that this right to rule cannot, in these circumstances, ever be transmuted into the power to rule, it is at this point that the left confronts complex questions which it has so far probed only very imperfectly: it is here that slogans, rhetoric and incantation have most readily been used as substitutes for the hard grind of realistic political cogitation. From this point of view, Chile offers some extremely important pointers and 'lessons' as to what is, or perhaps what is not, to be done.

The strategy adopted by the forces of the Chilean Left had one characteristic not often associated with the coalition, namely a high degree of inflexibility. In saying this, I mean that Allende and his allies had decided upon certain lines of action, and of inaction, well before they came to office. They had decided to proceed with careful regard to constitutionalism, legalism and gradualism; and also, relatedly, that they would do everything to avoid civil war. Having decided upon this before they came to office, they stuck to it right through, up to the very end, notwithstanding changing circumstances. Yet, it may well be that what was right and proper and inevitable at the beginning had become suicidal as the struggle developed. What is at issue here is not 'reform versus revolution': it is that Allende and his colleagues were wedded to a particular version of the 'reformist' model, which eventually made it impossible for them to respond to the challenge they faced. This needs some further elaboration.

To achieve office by electoral means involves moving into a house long occupied by people of very different dispositions – indeed it involves moving into a house many rooms of which continue to be occupied by such people. In other words, Allende's victory at the polls – such as it was – meant the occupation by the left of one element of the state system, the presidential-executive one – an extremely important element, perhaps the most important, but not obviously the only one. Having achieved this partial occupation, the President and his administration began the task of carrying out their policies by 'working' the system of which they had become a part.

In so doing, they were undoubtedly contravening an essential tenet of the Marxist canon. As Marx wrote in a famous letter to Kugelmann at the time of the Paris Commune, '. . . the next attempt of the French Revolution will be no longer, as before, to transfer the bureaucratic-military machine from one hand to another, but to *smash* it, and this is the preliminary condition for every real people's revolution on the continent.'[21] Similarly in *The Civil War in France*, Marx notes that 'the working class cannot simply lay hold of the ready-made state machinery, and wield it for its own purposes';[22] and he then proceeded to outline the nature of the alternative as foreshadowed by the Paris Commune.[23] So important did Marx and Engels think the matter to be that in the Preface to the 1872 German edition of the *Communist Manifesto*, they noted that 'one thing especially was proved by the Commune', that thing being Marx's observation in *The Civil War in France* that I have just quoted.[24] It is from these observations that Lenin derived the view that 'smashing the bourgeois state' was the essential task of the revolutionary movement.

I have argued elsewhere[25] that in one sense in which it appears to be used in *The State and Revolution* (and for that matter in *The Civil War in France*) i.e. in the sense of the establishment of an extreme form of council (or 'soviet') democracy on the very morrow of the revolution as a substitute for the smashed bourgeois state, the notion constitutes an impossible projection which can be of no immediate relevance to any revolutionary regime, and which certainly was of no immediate relevance to

Leninist practice on
and it is rather hard
doing something whi
to blame them in the
the promise, and co
The State and Revol

However, disgra
suggest it, there ma
the discussion of
experience, and wh
'reformism' adopte

Thus, a governm
political changes
possibilities, even
bourgeois state'.
considerable chan
state system; and
tional and politic
existing state app
and it must event
of all, namely the

The Allende
could have done
a matter of argu
willing to tackle
military. Instea
support and go
to the time o
evidence of the
8 July of this ye
article, Luis C
begun to seek
and the armed
to replace the
the absolutely
Their enemies
reactionary ca
this view: on
to release the
who had bela
Similar stat
mindedness

the coalition, an
Corvalan were u
expect from the
most of them t
and that it was
American' patter

Regis Débray
Allende had a 'v
to be said about
ally crippled in th
or consider it igno
There are differe
may be occasions
also writes (and
Allende) was not
and he did not w
useless deaths: th
he refused to liste
useless manoeuvri
offensive.'27

It would be use
'popular power' is
should not be 'du
offensive'. But at
war, as Débray doe
for conciliation and
as to any possible
the argument that
has a revealing para

'Disarm the plo
'Give me first the
from all sides. Fo
that he was glidin
masses without id
'Only the direct
d'Etat.' 'And how
Allende would rep

Whether one agree
superstructures' or

by Allende himself. Of course, neither they nor
…der much illusion about the *support* they could
…military: but it would seem nevertheless that
…ought that they could buy off the military;
…not so much a coup on the classical 'Latin
…a that Allende feared as 'civil war'.

…has written from personal knowledge that
…sceral refusal' of civil war; and the first thing
…his is that it is only people morally and politic-
…ir sensitivities who would scoff at this 'refusal'
…ble. This however does not exhaust the subject.
…t ways of trying to avoid civil war; and there
…where one cannot do it *and* survive. Débray
…is language is itself interesting) that 'he (i.e.
…uped by the phraseology of "popular power"
…nt to bear the responsibility of thousands of
…blood of others horrified him. That is why
…to his Socialist party which accused him of
…g and which was pressing him to take the

…ul to know if Débray himself believes that
…necessarily a 'phraseology' by which one
…ped'; and what was meant by 'taking the
…ny rate, Allende's 'visceral refusal' of civil
…make clear, was only one part of the argument
…compromise; the other was a deep scepticism
…alternative. Débray's account, describing
…vent on in the last weeks before the coup,
…graph on this:

…ers?' 'With what?' Allende would reply.
…orces to do it.' 'Mobilize them,' he was told
…it is true (this is Débray speaking – R.M.)
…up there, in the superstructures, leaving the
…eological orientations or political direction.
…action of the masses will stop the coup
…many masses does one need to stop a tank?'
…y.[28]

…s that Allende was 'gliding up there, in the
…ot, this kind of dialogue has the ring of

truth; and it may help to explain a good deal about the events in Chile.

Considering the manner of Salvador Allende's death, a certain reticence is very much in order. Yet, it is impossible not to attribute to him at least some of the responsibility for what ultimately occurred. In the article from which I have just quoted, Débray also tells us that one of Allende's closest collaborators, Carlos Altamirano, the general secretary of the Socialist party, had said to him, Débray, with anger at Allende's manoeuvrings, that 'the best way of precipitating a confrontation and to make it even more bloody is to turn one's back upon it.'[29] There were others close to Allende who had long held the same view. But, as Marcel Niedergang has also noted, all of them 'respected Allende, the centre of gravity and the real "patron" of the Popular Unity coalition';[30] and Allende, as we know, was absolutely set on the course of conciliation – encouraged upon that course by his fear of civil war and defeat; by the divisions in the coalition he led and by the weaknesses in the organization of the Chilean working class; by an exceedingly 'moderate' Communist party; and so on.

The trouble with that course is that it had all the elements of self-fulfilling catastrophe. Allende believed in conciliation because he feared the result of a confrontation. But because he believed that the left was bound to be defeated in any such confrontation, he had to pursue with ever-greater desperation his policy of conciliation; but the more he pursued that policy, the greater grew the assurance and boldness of his opponents. Moreover, and crucially, a policy of conciliation of the regime's opponents held the grave risk of discouraging and demobilizing its supporters. 'Conciliation' signifies a tendency, an impulse, a direction, and it finds practical expression on many terrains, whether intended or not. Thus, in October 1972, the Government had got the National Assembly to enact a 'law on the control of arms' which gave to the military wide powers to make searches for arms caches. In practice, and given the army's bias and inclinations, this soon turned into an excuse for military raids on factories known as left-wing strongholds, for the clear purpose of intimidating and demoralizing left-wing activists[31] – all quite 'legal', or at least 'legal' enough.

The really extraordinary thing about this experience is that the policy of 'conciliation', so steadfastly and disastrously pursued, did not cause greater and earlier demoralization on the left. Even as late as the end of June 1973, when the abortive military coup was launched, popular willingness to mobilize against would-be putschists was by all accounts higher than at any time since Allende's assumption of the presidency. This was probably the last moment at which a change of course might have been possible – and it was also, in a sense, the moment of truth for the regime: a choice then had to be made. A choice *was* made, namely that the President would continue to try to conciliate; and he did go on to make concession after concession to the military's demands.

I am not arguing here, let it be stressed again, that another strategy was bound to succeed – only that the strategy that was adopted was bound to fail. Eric Hobsbawm, in the article I have already quoted, writes that 'there was not much Allende could have done after (say) early 1972 except to play out time, secure the irreversibility of the great changes already achieved (how? – R.M.) and with luck maintain a political system which would give the Popular Unity a second chance later . . . for the last several months, it is fairly certain that there was practically nothing he could do.'[32] For all its apparent reasonableness and sense of realism, the argument is both very abstract and is also a good recipe for suicide.

For one thing, one cannot 'play out time' in a situation where great changes have already occurred, which have resulted in a considerable polarization, and where the conservative forces are moving over from class struggle to class war. One can either advance or retreat – retreat into oblivion or advance to meet the challenge.

Nor is it any good, in such a situation, to act on the presupposition that there is nothing much that can be done, since this means in effect that nothing much *will* be done to prepare for confrontation with the conservative forces. This leaves out of account the possibility that the best way to avoid such a confrontation – perhaps the only way – is precisely to prepare for it; and to be in as good a posture as possible to win if it does come.

This brings us directly back to the question of the state and the exercise of power. It was noted earlier that a major change in the state's personnel is an urgent and essential task for a government bent on really serious change; and that this needs to be allied to a variety of institutional reforms and innovations, designed to push forward the process of the state's democratization.

But in this latter respect, much more needs to be done, not only to realize a set of long-term socialist objectives concerning the socialist exercise of power, but as a means either of avoiding armed confrontation, or of meeting it on the most advantageous and least costly terms if it turns out to be inevitable.

What this means is not simply 'mobilizing the masses' or 'arming the workers'. These are slogans – important slogans – which need to be given effective *institutional* content. In other words, a new regime bent on fundamental changes in the economic, social and political structures must from the start begin to build and encourage the building of a network of organs of power, parallel to and complementing the state power, and constituting a solid infra-structure for the *timely* 'mobilization of the masses' and the effective direction of its actions. The forms which this assumes – workers' committees at their place of work, civic committees in districts and sub-districts, etc. – and the manner in which these organs 'mesh' with the state may not be susceptible to blue-printing. But the need is there, and it is imperative that it should be met, in whatever forms are most appropriate.

This is not, to all appearances, how the Allende regime moved. Some of the things that needed doing were done; but such 'mobilization' as occurred, and such preparations as were made, very late in the day, for a possible confrontation, lacked direction, coherence, in many cases even encouragement. Had the regime really encouraged the creation of a parallel infra-structure, it might have lived; and, incidentally, it might have had less trouble with its opponents and critics on the left, for instance in the MIR, since its members might not then have found the need so great to engage in actions of their own, which greatly embarrassed the government: they might have been more ready to co-operate with a government in whose revolutionary will they could have had greater confidence. In part at least, 'ultra-leftism' is the product of 'citra-leftism'.

Salvador Allende was a noble figure and he died a heroic death. But hard though it is to say it, that is not the point. What matters, in the end, is not how he died, but whether he could have survived by pursuing different policies; and it is wrong to claim that there was no alternative to the policies that were pursued. In this as in many other realms, and here more than in most, facts only become compelling as one allows them to be so. Allende was not a revolutionary who was also a parliamentary politician. He was a parliamentary politician who, remarkably enough, had genuine revolutionary tendencies. But these tendencies could not overcome a political style which was not suitable to the purposes he wanted to achieve.

The question of course is not one of courage. Allende had all the courage required, and more. Saint Just's famous remark, which has often been quoted since the coup, that 'he who makes a revolution by half digs his own grave' is closer to the mark – but it can easily be misused. There are people on the left for whom it simply means the ruthless use of terror, and who tell one yet again, as if they had just invented the idea, that 'you can't make omelettes without breaking eggs'. But as the French writer Claude Roy observed some years ago, 'you can break an awful lot of eggs without making a decent omelette'. Terror may become part of a revolutionary struggle. But the essential question is the degree to which those who are responsible for the direction of that struggle are able and willing to engender and encourage the effective, meaning the organized, mobilization of popular forces. If there is any definite 'lesson' to be learnt from the Chilean tragedy, this seems to be it; and parties and movements which do not learn it, and apply what they have learnt, may well be preparing new Chiles for themselves.

October 1973

Notes

1. Had it not been for international pressure and protest, it may well be that Corvalan would have been executed by now (October 1973), like so many others, after the semblance of a trial, or without a trial.
2. *The Times*, 13 September 1973. My italics.
3. ibid., 20 September 1973.
4. *Le Monde*, 29 September 1973.
5. Quoted by K. S. Karol in *Nouvel-Observateur*, 8 October 1973.
6. *Le Monde*, 23–4 September 1973.
7. ibid.
8. ibid.
9. *Le Monde*, 13 September 1973.
10. *The Guardian*, 19 September 1973.
11. E. J. Hobsbawm, 'The Murder of Chile', in *New Society*, 20 September 1973.
12. *Le Monde*, 29 September 1973.
13. ibid.
14. K. Marx, *The Civil War in France*, in *Selected Works* (Moscow 1950), vol. I, p. 485.
15. Quoted in *The Times*, 5 October 1973. This of course is not an isolated account: *Le Monde*, for instance, has carried dozens of horrifying reports

of the savagery of the repression.

16. *The Times*, 5 October 1973.

17. *New Society*, op. cit.

18. Jean-Paul Sartre, *L'Idiot de la Famille, Gustave Flaubert de 1821 á 1857* (Paris 1972), vol. III, p. 590.

19. Marcelle Auclair, 'Les Illusions de la Haute Société' in *Le Monde*, 4 October 1973.

20. ibid., 20 September 1973.

21. *Selected Works*, op. cit., vol. II, p. 420.

22. ibid., vol. I, p. 468.

23. ibid., pp. 471 ff.

24. ibid., p. 22.

25. 'The State and Revolution' in *Socialist Register*, 1970.

26. *Marxism Today*, September 1973, p. 266 but see footnote 29.

27. *Nouvel Observateur*, 17 September 1973.

28. ibid.

29. ibid. It may be worth noting, however, that Altamirano is also reported as having declared after the attempted coup of 29 June that 'never has the unity between the people, the armed forces and the police been as great as it is now . . . and this unity will grow with every new battle in the historic war that we are conducting'. *Le Monde*, 16–17 September 1973.

30. *Le Monde*, 29 September 1973.

31. ibid., 16–17 September 1973. This is a reference to an article in *Rouge*, by J. P. Beauvais, who gives an eye-witness account of one such army raid, on 4 August 1973, in which one man was killed and several were wounded in the course of what amounted to an attack by parachute troops on a textile plant.

32. *New Society*, op. cit.

Select Bibliography

Since there is an immense literature on the topics covered in this volume this bibliography will seek only to furnish some guide to further reading and will concentrate largely on works by Marxists and socialists; no attempt is made to indicate the important body of literature concerning Marxist philosophy and aesthetics, and the works cited are for the most part strictly political in character. Thus the voluminous literature on trade unions and the women's movement is not included.

For Marxist discussion of classical political theory see in particular: Louis Althusser *Politics and History: Montesquieu, Rousseau, Hegel and Marx*, London 1972; Lucio Colletti *From Rousseau to Lenin: Studies in Ideology and Society*, London 1972, especially Part Three; C. B. Macpherson *The Political Theory of Possessive Individualism: Hobbes to Locke*, Oxford 1962; Herbert Marcuse 'A Study on Authority' *Studies in Critical Philosophy*, London 1972; Antonio Gramsci 'The Modern Prince' *Prison Notebooks*, edited by Quintin Hoare and Geoffrey Nowell Smith, London 1971.

The writings of Marx and Engels on directly political questions are now assembled in a three-volume edition in the Pelican Marx Library: *The Revolutions of 1848*, Harmondsworth 1973; *Surveys from Exile*, Harmondsworth 1973; *The First International and After*, Harmondsworth 1974; these volumes are each edited and introduced by David Fernbach. The volume of Marx's *Early Writings*, Harmondsworth 1974, introduced by Lucio Colletti, contains much material on Marx's early political philosophy. Engels's writings are not systematically covered in the Pelican Marx Library: his important later texts will be found in Marx/Engels *Selected Works*, Moscow 1968; see also Frederick Engels *The German Revolution*, with an introduction by L. Krieger, New York 1965. The letters of Marx and Engels contain much important political discussion; see *Selected Correspondence*, Moscow 1957. The Moscow Foreign Languages Publishing House also publishes a number of collections of the writings of Marx and Engels on various political themes; for example Marx/Engels *On Britain*, Moscow 1962 and (a slimmer volume) Marx/Engels *On Colonialism*, Moscow 1968.

It is important to set the political development of Marx and Engels in its historical context: for an overview see E. J. Hobsbawm *The Age of Revolution 1789–1848*, London 1968 and *The Age of Capital 1848–75*, London 1976. For the early history of the British working class see: E. P. Thompson *The Making of the English Working Class*, Harmondsworth 1969; John Foster *Class Struggle and the Industrial Revolution*, London 1974; E. J. Hobsbawm *Labouring Men*, London 1968. The French revolutionary tradition was of great importance to Marx: see Filippo Buonarroti *History of Babeuf's Conspiracy for Equality*, London 1836 and Prosper Lissagaray *History of the Commune*, New York 1971. For the early history of the German workers' movement see Theodore S. Hamerow *Restoration, Revolution, Reaction: Economics and Politics in Germany 1815–71*, Princeton 1966; and Theodore S. Hamerow *The Social Foundations of German Unification, 1858–71*, 2 vols, Princeton 1969 and 1972.

For the political activity of Marx and Engels see David Riazanov *Karl Marx and Frederick Engels*, New York 1975, B. Nicolaevsky and O. Manchen-Helfen *Karl Marx: Man and Fighter*, Harmondsworth 1976 and David McLellan *Karl Marx: His Life and Thought*, London 1973. The development of Marx's political ideas is discussed in Michael Löwy *La Théorie de la Révolution Chez le Jeune Marx*, Paris 1970; Fernando Claudin *Marx, Engels y la Revolucion de 1848*, Madrid 1975; R. N. Hunt *The Political Ideas of Marx and Engels*, London 1975.

Marxist politics is, of course, based on economic and social analysis: the most comprehensive discussion of the development of the capitalist world economy is Ernest Mandel *Late Capitalism*, London 1975; the social structure of advanced capitalist societies is investigated in Erik Olin Wright, *Class Interest and Class Capacity*, London 1977, and Nicos Poulantzas *Classes in Contemporary Capitalism*, London 1975. For a critical survey of recent Marxist thought in Europe see Perry Anderson, *Considerations on Western Marxism*, London 1976. Recent Marxist investigation of the capitalist state is commanded by two works: Nicos Poulantzas *Political Power and Social Classes*, London 1972 and Ralph Miliband *The State in Capitalist Society*, London 1969. The historical succession of state forms is studied in G. Novack, *Democracy and Revolution*, New York 1971; G. Thersom *State Power and State Apparatuses*, London 1977.

For an outline of the Marxist analysis of contemporary imperialism see Ernest Mandel *Marxist Economic Theory*, London 1974, chapter 13. The best review of the classical Marxist approach is Tom Kemp *Theories of Imperialism*, London 1967. For the modern debate on imperialism see A. Emmanuel *Unequal Exchange*, London 1972; Hugo Radice (ed.) *International Firms and Modern Imperialism*, Harmondsworth 1975; Michael Barratt Brown *The Economics of Imperialism*, Harmondsworth 1975; a valuable survey of the contemporary discussion is contained in Ernest Mandel *Late Capitalism*, London 1975, chapter 11. For particular regions see Fred Halliday *Arabia Without Sultans*, Harmondsworth 1974; Robin Blackburn (ed.) *Explosion in a Subcontinent*, Harmondsworth 1975. For the background to the coup in Chile see Regis Débray *Conversations with Allende*,

London 1972; Tariq Ali *The Only Road to Socialism and Workers'
Power*, London 1975.

There are three selections of Rosa Luxemburg's political texts
available in English: R. Looker (ed.) *Rosa Luxemburg: Selected
Political Writings*, London 1972; D. Howard (ed.) *Selected Political
Writings of Rosa Luxemburg*, New York 1971; M.-A. Waters (ed.)
Rosa Luxemburg Speaks, New York 1970. The best discussion of Rosa
Luxemburg's political conceptions is Norman Geras *The Legacy of
Rosa Luxemburg*, London 1976. Luxemburg's political activity is
recounted in P. Frolich *Rosa Luxemburg*, London 1972 and J. P. Nettl
Rosa Luxemburg London 1966.

Lenin's most important political texts are available in the three-
volume *Selected Works*, Moscow 1967. The best introduction to
Lenin's political thought is Georg Lukacs *Lenin*, London 1970. An
important study of both Lenin's theories and his political practice is
Marcel Liebman *Leninism under Lenin*, London 1975; see also Tony
Cliff *Lenin*, London 1975 and Moshe Lewin *Lenin's Last Struggle*,
London 1969.

Trotsky's political ideas are usefully anthologized in *The Age of
Permanent Revolution*, introduced by Isaac Deutscher, New York 1974.
The works which contain Trotsky's most important political theses are
The Revolution Betrayed, London 1957; *The Struggle Against Fascism
in Germany*, Harmondsworth 1975; *The Permanent Revolution*, New
York 1965; *The Third International After Lenin*; New York 1957; *The
Spanish Revolution (1931–9)*, New York 1973; *The Transitional Programme for Socialist Revolution*, New York 1974. Trotsky's historical
writings should also be consulted: notably *1905*, Harmondsworth
1974, and *History of the Russian Revolution*, London 1967. Trotsky's
ideas and political activity are vividly presented in Isaac Deutscher's
biography *The Prophet Armed; The Prophet Unarmed; The Prophet
Outcast*, Oxford 1970.

For the class struggles in Italy after the First World War see Paolo
Spriano *The Occupation of the Factories*, London 1975; Gwyn A.
Williams *Proletarian Order: Antonio Gramsci, Factory Councils and
the Origins of Communism in Italy 1911–21*, London 1975; John
Cammett *Antonio Gramsci and the Origins of Italian Communism*;
Giuseppe Fiori *Antonio Gramsci: Life of a Revolutionary*; Georg
Lukacs 'The Crisis of Syndicalism in Italy' *Political Writings 1919–29*,
London 1972; Leon Trotsky 'Speech on the Italian Question', *The
First Five Years of the Communist International*. The editors' intro-
duction to Gramsci's *Prison Writings*, London 1971, contains a useful
account of Italian Communism in the twenties.

On the British labour movement in the twentieth century see Walter
Kendall *The Revolutionary Movement in Britain*, London 1969;
Bernard Semmel *Imperialism and Social Reform*, London 1960; James
Hinton *The First Shop Stewards Movement*, London 1973; James
Hinton and Richard Hyman *Trade Unions and Revolution*, London

1975; Michael Woodhouse and Brian Pearce *Communism in Britain*, London 1975; L. J. MacFarlane *The British Communist Party*, London 1966; Ralph Miliband *Parliamentary Socialism*, London 1973; David Coates *The Labour Party*, London 1974.

For a general history of the European labour movement see Wolfgang Abendroth *A Short History of the European Working Class*, London 1972 and Julius Braunthal *History of the International*, 2 vols, London 1966 and 1967. See also Ernest Mandel (ed.) *Fifty Years of World Revolution*, New York 1968.

On the fate of the Russian revolution see Victor Serge *Memoirs of a Revolutionary*, edited and introduced by Peter Sedgewick, Oxford 1967; Isaac Deutscher *Stalin*, Harmondsworth 1968; E. H. Carr *A History of Soviet Russia 1917–29*, London 1950–70; Stephen E. Cohen *Bukharin and the Bolshevik Revolution*, London 1975; Leon Trotsky *The Revolution Betrayed*, London 1957; Roy Medvedev *Let History Judge*, London 1972; Nikita Khrushchev *Khrushchev Remembers*, 2 vols, 1972 and 1974; Isaac Deutscher *The Unfinished Revolution*, Oxford 1967; P. G. Grigorenko *The Grigorenko Papers* London, 1977.

On the Third International and the Communist Parties the best overall account up to the nineteen-fifties is Fernando Claudin *The Communist Movement*, Harmondsworth 1975; also worth consulting is Franz Borkenau *The Communist International*, London 1938. For the early period and the policy of imperialism in central Europe see Arno Mayer *The Politics and Diplomacy of Peacemaking*, New York 1967; a selection of official documents of the Comintern is available in Jane Degras (ed.) *The Communist International (1919–43); Documents*, London 1956–65; see also Leon Trotsky *The First Five Years of the Communist International*, 2 vols, New York 1972.

For particular episodes and periods see Pierre Broué and Emile Temime *Revolution and Civil War in Spain*, London 1973; Nicos Poulantzas *Fascism and Dictatorship*, London 1974; Daniel Brower *The New Jacobins: the French Communist Party and the Popular Front*, New York 1968; Leon Trotsky *Whither France?*, London 1974; for the thirties as a whole see *Writings of Leon Trotsky 1930–40*, New York 1969–76; Josef Rothschild *The Communist Party of Bulgaria: Origins and Development*, London 1959; Ernst Fischer *An Opposing Man*, London 1974 (especially the sections on Vienna and Moscow); D. Eudes *The Kapetanios: Partisans and Civil War in Greece*, London 1972; C. Tsoucalas *The Greek Tragedy*, Harmondsworth 1969; Francois Fejto *A History of the People's Democracies*, London 1971; Jiři Pelikan *The Secret Vysocany Congress of the Czech Communist Party*, London 1971; Daniel Singer *Prelude to Revolution: France in May 1968*, Maria Antonietta Macciochi *Letters from Inside the Italian Communist Party*, London 1973; E. J. Hobsbawm *Revolutionaries*, London 1976.

For the United States see James Cannon *The First Ten Years of American Communism*, New York 1962; Studs Terkel *Hard Times*;

New York 1970; Farrell Dobbs *Teamster Rebellion*, New York 1972; James Cannon *The History of American Trotskyism*, New York 1970; George Charney *A Long Journey*, Chicago 1968; Joseph Starobin *American Communism in Crisis 1943–57*, Cambridge (Mass.) 1972; Tim Wolhfarth *The History of American Trotskyism*, New York 1968; Art Preis *Labor's Giant Step*, New York 1964. A valuable introduction to US policy in the post-war period is Gabriel and Joyce Kolko *The Limits of Power*, New York 1972. For an historical overview see James Weinstein *Ambiguous Legacies*, New York 1976.

On the Chinese revolution see Harold Isaacs *The Tragedy of the Chinese Revolution*, Stanford 1961; Edgar Snow *Red Star over China*, London 1966; Jack Belden *China Shakes the World*, Harmondsworth 1973; Lucien Bianco *Origins of the Chinese Revolution 1915–49*, Stanford 1971; Graham Peck *Two Kinds of Time*, Boston 1967; Stuart Schram *Mao Tse-tung*, Harmondsworth 1966; Livio Maitan *Party, Army, Masses in China*, London 1976. Mao's own writings are available in a four-volume edition published in Peking; the most important part of these official writings are the early social investigations and texts on military strategy. Also of interest are the 'unofficial' texts and speeches; see, for example, Stuart Schram (ed.) *Mao Unrehearsed*, Harmondsworth 1974.

The recent evolution of communism in Western Europe has produced a new debate on socialist strategy in the advanced countries. See, in particular, Santiago Carillo with Regis Debray and Max Gallo *Dialogue on Spain*, London 1976; Etiènne Balibar, with a comment by Louis Althusser, *The Dictatorship of the Proletariat*, London 1977; Ernest Mandel *The Revolution in Western Europe*, London 1977.

The best way to follow Marxist analysis of the contemporary world is to obtain the following publications: *New Left Review* (every two months), 7 Carlisle Street, London W1, V 6NL; *The Socialist Register* (annual) edited by Ralph Miliband and John Saville, Merlin Press; *Inprecor*, (every two weeks) 12/14 rue de la Buanderie, Brussels 1000, Belgium; *Intercontinental Press* (weekly), PO Box 116, Village Station, New York, NY 10014, USA. *Socialist Challenge* (weekly), 328/9, Upper Street, Islington, London N.1.; *International*, at the same address; *Samizdat Register* (annual) edited by Roy and Zhores Medvedev, Merlin Press; *Labour Focus on Eastern Europe*, 116 Cazenove Road, London N.16.

Notes on contributors

ROBIN BLACKBURN is an editor of *New Left Review*. He edited *Ideology in Social Science: Readings in Critical Social Theory* (Fontana 1972); formerly Lecturer in Sociology at the London School of Economics and Visiting Professor at the Department of Philosophy, University of Havana.

LUCIO COLLETTI is Professor of the History of Philosophy at the University of Salerno and Reader in Philosophy at Rome University. From 1958–62 he was an editor of *Societa*, theoretical journal of the Italian Communist Party. His writings include *From Rousseau to Lenin: Studies in Ideology and Society* (London 1972, awarded the Isaac Deutscher Memorial Prize), and *Marxism and Hegel*, London 1973.

ISAAC DEUTSCHER (1907–67) was in the twenties and thirties a member of the Polish Left Opposition. His writings include a three-volume biography of Trotsky: *The Prophet Armed*, *The Prophet Unarmed* and *The Prophet Outcast*, Oxford 1970; also *Stalin*, Harmondsworth 1968; *The Unfinished Revolution*, Oxford 1967; *Russia, China and the West*, edited by Fred Halliday, Harmondsworth 1972; *Ironies of History*, London 1966.

NORMAN GERAS is a Lecturer in Politics at the University of Manchester and author of *The Legacy of Rosa Luxemburg*, London 1976.

ANTONIO GRAMSCI (1891–1937) was editor of *Ordine Nuovo*, a paper which played an important part in the Workers' Council Movement of Turin in 1919 and 1920. He was later one of the founders of the Italian Communist Party and an important leader of it until his arrest in 1926; he was to spend the rest of his life in Mussolini's prisons. His writings include *Selections from the Prison Notebooks*, edited by Quintin Hoare and Nowell Smith, London 1971.

MICHEL LÖWY is a Lecturer in Sociology at the University of Vincennes and a leader of the Ligue Communiste Revolutionaire, French section of the Fourth International. His writings include *The Marxism of Che Guevara*, New York 1973 and *La Théorie de la Révolution Chez le Jeune Marx*, Paris 1970.

444   Notes on Contributors

ERNEST MANDEL has been a leading militant of the Fourth International since 1945; he was a member of the economic commission of the Belgian TUC from 1955–63. He has been invited to give the Marshall Lectures at Cambridge University for 1978. His writings include *The Formation of the Economic Thought of Karl Marx*, London 1972; *Marxist Economic Theory*, London 1968; *Europe versus America?*, London 1970; *Late Capitalism*, London 1975.

RALPH MILIBAND is Professor of Politics at the University of Leeds and co-editor of the annual *Socialist Register*. His writings include *Parliamentary Socialism*, new edition London 1973 and *The State in Capitalist Society*, London 1969.

TOM NAIRN is an editor of the *New Left Review*; his writings include *May '68: The Beginning of the End*, London 1969, *The Left Against Europe?*, Harmondsworth 1973 and *The Break-up of Britain*, London 1977.

JIŘÍ PELIKAN was a leader of the Czechoslovak Communist reform movement of 1967–8; he was director of the television services in 1968 and was elected to the Central Committee by the Vysocany Congress of the Communist Party, held clandestinely shortly after the Russian invasion. His writings include *The Secret Vysocany Congress of the Czech Communist Party*, London 1971.

The Modern Britain Series

Readers in Sociology

This original series is designed to show how the sociologist analyses and describes the main features of a complex, modern, industrial society. Each book contains extracts by British and foreign sociologists, and each chapter has a short introduction by the editors which discusses the main issues and problems and links the extracts together. This series is of great value to all those interested in contemporary society, and not only those engaged in formal courses.

The general editors of the series are Eric Butterworth, Reader in Community Studies at York University, and David Weir, Lecturer in Sociology at the Manchester Business School.

The Sociology of Modern Britain

Edited by Eric Butterworth & David Weir

This work introduces students to the study of their own society. The chapters cover the main institutional areas of contemporary Britain – the family, community, work, class and power. The book also includes a chapter on the values implicit in British society, around which much political and social conflict is inevitably centred.

Social Problems of Modern Britain

Edited by Eric Butterworth & David Weir

This book discusses such problems as inadequate housing, environmental depreciation, poverty, immigration, racial discrimination, crime, deviant behaviour and sets them in the context of the social attitudes and perspectives of the 'social problem' groups themselves.

Men and Work in Modern Britain

Edited by David Weir

Readings on organisational types, occupations and social status, recruitment, selection and training, career patterns, ideologies and values, deviance, leisure and unemployment, linked by critical editorial introductions.

Popper
Bryan Magee

Karl Popper has been acknowledged by professional colleagues as the most formidable living critic of Marxism; as the greatest philosopher of science there has ever been; as a thinker whose influence is acknowledged by men of action as well as by an almost bewildering variety of scholars—and yet he remains comparatively unknown to the wider audience for whom this series is intended. This book is therefore as timely as it is brilliant. Bryan Magee demonstrates Popper's importance across the whole range of philosophy; and in doing so provides a lively and up-to-date introduction to philosophy itself.

'. . . lucid, based on close study and deep understanding, the perfect pocket guide to a thinker whose importance it is impossible to over-estimate.'   *The Observer*

'Bryan Magee is a very successful populariser of serious ideas . . . It is not surprising, therefore, that *Popper* should be such a good little book . . . Magee does an excellent job of placing Popper's view of science within the wider context of his metaphysics.' Alan Ryan, *The Listener*

'Magee, writing about Popper with the zeal of the new convert, gives a lively account of Popper's philosophical battles with Marxist, logical positivist and linguistic philosophers.'
                                                      Times Higher Education Supplement

Into Unknown England 1866-1913

Selections from the Social Explorers

Edited by Peter Keating

How did the poor live in late Victorian and Edwardian England? In the slums of London and Birmingham? In the iron-town of Middlesbrough? In a Devon fishing village? In rural Essex?

This is a fascinating sequence of extracts from the writings of those individuals, journalists and wealthy businessmen, a minister's wife, and a popular novelist, who temporarily left the comfort of their middle-class homes to find out how the other half lived. Peter Keating includes material from Charles Booth, Jack London, B. S. Rowntree and C. F. G. Masterman as well as by such lesser-known figures as George Sims, Andrew Mearns and Stephen Reynolds.

'. . . a brilliant and compelling anthology . . . *Into Unknown England* is not only an education in itself, throwing into three-dimensional chiaroscuro the flat statistics of "scientific" history, but a splendid example of prose which is always immediate and alive.'
Alan Brien, *Spectator*

'The writers collected here used all the techniques they could to solicit sympathy. Their descendants are a thousand television documentaries.'
Paul Barker, *The Times*

'. . . a rich collection of passages, intelligently presented.'
Guardian

Fontana Modern Masters

General Editor: Frank Kermode

ARTAUD	*Martin Esslin*
BECKETT	*A. Alvarez*
CAMUS	*Conor Cruise O'Brien*
CHOMSKY	*John Lyons*
EINSTEIN	*Jeremy Bernstein*
ELIOT	*Stephen Spender*
ENGELS	*David McLellan*
FANON	*David Caute*
FREUD	*Richard Wollheim*
GANDHI	*George Woodcock*
GRAMSCI	*James Joll*
JOYCE	*John Gross*
JUNG	*Anthony Storr*
KAFKA	*Erich Heller*
KEYNES	*D. E. Moggridge*
LAWRENCE	*Frank Kermode*
LAING	*E. Z. Friedenberg*
LE CORBUSIER	*Stephen Gardiner*
LENIN	*Robert Conquest*
LEVI-STRAUSS	*Edmund Leach*
MARCUSE	*Alasdair MacIntyre*
MARX	*David McLellan*
ORWELL	*Raymond Williams*
POPPER	*Brian Magee*
POUND	*Donald Davie*
PROUST	*Roger Shattuck*
REICH	*Charles Rycroft*
RUSSELL	*A. J. Ayer*
SARTRE	*Arthur C. Danto*
SAUSSURE	*Jonathan Culler*
SCHOENBERG	*Charles Rosen*
WEBER	*Donald MacRae*
WITTGENSTEIN	*David Pears*
YEATS	*Denis Donoghue*